SINO-INDIAN EQUATION

Competition + Cooperation – Confrontation

SINO-INDIAN EQUATION

Competition + Cooperation – Confrontation

Brigadier (Dr.) Rajeev Bhutani

Foreword by

Lieutenant General Vinod Bhatia, PVSM, AVSM, SM
Director, Centre for Joint Warfare Studies (CENJOWS)

CENTRE FOR JOINT WARFARE STUDIES (CENJOWS)

PENTAGON PRESS LLP

Sino-Indian Equation (Competition + Cooperation – Confrontation)
Brigadier (Dr.) Rajeev Bhutani
E-mail: rajeev.deepa19@gmail.com

ISBN 978-93-86618-75-7

First Published in 2019

Published by
PENTAGON PRESS LLP
206, Peacock Lane, Shahpur Jat,
New Delhi-110049
Phones: 011-64706243, 26491568
Telefax: 011-26490600
email: rajan@pentagonpress.in
website: www.pentagonpress.in

Cover conceptualized by Akanksha Bhutani

Printed at Aegean Offset Printers, Greater Noida, U.P.

Dedicated to
My mother Late Mrs. Raj Kumari Bhutani

Contents

Foreword

In the emerging strategic construct and jostling for world leadership, China is readying to challenge the United States. In this game of 'Balance of Power', other global players like India, Russia and Japan will be the Balancing Powers. India may do well to ensure a balance between the 'Balance of Power' and 'Balance of Interests' in the great game being played out by the United States and China. To this end, Brigadier (Dr.) Rajeev Bhutani has produced a very comprehensive and contemporary work on Sino–India relations.

Having resolved the Doklam Standoff at the politico-diplomatic level, the informal summit between Prime Minister Narendra Modi and President Xi Jinping in the Chinese city of Wuhan in April 2018 paved the path of cooperation between the two countries. Since then both the leaders have met four times in 2018, being described as a milestone in bilateral relations. Consensus is being built up between Prime Minister Modi and President Xi to replace confrontation and competition between the two countries with cooperation. In his keynote address at the Shangri La Dialogue in Singapore in June 2018, Prime Minister Modi made a specific mention, *"In April, a two-day Summit with President Xi helped us cement our understanding that strong and stable relations between our two nations are an important factor for global peace and progress."* He further said, *"I firmly believe that Asia and the world will have a better future when India and China work together in trust and confidence, sensitive to each other's interests."*

This positive outlook and the bonhomie in the bilateral relations are only short-term measures unless the key issue of boundary dispute between the two nations is resolved. Continued presence of Dalai Lama in India will be a further source of irritation for China. In bilateral trade, India has no solution in sight to significantly reduce its trade deficit with China.

In the immediate neighbourhood, China is actively influencing the South Asian states through its predatory economic intervention for gaining ports / bases – 99 years lease of Hambantota port in Sri Lanka and 40 years lease of Gwadar port in Pakistan are the recent examples. This is supported by increasing deployment of Chinese warships and submarines in the Indian Ocean. Influencing the political leaders of small states to gain a foothold is an art, which Chinese leadership has mastered with great finesse, for which there cannot be better examples than the Maldives and Nepal.

In the global arena, world is passing through a turbulent phase, encompassing varied issues: Trade war between the United States and China; the United States-Russia tensions and the conflict in Ukraine; Differences over climate change; China's militarization of artificial islands in the South China Sea resulting in to conflict with rule based international maritime order and freedom of navigation. The latter has brought together India, Japan, the United States and Australia in to a "Quadrilateral Security Dialogue" or "QUAD" which is being viewed by China with suspicion as 'ganging up' of these powers against her.

The ongoing shift in the balance of power in Asia is of concern to the United States, Japan and India and it has to be addressed on both the economic and security fronts. Ultimately, it will be the 'Balance of Interest' and not 'Balance of Power' which should influence India's stance with China vis-à-vis other powers. In this context, Prime Minister Modi's recent trilateral meetings on the sidelines of G20 Summit at Buenos Aires, Argentina on 30 November – 01 December 2018 hold special significance. For India's economic development, the United States and Japan are vital partners hence a common understanding on this trilateral format would enable India to achieve its goal of becoming a $ 5 trillion economy by 2025. Japan and India have committed themselves for collaborative infrastructural projects in Sri Lanka, Myanmar, Bangladesh and Africa. The United States, under its BUILD Act, is also endeavouring to forge its participation in building infrastructure in developing countries. Prime Minister Modi termed the first trilateral meeting held between Japan, America and India on the sidelines of G20 in Buenos Aires on 30 November 2018 as "JAI" (Hindi for success or victory). Hopefully, the trilateral cooperation between these nations will create a formidable base on which the security edifice of QUAD will be established to ensure a peaceful and prosperous Indo-Pacific region where international law and freedom of navigation will be respected.

Another trilateral meeting was held between President Vladimir Putin, President Xi Jinping and Prime Minister Modi on the sidelines of G20 Summit on 01 December. The Russia-India-China (RIC) meeting took place after a gap of 12 years, which consolidated India's position as an independent player in the global arena and it is indicative of the success of India's all-round diplomacy under Prime Minister Modi. Interestingly, New Delhi and Moscow will soon sign a logistic supply agreement that will allow their military forces to share each other's facilities. India has similar agreements with the United States and Singapore.

Against this backdrop, I found it most heartening that Brigadier (Dr.) Rajeev Bhutani has selected this subject, which is most contemporary and is appropriately timed. A keen and devoted China watcher, he did his Doctor of Philosophy (D.Phil) from the Central University of Allahabad and authored his first book titled "RISE OF CHINA: 2030 and Its Strategic Implications" – widely acclaimed as an enriched reference book on 'Rise of China' adorning the libraries world-wide including those of Stanford and Princeton Universities.

Rajeev has analysed the Sino-Indian relations in great detail by deliberating upon the sources or rather drivers of conflict between the two nations first, and then discussed all possible fields of cooperation and competition threadbare. Finally, he has put across strategic initiatives which Modi government has adopted in the emerging Indo-Pacific Region – their likely influence on the Asian balance of power and what more can be done to further strengthen the comprehensive national power of India.

Brigadier (Dr.) Rajeev Bhutani deserves to be commended for his detailed research and lucid expression. This book is loaded with authenticated and useful data and illustrations, which the author has utilized to forcefully build up his arguments in a very absorbing and effective manner. The book will be of immense value to research students, strategic planners and policy makers.

New Delhi
07 January 2019

Lt Gen Vinod Bhatia, PVSM, AVSM, SM
Director, CENJOWS

Preface

Writing a book on a contemporary and thought provoking subject that should be based on analysis of events spread over decades and copious data needs tremendous motivation. Since I had written a voluminous book on 'Rise of China' earlier, one of my friend, Dr. Shivendra Shahi requested me to write an article on 'Future of India-China Relations' with a limit of 2500 words for his book. When I started writing, I realized that one could not do justice for such a vast subject in a short article.

Then I discussed with Director Center for Joint Warfare Studies (CENJOWS), Lt Gen Vinod Bhatia that I wanted to write on 'India-China Relations'. Without getting in to any nitty-gritty, he said, "Go Ahead, you write anything, we will publish it for CENJOWS". General Bhatia, a paratrooper and former Director General of Military Operations (DGMO) is a leader par-excellence. In CENJOWS, he encourages senior fellows to express their views without any restraints irrespective of whether during discussion or in their writings. Free flow of thought rejuvenates a creative mind resulting in to innovative solutions. One cannot find a better thinking environment.

With my Director's motivation, I engrossed myself in to writing, which resulted in to this book. Selecting a suitable title for my book was an exercise in itself. I found various analysts and authors have defined Sino-Indian relations in terms of competitive cooperation or defining various aspects of their relations in terms of 3Cs i.e., cooperation, competition and conflict. Irrespective of wherever you reach in your career, your initial academic background stays firm in your mind and provides you intellectual strength. Having done my Masters in Chemistry, I thought why not to balance 'Sino-Indian Relations' like an equation. After all, the complete nature, the whole world and the complete planetary systems are based on balance. There is continuous movement in the nature to achieve or retain the balance. In an atom of every element in the Universe, electrons are continuously moving from one orbit to another to become saturated either within itself or by combining with the atom of another element and that is how the equation is balanced. International order is also based on 'Balance of power', wherein nations strive to establish their position or identity in that hierarchy. Chinese also achieve harmony through balancing of Yin and Yang. That's why I decided to have the title of my book as "Sino-Indian Equation: Competition +Cooperation – Confrontation". Moreover, my deep interest in China has been kindled by none other than renowned sinologist Dr Mohan Malik, Professor in Asian Security at Asia Pacific Center for Security Studies (APCSS), Honolulu, Hawaii, whom I always consider as my guide, philosopher and mentor and seek his guidance and blessings.

I benefitted immensely from the 'Environment scans', conducted every fortnight in CENJOWS, which ensure that you don't miss out on any important event happening anywhere in the world and interaction with colleagues sharpens your analytical ability. I am thankful to my colleagues (all senior fellows) viz., Gp Capt G D Sharma, VSM (retd.), Air Cmde T Chand (retd.), Brig Navjot Singh Bedi, Col Harpreet Singh, Col Sumit Rana, Col Shyamji Yadav, Col Arvinder Singh, Col Karan Singh, VSM, Capt K K Agnihotri, IN, Capt Ranjit Seth, IN, Shri R Chandrashekhar and Col Y S Pathania, Secretary CENJOWS for providing their valuable support in my endeavor. I am extremely thankful to Brig H S Cheema, a dedicated China watcher for sharing his views from time to time in my more than a year-long effort.

My first book on China, which turned out to be 507 pages after printing, was written in hand by me – an habit of writing with pencil so that you can correct and recorrect time and again, had been developed since my Staff College days and continued through out. My daughters Akanksha and Srishti, both engineers – Elecronics & Communications, and civil engineer respectively, had put in almost 80 percent of the book on computer. Though I had a personal computer at home but my elder daughter sprung a surprise by gifting me Apple Mac pro laptop and stated that I should do my next book myself on that laptop. I started writing articles on google docs because I found my laptop not compatible with MS Word. One of my colleague Brigadier Jai Singh Yadav, SM, VSM, who is a keen China watcher not only enriched my knowledge on China's BRI but his son Dhruv Jai Singh doing graduation in Political Science from Delhi University and a budding software enthusiast made my laptop MS Word friendly, for which I will always remain indebted to him. Though I continue to write in hand because 'old habits die hard' but I can say with pride that I could put my complete book on computer myself, leaving aside the maps and drawings as my daughters are always there to do my work. Interestingly, the day I gave my book script for publishing to Pentagon Press, my daughter Akanksha also completed her doctoral thesis on 122 GHz Microwave antenna (five years hard work) and submitted it to her examiners at Karlsruhe Institute of Technology, Germany.

In today's world of internet, any book, paper or document can be accessed on your computer through a click of the mouse but availability of a good library is a great asset and nothing can match the physical feel of a book in your hand. The Institute for Defence Studies and Analyses (IDSA), New Delhi has an excellent library stocked with well-documented publications on any subject for which I am grateful to the organization and in particular to Mr. Mukesh Kumar Jha, the librarian, who has been extremely prompt and resourceful in providing me the reference material in no time. Subedar Yogendra Singh Rathore, a former para commando, Indian Army of Jaffna fame – a dedicated soldier capable of wielding a rifle and computer mouse with equal dexterity -is presently the Office Superintendent at CENJOWS. I am extremely thankful to him for helping me out in formatting and editing my book script.

My wife Deepa has been a constant source of support in all my professional and academic endeavors and it is because of her encouragement that I could take up the challenge of writing a second book and complete it well in time. Most importantly, it is the youngest member of our family 'Gullu' who deserves credit for giving his silent blessings and imbibing patience in me through his aura.

Finally, I will like to express my heartfelt gratitude to Lt Gen Vinod Bhatia, PVSM, AVSM, SM for devoting his precious time to go through the complete script of my book and commending me for my work.

Brigadier (Dr.) Rajeev Bhutani

1

Introduction

"*Chinese 'dragon' and the Indian 'elephant' should join each other in a duet, not a duel.*"

—President Xi Jinping

"*When India and China work together, 1+1 is not two, but 11*"

—Prime Minister Narendra Modi

CHINA and India have some striking similarities. Both the countries are ancient civilizations of the world having a glorious past and again reincarnated as modern republics in the mid-twentieth century. Demographically being the two largest countries in the world, China and India are together accounting for more than a third of world's total population. In economic retrospect, both were great economic powers accounting for nearly half of the world's GDP from 1000 to 1820 AD.[1] In fact, in 1700 AD India with a population of 165 million was the world's largest economy whereas China with 138 million people was the world's second largest economy after India.[2] Again in 1978, when China was placed on the path of reform, it was economically and institutionally a very weak state and its economy was smaller than India's. However, India took the decision to liberalize its economy in 1991, thirteen years after China. Today, China's economy is about five times larger than India's.[3] In recent years, when China's economic growth is slowing down, India is emerging as the fastest growing economy in the world. Riding on the cusp of sustained and high economic growth rates, both the nations have reemerged as major global and economic powers. This makes the Sino-Indian relationship critical not only for those living in China and India but also for the whole world.

Over last five decades, Sino-Indian relations have been progressed on the basis of a balanced and mature consideration of geo-political realities, which has resulted in short-term stability on the borders and an increased level of trade. However, due to unresolved territorial and boundary dispute between the two countries, the relations remain strategically uncertain. With the arrival of Xi Jinping as the most powerful leader since Deng Xiaoping, things have started looking different. Addressing the 19th National Congress of the Communist Party of China (CPC), Xi Jinping declared that China's international standing has risen as never before and he said "*China is moving closer to center stage*"[4] – implying that China is ready to claim its share of global leadership. Under his leadership, China has become more assertive on the global stage – from its continued dominance in the South China Sea despite international protestations to its exercise of economic power through his flagship Belt and Road Initiative. Interestingly, closer home the increased border intrusions including the military stand-offs at Daulat Beg Oldi, Eastern Ladakh (April 2013), Chumar, Eastern Ladakh (September 2014)[5] and Doklam near Sikkim (June 2017) took place after Xi assumed the leadership of China in 2013 – wearing three hats i.e., General Secretary of the CPC, Chairman of the Central Military Commission (CMC) and President of China.

In the current decade, the world is also not the same – leading to changing global alliances and shifting power balances. If China is gearing up to challenge America's global hegemony, starting first in the Asia-Pacific by expanding its economic and military influence and trying to transform the strategic geography on its periphery to its own advantage, the United States is also moving fast to 'nip in the bud' the China's ulterior designs. Taking cognizance of the vast potential of India and the Indian Ocean, the United States has now given due importance to India, which was long since overdue. The whole region is now being increasingly referred to as "Indo-Pacific" in all the international forums. The term has been in vogue since 2010 AD or historically may be even much before but it got officially adopted by the United States in 2017.[6] It is estimated that if India's economic growth stays on course, by mid of this century, India's economy could surpass that of the United States and be second only to China. And one can be rest assured that India's military and technological power will not lag behind.

Subsequent to 1962 Sino-Indian Border Conflict, though the bilateral relationships were reestablished somewhere in 1976 but the relationship always remained fragile due to lack of trust having emanated from Chinese betrayal. Consequent to India's nuclear tests in May 1998, China was referred to as a main threat to India, in that famous Prime Minister Atal Bihari Vajpayee's maladroitly drafted letter to the U.S. President Bill Clinton and eventually leaked by Washington. The then Defence Minister George Fernandes identification of China as Enemy Number One further added fuel to the fire.[7] In the *Shanti Parva* of Mahabharata, Bhishma Pitamah had stated "*In international politics, there are no natural friends or enemies and only circumstances create them.*"[8] If the Geography has destined China and India to be neighbors, then they must do everything in their power to create circumstances in which both can co-exist and prosper peacefully. If the US and Western nations consider that there is enough political space for a risen China and India and a recovered Japan, then the 'China threat' discourse which started perhaps in the late 1990s, will become inconsequential. India's former Prime Minister Manmohan Singh had aptly said, "*The world is large enough to accommodate the growth and ambitions of both our countries.*"[9]

Deriving an analogy from human relations, neighbors need not be friends but at the same time they don't have to be enemies also. Sometimes, they cooperate and some other times they compete. We have to determine whether China is our enemy or adversary? Michael Ignatieff, a former leader of the Liberal Party of Canada wrote in 2013 "*An adversary is someone you want to defeat. An enemy is someone you have to destroy. With adversaries, compromise is honorable: Today's adversary can be tomorrow's ally. With enemies, on the other hand, compromise is appeasement.*" He further wrote, "*Between adversaries, trust is possible. They will beat you if they can, but they will accept the verdict of a fair fight... Between enemies, trust is impossible. They don't play by the rules (or if they do, only as a means to an end) and if they win, they will try to rewrite the rules.*"[10] India's former foreign secretary Nirupama Rao has opined, "*India and China, have essentially attempted to build a "partnership" on the foundations of what is an adversarial relationship.*" If post-1962 China was regarded as enemy, today it is an adversary with which we must seek solutions.[11]

Innumerable analysts have predicted that the 21st Century is an Asian Century and it will belong to China. It can also be regarded as an Indian Century given the strength it projects in to future:

> First, India is one of the youngest nations in the world with more than 54 percent of the total population below 25 years of age. For the next few decades, India will have a youthful and productive labor force. India's demographic window of opportunity is between 2015 to 2050, whereas China's is 1990 to 2025, India's median age in 2010 was 26

and it will be 32 by 2030, the lowest among top ten economies of the world;[12]

Second, In India consumer spending grew from US$ 549 billion to US$ 1.06 trillion between 2006 and 2016, putting India on the path of becoming one of the largest consumer markets by 2025.[13] According to the International Monetary Fund, the household consumption share of the economies of Brazil, Russia, India and China were 62.8 percent, 54.1 percent, 57.3 percent and 35.1 percent respectively. Though, China has embarked upon rebalancing of its economy but some analysts believe that transition to higher household consumption will take many years – if GDP grows by 6 percent per year and consumption outpaces overall growth by 2 percent, it would not be until 2038 that consumption reaches a level of 60 percent of GDP, near the level of India, Brazil, Japan and Taiwan today.[14] Whereas India's consumption is expected to rise 7.3 percent every year over the next 20 years;[15]

Third, Given the labor supply-side flexibility and comparative wage rate differential, India has the ability to become the world's new manufacturing hub.

After having indulged in a harsh and threatening rhetoric during the Doklam crisis, China's popular daily tabloid newspaper, Global Times has now written "*India is poised to become one of the world's largest consumption markets over the next decade, and the Chinese companies don't want to miss out.*" It further added "*India has several weak points, but it also has unique advantages in labor costs. China and India have broad potential for cooperation in fields such as manufacturing. Chinese enterprises are happy with India's economic miracle.*"[16]

With the Doklam crisis having been resolved diplomatically, President Xi Jinping and Prime Minister Narendra Modi had an especially important meeting in Xiamen City of China on the sidelines of the 9th BRICS Summit on 5 September 2017, which is now being popularly termed as "Xiamen Consensus". President Xi emphasized that we (China and India) should be each other's development opportunities rather than be threats to each other – "*dragon and elephant should dance together*". Prime Minister Modi shared the same idea and believed that the political effects of "*making one plus one eleven*" could be achieved in China-India relations.[17]

To take this spirit of 'Cooperation' and 'Reconciliation' between the two nations forward, Chinese Foreign Minister Wang Yi, and the new member of Political Bureau of the CPC and State Councilor Yang Jiechi, visited India within ten days in December 2017[18] and it was reciprocated by India's newly appointed Foreign Secretary Vijay Gokhale by making a surprise visit to Beijing on 23 February 2018. Incidentally, Gokhale, a fluent Mandarin speaker, had played a key role in the disengagement at Doklam.[19] Simultaneously, conciliatory statements and friendly overtures were made by Chinese diplomats and were accordingly reciprocated in equal amount by their Indian counterparts.

2018 can be earmarked as a watershed year in the Sino-Indian relationship, commencing with now famous informal summit between Prime Minister Narendra Modi and President Xi Jinping in the central Chinese city of Wuhan in April. Though the exact nature of discussion between the two leaders was not made public and there was no joint declaration but as the events are getting unfolded in the following months, it is emerging that the two countries are appearing to move on a path of cooperation. For instance, it was widely reported that at Wuhan, possibility of India and China working together on a project in Afghanistan was discussed. A few weeks later, both the leaders met again on the sidelines of the SCO Summit in the coastal city Qingdao and Indian foreign secretary Vijay Gokhale announced that the two countries would undertake a capacity-building project in war-ravaged Afghanistan – their first third-country joint venture.[20]

Moving from 'Doklam Confrontation' to a phase of cooperation has involved not only lot of diplomatic maneuvering but the Indian government has traveled an extra mile: Subsequent to India's foreign secretary Vijay Gokhale's visit to Beijing in February, India had asked its officials not to attend Tibetan leader Dalai Lama's events, related to commemoration of his 60 years of exile calling it 'Thank You India', at Dharamsala; and later this year Indian government ordered its national carrier Air India to change over to the name "Chinese Taipei" from Taiwan on its website – as demanded by China.[21]

Narendra Modi met Xi Jinping on the sidelines of 10th BRICS Summit at Johannesburg on 26 July 2018 – third time in nearly three months. Recalling his recent meetings with Mr. Xi, Prime Minister Modi said that they had given a new strength to India-China ties and also provided new opportunities for bilateral cooperation.[22] President Xi accepted the invitation to visit India for an informal summit next year. On 30 November, the two leaders met again on sidelines of the G20 summit in Buenos Aires, Argentina – their fourth meeting in 2018 and discussed joint efforts to further enhance mutual trust and friendship across all aspects of their ties.[23]

Stalled dialogue mechanisms between the two countries are being revived and the bilateral military exercise will be held again during the year. Several high-level exchanges have been planned.

It is apparent that consensus is replacing confrontation and competition, in redefining the Sino-Indian relationship. Prime Minister Narendra Modi at Shangri La Dialogue on 01 June 2018 had concluded his keynote address by stating that, "*Competition is normal. But, contests must not turn in to conflict; differences must not be allowed to become disputes...It is normal to have partnerships on the basis of shared values and interests.*"[24]

With the aforesaid as a backdrop, it is intended to analyze the Sino-Indian Equation as under:

- Sino-Indian Relations – Sources of Conflict.
- Areas of Cooperation vs. Competition.
- India's Strategic Initiatives.

2

Sino-Indian Relations: Sources of Conflict

THE rise of China was unmistakably foreseen by India even before the People's Republic of China (PRC) was formally proclaimed on 01 October 1949 – it resonated in the portals of the Indian Parliament when on 04 December 1947 Congress Member Brajeswar Prasad said in the Lok Sabha, "*India and China are destined to be the leaders of Asia. Joined together, they will be (a) force to be reckoned with.*"[1] India was the second non-communist country to accord recognition to the PRC. Mao Zedong, speaking in 1951 in honor of the first anniversary of India's constitution, declared that 'excellent friendship' had existed between the two countries 'for thousands of years'.[2] In the 1950s, this friendship was affirmed by the "*Hindi Chini Bhai Bhai*" slogan but then occurred the "betrayal" of 1962, turning China in to a foe. On May Day 1970, Chairman Mao Zedong engaged India's Charge' d affaires in Beijing, Brajesh Mishra on the rostrum at Tiananmen Square, to say, "*We cannot keep on quarrelling like this. We should try and be friends again*" to which the latter replied, "*We are ready to do it today.*" It took six years before the two countries could restore their diplomatic relations to ambassadorial level, with the initiative taken by Mrs. Indira Gandhi, the then Prime Minister.[3]

India and China share a 3488 km (4,057 Km border according to The United States Department of Defense)[4] long disputed border. China also lays claim to a little over 110,000 sq. km of India's territory but as per China's stance the disputed border is only 2000 km.[5] The Sino-Indian border is the longest disputed, but at the same time the most peaceful border in the world, with the last shot having been fired in anger, way back in October 1975 (when four Assam Rifles personnel lost their lives in a Chinese ambush at Tulung La, Arunachal Pradesh).[6] The normalization phase began with the reinstitution of the offices of ambassadors. In 1979, the then Foreign Minister, Shri Atal Behari Vajpayee paid a historic visit to China but it coincided with China's attack on Vietnam because of which he had to cut short his visit as a mark of protest.[7] This was followed by a visit to India by the Chinese foreign minister Huang Hua in 1981 and Deng Xiaoping made his "package proposal" to resolve the border dispute, which was out rightly rejected by India.[8] Border talks commenced with the signing of various agreements between 1993 and 2013 but little to show by way of progress on ground. The disputed borders are being ever present as the potential source of conflict. A lack of trust remains in the shadow as a remnant from the Sino-Indian Border Conflict of 1962, resulting in a fragile relationship.

China considers India as an impediment to her aspirations of becoming a Super Power. Hence, she wants to marginalize India by exploiting border tensions and building up neighboring countries as a politico-military counter. The Sino-Indian relationship is complex as it can be seen both as competitive and cooperative. They are cooperative in trade ties and on issues of global commons in the international forums, but competing for influence in the Indian Ocean, the Persian Gulf, Africa, Central Asia and East Asia. Thus, their relationship can best be analyzed by studying the sources of conflict and areas of mutual cooperation.

Border and Territorial Dispute

At the first Afro-Asian Conference at Bandung, Indonesia in 1955, China was reported to have reached a 'strategic understanding with Pakistan founded on their convergent interests, vis-à-vis, India'.[9] After Bandung, the emerging competition between China and India contributed to an increasingly strained bilateral relationship that was soon put to the test in addressing a serious irritant – the Sino-Indian border. However, there were other underlying reasons also behind the roots of the Indo-Chinese border dispute, such as, the Chinese invasion of Tibet in 1950 and subsequently, the Dalai Lama fleeing in March 1959 and given shelter in India. After the failure of Chairman Mao's Great Leap Forward Program, China decided to resolve the Sino-Indian border issue by use of force when it attacked Indian positions on 20 October 1962. On 21 November, China unilaterally declared a ceasefire and withdrew after taking possession of approximately 36,000 square kilometer area of Aksai Chin – Indian Territory in the Western Sector. In the Eastern sector, Chinese forces withdrew behind the McMahon Line, though Beijing still claims some 90,000 square kilometer south of that line in the Indian State of Arunachal Pradesh.[10] For Mao Zedong, that war was a means to humiliate and demolish India as an alternative democratic model to totalitarian China.[11]

The Sino-Indian war was a watershed moment in Indian foreign policy, after which Nehruvian idealism gave way to the pragmatic approach of subsequent administrations. After the war, India began to align itself more closely with the Soviet Union, which had begun to split from China within the international Communist movement; meanwhile, China and Pakistan developed closer ties. When India-Pakistan war broke out in September 1965, China came down heavily on Pakistan's side, the PLA sent probing missions on the entire Sikkim-Tibet border. Two years later, in September 1967, the PLA launched a direct attack on the Indian armed forces at Nathu La, on the Sikkim-Tibet border. The attack was repulsed at all points and the Chinese were known to have suffered at least twice as many casualties, as the Indians in this encounter.[12]

In mid-1986, it came to the notice of India that the PLA had built a helipad at Wangdung in Sumdorong Chu Valley in Arunachal Pradesh and about 40 Chinese personnel had intruded approximately two-three km in the same area. India reacted swiftly and the PLA had an eyeball-to-eyeball confrontation with the Indian Army in Sumdorong Chu Valley in August 1986. After a week of tense moments both sides mutually agreed to withdraw their forces inside their respective territories and create a no man's land. Beijing quickly realized that 1962 cannot be repeated.[13] In December 1988, Prime Minister Rajiv Gandhi travelled to Beijing, where he was received by top Chinese leaders, including Deng Xiaoping and in-depth talks on the boundary issue were held. It was agreed that these would be settled through peaceful, friendly discussions.

Narasimha Rao, as Prime Minister, pushed the process further in September 1993, with the 'Agreement on the Maintenance of Peace and Tranquility along the Line of Actual Control in the India-China Border Areas'. This 'Land mark' agreement specified that "*neither side shall use or threaten to use force against the other*" and pending an ultimate solution to the border question, both "*shall strictly respect and observe the line of actual control between the two sides*". Further "*no activities of either side shall overstep*" this line and, in case they do, they "*shall immediately pull back to their own side*" on being cautioned by the other side. It clarified that "*references to the line of actual control in this agreement do not prejudice their respective positions on the boundary question.*"[14] These agreements established a foundation for greater economic cooperation that withstood the shock of India's May 1998 nuclear tests. After some strident criticisms of the tests and India's justifications, Beijing quickly resumed relations with New Delhi.[15]

The new millennium saw the resumption of high-level diplomatic exchanges and agreements – the 2002 Agreement on Providing a Political Push to Settling the Border Problems; the 2005 Agreement on the Political Parameters and Guiding Principles for Settlement of the India-China Boundary Question; as well as a raft of economic and cultural agreements.[16] In April 2005, Chinese Premier Wen Jiabao during his meeting with Indian Prime Minister Dr. Manmohan Singh in India, stated that China regarded Sikkim as an "*inalienable part of India*" and that Sikkim was no longer an issue in India-China relations and the Chinese side had officially handed over a revised map showing Sikkim as within the international boundaries of India.[17] Further, Mr. Wen Jiabao agreed to a boundary settlement along "easily identifiable natural geographical features", adding that in reaching a boundary settlement, "the two sides shall safeguard the interests of their settled population in border areas". This was interpreted by most of the Sinologists as a more or less, Chinese commitment to soften their claims on population centers like Tawang.[18]

But soon China upped its border claims by asserting that the whole of Arunachal Pradesh was a part of "South Tibet". In May 2007, China declined to issue visa to an IAS officer from Arunachal Pradesh, treating him instead as a Chinese citizen from Southern Tibet who did not require a visa.[19] The official was part of a group of 107 officers scheduled to visit China on a study tour. In retaliation, the Indian Government cancelled the entire visit. In 2008, Prime Minister Dr. Manmohan Singh invited Chinese displeasure by visiting Arunachal Pradesh and President Pratibha Patil's visit to the State and to Tawang aroused similar complaints. Matters came to a head, when China formally blocked the passage of $ 2.9 billion assistance program for India from the Asian Development Bank (ADB), merely because it contained provisions for aid to developmental projects in "Southern Tibet". New Delhi reacted strongly and China stood isolated, when every other ADB member including Pakistan rejected its objections and endorsed the assistance package for India.[20]

Subsequently, China started granting stapled visas to residents of Jammu & Kashmir and even Northern Army Commander was denied visa. The Indian foreign secretary openly referred to the need to show mutual sensitivity, arguing that "*the Chinese side needs to be sensitive to our concerns in Jammu & Kashmir, like India has been sensitive to Chinese concerns on Taiwan and Tibet.*"[21] Unwilling to reopen questions over the status of Tibet, China quietly dropped the stapled visa policy for J&K residents.

With the coming in of Xi Jinping as the paramount leader of China, there appears to be a change in the China's established position on the India-China Boundary Question or even relations, as the pattern of events over his complete tenure indicate. On 28 March 2013, President Xi Jinping met the then Indian Prime Minister Manmohan Singh at Durban on the sidelines of the BRICS Summit and told him "*China and India should improve and make good use of the mechanism of the Special Representatives to strive for a fair, rational solution and framework acceptable to both sides As Early As Possible*". Introduction of this new phrase of 'As Early As Possible' was a departure from the decades old position till then, which considered Boundary dispute to be a complex historical legacy needing time to resolve and should not hamper the China-India relations. The same was reiterated during the meetings between President Xi and Prime Minister Modi later.[22] Further the border incidents, which followed on ground after these meetings had striking similarity and need to be viewed in detail. A standoff took place between Indian and Chinese troops in Eastern Ladakh, in the Daulat Beg Oldi area in April 2013 as a Chinese military unit had apparently set up a camp fairly deep into what New Delhi considered was its side of the Line of Actual Control.[23] The situation was diffused after diplomatic intervention at the highest level. Eastern Ladakh continues to be a flashpoint between India and China. Just a week before Chinese President Xi Jinping's three-day visit to India, a military standoff started at Chumar in Eastern Ladakh, with around 1,000 Chinese soldiers ranged against an equal number of Indian troops. The 30 R position, at an altitude of 14,500 feet, was the site of the initial confrontation after Indian soldiers prevented PLA troops from building a road in the "disputed area" ahead of Chepzi towards Chumar on 10 September 2014.[24] Despite the bonhomie achieved between Indian Prime Minister Narendra Modi and Chinese President Xi Jinping during the latter's visit, it took almost 17 days when troops from both sides agreed to pull out in order to restore the pre-September 10 status quo. There had been a speculation in some circles that the PLA was acting independently of the leadership in Beijing. President Xi only supported this feeling when he appeared ignorant of the intrusion during his private conversation with Prime Minister Modi. Even more conspicuously, on his return from India Xi appeared to have given a dressing down to the PLA brass, exhorting them "*military commanders should have a better understanding of international and domestic security situations as well as the latest military development.*" He also said, "*Headquarters of PLA forces must have absolute loyalty and firm faith in the Communist Party of China, guarantee a smooth chain of command and make sure all decisions from the central leadership are fully implemented.*"[25] However, there is sufficient reason to discard this conjecture. Firstly, Xi has accumulated enough power and authority over various organs of the State including the PLA that none of them would dare act without his acquiescence or even knowledge. Secondly, if someone has analyzed Xi's profile; he has imbibed the traits of both Chairman Mao as also Deng Xiaoping and applies principles of their ancient strategist-philosopher Sun Tzu in the modern context. He has the ability to listen to everyone without giving away his intentions or emotions. Thus appearing ignorant during discussion with Prime Minister Modi has no relevance. Thirdly, he has not shied away from punishing the corrupt or rather disloyal officials as is evident from the most robust purge of senior party figures and military officers carried out by him. On the contrary, nine officers in the Lanzhou Military Region responsible for that portion of China-India border made the significant jump from senior colonel to the rank of major general on 12 January 2015.[26] And as the events would unfold later, the standoff at Doklam was not only a continuation of such incidents and intrusions, which started after the arrival of Xi but appeared to be a part of greater Chinese design.

Doklam Standoff

On 16 June 2017 Chinese troops with construction vehicles and road-building equipment began extending an existing road southward in the Doka La area of the Doklam plateau. On 18 June 2017, Indian troops entered Doklam, on behalf of its Ally Bhutan, to stop the Chinese troops from constructing the road, leading to a standoff between units of the Indian Army and the People's Liberation Army of China. China attempted to extend a road that previously terminated at Doka La towards the Bhutan Army camp at Zompelri near the Jampheri Ridge 2 km to the south; that ridge, viewed as the border by China but as wholly within Bhutan by both Bhutan and India, extends eastward approaching India's highly strategic Siliguri corridor. Indian strategic planners remain particularly concerned given the proximity to the vulnerable Siliguri Corridor – a geographic choke point between Northeast India and the rest of the country measuring just 23 km at its narrowest point. On 29 June 2017, Bhutan protested to China against the construction of a road in the disputed territory.[27] On 28 August, Indian and Chinese troops agreed to disengage, ending a 73-day standoff. At the height of the Doklam standoff, while China indulged in shrill rhetoric and threatening stance, India pursued a three-pronged strategy: One, it maintained restraint in its public statements and continued with behind-the-scenes diplomacy; Two, it stopped China's road construction through the crude means of physical denial, leaving the onus of escalation on Beijing;[28] and Three, India also had quietly stepped up its military preparedness just in case the diplomacy and physical denial did not work – a village near the face-off site was evacuated and mountain divisions of the army were moved to the border regions. India's three-pronged strategy was very well crafted and had all the ingredients for success but viewing it in the hindsight it may best be regarded as a tactical victory. Satellite images now show that China has considerably beefed up its military presence in the region just to the North of the standoff site. In addition to several military structures, some road construction machinery could also be spotted.[29] While the 28 August disengagement was carefully projected as a peaceful resolution at the politico-diplomatic level so as not to define a winner or a loser but it may not be off the mark to state that it was a retreat for China. To overcome the setback suffered, China's response is on expected lines.

China's Growing Strategic Ambitions in the Indian Ocean Region

With the rapid growth in its economy and political influence, China's previous pre-occupation with 'border security' has now been transformed into 'security boundary', which entails increasing importance being given to maritime domain. In 2015, China became the world's largest importer of crude oil surpassing the United States.[30] The U.S. Energy Information Administration (EIA) estimates China to import about 80 percent of its crude oil by 2035. Each year, more than 60,000 merchant vessels or about three-quarters of China's oil imports traverse long and vulnerable Sea Lines of Communication (SLOCs) through the Indian Ocean and Malacca Straits, before reaching the South China Sea.[31]

The "Malacca Dilemma" articulated by former Chinese President Hu Jintao for the first time in 2003, is not only related to China's concern for piracy alone but emphasizes the region's strategic importance. Since then, the "Malacca Dilemma" has become an inseparable feature of China's strategic discourse. Chinese analyst Shen Dingli brought out "*the real threat to us is not posed by the pirates but by the countries which block our trade route*". He further added "*The situation requires us be able to hit the vulnerable points of our potential opponents by restricting their international waterway. So we need to set up our own blue-water navy and to rely on the overseas military bases to cut the supply costs*".[32] It may be of interest to note that while participating in "Galle Dialogue 2012" in Sri Lanka on 13 December 2012, Vice Admiral Su Zhiqian, Commander of the East China Sea Fleet, People's Liberation Army's Navy (PLAN) had stated "*The freedom and safety of the navigation in the Indian Ocean play a very important role in the recovery and development of global economy and the Chinese Navy will actively maintain the peace and stability of the Indian Ocean.*"[33] The formal shift in China's strategic thinking became evident from its White paper on China's Military Strategy released in May 2015. It states, "*The traditional mentality that land outweighs sea must be abandoned, and great importance has to be attached to managing the seas and oceans and protecting maritime rights and interests.*" It has further emphasized the necessity for developing a modern maritime military force structure to protect the security of strategic SLOCs and overseas interests.[34]

The PLAN started its first foreign port calls with Indian Ocean between November 1985 and January 1986, when its warships made port calls in Pakistan, Sri Lanka and Bangladesh. In 2000, a Chinese destroyer made the PLAN's first full transit of the Indian Ocean and in 2001 a PLAN submarine made an unannounced port call to Myanmar. In 2005, two PLAN ships made their first port call in India. In 2008 a naval coalition was formed by the international community to combat the growing threat of piracy off the Horn of Africa and China was invited to join the anti-piracy operations. Beijing dispatched a PLAN escort fleet to participate but it chose to operate independently from the coalition. As of February 2016, 23 PLAN escort fleets have rotated through the Indian Ocean.[35]

Not only China's critiques but their own officials and strategic thinkers had stated in various forums that combating piracy is not the only objective of PLAN in the Indian Ocean but the main purpose is the security of Strategic SLOCs and power projection. In 2012, the PLAN for the first time began deploying maritime intelligence collection ships to the Indian Ocean. These ships were likely to have the equipment for collecting signals and electronic intelligence and for mapping the ocean floor.[36] In 2014, China deployed submarines to the Indian Ocean for the first time, ostensibly in support of its counter-piracy patrols. A SHANG-class nuclear-powered attack submarine (SSN) conducted a two-month deployment in the Indian Ocean between

December 2013 and February 2014, surfacing twice near Sri Lanka and in the Persian Gulf before returning to the Western Pacific. A SONG-class diesel-powered attack submarine (SS) patrolled in the Indian Ocean in September and October 2014. The SONG also conducted the first foreign port call by a PLAN submarine with two stops in Colombo, Sri Lanka. The Chinese Ministry of National Defense assured regional nations that the submarines were deployed to the Indian Ocean in support of China's counter-piracy patrols.[37] However, China likely used these deployments to test the submarine and its crew's ability to operate for long durations at extended distances from China and to prepare for potential crises and wartime operations in the Indian Ocean. Since then, at least one and potentially two additional PLA Navy submarines have deployed to the Indian Ocean, indicating Chinese submarine patrols in the region are becoming routine.[38]

Acquisition of overseas military bases had been the most taboo of subjects in Beijing. It was believed that Beijing would likely avoid the complications inherent in establishing permanent foreign bases and might probably follow a **'places, not bases'** strategy in developing strong relationships with key allies and partners so as to allow its naval vessels to dock, replenish and refit in key locations.[39] Notwithstanding the above observation by a reputed international strategic institute, concerns over Chinese interests in establishing regional military bases had, in fact, surfaced more than a decade ago. In 2004, the U.S. defense contractor Booz Allen Hamilton coined the term **"String of Pearls"** in his report "Energy Futures in Asia" submitted to the Office of Net Assessment at the U.S. Department of Defense. The study was commissioned by Defense Secretary Donald H. Rumsfeld and this internal report was previously undisclosed. However, the Washington Times got a copy of the report and published its contents in its edition of 17 January 2005. The Report stated that China was adopting a "string of pearls" strategy of bases and diplomatic ties stretching from the Middle East to Southern China that included a new naval base under construction at the Pakistani port of Gwadar (See Map at Annexure 1). Beijing already had set up electronic eavesdropping posts at Gwadar and was monitoring ship traffic through the Strait of Hormuz and the Arabian Sea. Other "pearls" in the sea-lane strategy, according to the report, include:

- Bangladesh: Building of a container port facility at Chittagong.
- Burma: China is building naval bases in Burma and has electronic intelligence gathering facilities on islands in the Bay of Bengal and near the Strait of Malacca.

- Cambodia: China signed a military agreement in November 2003 to provide training and equipment.
- South China Sea: Building up its military forces in the region to be able to "project air and sea power" from the mainland and Hainan Island. China upgraded a military airstrip on Woody Island and increased its presence through oil drilling platforms and ocean survey ships.
- Thailand: China is considering funding construction of a $20 billion canal across the Kra Isthmus that would allow ships to bypass the Strait of Malacca. The canal project would give China port facilities, warehouses and other infrastructure in Thailand aimed at enhancing Chinese influence in the region.[40]

In spite of these disclosures, Beijing repeatedly insisted that it would never establish military bases abroad and its portfolio of Indian Ocean investments carried no military arrangements. Chinese Defense Minister Liang Guanglie in an interview with The Hindu in September 2012 said "*China would consider having logistic supply or short rest at appropriate ports of other countries*". He further added, "*Such logistic supply activities do not have any connection with establishing military bases overseas.*"[41] China formally opened its first overseas military base on 1 August 2017 in Djibouti in the Horn of Africa, the same day as the PLA marked its 90th birthday. Although, Beijing officially describes it as a Logistics Support Base for resupplying Chinese vessels on peacekeeping and humanitarian missions but satellite imagery and unofficial reports have shown that the base has military infrastructure and docking facilities that can handle most vessels in its naval fleet.[42] Ironically, China is the seventh country to establish a military presence in the small African nation, following the United States, France, Italy, Spain, Japan and the latest being Saudi Arabia. Since 2015, Beijing has poured over $14 billion into infrastructure development in Djibouti, a resource-poor nation of 14,300 square miles with just 875,000 people. This, far exceeds U.S. spending in that country. In January 2016, the People's Liberation Army (PLA) had conducted a 72-hour exercise involving thousands of marines and the navy special operations regiment in the Gobi Desert in the Xinjiang Uyghur Autonomous Region. The area's topography and climate resemble much of North Africa and the Sahel. With China's stated goal of housing up to 10,000 Chinese servicemen in Djibouti, such exercises offer ample basis for concern.[43] Acquisition of a naval base at Djibouti has only reconfirmed China's geopolitical ambitions overseas and analysts opine that Beijing could use the base to project its power into North Africa, as also to strengthen its position in the Indian Ocean.

Strategic Encirclement of India

China has made concerted efforts to create a ring of anti-Indian influences around India through military and economic assistance programs to neighboring countries, combined with complementary diplomacy. Pakistan, Bangladesh, Nepal, Sri Lanka and Myanmar have been assiduously and cleverly cultivated towards this end. It has been widely termed as "Strategic Encirclement of India"[44] because China gained strategic advantage over India by progressively making India's neighbors dependent on her to a large extent for their economic and defense needs.

Although China's direct support for counter-insurgency movements in India has definitely dwindled, but China is seeking to keep India strategically engaged through her neighbors. The large-scale supply of cheap small arms to regimes inimical to India, is an ingenious method of indirect involvement as these small arms eventually find their way to militant organizations in Jammu & Kashmir, the North-Eastern States and Naxal affected states of India through agencies like Pakistan's Inter Services Intelligence (ISI). Further, in search of an assured energy supply and safe routes so essential for its rapid economic growth and regime stability, China has been working on securing its interests around the Indian Ocean littoral. Strategists have been referring to this as 'String of Pearls' policy of China as described above in the preceding paragraphs.[45] How China has established its influence on various littoral states of Indian Ocean as also surrounding India needs to be studied in detail.

Pakistan

China's relationship with Pakistan is driven primarily by its interest in countering Indian power in the region and diverting Indian military force and strategic attention away from China. The China-Pakistan partnership serves both Chinese and Pakistani interests by presenting India with a potential two-front theater in the event of war with either country.[46] Chinese officials also view a certain degree of India-Pakistan tension as serving their own strategic interests as such friction would bog India down in South Asia and interfere with New Delhi's ability to assert its global ambitions and compete with China at the international level.[47]

China is Pakistan's largest defense supplier. China and Pakistan have been jointly developing FC-1 Xiaolong (called JF-17 Thunder in Pakistan) a lightweight and multi-role combat aircraft. The PAF plans to induct 150 JF-17 combat aircraft in the coming years. JF-17 is being specifically developed to replace the PAF's Dassault Mirage III/5 Fighter jets by 2020.[48] China has also been jointly developing MBT-2000 (Al Khaled) tanks, K-8 Karakoram advance training aircraft & Babur cruise missile.[49] Beijing has agreed to sell eight modified diesel-electric attack submarines to the Pakistan Navy by 2028, half of which will be built in Karachi. The majority of analysts speculate that these submarines will be a lighter export version of the PLAN's Type 039 and Type 041 Yuan-class conventional submarine.[50] China's help to Pakistan in the nuclear-missile field is a well-documented fact. China supplied Pakistan the complete design of a nuclear weapon – a 25kt implosion device, possibly a Chic-4 in 1983 and 34 M-11 short-range ballistic missiles in 1992. China had even helped Pakistan to develop its indigenous ballistic missiles, viz., HATF-1, HATF-2 and HATF-3.[51] Beijing also built a turnkey ballistic missile manufacturing facility near Rawalpindi and helped Pakistan develop the 750km range Shaheen-I ballistic missile.[52] The close nuclear and missile proliferation relationship between Pakistan and North Korea, as also the supply of centrifuges for Uranium enrichment to Libya and North Korea through the so-called A.Q. Khan network, were all through the more or less acquiescence of China.[53] Pakistan's nuclear weapons and missile capabilities are being upgraded by China. India has to carefully monitor if China is assisting Pakistan to shift its nuclear weapons from the growingly unstable Baluchistan Province, to tunnels in the remote parts of Gilgit-Baltistan.[54]

China and Pakistan had jointly built Gwadar Port, which is strategically located at the confluence of Gulf of Oman and the Arabian Sea and is in close proximity to the vital Straits of Hormuz, through which an estimated 40 percent of the world's oil supply passes. In its first phase, the port was developed jointly by the governments of Pakistan and China at a cost of 17 billion rupees ($288 million) and inaugurated in March 2007. China financed 80 percent of the amount for the first phase and reportedly is funding most of the second phase of the project as well. Much of the amount is reportedly through loans given on strict conditions. Control of the port was transferred to the state-run Chinese firm China Overseas Port Holding Company (COPHC) in 2013. Though the port at Gwadar is owned by the Pakistan government's Gwadar Port Authority (GPA) but China has got the operation rights of Gwadar port for 40 years.[55] The revenue sharing and control agreement for Gwadar port shows that, for the next 40 years, COPHC will get a 91 percent share of the revenue and the Gwadar Port Authority just the remaining 9 percent. Although this is a 40-year build-operate-transfer (BOT) agreement and technically different from a lease; Pakistan has still lost control of the port for the next four decades. Pakistan's total external debt is around US$82 billion, and Chinese loans will further inflate this.[56] It's quite possible that, in the near future, Pakistan will be left with no choice but to hand over Gwadar port to China, in the same way as the Chinese have got hold of Hambantota from Sri Lanka, even though the government of Pakistan rejects such fears. Alternately, China may turn its investments in Gwadar Port into access for its warships.

At any given time, the port can berth two or three large ships with capacity of 50,000 DWT (dead weight tonnage). Gwadar will be able to handle about one million tons of cargo annually by the end of the year. By 2045, the port will be able to berth 150 ships and handle cargo up to 400 million tons annually, and will have multiple logistics services, a huge storage facility and a nine-square kilometer industrial free trade zone (GPFZ).[57]

As part of China's Belt and Road Initiative (BRI), Chinese President Xi Jinping during his visit to Islamabad on 20 April 2015, had announced investments worth $46 billion for China-Pakistan Economic Corridor (CPEC), which was later increased to $62 billion. CPEC is a 3,000-kilometer corridor from Kashgar in Western China to Gwadar in the Baluchistan province of Pakistan (See Proposed Plan of CPEC at Annexure 2). Out of 39 "early harvest" projects under CPEC, 19 have since been completed or are under construction with a Chinese investment of about $18.5 billion. The progress makes it the fastest developing of all of at least six BRI's corridors China plans to establish. The CPEC became partly operational on 13 November 2016 when Chinese cargo was transported over land to Gwadar Port for onward maritime shipment to West Asia and Africa. Chinese naval ships will be anchored at Gwadar to safeguard the port and trade under the CPEC. Pakistani officials have trained and deployed about 15,000 troops and paramilitary forces to guard CPEC-related projects and the Chinese working on them.[58] However, Pakistani newspapers have now been reporting, citing documents of Ministry of Planning and Development, that unlike the earlier claims of $ 50 billion to $ 62 billion CPEC investment, the actual investment is likely to remain half of the initially announced investment figures. Rather, Pakistan will pay $ 39.83 billion to China in 20 years as repayments of debts and dividends on a $ 26.5 billion investment under the CPEC. The loans have been given at an interest rate as high as 5.2 percent and Pakistan on an average will return $ 2 billion per annum to China. It is reported that the only major project that can materialize in the next few years is the $ 8.2 billion Mainline-I Project of Pakistan Railways and the project cost has not been included in these estimates.[59]

Besides serving as a deep water cargo port and naval base, it will also serve as a key base to secure greater Gulf energy resources for China. It takes 16 to 25 days for Chinese oil tankers to reach the Gulf through sea access, but when high-speed rail and road links through Gilgit and Baltistan are completed, China will be able to transport cargo from Eastern China to the new Chinese-built Pakistani naval bases at Gwadar, Pasni and Ormara, just east of the Gulf within 48 hours.[60] Washington-based political activist Senge H. Sering, a former visiting fellow at the Institute for Defense Studies and Analyses (IDSA) warned that when Gwadar-Karakoram Corridor would be linked to the upcoming Urumqi-Beijing rail link, the commute time from Central and Eastern China to the Pakistani ports would come to a "mere few hours."[61] The Gwadar port will also facilitate trade between China and the Central Asian and Middle Eastern nations. Protected by cliffs from three sides, Gwadar will not only provide critical strategic depth to Pakistan against a 1971-style Indian attempt to bottle up its navy, but will also open the way to the arrival of Chinese submarines in India's backyard. Beijing admitted that Gwadar's strategic significance was equivalent to the Karakoram Highway, which since opening in 1969, had helped strengthen the Sino-Pakistan nexus and served as the route for covert Chinese nuclear and missile transfers.[62]

Sri Lanka

While India was selective and conditional in extending support to Sri Lankan government for its fight against the Liberation Tigers of Tamil Eelam (LTTE), China provided wholehearted support to Mahinda Rajapaksa (who became president in 2005), including supply of all the hardware on its military wish-list. In the post-war period, Beijing was a key defender of Sri Lanka at various international human rights forums when President Mahinda Rajapaksa came under criticism over its rights record and allegations that 40,000 Tamil civilians were killed at the end of the war.[63] The then Prime Minister Manmohan Singh, not only shunned a Commonwealth summit hosted by Rajapaksa in 2013 over the treatment of Tamils but also abstained from voting on the US-sponsored resolution against Sri Lanka on alleged human rights violations, instead of opposing it in March 2014.[64] This exacerbated mistrust of New Delhi in Colombo. It is apparent that as relations between India and Sri Lanka became strained, China moved in to the former's sphere of strategic influence by supporting Sri Lanka on human rights issue in international forums and providing substantial economic and developmental assistance for its infrastructure projects.

Chinese funds have been channeled into roads, airports, and seaports, the two highest profile initiatives being the Hambantota Port Development and the Colombo Port Project. The Hambantota Port was built on a turnkey basis by Chinese state-owned contractors. It is the state-owned Export-Import Bank of China, which provided construction loans worth US$1.2 billion to the Sri Lankan government to build the Hambantota deep-seaport and a 2,000-hectare investment zone. This seven-year-old loss making deep-water container port was owned and operated by the Sri Lankan government's Port Authority. It has been a bust, a half-finished commercial extravagance, where few ships called. The Port lost more than $300m since it opened.[65] The new president, Maithripala Sirisena had faced a serious problem: Sri Lanka's debt was almost 80 percent of its GDP in 2016. The rating agency Moody warned in August that Sri Lanka would have to repay loans worth US$13.8 billion between 2019 and 2022. In 2017, after five months of discussions, one of China's largest and most powerful state-owned companies, China Merchants Group, with total assets of $855bn, signed an agreement to take over Hambantota port for US$1.12 billion on a 99-year operating lease.[66] China Merchants will effectively pay off the construction loans granted by the Export-Import Bank of China to the Sri Lankan government. China Merchants plans to invest at least another $1bn, but perhaps as much as $3bn, to complete Hambantota port and turn it into the key Indian Ocean deep water port for ships plying the route between Suez and East Asia. Hambantota is only 10 to 12 nautical miles from the main Indian Ocean sea-lane linking the Suez Canal and the Malacca Straits.[67]

Its port operations subsidiary, Hong Kong-listed China Merchants Port Holdings (CMP) has taken over management of Hambantota in December 2017. The company also agreed to invest a further US$600 million into port operations. But the proposed deal was heavily criticized by opposition politicians and port workers; concerned about ceding control over land to CMP and the handling of security. Under pressure, the government agreed to set up two companies that would be owned by the Sri Lanka Port Authority (SLPA) and CMP.[68] A joint venture between state-controlled CMP and the SLPA owns the leasehold for the port and 15,000 acres of adjacent land (which is over and above 2,000-hectare investment zone). In the deal, the Chinese partner actually holds a 70 percent stake[69] (80 percent by another account)[70] and it has been criticized for undermining Sri Lankan sovereignty. China's exports may be able to come in via the Sri Lankan backdoor. India and Sri Lanka have a free-trade agreement that in theory lets Sri Lankan goods enter the vast market duty-free. Chinese manufacturers could turn the Hambantota free trade zone into a giant Mexican Maquiladora and export finished products to India. This would flood India with lowered priced consumer goods, autos, chemicals and clothing.[71]

The port deal is just one of a series of infrastructure forays China has made into Sri Lanka. Next door, China has earmarked US$1.4 billion for the Colombo Port City, since renamed the Colombo International Finance Center (CIFC) along the lines of Dubai's International Finance Center. This is the single largest Foreign Direct Investment (FDI) Sri Lanka has ever received and the project is expected to become the first mid to high-end financial hub in South Asia and home 250,000 people. It is expected to attract US $13 billion worth of investments over the 30-year period of the project cycle.[72] In total, China has invested more than US$6 billion[73] (US$8 billion by another account)[74] into Sri Lankan infrastructure projects, which includesUS$500 million China-owned container terminal at Colombo port, US$455 million coal power plant, highways and expressways, and a National Theater.[75]

China has replaced India as Sri Lanka's single largest trading partner, which is largely due to massive imports from China for the Chinese-funded infrastructure projects. Sri Lanka's bilateral trade with China amounted to US$ 4,426 million as against India's US$ 4,369 million in 2016. Sri Lanka, at the same time has trade deficit with China (US$ 4,004 million in 2016) followed by with India amounting to US$ 3,261 million. The trade deficit of Sri Lanka with China is expected to continue to rise in the next decade and beyond because of large-scale public investments by the Chinese state-owned companies.[76]

But there are concerns over the military implications of such deals. In September 2014, two Chinese submarines docked in Colombo, just as Sino-Indian ties were strained by territorial disputes in Ladakh on Indian's northern border. In an attempt to ease Indian concerns, Sri Lankan officials had said the Hambantota would not be used for military purposes.[77] But it is apparent that with two strategic seaports of Sri Lanka under its control, China will pose a direct challenge to India's influence in its strategic backyard.

Myanmar

In the 20th century, Xinjiang was the New Territory and Tibet was the New Treasure (In fact, the Chinese name for Tibet is Xizang, which translates roughly as "Western treasure house"). In the 21st century, Pakistan is the New territory and Myanmar is the New Treasure. Initially, China had exploited the Burma route for instigating tribal insurgencies in India's Northeast, particularly for training and arming Naga and Mizo guerrillas. During World War II, the Allied and Axis powers had rightly classified Burma (now Myanmar) as a 'back door to India'.[78] Ever since Myanmar's military junta was reduced to a pariah status by the international community following its ruthless suppression of democracy in 1988, China had assiduously built up a close alliance, backing the junta in the international arena and in return won control over Myanmar's vast natural resources[79] – chopping down the forests in its North and East, having denuded the jade mines of the Kachin Hills and hunted and shipped many endangered species.

Myanmar flanks the Bay of Bengal and the Malacca Straits. For China, Myanmar is an advanced strategic post, where geography is on China's side. Myanmar's strategic location has allowed China a valuable corridor to the Bay of Bengal, allowing it to build oil and gas pipelines connecting to its interior. Commencing in late 2008, the two countries had built a $1.5 billion oil pipeline and a $ 1.04 billion gas pipeline. The pipelines run parallel to each other.[80] The 771-kilometer (479-mile) oil pipeline, which is designed to carry 22 million tons of crude a year or about 442,000 barrels a day (Myanmar can take 2 million tons of crude annually from the line), terminated in Kunming, capital of Yunnan, while the 2,806-km natural gas pipeline, designed to carry 12 billion cubic meters (bcm) of Burmese-produced natural gas every year, will extend to Guizhou and Guangxi. The first phase of the gas pipeline up to Yunnan became operational on 20 October 2013, and it shipped 3 bcm of gas in 2014. In 2014, construction was finished on Burma-China oil pipeline. After a long delay, only when the government of Myanmar agreed to lower transit fees, the process of filling the pipeline with crude oil could commence in April 2017. This pipeline eliminates 3,000 miles of sea travel through the Malacca straits by transporting crude oil from Kyaukpyu (Made Island Oil Terminal) Burma to Kunming, China. More importantly, the crude oil for this pipeline will be supplied by Saudi Arabia and other Middle Eastern and African countries.[81] Chinese security agencies have positioned personnel at several Burmese coastal points, including the Chinese built harbors at Kyaukpyu and Thilawa. These agencies already operate a Signals Intelligence Listening

Post and maritime reconnaissance facilities on the two Coco Islands in the Andaman Sea near the Indian Ocean[82] – transferred by India in the Fifties to Myanmar, which then leased these to Beijing in 1994. It allows China to monitor Indian missile tests and naval communications. Through Myanmar, China could in the future put pressure on India's Northeast, on the Bay of Bengal and on the Malacca Straits in a worst-case scenario.[83]

Bilateral trade between China and Myanmar reached $10.7 billion in FY 2016-2017, making China, Myanmar's top trading partner. Their bilateral trade had already reached $5.5 billion in the first half of the 2017-2018.China is also a major investor in Myanmar. It has invested over $14 billion since 1988, accounting for one-third of the total foreign investment in the Southeast Asian country.[84] However, in September 2011, Myanmar's new president Thein Sein shocked Beijing by cancelling the $ 3.6 billion Chinese hydroelectric dam project, even at the cost of a hefty cancellation fee of $ 42.5 million. Tremendous public opposition to the project, which planned to send most of its power to China but had already displaced tens of thousands people, forced the regime to choose between its legitimacy in the people's eyes or its friendship with China.[85] Since then, a succession of developments have taken place in Myanmar resulting in its opening up to the world, particularly warming up of US-Myanmar relations.[86] Myanmar had begun to look at other alternatives to China even before its democratic transition took place. In the economic sphere, countries like Japan and Singapore are investing heavily. A strong reiteration of this point is that for the first six months of FY2017-2018, Singapore has even overtaken China in terms of investment.[87] And dealing a blow to China's trade-linking project, the "One Belt, One Road" initiative, Myanmar announced last month that it is no longer interested in big hydroelectric power projects.[88]

Bangladesh

Chinese arms trade with Bangladesh is one of the major dimensions of Bangladesh-China relationship and in fact it was a precursor to deepening of relations further. When the Indo-Soviet security crust over Bangladesh was withdrawn in 1975 after the assassination of Sheikh Mujibur Rahman, the vacuum, which aroused in the defense sphere, was immediately filled up by China. In late 1980s China emerged as one of the major arms supplier of Bangladesh. Initially, most of the Chinese exported items to Bangladesh were small and conventional arms. Later China provided majority of the equipment such as: F-6, F-9, A-5 and F-7M Fighter aircraft for Bangladesh Air Force;

frigates, missile boats and submarine (a second hand Romeo Class in 1984) for its navy; and 36Type-59 main battle tanks (MBTs) for its army.[89] Beijing's 'Defense Cooperation Agreement' signed with Dhaka in 2002 – Bangladesh's first such accord with any country – was apparently to gain a strategic foothold on India's Eastern flank in Bangladesh.[90] In its report submitted to the United Nations in 2006 by China, Dhaka has emerged as a major buyer of weapons from China.[91] In 2006, China supplied 65 artillery guns and 114 missiles and related systems.[92] In 2008, Bangladesh set up an anti-ship missile launch pad near the Chittagong Port with assistance from China and it successfully test fired anti-ship missile C-802A (modified version of Chinese Ying Ji-802) with a strike range of 120 km from the frigate BNS Osman (a 1500-ton Chinese built Jianghu class Frigate) near Kutubdia Island in the Bay of Bengal with active participation of Chinese experts.[93]

Since 2010, Beijing has supplied Dhaka with five maritime patrol vessels, two corvettes, 44 tanks, and 16 fighter jets, as well as surface-to-air and anti-ship missiles, according to the Stockholm International Peace Research Institute.[94] Bangladesh is the second largest importer of Chinese weapons (after Pakistan) and accounted for 82 percent of all Bangladesh weapons purchases between 2009–2013.[95] Bangladesh Army is in the process of acquiring Chinese VT5 light MBTs for equipping its 2 to 3 regiments. China is helping Bangladesh to build a formidable navy in the Bay of Bengal. According to some credible sources, Bangladesh is going to build Chinese PLAN Type 056 Jiangdao class stealth ASW corvettes in Khulna Shipyard and PLAN Type 054A Jiangkai II multipurpose guided missile stealth frigates in Chittagong Dry Dock Limited.[96] In 2013, Bangladesh Prime Minister Hasina Sheikh signed a contract with China for the purchase of two Type 035G Ming Class submarines worth $203.5 million to boost country's naval power. Both of these submarines were reportedly received in January 2017. The Ming-class submarines (Type 035) are medium sized diesel-electric submarines. In the 1960s China reverse engineered the Russian Romeo Class into the Chinese Romeo-class Type 033. The Ming-class Type 035 were developed in the 1970s from the Romeo Type 033.[97] These submarines, in all likelihood, are ex-Chinese navy, which were either decommissioned or placed in reserve since the Chinese navy itself is going through a modernization phase. These diesel-electric submarines displace 2110 tons and have a surfaced endurance of 8000 nm allowing them to stay at sea for about 60 days. Besides providing training to the Bangladeshi crews, the Chinese are also likely to be deeply involved in setting up the shore infrastructure like repair yards, training facilities and operational support establishments – a basic necessity for smooth conduct of submarine operations.[98] Thus India's main concern is not about two Bangladeshi submarines entering in to Indian waters but it is about the long-term Chinese naval presence, in terms of personnel and possibly ships, in the Bay of Bengal. Gathering of tactical intelligence in Indian waters will become much easier for them. China has reportedly offered $1 billion in soft loan to Bangladesh Air Force to buy 16 Chengdu J-10B, 1 Xian Y-20 heavy lift military transport aircraft and many more.[99]

China too eyes Bangladesh's oil and gas reserves of 15.51 trillion cubic feet.[100] The incentive for harnessing these reserves has prompted China to go beyond providing the defense component. The bilateral trade between the two countries is heavily in favor of China with Bangladesh having imported $14 billion goods from China and exported as little as $800 million in 2016. Going forward, under even a conservative trade growth scenario, according to Dhaka's popular newspaper Daily Star, the two-way trade between the two countries could exceed US$ 30 billion by 2021.[101]

China and Bangladesh are reportedly developing road and rail links between Kunming to Chittagong via Myanmar, which called the Chittagong-Kunming Road and Railway Link, could be a boon for Bangladeshi infrastructure and trade. It would also provide a cheaper alternative than is presently available for shipping goods between China and its western neighbors.[102] Further, Bangladesh is also an important part of China's "Belt and Road" both in the overland component – via the Bangladesh-China-India-Myanmar (BCIM) corridor – and as a port hub for the Maritime Silk Road. The latter, in particular, has military overtones, as observers have often worried that China's investments in maritime infrastructure are expected to bear fruit as military assets as well (the basis for the "string of pearls" theory). China played a large role in developing Bangladesh's port at Chittagong even before the "Belt and Road" initiative came along.[103] However, China's plans for construction of a deep-sea port at Sonadia, south of Chittagong suffered a setback in February 2016 when Bangladesh government shelved the project. China was hoping to design, build and operate the port at Sonadia, which was expected to emerge as an important transshipment hub for the Maritime Silk Road. It would have been an alternative to the deep-sea port at Kyaukpyu that Beijing is building to link its underdeveloped southern provinces to the Bay of Bengal and the Indian Ocean. The port at Sonadia would have been Bangladesh's first deep-sea port as its existing ports at Chittagong and Mongla have a shallow draft and are heavily congested and inadequate to meet the mounting needs of its growing economy, which is reliant on sea-borne trade. The reason for cancelling the deal with China lies in the fact that in 2014, Japan came up with a proposal for a project at Matarbari, 25 km from Sonadia, which would include not only a deep-sea port but four coal-fired power plants and an LNG terminal. It offered to provide 80 percent of the funding for the $4.6 billion port on easy terms. Building two ports just a few kilometers apart was seen as economically unviable, and as Japan's terms were more favorable, the Bangladesh government chose the Matarbari project and scrapped a port at Sonadia (See Map Bangladesh & Myanmar at Annexure 3). Moreover, it is obvious that the U.S. and India would have applied pressure on Bangladesh to cancel the deal with China in favor of Japan.[104]

During Xi Jinping's visit to Bangladesh in October 2016, the *'closer comprehensive partnership of cooperation'*, which was forged in 2010 was elevated to *'strategic partnership of cooperation'* between the two countries.[105] Incidentally, Bangladesh does not have any such formal strategic partnership with India.[106] During Xi's visit, China had signed nearly $24bn in bilateral business deals but after one year, it has been evaluated that there has been no significant progress upon the soft loan of $21.5bn promised by China for 27 projects in Bangladesh.[107] Although Bangladesh has signed a huge number of loan agreements, it must be well aware that loan burden will not only affect the quality and strength of development but once it starts accumulating the country will fall into a unfathomable debt trap with unknown consequences.

Geostrategic Importance of Rakhine State of Myanmar and China's Role

China's interest in the Rakhine state is due to its strategic location and rich resources. The state is located on the Bay of Bengal, which opens into the Indian Ocean. Like Pakistan's Gwadar port, which enables Beijing to transport West Asian oil, gas and other commodities through a shorter route via Pakistan to underdeveloped western China, the long Rakhine coastline (with its Kyaukpyu port) provides Southern China with access to the sea and Eastern China with a shorter route to the Indian Ocean. Covering 36,762 km^2 of Myanmar's Western coast, Rakhine state is rich in natural resources. In 2004, South Korean company Daewoo discovered 4.5 trillion cubic feet of gas reserves off the state's coast. This sparked the interest of China. Starting from 2008, China's state oil company, the China National Petroleum Cooperation (CNPC), was permitted by the Myanmar military government at the time to buy gas from the Shwe reserve, in Rakhine's offshore basin. China's project to extract gas from Rakhine directly into its territory was realized in 2013 when gas was transported from Kyaukpyu on Rakhine's coast to China's Yunnan Province through the Myanmar-China Gas Pipeline. This gas meets the needs of China's Yunnan, Guizhou and Guangxi provinces as well as that of other counties and cities. China-Myanmar oil pipeline, which is running parallel to gas pipeline, began transporting oil from Rakhine's Made Island port towards Yunnan in April 2017, four months before the escalation of the crisis in Rakhine. Besides having spent an estimated US$2.5 billion on the China-Myanmar oil and gas pipeline projects, China plans on investing US$10 billion into the Kyaukpyu Special Economic Zone (SEZ), which will include a deep-sea port and an industrial park around the city of Kyaukpyu in Rakhine. It aims to turn the area, which extends over 17 km^2, into a maritime economic hub.[108] Rakhine's natural resources and geostrategic location are equally important for India also to develop its Eastern strategy.

The "stability of Rakhine" is regarded as "important" to the success of the BRI. The Rohingya crisis began on August 25, 2017 when the Myanmar government declared the Arakan Rohingya Salvation Army (ARSA) a terrorist organization and launched a military crackdown in Rakhine. However, horrific violence having been unleashed on Rohingya civilians, including women and children led to the exodus of over 600,000 of the estimated 1.1 million Rohingya from Myanmar to Bangladesh. Concerns over the impact that violence and unrest in Rakhine could have on the success of its projects in Myanmar and the BRI, in particular, underlie China's interest to end the Rohingya crisis and restore stability in the region. Further, Beijing is worried about the intervention of other powers in the Rakhine region. Hence, after having praised the Myanmar's military action against Rohingyas, Beijing now acted as a mediator between Myanmar and Bangladesh. China's new role as an international mediator, is motivated by economic interests rather than by humanitarian reasons.[109]

The areas that are the worst affected by the ongoing violence are in the North of Rakhine, near Myanmar's border with Bangladesh. Although neither Kyaukpyu nor the oil and gas pipelines are located in or run through these restive areas, Beijing is still concerned. The rise of ARSA and its mounting capacity to carry out attacks on well-secured targets indicated that it was only a matter of time before it could struck outside its stronghold. This had triggered concern in Beijing over the safety of infrastructure it has invested and built in the Rakhine state. Further, China has established strategic partnership with

Bangladesh. Therefore, Chinese leaders got concerned with Bangladesh's attempts to draw extra-regional powers to intervene in the crisis, prompting Beijing to accelerate efforts to bring Myanmar and Bangladesh to the negotiation table and end the refugee problem. During his visits to Dhaka, Bangladesh and Naypyitaw, Myanmar on November 18 and 19, 2017 China's Foreign Minister Wang Yi put forward a three-phase plan to resolve the Rohingya crisis: First, a ceasefire in Myanmar's Rakhine state, aimed at restoring order and stability, so as to halt the flow of Rohingya refugees to Bangladesh; Second, negotiations between Myanmar and Bangladesh to address the refugee problem; and Third and final stage will involve the economic development of the Rakhine state to address the underlying causes of the violence. China's plan has reportedly found acceptance in Naypyitaw and Dhaka and marks the start of a new phase in Beijing's involvement in the Rohingya conflict. Uptil now, to ease Dhaka's burden of looking after the Rohingya refugees, China was providing aid, including tents and blankets to Rohingya refugees in Bangladesh and on the other hand protecting Myanmar from international censure.[110]

Nepal

With China to its North and India to its South, Nepal is sandwiched between the two Asian giants, where both the countries are competing to enhance their influence. China's strategic interest in Nepal is also heightened due to it being the gateway into its restive Tibetan regions – 22 of the 30 counties in the Tibet Autonomous region (TAR) share border with Nepal.[111] For China the destabilization of its Tibet region bordering Nepal is one of its major concerns. Even though Kathmandu itself has no political interest in Tibet, a lot of Nepalese are sympathetic to the Tibetan cause. There are about 20,500 Tibetan refugees living in 12 settlements across the country in Nepal. However, the true number of Tibetan refugees is unknown. Some estimates show that 30,000 Tibetans live in Kathmandu alone.[112] It forms a major security issue for China. Further, till 2006, almost 2900 Tibetans escaped into Nepal enroute to India. Then, there were Tibetan Khampa resistance fighters based at Mustang (known to the world as the other Tibet and lies in North-Central Nepal), who backed by the Central Intelligence Agency (CIA) carried out attack on the PLA in the 1970s. Not only Khampa problem was curtailed, Beijing had been successful in its approach, as the number of Tibetan refugees crossing into Nepal from China after 2008 fell from 3000 to about 800 a year.[113]

China in 1988 had offered military hardware to Nepal and thereafter its defense supplies and military exchanges escalated after the visit of the Royal Nepal Army Chief to Beijing in 1999. By 2005, a major shift was seen in Nepal's weapons procurement policy, when it became entirely dependent on China for military supplies, which was earlier enjoyed by India. In 2007, China announced military aid worth of $ 1.3 million which was increased to $ 2.6 million with the Maoists coming to power.[114] Subsequently, during the Chinese Army Chief General Chen Bingde's visit to Nepal in 2011, China signed an agreement for providing military aid to the tune of US$ 7.7 million to the Nepal Army. Leading a 19-member high-level military delegation, the Chinese Defense Minister and State Councillor General Chang Wanquan undertook a three-day official visit to Kathmandu from March 23 to 25, 2017. The visit saw China offer a grant assistance of US$ 32.3 million to the Nepal Army for the purpose of strengthening its capacity. Chang's is the first defense ministerial visit since the two countries established diplomatic relations in 1955. Akin to Sri Lanka and Bangladesh, China has upgraded its relationship with Nepal to the level of 'Strategic Partnership' and during this phase, China is attempting to deepen military cooperation with the Nepal Army, which has been traditionally close to the Indian and US Armies.[115] The first ever Nepal-China special forces joint military training named 'Sagarmatha Friendship-2017' was conducted in Kathmandu, as part of their preparedness against terrorism, for a period of ten days in April 2017.[116] The joint training with China marks Nepal Army's extension of military diplomacy.

Nepal shares 1,415 Km. long border with China along the length of the Himalayan range in the North, with 18 passes. Nepal and India have an open border and free mobility of populace across borders. Nepal's trade is highly dominated by India. In 2011-12, India-Nepal trade was $ 3 billion and the total volume of trade between Nepal and China amounted to $ 1.2 billion.[117] Although, Nepal's trade with China is in increasing trend, it is far below the potential. This is due to less developed transport system and because of only one road link between Nepal and China i.e., the Arniko Highway and the absence of dry port in Nepal.[118] China is increasingly working to take over India's position of the largest trading partner of Nepal. To achieve this, China has offered zero-tariff treatment to 60 percent products of Nepal.[119] When there was blockade of fuel and necessary supplies on India-Nepal border due to protest by Madhesi, Beijing gave 1.3 million liters of petrol to Nepal as a grant, with the promise of following up after a commercial arrangement was signed between companies on the two sides.[120] In 2014, China had overtaken India to become the largest contributor of FDI to Nepal.[121] According to

Nepal's Department of Industry (DoI) statistics, Nepal received FDI pledge of 8.08 billion Nepali Rupees (79.26 million USD) from China in the first half of the fiscal year 2017-18, which is 57.73 percent of the total FDI pledges received by the Himalayan country during the period. India came second with FDI pledges of 3.73 billion Nepali Rupees (36.63 million USD).[122] China's open diplomatic policy in Nepal remains to exploit the resources of Nepal and take advantage of Indian market. Hence, it has completed 22-km road in central Nepal connecting its southern plains with Kyirong, county of Tibet, making the shortest motorable overland route between China and India.[123]

As part of its ambitious "One Belt, One Road" (OBOR) initiative, Beijing is looking into the possibility of connecting Kathmandu to Lhasa in Tibet via railways. Kathmandu's support for OBOR materialized in May 2017 when Nepal had officially signed a framework agreement with China, to be part of President Xi Jinping's BRI.[124] Soon after 19th National Congress of the Communist Party of China, a high-level Chinese delegation was dispatched to Nepal to carry out an inspection of the technical feasibility of the railway. According to reports in the Chinese and Nepalese media, the Qinghai-Tibet railway would be extended from Lhasa to Shigatse and then to Kyirong (Chinese: Gyirong) on the Nepal border, and Yatung (Dromo in Tibetan) in the Tibet Autonomous Region, on the border with Sikkim, India, and Bhutan.[125] Yug Raj Pandey, an undersecretary at Nepal's Ministry of Finance, told Reuters "*the proposed 550 kilometer-long railway...could cost $7-8 billion and take up to eight years to complete.*"[126]

As to the further development, the authority of Nepal emphasized the hope to link the three main cities in Nepal, Kathmandu, Pokhara and Chitwan with this international line many times. Since 30th August 2017, Gyirong Port (Rasuwa Port on Nepal side) has been opened to foreign travelers, which means that travelers can travel between Tibet and Nepal directly by land.[127] Although the Chinese government has generally sought to depict the purpose of the new lines to India and Nepal in terms of deepening of trade and tourism, the Chinese state media characterizes the plans overall as a "strategic rail network."[128] China has also funded the establishment of 35 China Study Centers in Southern Nepal especially near the borders with India to popularize the Chinese language as well as disseminate anti-India propaganda. It has also set up the China Radio International's local FM radio station in Kathmandu and a Nepal China Mutual Co-operative Society. The Business School of Kathmandu University also opened its Confucian Institute.[129]

Extension of the railways as well as the construction of All Weather expressways in Tibet will be the alternative trade linkages to Nepal, thereby, reducing dependence on India. China has also opened seven dry ports for Nepal inside Tibet. Chinese expansion in the region is a plot to fulfill Beijing's bigger and long-term ambition to use Nepal as a corridor connecting China to South Asia or more precisely to enter the huge markets in the Indian plains and de-stabilize security in the region through both covert as well as overt means.[130]

Commencing on 12 January 2018, China has provided the internet access to Nepal by opening a fiber optic link from Kathmandu to the border point Rasuwagadhi into the Tibet region. Nepal line is connected via Hong Kong bandwidth, which is not restricted by the infamous "Great Firewall". Previously, all internet connections to Nepal were provided by India's Bharti Airtel and Tata Communications through the cities of Bhairahawa, Biratnagar and Birgunj in Southern Nepal.

The communications link with China would have been established in December 2014 but it was completely destroyed in a devastating earthquake in April 2015. The link was scheduled for launch by the middle of last year but it was delayed due to the difficulties of working at high altitudes above 4,000 meters. It came after a coalition of two communist parties that are considered pro-China won Nepal's election. The new government is ready to revisit the Chinese company-funded Budhi Gandaki dam project, which was cancelled on the eve of the election.[131]

Maldives

South west of India, the Republic of Maldives is strategically located, sitting along major sea lines in the Indian Ocean. China has been working on the Maldives for a long time. Somewhere in 2001, China had coaxed Maldives' Abdul Gayoom Government to let it establish a base in Marao. Marao is one of the largest of the 1192 coral islands grouped into atolls that comprise Maldives and lies 40 km South of Male, the capital. Coral islands make fine submarine pens. The PLAN's objective was to deploy nuclear submarines fitted with sea-launched Dong Feng-44 missiles and ballistic missiles in Marao. The base deal was reportedly finalized after two years of negotiations when Chinese Prime Minister Zhu Rongji visited Male on 17 May, 2001.[132] A Chinese base in Marao islands would have placed it in a direct position to influence oil commerce. The naval base was expected to be operational by 2010, but the deal appeared to have run into trouble in 2002. Both the Maldivian and Chinese governments denied the reports and have since maintained that the deep sea surveys were carried out for environmental protection and not for military purposes.[133]

China and Maldives established diplomatic relations in 1972 but it was only in 2011 that China opened its embassy in Maldives, under the invitation of former President Nasheed. The Chinese ambassador to the Maldives, Wang Fukang, mentioned three critical areas where Beijing and Male should increase their cooperation: tourism, infrastructure projects, and, finally, closer maritime cooperation between the two nations.[134] Maldives attracts a million tourists annually, of which Chinese tourists numbered 35,000 in 2008-9 but it increased to 363,626 in 2014, accounting for one-third of arrivals.[135] Investing in infrastructure projects in the Indian Ocean is Beijing's preferred approach for obtaining a strong foothold in the region and Maldives holds an important place in China's Indian Ocean game. After taking over as the President, Mr. Mohammad Waheed Hassan had visited Urumqi, Capital of Xinjiang in the first week of September 2012 to attend the second China-Eurasia Expo, where three agreements were signed, providing for Chinese assistance worth $ 500 million. The decision of the Government of President Mohammad Waheed in Nov 2012 to unilaterally terminate the contract given to a consortium headed by an Indian Company (GMR Infrastructure Ltd) to operate and modernize Ibrahim Nasir International Airport in Male worth $ 511 million, was said to be at the behest of China, to ultimately benefit a Chinese company.[136] The relationship with China bloomed when the current Yameen government took over and had been actively courting China while moving away from India. When President Xi Jinping visited Maldives on 15 September 2014, the two leaders agreed to upgrade the main airport and to build a bridge, connecting Male to Hulhule – the island where the Male International Airport is located – dubbed as the "China Maldives Friendship Bridge". The initial agreement to upgrade was later reportedly changed to building of a whole new airport with a second runway.[137] It is reported that $ 373 million loan for the Male airport and $210 million for the Male – Hulhule Bridge have been granted from China's EXIM bank. In addition, China is also building a 7,000-home housing project.[138] There is no transparency on how these loans or aid would be repaid by the receiving countries. Most of the loans are controlled by government-held institutions and were, apparently, given at a very high rate of interest that Male certainly would not be able to meet without a unilateral waiver. This is a common tactics applied by China – relaxing loan conditions in exchange for control over maritime projects it helps finance, for instance, Hambantota and Gwadar are the latest examples.

Significantly, the Maldives also accepted Xi's request to join the Chinese Maritime Silk Route (MSR) program, which envisions development of a sea route from China's Fujian province to the Mediterranean Sea via South Asia and East Africa. By endorsing MSR, Maldives seeks to promote itself as a vital trade cum transit port. This fits in well with Male's ambition of transforming itself into an international trade hub on par with Singapore. The link to China's MSR is through the Ihavandhippolhu Integrated Development Project or iHavan which is located in the Haa Alif Atoll situated in the North of Maldives and are closest to India and Sri Lanka. The design of the MSR project seeks to capitalize on the location of the atoll, which lies on the seven-degree channel through which the main East-west shipping routes connect China to the Middle East and Europe.[139] Interestingly, iHavan, located centrally at the IOR, has over US$18 trillion worth of goods passing through its waters annually.[140] Beside iHavan, China has also shown interest in the development of Maarandhoo Islands (in the Haa Alif Atoll) with transshipment ports among other things as also contributing to the development of Maldives' second international airport at Hanimaadhoo.[141]

China-Maldives economic cooperation is gaining momentum. Bilateral trade increased to US$ 98 million in 2013 and US$ 104 million in 2014.[142] The latest deal was a controversial and hurriedly signed country's first-ever free trade agreement (FTA) during the first Maldives-China Joint Commission meeting held in Beijing in December 2014. It will exempt Maldivian imports, mostly fisheries products, from taxes, while Maldives on its part would waive off tariffs on Chinese imports.[143] Talks are on between Male and Beijing on oil exploration. Defense collaboration is already underway, since the two countries signed a military aid agreement in 2012.[144] Post-2014, China has already started offering training to maritime personnel in the Maldives.[145] Around the time, when the FTA was signed, China and Maldives had officially agreed to establish a Joint Ocean Observation Station, which is reportedly coming up in Makunudhoo, the Western most atoll in the North. According to opposition leaders, the observatory will also have military applications with provisions even for a submarine base. There are also reports that China is seeking a port in the Southern part of the country as people from the Gadhoo island (Laamu atoll) have been evacuated and Chinese have been found building roads in that region. This island is located at the entrance to the one-and-a-half degree channel, a major international shipping passage that crosses the

Maldives.[146] With enhancement of ties with the Maldives, China may attempt to dock its naval assets at the island state, similar to the PLAN's trysts with Colombo; posing a threat to India's regional security. The concerns are not without substance; in August 2017, three Chinese naval vessels docked at the Maldives' capital, Male.[147] Another significant offer from Male is to help China play a bigger role in the South Asian Association for Regional Cooperation (SAARC), a move which poses dilemma to Indian leadership, which has tried to preclude Chinese influence in the South Asian region. Simultaneously, the Maldives has expressed its interest in the Shanghai Cooperation Organization (SCO).[148] Shift in the Maldives' foreign policy became apparent when President Abdulla Yameen announced in November 2014 that compared to "Western colonial powers", economic cooperation with China did not challenge Maldives' Islamic identity.[149] In a significant move, on 22 July 2015, the Maldivian Parliament (Majlis) amended the constitution and approved by 70 votes (14 against) foreign ownership of land in the country, including investments of over 1 billion dollars for projects where 70 percent of the land has been reclaimed. Looking at the parameters, China will be the obvious beneficiary. Members of Parliament voting against the move said that allowing investment of more than $1 billion could be used by China for its military expansion in the Indian Ocean region and would be detrimental to Maldivian national security interests.[150] Maldives has already leased an island close to the Male airport, Feydhoo Finolhu to China for 50 years. The islands are being leased to China for a fraction of estimated value, such as Feydhoo island was leased for only $4 million.[151]

Maldives had been in a state of emergency since 5 February 2018. Problem began on 1 February, when the Supreme Court quashed the conviction of former President Mohamed Nasheed (convicted on terrorism charges in 2015 and sentenced to 13 years in jail, living in self-exile in Sri Lanka since 2016) and ordered reinstatement of 12 parliamentarians who had been stripped off their seats last year, when they left Yameen's Progressive Party of Maldives to join the opposition. President Abdulla Yameen rejected the decision and declared a 15 day emergency, arresting two Supreme Court judges as well as his half-brother and former President Maumoon Abdul Gayoom. The emergency was extended for another 30 days. Restoring the seats of the 12 lawmakers would have effectively reduced Yameen's party to a minority. President Yameen feared he would be defeated by a strong opposition campaign targeting him on issues of corruption, illegal sale of natural resources and on his controversial deals with China. The United States, United Kingdom and India rallied against the Yameen government, calling for a roll back of the state of emergency. China, on the other hand, provided indirect yet firm support to Yameen – urging all relevant parties in Maldives to resolve differences "through dialogue and negotiations" and warning other countries like India against getting involved. Of late, China instead offered to mediate between the feuding parties in the archipelago, moving away from its initial stance of letting the parties resolve differences among themselves. It was reported that the opposition rejected such an offer. China was apprehensive that if the exiled President Nasheed returned to power, its Belt and Road Initiative would come under threat as Nasheed had rallied against China, accusing it of land grabbing in Maldives. In a recent interview, Nasheed said that China had already acquired 17 islands and Maldives was falling into a Chinese debt trap, with more than 70 percent of foreign debt owed to Beijing. There is no disclosure of sovereign guarantees given by Yameen to commercial loans given by Chinese banks.[152]

Seychelles

Seychelles is another island nation in the Indian Ocean, which hosts a US drone base, has a strategic position between Asia and Africa and has substantial Indian population. There were reports in 2012 about an offer from Seychelles to China for a base to provide relief and resupply facilities to the PLAN.[153] Though promptly denied by Beijing, the offer underscored the changing balance of power in the region. India has traditionally been the main defense provider of Seychelles – providing armaments and training to its Peoples' Defense Forces or SPDF. India extended a $ 50 million line of credit and $ 25 million grant to Seychelles in 2012 in an attempt to strengthen strategic ties. Subsequent to former Chinese President Hu Jintao's visit to the island nation in 2007, China became proactive in courting Seychelles. Much to India's discomfort, Beijing now participates in training SPDF and provides military hardware. China has expanded military cooperation with Seychelles, providing two Y-2 turboprop aircraft for surveillance of the Exclusive Economic Zone (EEZ).[154] China, as part of its efforts to bolster the island nation's maritime security capacity, has delivered the Type 62 patrol boat Etoile (607) to the Seychelles Coast Guard in June 2014.[155]

It has become increasingly evident that China is determinedly encroaching on India's strategic backyard by assembling a 'String of pearls' in the form of ports, electronic listening / monitoring stations, and naval bases stretching from Gwadar in Pakistan and Hambantota in Sri Lanka to Chittagong in Bangladesh and Kyaukpyu in Myanmar and further to Cambodia, Thailand and in the South

China Sea. Seeking bases in Maldives and Seychelles could be part of China's strategy of securing the sea-lanes in the IOR through which its oil tankers pass. China reinforces her relationship with these countries through colossal monetary inducements, leading to debt trap. In these pearls of littoral states, Nepal is an exception, but it provides an easy entry to China into South Asia beside its Tibet specific role. China's 'Belt and Road' initiative is the emboldened avatar of its erstwhile disguised "String of Pearls" strategy. Instead of the hardened military bases of the Cold War and earlier epochs, dual-use civilian-military facilities, where basing arrangements are implicit rather than explicit, are being employed and these are completely dependent on the health of the bilateral relationship in question.[156] *In fact, China's New Silk Road shall be regarded as overt expression of China's power ambitions in the 21st Century.*

Employment of Infrastructure as a Tool of Strategic Power

Xi Jinping's vision of OBOR or Yidai Yilu, where the Road refers to ancient maritime routes between China and Europe and the Belt describes the Silk Road's better-known trails overland, comprises a network of high-speed rail, motorways, oil and gas pipelines, ports, transmission lines and fiber optic cables. Apparently, China's visualization is that infrastructure power is the key to economic power and in turn economic power leads to the strategic power. With a view to create new markets for Chinese firms and a Eurasian trading bloc as also to establish new spheres of influence for his government, OBOR or BRI has become the centerpiece of Xi Jinping's foreign policy and it has been enshrined in to Party's constitution during the 19th National Congress of the Communist Party of China.[157] China's FDI is increasingly moving to OBOR countries. Its OBOR contracts are now more likely to involve Chinese firms managing the infrastructure they build, rather than building and handing over, a practice being followed in the past.[158] An outline plan of OBOR is shown in the Annexure 4.

In close proximity, China has been building a web of rail and road infrastructure around India, which is creating strategic pressure on the latter's periphery on three separate flanks. China is developing two North-South strategic corridors on either side of India: the Trans-Karakoram Corridor stretching right up to Gwadar at the entrance to the Strait of Hormuz, which has now been absorbed in CPEC; and the Irrawaddy Corridor involving road, river and rail links from Kunming in Chinese Yunnan province to Myanmar ports (Sittwe in Western Myanmar and Thilawa near Rangoon on the Bay of

Bengal). In addition, it is building up an East-West strategic corridor in Tibet across India's Northern frontiers: China constructed the world's highest 1,142 km Golmud-Lhasa rail line, which was opened in July 2006 and further extended it westward by a 252 km link to Xigaze, Tibet's second largest city and is pushing ahead with seven other rail-road projects adjoining the Indian border. It is planning to have a further 400 km extension not only to Kyirong (Chinese Gyirong), on the border with Nepal but a probable 120 km link to Kathmandu. It could also come to Yatung (Dromo in Tibetan), a trading center close to Bhutan and barely a few kilometers from Nathu La, a mountain pass that connects Tibet with Sikkim. There is a proposal too to extend the line to Nyingchi, an important trading town North of Arunachal Pradesh, at the tri-junction with Myanmar. These rail lines will bring the Chinese trains up to Sikkim and Arunachal Pradesh[159] (See China's Rail-Road Network from Tibet to India's Northern Borders at Annexure 5). China-Tibet railway is designed not only to aid the mineral exploitation of the Tibetan plateau, but also to strengthen China's hold on Tibet. Just as the newer highways into Tibet had helped in significant increase of Han migration, the railway to Lhasa and Xigatse will further accelerate Tibet sinocization and the economic marginalization of its native people. Ten years after the railway was built, Tibet now has close to 100 mining sites spread around the country. Tibetan copper and gold deposits are worth nearly one trillion dollars to China. Tibet is rich in Silver, Lead, Zinc, Lithium and other raw materials used in consumer products. The new infrastructure has also allowed the Chinese government to introduce large numbers of Han Chinese workers into Tibet. China has moved more than 2 million Tibetan nomads off their land to open it up for exploitation.[160] The fragile ecology of Tibet had already been made more vulnerable by the passage of railways. The Tibetan railway along with strategic corridor has significant strategic ramifications for India:

- It has augmented China's military-transport and reinforcement capabilities against India. At short notice, China will be able to intensify military pressure on India by rapidly mobilizing up to 12 divisions.[161]
- The new rail-road facilitates the easy transport of IRBMs and allows China to rail-base in Tibet some of its ICBMs, its latest ICBM, the DF-31A is also rail mobile. To engage any targets in India, China does not require to move its ICBMs in Tibet because of their extensive range, but availability of launch sites now in the mountainous region of TAR as also because of greater dispersion will enhance their survivability against any anticipated first strike.

- Improved potential to meddle in India's restive North-east and the ability to dump goods in the Indian market via Chumbi and Nepal. China would like to extend the Tibetan railway to Kathmandu.

Tibet

Tibet has played a vital role in the relationship between China and India since China's occupation of Tibet in the early 1950s. In March 1959, Lobsang Yeshi Tenzin Gyatso, His Holiness the 14th Dalai Lama, Tibet's political and spiritual leader and some 80,000 Tibetans sought refuge in India, Nepal and Bhutan, to avoid the Chinese government's crackdown on a popular armed revolt against Chinese rule in Lhasa, the capital of Tibet. Following the revolt, China established complete military and political control over Tibet. The influx of refugees continues even today. Currently, the Tibetan exile population is over 140,000, of which about 100,000 are based in India (However, according to a reputed international think tank, more than a million Tibetan refugees live in India today).[162]

On 29 April 1959, His Holiness the Dalai Lama established the Tibetan exile administration in the North Indian hill station of Mussoorie. Named the Central Tibetan Administration (CTA) of His Holiness the Dalai Lama, this is the continuation of the government of independent Tibet. In May 1960, the CTA was moved to Dharamsala, India. Right from its inception, the CTA has set itself the twin task of rehabilitating Tibetan refugees and restoring freedom and happiness in Tibet.[163]

From China's perspective the "Tibet issue" and the presence of Dalai Lama in India are the main causes of tension in China-India relations:

- After the Sino-Indian border conflict, Chinese Premier Zhou Enlai told an assembly of socialist countries that the "center of the Sino-Indian conflict" was not the border dispute but India's efforts to "oppose reform in Tibet" and its desire to keep Tibet as a "buffer state."[164]
- Insecure about its control over Tibet, China fears that India would use the presence of the Dalai Lama and the large Tibetan refugee population in India to foment unrest in Tibet. China asserts its claim over Arunachal Pradesh, considering it as part of Tibet.
- The succession of the 84-year old Dalai Lama is the potential source to complicate the relations further. The Dalai Lama had once stated

that he might be the last to hold the position and the tradition of the post could end with him.[165] But later he believed the time had come for him to choose his successor. Addressing the annual Rajendra Mathur memorial lecture organized by the Editor's Guild of India on 9 August 2017, the Dalai Lama said that some of the 'preparation work' to select his successor, the 15th Dalai Lama, would begin in as early as 'one or two years'. In the same breath, he said that the process to choose his successor would begin only after he turned 90, in the year 2025.[166] However, Dalai Lama's statement to the media should not be taken as sacrosanct. In a recent interview to Mr Shishir Gupta, Hindustan Times (25 December 2018) the Dalai Lama has stated that the process of reincarnation is not his business and it was up to the Tibetan people to decide whether the very institution of Dalai Lama should continue or not. He further said, "*As the Dalai Lama institution is close to Mongolia, Mongolian people should be involved. I think there should be an international Buddhist conference involving Himalayan people and other Buddhist countries to decide on this.*" He also half-seriously said that the institution could voluntarily and democratically cease with the 14th Dalai Lama. He admitted that the dialogue process for reincarnation had not even started.[167]

- The Chinese government wants to continue with the tradition of reincarnation but it has, however, asserted that its officially atheist Communist leaders have only the right to approve the Dalai Lama's successor, as a legacy inherited from China's emperors.[168]
- Additionally Beijing is concerned that the death of the 14th Dalai Lama might pave the way for the rise of a new generation of more radical Tibetan leaders who will embrace less conciliatory positions towards the Chinese government. Together with the rekindled instability in ethnically Tibetan areas since 2008, all of this has impelled China to reaffirm its sovereignty over the Tibet Autonomous Region and to adopt a more rigorous position regarding its claim to Arunachal Pradesh.[169]
- Beijing has time and again accused the Dalai Lama for promoting unrest in Tibet and demanded India to prevent him from engaging in any political activities. Thus, every time the Dalai Lama meets the senior Indian officials or delivers a prominent speech in Delhi, or is

permitted to visit Arunachal Pradesh, Beijing perceives an Indian-designed strategy to undermine Chinese sovereignty and authority. For instance, latest in the series is the high-profile event by the Tibetan government-in-exile commemorating Dalai Lama's 60 years of exile naming it 'Thank You India', which was earlier planned at New Delhi but shifted to Dharamshala.[170]

- For China, Tibet is a "core" issue, just as Kashmir is to India. Dr. John Garver has said, "*Tibet is virtually the only effective mechanism of leverage India has against Beijing.*"[171]

Another reason Tibet plays an important part in Sino-Indian relations is that Tibetan Plateau is considered as the 'Water Tower' of Asia from where largest rivers of the Indian sub-continent are originating. This aspect is being covered in detail in the succeeding paragraphs.

Water as a Source of Conflict

The Tibetan Plateau is the world's highest and largest plateau. With an average altitude of 3,650 meters above sea level, the land extends over 2.5 million square kilometers. Stretching 2,400 kilometers from East to West and 1,448 kilometers from North to South, the Plateau encompasses an ecological abundance unmatched anywhere on earth. An estimated 46,000 glaciers and hundreds of the snow-capped tallest mountains on earth feed nine of the biggest Asian rivers. Four of the largest rivers of the Indian sub-continent originate in Mount Kailash in Western Tibet: Indus, Sutlej, the Ganga and the Brahmaputra (Yarlung Zangbo or Tsangpo). The Salween (Nu), Irrawaddy and the mighty Mekong (Lancang), originating from the Changtang (Northern plains), form the main water arteries of Myanmar, Thailand, Laos, Cambodia, and Vietnam. China's two main rivers the Yangtze and the Huang He (Yellow River) originate in the North Eastern area of the Tibetan Plateau. In addition, hundreds of their tributaries such as the Koshi, Karnali, Gandaki, Mechi and Mahakali, transect the Himalayas to create the world's deepest gorges and the most fertile land of the Indo-Gangetic Plains.[172] Its river-waters are a lifeline to twelve countries, stretching in a contiguous arc from Afghanistan to Vietnam, which together constitute 47 percent of the global population.[173]

China and India already are water-stressed economies. Both of them are facing the prospect that their rapid economic modernization may stall due to inadequate water resources. If their industrial, agricultural and household demand for water continues to grow at the present frenetic pace, the day is not far when this prospect may become a reality. Against this background, water is likely to become a key security issue in Sino-Indian relations and a potential source of enduring discord. China's control over Tibet enables it to claim sovereign right to control the world's largest fresh water resources outside the Polar Regions. But while the water in the icecaps is all locked up, much of the water in Tibet is accessible.[174] Having extensively contaminated its own major rivers through unbridled industrialization, China now threatens the ecological viability of river systems linked to Southern and South-eastern Asia in its bid to meet its thirst for water and energy.

China possesses a robust glaciological program and knows fairly well how long Tibet's snow and ice resources will last. It has embarked on integrated water resource management of all rivers emanating from Tibetan plateau. China has been building dams on a staggering scale and at an extraordinary rate. By 2000, China had built 22,104 large dams (defined as having a wall height of over 15m), providing a total of 77GW electricity generating capacity. For comparison, the US, the world's second most prolific dam builder, had 6,390 dams, and India 4,000. By 2010 China had installed 220GW of hydropower. It met its 2015 target of 290GW a year ahead of schedule and plans to reach 430GW (increasing its earlier target of 380GW) by 2020. China has built more large dams than the US, Brazil and Canada combined and shows no sign of slowing down.[175] It has planned / completed dam construction and water diversion projects on the Salween and Mekong Rivers, despite regional and global criticism that these will be socially and economically devastating downstream.[176] For example, Xiaowan dam on the Mekong completed in 2010, has a wall height of 292m – around the height of an 80-storey building – and with 4,200 MW producing more electricity than the installed hydropower generating capacity of all of the lower Mekong countries together.[177] Next in progress on Mekong is the 5,850 MW Nuozhadu, which when complete will be even bigger in storage volume, but not in height.[178]

In March 2009, the Chairman of the Tibetan regional government unveiled plans for major new dams on the Brahmaputra. A series of six big dams have been planned to come up in the upper middle reaches of the Brahmaputra, to the South-east of Lhasa. The Zangmu Dam is a gravity dam on the Brahmaputra River, located in the Gyaca County of Shannan Prefecture in Tibet. The purpose of the dam is hydroelectric power production using run-of-the-river technology. It is part of the Zangmu Hydropower Project and supports a 510 MW power station costing $1.5 billion. Construction began in 2009 and the first generator was commissioned in November 2014. The last became operational on 13 October 2015. It is the first dam on the Brahmaputra River and being 390 meter long and 116 meter high; Zangmu is regarded as the world's highest-altitude hydropower station and the largest of its kind, is set to generate 2.5 billion kilowatt-hours of electricity per year. As part of this cascade, four other new dams will come up downstream from Zangmu. In January 2013 China approved three more dams on the river as part of its Twelfth Five Year Plan. The Dagu (640 MW) and Jiexu (560 MW) dams will be constructed upstream of Zangmu and the Jiacha Dam (320 MW) downstream. (See Annexure 6) This cascade is in addition to more than a dozen smaller dams that China has already built on the Brahmaputra and its tributaries.[179]

China has started construction of its USD three billion Suwalong hydropower project over the Jinsha river. The Jinsha is a tributary of the Yangtze River. The Suwalong project is located at the junction of Mangkam county of Tibet and Batang county of Sichuan province in southwest China. It will be the largest power station in Tibet upon completion. The power station has a design capacity of 1.2 gigawatts (1.2 million kilowatts) and will be able to generate about 5,400 gigawatts hours (5.4 billion kw/h) of electricity a year when completed in 2021. The design capacity of Suwalong dam is more than double that of the Zangmu hydropower plant on Brahmaputra River, which is Tibet's largest existing hydro project.[180]

Another one is the Lalho project on the Xiabuqu River in Xigaze (close to Sikkim), which is under construction at an investment of $740 million. The Xiabuqu river, 195-km long, flows from Bainang in Tibet Northwards and joins the Yarlung Zangbo near the region called Xigaze, also known as Shigatse. Xigaze is the city from where China intends to extend its railway towards Nepal. This tributary was blocked for the Lalho hydel project that was launched in June 2014 and is scheduled to be completed in 2019. The river's mean discharge is 25.8 cubic meters per second (cumecs), less than 0.15 percent of the Brahmaputra's mean discharge when it enters India. Its reservoir was designed to store up to 295 cumecs and it will irrigate 30,000 hectares, control floods and generate power.[181]

The most ambitious plan China is pursuing is the one to reroute a sizable portion of the River Tsangpo (Brahmaputra) northwards at the Great Bend, the point where the river makes a sharp turn to enter India. Metog (called Motuo in Chinese) will be the site of the mega project at the huge bend inside a giant canyon approximately 3.1 miles deep and 198 miles long, a canyon larger and deeper than the Grand Canyon in the US. This will involve construction of a series of tunnels, pipes, reservoirs and turbines that will generate 38,000 MW of power and exploit the spectacular 2,000-meter fall of the river as it winds down towards India.[182] This project was revealed by Tashi Tsering, an environmental studies scholar at the University of British Columbia, when he posted a map of potential dam sites and two Chinese proposals to harness the untapped hydroelectric potential of the Brahmaputra along the 'great bend'. He told that *'if or when the Motuo project is built, China will gain significant capacity to control the flow of Brahmaputra with a huge reservoir'.* The Motuo project proposal is unofficial, but backed by influential Chinese engineers such as Zhang Boting, deputy general secretary of the China Society for the Hydropower Engineering, who said *'research had been carried out on the project, but no plan has been drawn up and the said dam could generate energy equivalent to 100m tonnes of crude coal or all the oil and gas in the South China Sea'.* He had written *'We should build a hydropower plant, in Motuo ... as soon as possible because it is a great policy to protect our territory from Indian invasion and to increase China's capacity for carbon reduction.'* He listed an alternative proposal at a 2,400 m drop in altitude at Daduqia *'but it is near border with India and would be highly exposed, if there were another conflict'.*[183] There was another report stating that this water diversion project – an essential part of China's 10th five year plan – would cost $ 62 billion and the entire staff responsible for constructing the Lhasa-Beijing railway line had been assigned for executing this mega project quickly.[184]

China's 13th Five Year Plan calls for large-scale expansion of hydropower projects. Most of the new hydropower capacity on international rivers is expected to be added on the Lancang (Mekong) – with the rest on the Yarlung Zangbo (Brahmaputra). The controversial cascade of dams on the Nu River has been suspended for 10 years in a surprise announcement from the Yunnan provincial government in February 2016. China will push ahead with follow up work on the Central and Eastern routes of the "South-North Water Diversion Project" but there is no explicit mention of the more controversial Western route stretch over the Tibetan plateau.[185] The Brahmaputra flows into India and then Bangladesh before merging with the Ganga. Any hydropower project on this river will exacerbate tensions with downstream countries worried about their future water supplies.

Perhaps recognizing this, the new plan states the need to "*scientifically develop and harness international rivers*" and "*deepen cooperation with other riparian countries / along the rivers.*"[186] To balance between upstream and downstream interests, the UN General Assembly on 21 May 1997 had adopted the UN Convention on the Law of the Non-Navigational Uses of International Watercourses (with China voting against it). The convention commits state parties to the utilization of trans-boundary rivers in "an equitable and reasonable manner" and require them to take "all appropriate measures to prevent the causing of significant harm" to co-riparians, presently constituting large parts of Tibet, Northeastern India, Bangladesh and Mekong region countries.[187] China's upstream claim over the Brahmaputra has emerged as a threat to the environment, putting into jeopardy the livelihood of millions downstream. As with large hydropower projects the world over, local communities bear the brunt of these controversial projects and reap hardly any benefits. The electricity generated serves the needs of large cities and industrial centers rather than the local population. Dams not only disrupt the flow of water; they block the flow of silt which otherwise carries vital nutrients downstream. And with less silt being deposited at the delta, salt water encroaches on cropland.[188] Upstream, land is lost and communities get displaced by dam reservoirs. Habitats are destroyed and the ecosystem in the waters is also disturbed, dramatically affecting the life cycle of high altitude fish species. It is notable that in the most of these regions, fish is a major source of caloric intake, which means that rural food security in Northeast India, Bangladesh and Southeast Asia may be compromised.[189]

China has done little to engage its downstream neighbors over its dam building projects. It has not joined the Mekong River Commission – an intergovernmental agency that works directly with the governments of Cambodia, Laos, Thailand and Vietnam on the trans-boundary management and sustainable development of the Mekong.[190] However, in order to prevent escalation of threat to peace and stability in the Mekong region, China has taken recent steps to reach out to Mekong river countries by signing bilateral agreements.[191] But little progress has been made with India over the Brahmaputra, apart from the Chinese providing water flow data and flood warnings during the monsoon months. India and China signed two pacts in 2008 and 2010, which facilitated India with data on water levels and rainfall twice a day from June 1 to October 15 at three hydrological stations in Tibet.[192] The non-existence of a water-sharing agreement with China strategically also challenges India's claim on parts of Arunachal.

China's opaquely pursued hydro-engineering projects in Tibet threaten the interests of India as also of Bangladesh. Through its giant projects in Tibet, China is actually equipping itself to use water as a weapon against India. Such a weapon can be put to overt use in war or employed subtly in peacetime so that the level of cross-border water flows becomes a function of political concession.[193] A few strategic thinkers are of the opinion that there is very little historic evidence that water is a source of direct military conflict, although it is a source of political difficulties. However, there is an emerging opinion that 'water wars' may not be officially declared but '*water could be an underlying driver of conflict.*' Water causes problems between people and communities, even if these are not formally labeled water wars. '*Besides, history is not always a good predictor for the future.*' Water is already becoming an issue in the intra-state as also in inter-state bilateral relations. For instance, water was not an issue in the relations between India and China until India discovered that China had built all these dams of which India did not know. When President Hu Jintao came to India in 2006, water was on the agenda for the first time. Both countries agreed to set up a joint mechanism. This shows that water is an issue bilaterally between China and all its South-East Asian neighbors. It also is an issue between China and Nepal, and between China and Kazakhstan. '*The changing paradigm in Asia is making water an issue in interstate relations.*'[194]

Sino-Indian Trade Relations

Today, China is India's largest trading partner. Sino-Indian trade has galloped from only \$5 billion in 2002 to \$89.6 billion during 2017-18 but it is heavily loaded in favor of China. India imported \$76.27 billion worth of Chinese products while it exported just \$13.33 billion worth of goods to China. The trade deficit, which stood at –\$38.7 billion in 2012-13, now stands at a whopping –\$62.9 billion.[195] One of the main reasons for asymmetry in the trade relationship is that India's exports to China are mainly raw materials or primary and intermediate products while imports from China has a major share of manufactured goods as also the items to meet the demand of fast expanding sectors like telecom and power. The trade deficit can be reduced when India starts exporting manufactured products. Unfortunately, the Indian manufacturing industries have to go a long way before they are in a position to export high quality products at competitive rates to China.

India is one of the largest manufacturers of generic drugs and software. But it has not been able to export to China because of Beijing's protectionist policies. China's leadership has repeatedly promised to open up their markets to Indian exports of software and pharmaceuticals, but there is nothing on the ground. Indian firms, especially pharmaceuticals and IT companies, face huge registration problems, language barriers and a hierarchical business structure in China.[196] According to Jagat Shah, Secretary General, China India Trade and Investment Centre (CITIC) "*In most developed countries, registering a new drug takes a year or two, but in China there are petitions from Indian drug companies that have been pending for eight to 10 years*". He further added, "*They don't say yes and they don't say no. IT companies face similar barriers with their software.*" Former commerce minister Nirmala Sitharaman also confirmed the Chinese attitude by stating, "*China's restrictive, time-consuming practices have to be questioned.*" Her successor, Suresh Prabhu said "*We must seek greater access for Indian goods in China.*"[197] A colonial pattern is thus being perpetrated by China, which has been resented in India. According to officials involved in trade negotiations, "*China's greatest export to India is promises*".[198]

Only a limited range of primary, resource-based and low-end technology products are being exported to China like salt, sulphur, ores, slag and ash, cotton, pearls and precious stones, minerals fuels/oils, iron & steel and its articles, copper, nickel, aluminum, lead, zinc and its articles and organic chemicals. Products in the category of nuclear reactors, boilers and electric machinery & equipment are also being exported to China but the reciprocal import from China in the same category is almost 35 times that of India. China's exports to India are diversified and include high-value, finished products like telecom instruments, computer hardware, peripherals, fertilizers, electronic components and instruments, project goods, organic chemicals and drug intermediates, consumer electronics, electrical machinery and equipment, iron and steel etc. Composition of India's trade with China during financial years 2016-2017 and 2017-2018 is elucidated in Annexure 7.[199]

Increasing Trade Deficit with China

Mr. C.R. Chaudhary, Minister of State in Ministry of Commerce and Industry, in his reply to the Rajya Sabha, on 7 March 2018 had informed, "*Imports exceed exports because of shortages/non-availability of items domestically or because of the cost competitiveness of the foreign manufacturers.*"[200]

In solar energy sector, India has achieved a milestone20 GW on 30 January 2018, four years ahead of time (cumulative utility-scale installations about 18.4 GW, with rooftop solar accounting for another 1.6 GW). The government is now working to achieve the revised target of 100 GW (1 GW = 1,000 MW) solar by 2022.[201] In 2016-17, only 11 percent equipment that solar developers used came from local manufacturers, while over 80 percent of it was imported at a cost of around $3 billion from China alone. Indian entrepreneurs have set up the manufacturing units of solar modules but Indian developers prefer Chinese solar cells because these are 35 percent cheaper than the indigenous products; solar panels cost 10-15 percent less. Chinese annual manufacturing capacity of solar equipment has trebled from 23 GW to 70 GW over the past four years. In comparison, in the same period, India's panel manufacturing capacity increased from 3 GW to 8 GW, while cell-making capacity grew from 850 MW to 3 GW.[202] Due to the Chinese dumping, much of even this limited capacity lies unused (Dumping implies selling in a foreign country at a price lower than the cost of manufacture in the home country). Aggressive pricing on the back of state subsidy, a protectionist outlook and cheap finance have allowed Chinese manufacturers to out price the domestic counterparts. India's aggressive solar energy targets could mean business worth over $40 billion for component manufacturers over the next five years.[203] The Indian Solar Manufacturers Association (ISMA) wants the government to follow the example of the European Union and the US, both of which have imposed duties on Chinese solar products.

Chinese companies today dominate the telecom sector in India. In mobile handsets, they control 51 percent of India's $10 billion plus smart phone market. Several smart phone manufacturers from China such as Xiaomi, LeEco, Gionee, Vivo, Lenovo, OPPO and ONEPLUS have been established in India. In the FY 2016-2017, India imported some $11.3 billion worth of telecom instruments from China and some $4.4 billion worth of electronic components. In the power sector, in the 12th Plan alone, almost 30 percent of the generating capacity was imported from China.[204]

Having established itself in mature sectors like power and telecommunicat-ions, China is exploring other sectors now. Chinese carmaker Geely today is competing with Audi, BMW and Mercedes and eyeing the luxury car market with an all-electric thrust by 2019. The automobile sector has attracted the biggest Chinese foreign direct investment, with Shanghai Automotive Industrial Corporation (SAIC) recently buying General Motors' factory in Kalol in Gujarat.[205]

In mid-2016, Chinese pharma major Shanghai Fosun sought to acquire Hyderabad-based Gland Pharma – buying 86 percent stake for $1.4 billion. But the Foreign Investment Promotion Board (FIPB), following strong objections from the Swadeshi Jagran Manch (SJM), opposed it. After abolishment of the FIPB, the matter stayed pending at the Cabinet Committee of Economic Affairs (CCEA). In September 2017, Fosun decided to cut down the stake purchase to 74 percent, so that it can come via the automatic route.

However, even if the Chinese player manages to acquire the 74 percent stake, it would still require permissions from several Indian agencies before marketing the restricted drugs. Gland Pharma has around 76 restricted drugs.[206]

As per the FDI Data maintained by Department of Industrial Policy & Promotion (DIPP)/Reserve Bank of India (RBI), the Chinese FDI in India, though growing, has been insignificant compared to China's total FDI overseas. China presently ranks 17th in terms of FDI equity inflows into India. The cumulative FDI equity inflows from China since April 2000 to September 2017are to the tune of US$ 1.73 billion only, which is about 0.49 percent of the overall FDI equity inflows into India. The major sectors in which the investment has come from China are: Automobile Industry (53.79 percent); Metallurgical Industries (10.49 percent); Services (7.54 percent); Electrical Equipment (6.70 percent); Industrial Machinery (3.99 percent).[207] Modi government encouraged "cashless economy" in India, giving a fillip to players like Paytm. Chinese digital giants have been investing heavily in India's digital ecosystem. It is a known fact that 40 percent shares of Paytm are owned by the Chinese firm Alibaba and similarly CTrip has invested in Make-MyTrip. China's Tencent Holdings has so far invested $700 million in Flipkart. Chinese real estate firms like China Fortune Land Development Company and Dalian Wanda are entering India with multi-billion dollar plans for industrial townships and similar projects.[208]

Is Trade War an Answer to Rectify the Trade Imbalance?

In a range of sectors from steel to power to telecom, having not been able to match the price of cheap Chinese products, there is a rising demand from Indian manufacturers to the government for imposing anti-dumping duty and safeguard duty. In order to create a level playing field for Indian manufacturers, recently, India imposed anti-dumping duties on 93 Chinese products. The anti-dumping duties on chemicals and machinery items imported from China had already been in place for some time. Other Chinese products on which India has imposed anti-dumping duties include steel and other metals, fibers and yarn, rubber and plastic, electric and electronic items, and consumer goods.[209] An article in state-owned Global Times said that China could easily retaliate with restrictions on Indian products, but added that it "doesn't make much economic sense" for the country. State-owned Chinese media has urged Chinese firms to reconsider the risks of investing in India and warned New Delhi to be prepared for the "possible consequences for its ill-considered action"[210]

Is it advisable for India to indulge in a trade war with China at this juncture? India exports less to China (mainly raw materials) and imports more (mainly electronics and other manufactured goods which are in high demand). A trade war when Indian manufacturing ability is limited is not going to favor India. Any move to put a restriction on the import of Chinese goods will hit Indian industries hard. India's imports from China are crucial at this stage: First, India's pharmaceutical sector has critical dependence on Chinese imports used in drugs manufacturing; Second, as local manufacturing companies in India are not geared up to supply goods to the rising power and telecom sectors, India may be forced to import such goods from the United States and Europe at a prohibitive cost, which may put an additional financial burden on these two sectors; Third, Yet any step to impose unreasonable restrictions of imports from China would amount to a contravention of the World Trade Organization's laws.[211]

Before the festival seasons such as Holi and Deepawali, shrill calls for boycott of Chinese goods become louder, with the social media networks further amplifying the noise. If we talk of the Chinese items, which proliferate our markets during festive seasons, about a decade back, the traders often used to source products – toys, plastic items, idols of Indian gods, among others – from domestic manufacturers. Reportedly, they have all shut down and now import from China. Cheaper and better Chinese imports have wiped out the domestic industry, particularly toys.[212] Further, China's exports to India account for only 2 percent of its total exports.[213] So even if Indians boycott all the goods imported from China, it will not make a big impact on China. Rather India would stand to suffer more than China. Another popular impression is that China is dumping consumer goods into India. But the fact is that India depends on China for capital goods too. Reduction in import of cheaper capital goods will push up production costs and will hit Indian industries hard.[214] Despite Prime Minister Modi's "Make in India" initiative, India is finding it difficult to increase its manufacturing capabilities in a short time span. It may take even a decade to attain the manufacturing capability, when it can challenge China in a trade war.

Measures to Reduce the Trade Deficit with China

Ultra nationalists' advocacy for use of bilateral trade, as a weapon is only to provoke the public sentiments and will not in any way boost the economy. Presently, India has been importing almost six times more from China than the latter did from India. It obviously shows India's heavy dependence upon

Chinese imports. Trade deficit can be reduced only when India starts exporting value-added products and that can be achieved in the long-term because, unfortunately, the Indian manufacturing industries have to go a long way before they are in a position to export high quality products at competitive rates to China. To create a sound-manufacturing base in an earlier timeframe, India should avoid imposing unreasonable restrictions on Chinese goods until it has found an alternative source of supply for its capital goods at identical or even cheaper rates.

In short-term, Indian government is seeking "windows of opportunities" to push its exports to China. For instance, the ongoing trade war between the US and China can provide opportunities to India for export of cotton, oilseed meal and maize:

- China produces about 32 million bales of cotton and its textile mills consume around 45 million bales, allowing imports to meet the shortfall.[215] In 2016-2017, cotton was the second most exported commodity from India to China in terms of value, costing about $ 1.3 billion. In 2017-18, Indian cotton exports have further declined by 25.27 percent to $ 1.0 billion.[216] For the sake of records a peak of $ 4 billion was reached in 2011-12.[217] China's decision to impose 25 percent duty on cotton supplies from the United States comes as Beijing's own stockpile is depleting fast and it needs to shore up depleting domestic reserves. There is no duty on import of Indian cotton in China and thus it will be cheaper than that of the US.[218] India is looking to sell 2.5 million to 3 million bales, each of 170 kg, to China in the next season beginning in October 2018. India benefits from geographical proximity to China compared to other competitors. Beside lower freight rates, shipments from India reach China in about two weeks compared to an average of three to six weeks from other suppliers.[219]
- Soybean production has been flat in China since the 1990s as it grows only about 14 million tonnes of soybeans, mainly to make food for human consumption.[220] It relies on imports for about 90 percent of its annual soybean consumption of around 110 million tons. In 2017-18, the largest supplier of soybeans to China was Brazil, with the U.S. in the Number 2 spot at 33 million tons with a value of $12 billion. Millers in Chinese coastal cities such as Dalian turn U.S. soybeans

into cooking oil. The byproduct, soybean meal, is turned into livestock feed. Of the total soybean volume, about 20 percent becomes oil, while 80 percent becomes soy meal. Pork is a staple of the Chinese diet and soy meal for feed is a key to satisfying demand for pork. Higher duties on soybeans will raise the cost of pork production and put upward pressure on prices.[221] Outside of Brazil, the United States and Argentina, about 17 million tonnes of soybeans comes from a handful of countries.[222] While speaking at the 5th India-China Strategic Economic Dialogue held at Beijing on 14 April 2018 between the National Institution for Transforming of India (NITI) Aayog and China's National Development and Reform Commission (NDRC), chaired by He Lifeng, Niti Aayog Vice-chairperson Rajiv Kumar offered to export soybean and sugar to China amid the tariff spat between Beijing and Washington. He said, "*I was noticing that there are some tariffs you imposed on farmers from Iowa and Ohio. Maybe India can substitute for soybean and sugar, if we could access those exports with all the due quality considerations to our farmers*".[223] Interestingly, India produced around 8.3 million to 8.5 million tonnes of soybeans at the end of 2017, down from more than 11 million tonnes a year ago (and in 2016-17, India could export only 269,000 tonnes of soybean). As a consequence, India's soybean imports have hit a record high this year and more buying is expected as domestic supplies tighten following lower production last year. Traders have signed deals to sell up to 100,000 tonnes of soybeans to India since December, shipping mainly from the African countries of Ethiopia and Benin and more imports are expected to continue.[224] However, India exports soymeal and its total soymeal exports peaked to 2 million tonnes for oil year 2016-17 from a mere 320,000 tonnes during the previous year. Soymeal has become expensive because of rising soybean prices. India's cost of soymeal production works out to $500 a tonne as against exports from Argentina and the United States at $400 a tonne. Therefore, Indian soybean meal is more expensive by $100 a tonne when compared to the rest of the world. India has exported around 700,000 tonnes of soymeal between November 2017 and January 2018. However, further exports are impossible at the current uncompetitive price. Assuming that the current trend continues, India would not be able to achieve even 1 million tonnes of soymeal exports during the current oil year (November 2017-October 2018).[225] Further, China had reportedly placed some restrictions on Indian soymeal and rapeseed meal trade. During the meeting on the sidelines of the G20 Summit on 30 November between Prime Minister Narendra Modi and President Xi Jinping, the latter spoke about the possibility of greater import of soymeal and rapeseed. China has dropped a years-long ban on rapeseed meal imports from India as the government seeks to diversify sources of protein used in animal feed.[226] With the tightening domestic situation in respect of both soybean as well as soymeal, it is not understood how India can replace world leaders in respect of these commodities for supplying to China. It can be best left to the wisdom of India's commerce mandarins! In today's world of globalization, everything is possible, provided a country's leaders have better business acumen than their adversary's and they know how to exploit the global commerce to their country's advantage. However on China's part, it has accepted India's request and its State Council has announced reduction of tariffs on soybeans imported from India, South Korea, Bangladesh, Laos and Sri Lanka from the current 3 percent to zero.

- India is likely to produce a record 29.5 million tonnes of sugar in the 2017/18 season that ends on 30th September, up 45 percent from the previous year. India has 7 million tonnes of surplus sugar this year and with forecast of good rains the surplus stocks are expected to pileup further next year. China imports about 4.5 million tonnes of surplus stocks mostly from Brazil, Thailand and Cuba. Consequent to the informal summit between Prime Minister Narendra Modi and Chinese President Xi Jinping in Wuhan, about 50 officials of the 25 Chinese sugar companies attended a close door interaction with top officials of the Indian Sugar Mills Association (ISMA) to discuss the possibility to import about one million or 1.5 million tonnes of Indian sugar, which could fetch about USD 350 million. The meeting was organized by the Indian Embassy and according to the official sources during the informal summit, Prime Minister Modi had urged Xi to import Indian sugar, rice and pharmaceuticals. ISMA officials said India hopes to export its sugars to China under the 50 percent tariff category for which details are yet to be worked out. China charges 80 percent tariffs on sugar imports.[227]

- China has been buying Indian beef from Vietnam in the last few years and New Delhi was not getting any advantages in terms of changing the bilateral trade. Making China agree for direct import of bovine meat from India has been a top priority for Indian government since Narendra Modi took over in May 2014. After Prime Minister Modi's visit to China in May 2015, the matter was raised by New Delhi following which China had agreed to send its quality inspectors to see if Indian slaughterhouses adhere to the required quality norms. China has finally agreed to remove restrictions on beef export from India and has cleared 14 abattoirs for importing meat from here.[228] Exporters of frozen buffalo meat see an opportunity of $ 4 billion and more if China allows more number of centers.[229] The commerce ministry is hopeful that export of beef would make a considerable change in the bilateral trade deficit.
- China is the largest market for India's cotton yarn. From 2013-14 to 2016-17, India's cotton yarn exports to China have declined heavily from $2.17 billion to $1.1 billion respectively at a CAGR of 49 percent. During the same period, Vietnam's exports of the cotton yarn increased by 88 percent to touch $1.7 billion in 2016. Vietnam became the largest supplier of cotton yarn to China in 2016-17, surpassing India.[230] China has shifted from India to Vietnam and Indonesia as they have duty free access while Indian yarn carried 3.5 percent import duty. In 2013-14, Indian spinning mills performed well by taking advantage of various sops including the 2 percent incremental export incentive, 2 percent interest subvention and 3 percent focus market incentive. However, export incentives provided to Cotton yarn were withdrawn in 2014. Following this, yarn exports started declining and fell 26 percent to $3.3 billion in 2016-17.[231] Thus either the trajectory of India's export has to be shifted towards other major yarn importing nations such as Bangladesh, Turkey, Vietnam, Italy, Japan, etc., or it has to incentivize its imports to make these attractive to China.

To curb the excessive and uncontrolled flow of cheap Chinese imports that are impeding the growth of domestic manufacturers, Modi government has enforced certain regulatory measures: first, imposition of anti-dumping duties in last two years in response to complaints ranging from the one made by Reliance Industries – along with SRF Ltd – against Chinese polyester yarn to another by the Indian Fishnet Manufacturers Association against Chinese fishnets; second, the PMO has directed the ministries to assist the Bureau of Indian Standards (BIS) to lay down Indian standards for products, which are in their sphere and are being imported. Standards for steel, plastics and certain chemicals have already been set and the impact is visible, for example, according to industry estimates, toy imports from China have dropped to less than 50 percent after tougher quality norms and mandatory certification of compliance by accredited agencies have been effected from 1 September 2017. Before this, Chinese toys accounted for 70 percent of India's Rs 5000 crore toy industry; third, government procurement policies have been modified in May 2017, making it mandatory for government departments including public sector units and other state-owned entities to buy from local manufacturers only. In open tenders for high-priced items, even if foreign firms put in lower bids, the lowest bidding Indian company will get the contract if it agrees to match the lowest bid. Even for purchase of capital goods, government departments have been directed to source from companies with manufacturing facilities in India. Most of these imports have been coming from China until now. Effect of new rules is making the difference, for example in mid-June 2017, Public Sector GAIL intending to buy gas pipelines worth Rs 1000 crore in Phase one and Rs 3000 crore in Phase two, decided not to buy from Chinese companies. ONGC and Oil India have also decided not to buy tubular – rolled steel sheets from the Chinese. The new National Steel Policy, announced in May 2017, has sought to reduce Indian dependence on Chinese imports; fourth, foreign companies, including those from China, are welcome, if they are ready to set up manufacturing units in India, transfer the technology and create jobs; and lastly cyber security risks are being mitigated by instituting adequate measures while importing mobiles and other electronic items from China.[232]

Healthy trade between the two countries has the potential to reduce tensions. The two countries have developed a Five-Year Development Program for Economic and Trade Cooperation in September 2014 with the aim to strengthen cooperation and achieve trade balance over the next five years.[233] However, the trade deficit has increased from $ 48.46 billion in 2014-15 to $62.9 billion in 2017-18.Prime Minister Modi is leaving no stone unturned and seeking every possible opportunity to reduce this trade deficit; for instance on the sidelines of the two-day SCO summit (9-10 June 2018) at Qingdao, China, a protocol was signed in the presence of Prime Minister Modi and Chinese President Xi wherein India would also be allowed to export rice other than the premium Basmati variety to China[234] – a step toward reducing the trade deficit. The bureaucrats who are required to implement Modi's policies remain lethargic and indifferent, for example, China exports 'worn clothing or the so-called rags' to India six to seven times more than what it imports from India (China's $178.24 million vs. India's $23.52 million in 2016-17 and China's $170 million vs. India's $28.69 million in 2017-18).[235] Surely, these are not specialized high-tech components, which are indispensible for our industry. This clearly shows that Chinese are undoubtedly better businessmen. Unless Indian bureaucrats have professional commitment and dedication with a shrewd business mind, they will not be able to reduce the trade gap with China.

3

Areas of Cooperation vs. Competition

IN spite of many sources of friction, realpolitik demands that China and India should avoid conflict. Over the last few years, they have instituted measures to strengthen their relationship to include: drawing up of various agreements, establishing joint study groups, initiating strategic dialogues, regular high-level visits, conducting joint anti-terrorism training exercises and moving together on subjects of common interests in international forums e.g., climate change and environment protection. Having established themselves on a path of strong economic growth, both the nations are aspiring to uplift the living standards of their burgeoning population. For their economies to grow unhindered, maintenance of peace and tranquility on the borders is a prerequisite because any war in the modern context can set both the nations back by decades. But being in close geographical proximity to each other, their external spheres of influence are overlapping with each perceiving the other as a pursuing hegemony, trying to transgress into its own sphere. Further, both countries being ancient civilizations with the glorious past, their populations are being fed with aggressive nationalism by their respective leaders to enhance legitimacy of their regimes.

In the recent past, the Chinese had been perceiving their country as a global power solely on par with the United States and considered India as inconsequential, rather making disparaging comments about India's "unrealistic and unachievable 'big power dreams' (*daguomeng*)".[1] However, of late with India's economy surging ahead and being pronounced as the world's fastest growing economy by both International Monetary Fund and World Bank, the Chinese have taken note of it and see enough reasons for cooperation with

India in economic sphere. If India can leverage its favorable demographics, it will be in a position to close the strategic gap with China by mid of this century. In 2012, India's working-age population grew by twelve million while China's shrank by over three million.[2] A June 2013, UN report on world population prospects predicted that India's population would surpass China's by 2028.[3]

The rivalry between the two neighboring countries and that too of almost equal size and status is inevitable but both China and India have a lot to lose in an open conflict. India is required to concentrate on economic development as it intends to double its economy from the current \$2.5 trillion to \$5 trillion in a decade.[4] China has grown to about \$12 trillion and to expand further it has not only to enhance its domestic consumption substantially but is now looking outwards with its Belt and Road Initiative, needing a cooperative India. An open conflict could also coalesce many countries with concerns over China's growing ambitions, fuelled by growing nationalism at home.

Today China and India are more politically and economically engaged than at any time in recent history. They have periodically arrived at issues of converging interests like climate change negotiations, world trade talks, necessity to reform global governance institutions, primacy of state sovereignty, combating transnational crime, and controlling the spread of pandemic diseases.[5] Most importantly, both capitals have shown a commitment to mitigate recurring tensions in the relationship such as at Depsang (2013), Chumar (2014) and the latest one in Doklam (2017).

Post 1980s, Non-Traditional Security threats (NTS) have emerged as a strong factor affecting all nations and have created a comfortable zone of cooperation. NTS encompasses multitude of components like water-food-energy nexus, terrorism, piracy, transnational crimes, pandemics and climate change etc., which have compelled major powers to cooperate and work towards building consensus. This has facilitated multi-nation Humanitarian Assistance and Disaster Relief (HADR) exercises, as well as Standard Operating Procedure in case of any natural disaster or unforeseen accident.[6] There are issues under NTS, which have the potential to open up avenues for enhanced cooperation between the two sides and such cooperation might even help alleviate some of the protracted traditional security problems and thus improve overall relations.[7] However, going beyond purely bilateral dynamics, it must be appreciated that much of the potential for cooperation or competition between China and India in the NTS realm is increasingly taking place on the regional and global multilateral levels. Multinational organizations are the ideal platforms where the nations can cooperate on common issues and accordingly China and India have joined these. At the same time, there are areas where India and China are competing with each other such as energy resources, trade, soft power and space.

The issues or areas defining the cooperation or competition between China and India need to be analyzed in detail.

AREAS OF COOPERATION

Climate Change

China and India are the world's largest and third-largest green house gas emitters respectively. This implies that all necessary global efforts for climate change mitigation cannot succeed without the positive contribution of both India and China. However, under the current international climate change regime, the Kyoto Protocol, China and India have been in the group of so-called "Annex II Countries" (i.e., developing countries), which are exempt from any legally binding obligations to reduce emissions.[8] Reports of the Intergovernmental Panel on Climate Change (IPCC) and several other studies have concluded that the two countries face imminent threat in the form of ecological degradation, food and water scarcity, agricultural shifts, health hazards, etc., due to climate change. China and India have developed cooperative engagement on climate change both at the bilateral as well as the multilateral levels.

China and India signed a five-year agreement in October 2009 to jointly fight climate change and to negotiate international climate deals using common positions.[9] This agreement was made prior to the UN climate change summit in Copenhagen in December 2009. The BASIC nations (Brazil, South Africa, India and China) jointly opposed a proposal made at the Copenhagen Summit requiring developing countries, including India and China, to not increase their Greenhouse gas emissions after 2025. This was unacceptable for China and India, as they saw this as an attempt by Western powers to undermine their fast economic development. The BASIC countries prepared their counter-draft well in advance of the Summit, and India and China's cohesion on climate change remained throughout the Copenhagen Summit. They rejected calls by developed nations to set "legally binding" targets, and both countries signed a modified Copenhagen Accord afterward in March 2010.[10] The Copenhagen Accord reached between the US, China, India, Brazil and South Africa, contained no reference to a "legally binding" agreement. For instance, "verification" was replaced with "international consultations and analyses" after rephrasing in order to be accepted by India and China. Countries were asked to spell out by 1 February next year their pledges for curbing carbon emissions by 2020. The deal promised to deliver $30bn (£18.5bn) of aid for developing nations over the next three years. Subsequently, at Cancun Summit a year later an agreement was adopted by the majority to establish a "Green Climate Fund (GCF)" of $100bn a year by 2020 to assist poorer countries in financing emission reductions and adaptation and to build a "Climate Technology Center" for streamlining technology assistance. Shortly after the Cancun Conference, in December 2010 China and India signed a memorandum of understanding (MOU) on green technology as part of six agreements between the prime ministers of the two nations.[11]

In its Twelfth Five-Year Plan, China, for the first time, set for itself, a carbon-intensity reduction target of 17 percent by 2015. Similarly, the Government of India, in its Twelfth Five-Year Plan, recognized low carbon development and inclusive growth. Annexure 8 illustrates the policy objectives related to low carbon growth in China and India. It can be seen that China and India have taken similar approaches at the multilateral foras as well as in domestic areas of action.China and India both being developing countries, like other developing countries, have expressed intention not in terms of absolute emission targets but in terms of their development trajectories. China, with an ageing population, has expressed targets in terms of emission peaking and emission intensity of GDP. India, on the other hand, with a young workforce has expressed targets in terms of emission intensity of GDP.[12]

The existing agreements – namely, the UN Framework Convention on Climate Change (UNFCCC) and the Kyoto Protocol are solidly based on the principle of equity. They recognize that the bulk of greenhouse gas concentrations in the atmosphere have originated in the developed countries and, therefore, in accordance with the principle of 'common but differentiated responsibilities', these countries must "take the lead" in tackling climate change. More specifically, the developed countries are required to reduce their emissions (the Kyoto Protocol sets out time-bound emission reduction obligations for each developed country). They are also required to provide financial support and technology transfer to the developing countries. The UNFCCC specifically notes that per capita emissions of developing countries remain low and that these will increase as a result of economic and social development. Developing countries are not required to divert scarce resources from their development and poverty eradication priorities in order to reduce emissions. The developed countries are now insisting on a new agreement, which will break down the firewall between the developed and developing countries and undermine the principle of differentiated responsibilities between the two categories.[13] The life of the Kyoto Protocol, which was due to expire at the end of 2012, got extended up to 2020, through an agreement reached at the Doha Conference (26 November to 8 December 2012).[14]

China and India reaffirmed their commitment to work together on climate change. Climate change figured as an important element at high-level bilateral talks during the Chinese President's visit to India in September 2014. In their joint statement, Prime Minister Modi and President Xi recognized the need to "achieve a balanced, comprehensive and equitable agreement under the UNFCCC in 2015".[15] During Prime Minister Modi's visit to China in May 2015, a joint statement was signed, which reaffirms that "the 2015 agreement shall be in full accordance with the principles, provisions and structure of the UNFCCC, in particular the principles of equity and common but differentiated responsibilities and respective capabilities, reflecting different historical responsibilities, development stages and national circumstances between developed and developing countries".[16] To strengthen the bilateral ties between the two countries the Indian government has set the goal of "INCH (India–China) towards MILES (Millennium of Exceptional Synergy)".[17]

In November 2014, United States and China had a joint announcement on climate change in which the two countries expressed their intention to reduce emissions in a time-bound manner. United States expressed intention to achieve an economy-wide target of reducing its emissions by 26–28 percent below its 2005 level in 2025 and to make best efforts to reduce its emissions by 28percent. China intends to achieve the peaking of CO_2 emissions around 2030 and to make best efforts to peak early and intends to increase the share of non-fossil fuels in primary energy consumption to around 20 percent by 2030.[18] From India's perspective, it would not want to be equated with a country that is the largest green house gas emitter (in aggregate terms) and whose per capita emissions are far higher than its own. Taking these factors into account, former special envoy to the India's Prime Minister on climate change, Shyam Saran, brought out that if China had agreed to peak its emissions in 2030, the India could agree to do the same 15-20 years after 2030. Thus there are conflicting interests between the two countries but at the same time issues of convergence are also there such as development, deployment and promotion of clean energy, bottom-up approach to climate action and climate finance.[19]

With the United States' President Donald Trump having abandoned the Paris Accord on climate change, it is assessed that neither China nor India is in a position to fill the void left by American leadership, or to foot the bill in terms of financial incentives the United States had offered poorer nations.[20] However, both the countries can combine their resources to invest in green R&D and assume collective leadership to fight the global climate change. In view of Trump's disinclination to commit to the Paris Climate Agreement, Global Times, one of the mouthpieces of China's People's Daily, the official newspaper of the Chinese Communist party, came up with a report appealing, "*China and India should play a much stronger leading role in the international effort against climate change.*"The Global Times report further said, "*China and India should encourage scientific institutions, environmental groups and firms to cooperate on research to develop environmentally friendly techniques that are tailored for both countries.*"[21]

World Trade Talks

India has been a member of the World Trade Organization (WTO) since its inception but China joined the WTO in the year 2001. China's entry into the WTO provided new opportunities and challenges for both the countries to establish cooperation in the areas of negotiations. The initiative to foster economic relations started after the Indian Prime Minister Atal Behari Vajpayee's visit to the PRC in June 2003. In a declaration, both the countries expressed their intention for good bilateral relations through enhancing economic cooperation. The two countries decided not only to step up bilateral trade but also to increase cooperation for safeguarding the interests of developing nations at the WTO. The then Minister of Commerce Mr Arun Jaitley, who was part of the prime ministerial delegation to China, had coordinated with his Chinese counterpart, Lu Fuyan and had said, "*We have decided to explore how to cooperate with China at the WTO.*"[22] To implement the aforesaid, a Joint Study Group (JSG) was formed by China and India in June 2003. On 21 March 2005, the JSG prepared a report on the India-PRC JSG on Comprehensive Trade and Economic Cooperation. The JSG also recommended the appointment of a Joint Task Force (JTF), which had been set up and its first meeting was held in New Delhi on 13 March 2006.[23] That trend continues and the 11th meeting of IndiaChina Joint Group on Economic Relations, Trade, Science and Technology was held at New Delhi on 26 March 2018.[24]

The common issues foreseen on which, India and China could cooperate are: agriculture subsidies, trade related aspects of intellectual property rights, trade facilitation, trade in services and trade dispute settlement etc.

Most important issue is the huge agriculture subsidies that the United States and the European Union have been giving to their farmers, which leads to increased export production and artificially low prices and this in turn hurts the developing countries that are competing against them in the global markets. Under the WTO, there are two categories of subsidies: ***Green box*** that are considered as minimally or non-trade distorting and these subsidies can be given in an unlimited manner; ***Amber box,*** which represents trade distorting type of subsidy and can be product specific – in favor of special type of producers, and non-product specific which provides for supporting agriculture in general. Amber box support is also known as Aggregate Measurement of Support (AMS). According to the rules of the WTO, Amber box subsidies given by developed countries should fall to 5 percent of the total value of agricultural production and for developing countries, these subsidies have to be limited to 10 percent (de minimis) level of the total value of production of that particular crop.[25] Further, according to the current WTO norms, the support is calculated at 1986-88 prices. The G-33, a grouping of 46 developing countries, has sought a revision of the base to a more recent year or the accommodation of high inflation since that period.[26]

Under the WTO's Agreement on Agriculture (AOA), billions of dollars are being given to farmers as direct subsidy both by the United States and the European Union and it is 'delinked' from production, which means that farmers can produce as much or as little as they want and still receive their subsidy. This encourages unviable farming practices, thereby flooding the global markets with cheap products. Production support given by developed countries to their agriculture has exceeded the value of their production in some years. According to the Organization for Economic Cooperation and Development (OECD) agricultural support estimates statistics (2016) US spent $38.7 billion on farm subsidies given directly to products like soya, wheat, rice, corn and cotton; EU spent $89.9 billion; and Canada $4.2 billion.[27] China and India had circulated a joint paper in Geneva on July 17, 2017, in which they pointed out that developed countries' subsidies under the Green Box, constitute more than 90 percent of their total entitlements, which had resulted in a major asymmetry in the WTO's Agreement on Agriculture. India and China have demanded a reduction of such subsidies and this needs to be capped.[28] Further, as a matter of fact, under the category of AMS regime of WTO, farm subsidies provided by developed countries are over 50 percent and in some cases more than 100 percent of value of production concerned, while developing countries are forced to limit it within 10 percent of the value of production. It is resulting in a major asymmetry in the rules on global agricultural trade. Developed countries are consistently providing trade-distorting subsidies to their farmers at levels much higher than ceiling applicable to developing countries.[29]

Another anomaly is in respect of per capita subsidy. In Asian countries like India and China where the number of farmers is much larger, the per capita subsidy works out to be much less. According to a research paper by South Centre, Geneva ('The WTO's Agricultural Domestic Supports Negotiations', January, 2017), the European Union spends $12,384 a year per farmer whereas the United States, where there are fewer farmers, spends $68,910 per farmer a year (in 2013). India spends $306 per farmer and China $348 per farmer (in 2010-11) a year.[30]

On the issue of the farm subsidies, Beijing and New Delhi had submitted a joint proposal in August 2017, which called on developed countries to eliminate their "amber box" support. Both countries have argued that eliminating this type of support would remove one of the biggest imbalances in the current farm trade rules by obliging the biggest "subsidizers" to reduce their special entitlements.[31]

However, cooperation between the two countries is not always guaranteed. For instance, India had blocked the adoption of the trade facilitation pact on July 31,2014 in the face of heavy criticism. It wanted a deal on finding a permanent solution to public stockpiling simultaneously with the adoption of the trade facilitation agreement. But at the time, it didn't get the backing of China or any of the other G-33 nations, including Indonesia.[32]

Multinational Organization: BRICS

Way back in November 2001, former Goldman Sachs' chief economist, Jim O'Neill coined the term BRIC in his seminal work "Building Better Global Economic BRICs".[33] Since then the grouping has come up a long way. In 2006, the first BRIC Meeting was held among the foreign ministers of China, Brazil, Russia and India on the margins of the 61st United Nations General Assembly session, which drew the prelude for BRIC cooperation. In 2009, the first BRIC Summit was held in Yekaterinburg, Russia. In December 2010, China, being at the helm, invited South Africa to join BRIC and attend the Summit in Sanya, China. BRIC was officially enlarged to include five countries and the acronym changed to BRICS.[34] According to International Monetary Fund's latest update, BRICS countries had a combined GDP of US$ 18.557 trillion in 2017, equivalent to approximately 23.4 percent of the global GDP. As regards the individual countries' share of BRICS total GDP (2017), China is clearly number one having contributed 64.7 percent while India is at number two with 14.07 percent (See Annexure 9 for all BRICS countries share of the GDP).[35] BRICS members have collectively contributed to more than 50 percent of world economic growth during the last decade.[36] Thus consolidation of the BRICS initiative is a means for China to carve its own path to global economic governance and counter US hegemony without direct confrontation.

India's initial response to the original four nations BRIC framework was cautious. Even when the BRIC grouping was elevated to a leaders' level summit at Yekaterinburg in June 2009, Prime Minister Manmohan Singh adopted a low-key approach. However, when India took on the role of host nation for the fourth BRICS summit in New Delhi, its approach changed from a largely defensive one to that of a leading role and it proposed a "South–South" or development bank in March 2012.[37]

With a desire to exercise financial dominance, China had number of proposals, which were not agreeable to India: First, at the 2014 Fortaleza summit in Brazil, the BRICS nations decided to create an initial USD 50 billion fund with equal stakes for each of the BRICS members. The BRICS economies also agreed to establish the Contingent Reserve Arrangement (CRA), amounting to USD 100 billion to deal with any future financial crisis. China had proposed an alternative model encouraging contributions based on each country's financial capacity as it would provide China with an opportunity to contribute more to the bank's capital base and thus, would give it an asymmetric power advantage over the founding members of the bank. India's legitimate concern was that China's leading role would eventually make the bank more like other international financial institutions where big members' voting rights overshadow those of smaller members.[38] Second, another contentious issue was regarding the location of the bank. China took the stand that the bank headquarters should be located in Shanghai as physical location of the bank had the potential to give a moral ascendancy to the host nation in relation to the bank, while India wanted the headquarters for itself. Third, contestations about control later spilled over into the issue of which currency would be the bank's functional currency. During the New Delhi summit in 2012, a memorandum of agreement was signed, which had paved the way for the

BRICS member development banks to use their respective currency denomination for extending loans. The process of moving away from the US dollar led to speculation about Chinese control through the internationalized Chinese Yuan. India was against this as the bank's goal would then become a means to "legitimize" the use of Chinese currency overseas.[39]

In spite of the above differences between China and India, the bargaining process ultimately led to the finalization of the New Development Bank (NDB) with its headquarters in Shanghai and its first president an Indian national, viz., Mr K.V. Kamath.[40] India had also joined the Beijing-backed Asian Infrastructure Investment Bank (AIIB) as a founding member along with 20 other countries. Founder members would initially contribute one-fifth of the AIIB'S $50 billion initial subscribed capital, eventually to be raised to an authorized capital of $100 billion.[41] Interestingly, it was discussed during the meeting held on 10 June 2014 in Shanghai under the aegis of China that the AIIB would ultimately meet Asia's US$ 8 trillion need for infrastructure development.[42] AIIB started functioning in 2016 and has 84 members now. Presently, India holds 7.74 percent equity in the multilateral bank, next only to China (29.9 percent).[43]

It is the membership of the AIIB, as also the economic cooperation under BRICS, which has brought India and China closer due to their converging interests in national financial security. In the past, India had endured an acute balance of payment crisis in 1990-1991 due to a combination of domestic factors and external shocks. While the International Monetary fund (IMF) was India's last-minute savior but in return India had to adopt neoliberal reforms. It was in India's interests to have an alternative "safety net" in the form of the currency reserve for any future financial crises. Furthermore, cash-starved India has been in acute need of infrastructure investment to enable broader economic development and security. Meanwhile, China needed to diversify its massive foreign reserve away from its investment in US Treasury bonds. Financing the NDB and the AIIB projects provided China with an alternative investment avenue: firstly, it helped to diversify China's foreign reserve investment and further supplemented its foreign policy objectives; and secondly, the BRICS reserve currency pool of US$ 100 billion furthered India and China's cooperation on common financial interests.[44]

In September 2017, the 9th BRICS summit was scheduled to be held in Xiamen city of China, with China assuming the rotating chair of the influential group. In the light of ongoing military standoff at Doklam between the two countries and certain other pinpricks, at one time it looked as if the strained relations between China and India might jeopardize the BRICS summit in Xiamen. However, the timely and peaceful resolution of the Doklam incident and decision by Prime Minister Modi to attend was a boost for the group. Xi Jinping complimented Modi and India and in a firmly positive speech he made no mention of Doklam. Xi praised the encouraging "development momentum of China-India relations," heralding cooperative ventures in industry, culture and international organizations.[45] Surprisingly, India secured a big concession with the BRICS joint statement that for the first time condemned the Pakistan-based terrorist outfits like Lashkar-e-Taiba (LeT) and the Jaish-e-Mohammed (JeM) among groups responsible for committing, organizing or supporting terrorist acts.[46] In short-term, the visuals at BRICS indicated that China has realized that hostility with India would only be a hindrance to China's strategic interests.[47] Further, it was very much on Beijing's agenda to make BRICS Plus, consisting of new members from among China's allies or other developing countries, a permanent feature of the group and China had been preparing for it since March 2017. But it apparently backed off from its plans in the wake of resistance from existing members, including India.[48]

Significance of G20

The Group of Twenty (G20) is an international forum that comprises of world's 20 leading industrialized and emerging economies. The group accounts for two-thirds of the world's population and combined GDP of its members is 85 percent of the global GDP. Established in the aftermath of the Asian financial crisis (July 1997), the first G20 summit was held in Berlin in December 1999 and was hosted by the German and Canadian finance ministers. Initially, attendance at G20 summits was limited to the finance ministers and central bank governors of member countries. The group was upgraded at the suggestion of the then U.S. president, following the 2008 global financial crisis (after the fall of Lehman Brothers in September 2008) and an inaugural meeting between G20 leaders took place in Washington DC.[49] In 2009 and 2010 the summit was held twice a year. Since 2011 however, it has been held annually.[50]

The G20 has no Secretariat or any permanent staff of its own and its chairmanship rotates annually between nations divided into regional groupings. The Eleventh G20 summit was held in the picturesque city of Hangzhou, the capital of Zhejiang province, in China on 4-5 September 2016.[51] In 2017, Germany held the chairmanship and the Twelfth summit was held at Hamburg from 7 to 8 July 2017. Although Berlin hosted ministerial-level G20 meetings in 1999 and 2004, the Hamburg event was the first time Germany had hosted G20 heads of government. The Thirteenth G20 Summit was hosted by Argentina in the city of Buenos Aires on 30 November and 01 December 2018, as Argentina became the first South American nation to host a G20.[52]

The member nations are: Argentina, Australia, Brazil, Canada, France, Germany, India, Indonesia, Italy, Japan, Mexico, Russia, Saudi Arabia, South Korea, Turkey, United Kingdom, United States of America, China, South Africa and the final member is the European Union, represented by the European Commission, rotating Council presidency and the European Central Bank (ECB). Spain as a permanent non-member invitee also attends leader summits. Fearing deadlock in a larger decision-making body, not all countries are invited to the G20.[53]

Having been born in the aftermath of the 2008 global economic crisis, G20, in the initial few years of its establishment, had produced tangible results in crisis management, coordinated policy making and follow up action in the sphere of trade, finance and economy. Aim of G20 was to make economic global governance more democratic and effective. However, with the passage of time, the scope of G20 got enlarged to cover political and social issues also including terrorism, terror financing, health, education, water and agriculture etc.[54] China and India play very crucial role in the G20 by delicately balancing their national interests with the imperatives of global economic integration. The G20 Summits provide much needed chance to China and India for improving their relationship and achieving greater cooperation on issues of common interests such as: promoting a transparent, equitable, non-discriminatory, open, inclusive and rule-based global trading architecture which positively responds to needs and priorities of developing nations; ensuring climate change decisions based on the principles of equity and Common But Differentiated Responsibility (CBDR) and so on.[55] India's priority in G20 forum ranges from deploying global surpluses for infrastructure development and inclusive development to energy efficiency.[56]

Though at multilateral level, G20 is believed to have lost focus but its significance has however continued to grow because of the opportunity it provides to world leaders to meet bilaterally with their major partners to discuss and resolve urgent issues of concern and interest. Interestingly, much of the important business takes place on the sidelines and in informal meetings.[57] For instance, China had exploited the G20 as a means of conducting bilateral and multilateral relations both. The most striking illustration of this strategy was visible immediately before the November 2014 Brisbane G20 summit, with the deal between US President Barack Obama and Chinese President Xi Jinping, in which China agreed to cap its greenhouse gas emissions by 2030 at the latest and to diversify its energy supply to include more non-fossil fuels. At the multilateral level, China used the G20 meetings to build autonomous activity by the BRICS countries.[58] However, at the Hamburg summit, there was an informal meeting of the BRICS leaders, wherein PM Modi "*appreciated momentum in BRICS under the chairmanship of President Xi and extended full cooperation and best wishes for the BRICS Xiamen Summit*" and President Xi reciprocated by appreciating "*India's strong resolve against terrorism*". He also praised the "momentum" in BRICS introduced under India's chairmanship. However, there was reportedly no bilateral meeting between the two leaders on the sidelines of the summit to resolve the Doklam standoff.[59]

Shanghai Cooperation Organization: A Complex Web of Multilateralism

Originally organized as Shanghai Five in 1996, Shanghai Cooperation Organization (SCO) is a Eurasian politico-economic and security-oriented organization, which was officially founded in Shanghai in 2001 at the behest of China with Russian support; and the other members were Kazakhstan, Kyrgyzstan and Tajikistan. Uzbekistan joined the group later.[60] Objective of China and Russia was to prevent the former Soviet republics of Central Asia from falling under the United States' influence. It was seemingly quick and easy U.S. victory in Afghanistan, which had brought Russia and China together. Then Russia's young and energetic leader Vladimir Putin wanted to restore his country's old glory and China was militarily weak and isolated, looking for support.[61]

India, along with Pakistan and Iran, was admitted as an observer in 2005. Initially, India was reluctant to become a member of the SCO, while the other two countries were extremely keen to join the grouping as early as possible and Pakistan and Iran had submitted their papers for membership in 2006 and 2008 respectively. India's leaders never attended any SCO summit in the capacity of an Observer while the Presidents of Pakistan (Musharraf and Zardari) and Iran (Ahmadinejad and Rouhani) attended several summits in different capitals to underscore their keenness for full membership of the organization. India's former Prime Minister Dr. Manmohan Singh attended

2009 SCO Summit in Yekaterinburg, Russia, while India was still an Observer, for which the credit goes to Russia. Respecting India's policy of not attending a summit, in which it had no decisive capacity, Russia had organized the BRICS and SCO summits together in 2009 at Yekaterinburg, which enabled India's Prime Minister to attend both the summits.[62] It was only in September 2014, India had formally submitted its application. Presumably a proactive policy decision by the Modi government; while knowing fully well that it is a China dominated organization and the nexus between China and Pakistan was well established and is even growing stronger.

In 15 years, the power equation between China and Russia got reversed: chronically low oil prices, tightening economic sanctions, and the meteoric rise of China dramatically worsened Russia's strategic position. Russia was desperately in need of balancing China lest its Central Asian client states be lured into the Chinese ambit.[63] Therefore, Russia wanted India into the SCO as a counterweight to China. China has long viewed the SCO as a building block of its hegemonic ambition in Central Asia. It has always considered India as a rival on its path to great power status hence it resisted India's membership in the SCO. Rather China preferred Pakistan but could only get the latter as part of a package deal whereby both India and Pakistan entered the SCO, in turn satisfying Russia, being India's principal supporter.[64] In fact, India's membership was supported by Kazakhstan and Russia both.[65]

However, nothing is permanent in international politics: With India moving closer to the United States and the Washington encouraging New Delhi to play a greater role not only in Afghanistan but in the entire Indo-Pacific region, this has resulted in strengthening of Sino-Russian relations and even Russia now embracing Pakistan. Russia had initially opposed Pakistan's membership because of the latter's role as a partner in terrorism but now it is acknowledging positively about Pakistan's anti-terrorism credentials and is even ready to sell weapons to Pakistan.[66] In the past, Russia as an all weather friend of India had always provided her an unstinted support in any crisis situation whether against Pakistan or China but with the changing dynamics of relations, the erstwhile equation appears doubtful.

That Pakistan has been given preference for membership over Iran and Afghanistan, which have major economic, cultural and direct security ties with Central Asian states reflects China's hold over the organization and its nexus with Pakistan.[67] However, it is a different thing that Iran's membership did not receive the go-ahead because of the UN sanctions against it. With the sanctions having been lifted in 2016, Iran will also likely join the grouping in the near future.[68]

With India and Pakistan, both having been admitted as full members of the SCO during its 17th Summit in Astana, the capital of Kazakhstan on 8-9 June 2017, addition of another 1.45 billion people has made the SCO, the world's largest regional cooperative organization representing the biggest section of the global population.[69]

Why 'Democratic' India has joined the 'Anti-Western' Organization?

Seen as a counterweight to North Atlantic Treaty Organization (NATO), the SCO is dubbed in the West as a "dictators' club" and it is often asked by various commentators as to what a vibrant 'democracy like India is doing in this organization?[70] The answer is simple: In today's world of globalization, a nation cannot stay aloof at the risk of being isolated. One cannot leave a geopolitical space vacant to be exploited by other nations at your expense. The SCO membership follows the same logic of working in all geopolitical spaces with a view to raising India's profile and enlarging its political, economic and security options.[71] Central Asian Republics have been regarded as India's 'Extended neighborhood' and hence of strategic necessity to maintain links with them. Further, India is following a pragmatic approach to international relations: exercise of "strategic autonomy". Therefore, India is trying to maintain a fine balance by strengthening military cooperation with the U.S. and forging a joint strategic vision in the Indo-Pacific by participating in the Quadrilateral (other two countries being Japan and Australia), preserving its traditional security ties with Russia and engaging with China positively despite differences.

Keeping in view the main objectives of the SCO,[72] India's primary aim as a member nation should be to promote trade and economic integration, regional connectivity, energy security, people-to-people contact through tourism and exchange visits in cultural and educational spheres, and military cooperation and counter-terrorism. However, unlike any other multilateral organization, SCO has complex linkages among its member states, which offer to India, opportunities and challenges both.

Opportunities. So far, the Central Asian states in the SCO were being dominated by China and Russia: China engaged in resource extraction, particularly oil and gas and promoting connectivity to support its exports; while Russia due to its tightening economic situation concentrated on security issues related to countering religious extremism and terrorism.[73] It is appreciated in strategic circles that India's entry in to the SCO club is likely to balance the preponderance of China and Russia, by offering alternate avenues to Central Asian states for their resources, diversify their markets and gain economic independence.

All the five Central Asian Republics are rich in natural resources and have abundance of hydrocarbons (oil and gas), minerals and water resources. Major areas of opportunity for India in Central Asia include oil and gas, hydro-power generation, energy transmission, minerals and metals, agricultural products, pharmaceuticals, textiles and chemicals.

- **Oil and Gas.** Kazakhstan is the twelfth-ranking oil power in the world with some 30 billion barrels of proved crude oil reserves. It also has sizeable gas reserves: 2.407 trillion cubic meter (Cu m) and ranking 15th in the world. Turkmenistan with proved natural gas reserves of 7.504 trillion cum is the sixth largest gas giant. The country's oil reserves are comparatively smaller, estimated at 600 million barrels. Uzbekistan too has substantial gas deposits: 1.841 trillion cu m with 20th ranking in the world and proved crude oil reserves of 594 million barrels.[74]

  However, the resources being mostly land locked, ferrying them across formidable mountain ranges and impenetrable deserts has been a challenge for centuries. In recent times, technology has enabled pumping of Kazakh oil and Turkmen gas through pipelines to far off areas – to the Atlantic coast and the Pearl River Delta.[75] India's pending energy project, the $ 10 billion Turkmenistan–Afghanistan–Pakistan–India (TAPI) gas pipeline, which was blocked, due in part to Pakistan's recalcitrant approach, should be able to get a much needed push through the SCO (See Map at Annexure 10). Interestingly, construction of the TAPI gas pipeline is reported to have commenced on 13 December 2015. India was represented at the ceremony by Hamid Ansari, the then Vice President while the Presidents of Turkmenistan and Afghanistan and Prime Minister of Pakistan represented their countries. The 1800 km long pipeline is expected to be completed by end 2019. It has a capacity to carry 90 million standard cubic meters a day (mmscmd). Both India and Pakistan will get supply of about 38 mmscmd whereas Afghanistan will get 14 mmscmd supply of natural gas.[76]

India had earlier attempted to build a presence in the region through its 'Connect Central Asia policy' of 2012 but could not succeed partly because of a lack of proper connectivity to the region as also due to lack of enthusiasm in the then UPA government. To the extent in 2013, Kazakhstan had blocked India's ONGC-Videsh Limited (OVL) from acquiring a stake in the Kashagan oilfield, after agreeing initially to sell, mainly due to slow response from Delhi to complete the acquisition. The stake was eventually sold to the China National Petroleum Corporation.[77] However, OVL had bought a 25 percent stake in Satpayev oil block of Kazakhstan and Prime Minister Narendra Modi during his visit to the country launched the first exploratory drilling by OVL in the Satpayev Block, along with Kazakhstan Prime Minister Massimov on 07 July 2015.[78] The SCO can provide an opportunity to India for seeking cooperation of China and jointly invest in Central Asian oil and gas fields as part of an international consortium, even if these fields end up supplying China. This will not be first time, as Indian national oil companies already have a stake in Myanmar's Shwe A1 gas field as also the pipeline carrying gas to Yunnan in China.[79] Indian oil companies with their expertise in setting up refineries can assist Central Asian states to establish refineries, which will add value to their crude before it is exported.[80]

- **Hydropower Generation.** Tajikistan is Asia's water giant, with its untapped rivers capable of generating more than 500 terawatt hours of electricity every year. That will be adequate to meet the entire electricity needs of not only all Central Asian Republics but much beyond.[81] Similarly, Kyrgyzstan also has hydropower potential but a little lower. Attracting investment in power plants is an uphill task. For example, the Rogun Dam is Tajikistan's most ambitious project, with an installed capacity of 3,600 MW and an estimated cost of at least US $ 3.9 billion. Originally envisioned by the Soviet government in 1968, progress in building the dam was slow and was retarded due to Tajikistan's independence and civil war in the 1990s. Tajikistan managed to raise US $ 500 million in its first issue of sovereign debt in September 2017. However, the amount is minuscule compared with the total cost of the Rogun Dam Project. The Kyrgyz Republic also has had its share of problems in raising funds for its dams on the Naryn River.[82] India and China both have expertise in hydropower generation. They can join hands, both in terms of finances as well as building of infrastructure for power generation in Tajikistan and Kyrgyzstan.

- **Power Transmission.** The power transmission using high voltage direct current (HVDC) lines between the five countries and beyond has got lot of potential. Central Asia Regional Cooperation (CAREC) program, established by the Asian Development Bank has funded the upgrading of high-tension power lines in Tajikistan and the development of power lines between Afghanistan and Turkmenistan. Power transmission through HVDC lines from Tajikistan and Kyrgyzstan to industries in North India had been discussed for many years in the past. CASA-1000 is a proposal to tap the electricity potential of Tajikistan for the benefit of South Asia but its fructification depends on the active financial and physical commitment of the participating countries along the way. India with its expertise in rapid rural electrification can offer assistance in establishing transmission grids over long distances.[83] Central Asian Republics will be very much interested in diversifying sale of their energy and surplus power to India and thus extend freedom to their economic domain.
- **Boost Bilateralism.** While the annual summits of such multi-lateral organizations provide valuable opportunity to heads of states to meet each other on a regular basis and arrive at a consensus to resolve common issues, it is in fact the bilateral engagements on the sidelines of summit that provide greater value to the relationship between the two states in the areas of mutual interest. Due to absence of shared physical borders as also because contacts between the top leadership of India and countries of Central Asia had been rather inadequate, that too under the previous government, India had not been able to expand its relations with the Central Asian Republics. Under Prime Minister Narendra Modi, the bilateralism has got a boost and now after having become a full member of the SCO, relations with each of the Central Asian Republics are expected to get proper attention by exploiting all possible aspects:
    - Kazakhstan has 12 percent of the world's Uranium resources and it became the world's leading Uranium producer in 2009, with almost 28 percent of world production, rising further to 39 percent

in 2016 producing about 24,560tU.[84] During Prime Minister Modi's two days visit to Kazakhstan, five agreements were signed between the two countries, which included the most important contract between Kazakh Uranium mining company KazAtomProm and India's Department of Atomic Energy (DAE) to supply 5000 tonnes of Uranium over the next four years i.e., until the end of 2019.[85]

- Uzbekistan has considerable Uranium deposits and is the world's seventh-ranking Uranium supplier.[86] India has signed an agreement with Uzbekistan for import of 2000 metric tonnes of Uranium ore concentrate over the next four years (2014–2018).[87] With Uzbekistan, India is exploring the possibility of extending the Friendship Railway Bridge to Herat in Western Afghanistan to give a push to the government's Afghanistan strategy. With Uzbekistan being the region's biggest military power, India is not only keen to expand the defense partnership with Uzbekistan, it is also seeking effective counter-terrorism partnership through the SCO counter-terror center based in Tashkent.[88]
- Tajikistan can be called India's 'Gateway to Central Asia' as a narrow strip of Afghan territory called the Wakhan Corridor, which is 200 km long and varying from 16 to 65 km in width,[89] separates India from Tajikistan (See Map at Annexure 11). Tajikistan became India's main point of entry in to the region, mainly due to former's close proximity and a special relationship, which it shared with Kabul. More than 30 percent of the 30 million plus population of Afghanistan is of Tajik origin.[90] The close cooperation between the two countries dates back to the late 1990s when they both supported the anti-Taliban resistance forces, the Northern Alliance, in Afghanistan. India had set up a field hospital at Farkhor Airfield, about 100 km Southeast of Dushanbe, capital of Tajikistan, where it treated the injured fighters of Northern Alliance forces of Ahmad Shah Massoud until 2002. India had reportedly used the airfield to supply the Northern Alliance with military equipment, munitions and to repair its combat helicopters.[91] Security relationship between India and Tajikistan got further strengthened when both the countries signed a bilateral

defense agreement in 2002. Based on that agreement, India refurbished a disused Soviet airbase Ayni, 15 miles West of Dushanbe. India spent $ 70 million to refurbish the airbase – lengthening its runway to 3200 meters and building hangars and an air traffic control tower.[92] Indian specialists handed over the refurbished facility to the Tajik Defence Ministry in 2010. New Delhi's support in upgrading the Ayni Airbase led to widespread speculation that India intended to use it as its first ever foreign military base. However, it was not confirmed by either of the government's sources. It is believed that under pressure from Russia, which considers Tajikistan within its sphere of "privileged interest", the Tajik government has denied India access to the airbase. Interestingly, Russia itself is in talks with Tajikistan government for the use of Ayni airfield but they have yet to resolve the excessive annual rent, which Dushanbe wants Moscow to pay.[93]

India's ties with Tajikistan have not been limited to revamping the airfield only. In 2003, New Delhi conducted its first Central Asian military exercise with Tajikistan. India had provided two Mi-8 helicopters along with critical spares, trucks and other vehicles, about 10,000 uniforms and computers to Tajikistan as military aid. In addition, hundreds of Tajik military cadets and officers have been trained at India's National Defence Academy since 1998. India also funded the refurbishment of the Tajik Military Institute in Dushanbe.[94] Though India's trade with Tajikistan has remained very low because of lack of physical connectivity, it has been providing aid to Tajikistan both in terms of cash and material from time to time in the fields of health, education and rural development etc. When Tajik President Emomali Rahman visited India in August 2012, the long-standing bilateral partnership was elevated to a strategic partnership, making Tajikistan third Central Asian country, the first two being Kazakhstan (2009) and Uzbekistan (2011).[95] Consequently, a 50-bed military hospital with medical stores, equipment and 55 personnel was airlifted and positioned as 'India-Tajik Friendship Hospital' at Ayni airbase. India already maintains over 100 Indian military personnel stationed at this base.[96]

Recognizing the importance of Tajikistan in India's strategic calculations, Prime Minister Modi visited Dushanbe on 12 & 13 July 2015. The President of Tajikistan Mr Emomali Rahman paid a return visit to India from 14 to 18 December 2016, interestingly his sixth visit to India, providing a significant impetus to bilateral ties.[97] India and Tajikistan have developed a broad convergence of views on security matters and counter-terrorism since 1990s, which need to be strengthened by India contributing more towards latter's economic prosperity. Tajikistan can provide valuable support to India in the SCO and as a counterweight to Pakistan.

- **Trade.** China's bilateral trade with Central Asian region in 2013 had reached $ 50 billion whereas India's trade with Central Asia was just $ 2 billion in the same year.[98] This comparison may be unfair, primarily due to two reasons: First, China shares a border of over 1,500 km with Kazakhstan, over 850 km with Kyrgyzstan and over 400 km with Tajikistan. Turkmenistan and Uzbekistan are also easily accessible through the land routes provided by these Central Asian states; On the contrary, there is no direct overland access between India and Central Asian states. Pakistan's reluctance in allowing Indian goods to pass through its territory has left India with no option other than routing through China or through Europe via Russia, thereby making it an expensive affair and putting constraints on India's trade interests from growing in the Central Asian Region. Second, China imports about 20 million tons of oil from Kazakhstan and 40 bcm of gas from Turkmenistan in addition to large quantities of Uranium and other minerals from these countries, whereas India has imported just 3,000 tons of Uranium from Kazakhstan and a 25 percent stake in Satpayev Oil Block in the same country.[99] Chabahar port in Iran has provided some relief but in a limited manner. India should look forward to use the SCO platform for exploring all the means to expand its trade with Central Asian Republics. The SCO Favorable Trade Agreement (FTA) is planned to be launched by 2020. India must take part in the negotiations and should make the best use of it.[100]

Challenges. Domination of the SCO by China is a well-known fact; rather it has got further strengthened by the presence of Pakistan. Their collaborative stance will impose severe restrictions on India's ability to achieve favorable outcome on various issues. Recent inclination of Russia toward Pakistan does not bode well for India. Challenges likely to be faced by India in the SCO are discussed as under:

- **Security and Counter-Terrorism.** India has shared interest with Central Asian Republics to counter threats from Islamic radicalism emanating from the Af-Pak region. The strong reemergence of the Taliban, aided once more by Pakistan presents a major challenge. Safe havens provided to the Al-Qaeda leadership on Af-Pak territory provided the staging grounds for the Islamic movements threatening Tajikistan and Uzbekistan.[101] The SCO charter and summits regularly decry terrorism and call for collaboration against it but China and Russia now embrace Pakistan, the sponsor of terrorism in Afghanistan and against India. It is still unclear as to how Pakistan, a promoter of terrorism itself, will cooperate with the framework of SCO to combat terrorism. India will be in a dilemma to participate along with Pakistan in SCO's joint military exercises.

  In 2005, the SCO had established Regional Anti-Terrorism Structure (RATS) at Tashkent. RATS works on information sharing and joint counter terrorism measures between member states. The SCO has successfully neutralized 600 would-be attacks and extradited more than 500 terrorists through the RATS mechanism. RATS will be useful for intelligence sharing, developing best practices and in capacity building to counter terrorism.[102]

- **Regional Connectivity.** Prime Minister Narendra Modi in his address at Astana Summit on 09 June 2017 expressed India's intent to deepen connectivity with SCO nations as top priority but success of connectivity initiatives would depend highly upon acceptance, solidarity, regional cooperation as well as inclusivity and sustainability.[103] India's refusal to participate in BRI is primarily due to incorporation of China-Pakistan Economic Corridor, which violates her sovereignty as it passes through Gilgit-Baltistan, an area claimed by India. BRI has received support from all SCO members less India. To avoid the risk of being isolated, India will have to be diplomatically suave and maintain strong bilateral relationships with Russia and five Central Asian Republics. India should avoid a confrontational situation with in the forum by emphatically articulating its position without endorsing the BRI project.[104] It appears Beijing has realized that New Delhi would not budge from its position as during the last SCO foreign ministers' meeting in Beijing in April 2018, India was the only country not to express support for the BRI while seven other foreign ministers reaffirmed support for China's BRI. In the light of the bilateral bonhomie achieved by the Modi-Xi informal summit, Chinese Vice-foreign minister Kong Xuanyou told, "*China does not think it is important whether India accepts China's Belt and Road infrastructure project and China won't force it to*". Apparently, China has reconciled to the fact India shared the common interests on connectivity for example, India does not oppose the Bangladesh, China, India, Myanmar (BCIM) Corridor, which predates the BRI but which Beijing has included as one of the six flagship economic corridors under the BRI and India is cooperating with China on it.[105]

- **Economic Integration.** Central Asian Republics, which constitute one-third of the SCO members, have been opposed to monopolization of regional geopolitics by a single country.[106] Proactive role by India in SCO and providing them an alternative option for economic expansion will be enthusiastically accepted. Speedy completion of the Chabahar Port (Due to the US President Donald Trump Administration's withdrawal from JCPOA treaty with Iran, India's development of Chahbahar port was likely to come under sanctions but due to strengthening of India-US relations, the US exempted Chahbahar from Iran-related sanctions in November 2018. As a result, rapid progress was made and Iran has formally handed over the port to India for operations on 24 December 2018), the much talked about International North-South Transport Corridor (INSTC) and membership of Free Trade Agreement with Eurasian Economic Union will be the corner stone of India's economic integration and all round cooperation with Central Asia. INSTC is a 7,200 km long, multi-modal (ship, rail and road) transportation system for connecting the Indian Ocean and Persian Gulf to the Caspian Sea via Iran and thereafter to Russia and North Europe. It is estimated that INSTC would be completely effective by the end of this decade. The Chabahar route along with INSTC are estimated to boost trade between India and Central Asia to around $ 170 billion.[107]

Undoubtedly, the SCO is a China-dominated organization and further China has made deep inroads in to Central Asia by investing heavily for construction of oil and gas pipelines through difficult terrain to transport Central Asian oil and gas to its Eastern seaboard. They are buying the hydrocarbons costlier but selling cheaper in their domestic market. Chinese national oil companies provide the necessary support while the political leadership handles the geopolitical aspects. Moreover, China has the geographical advantage of not having to transit through hostile Pakistan or unstable Afghanistan.[108] *In respect of a democratic setup like India, to undertake such a venture on foreign shores, political leadership has to take a decision based on geopolitical benefits vis-à-vis economic risks therefore the process is time consuming resulting in slow progress thereby creating impatience at the other end. One must know that Central Asian Republics are still evolving their political and legal systems and their tax and contract regimes are yet to be stabilized.*

India should not compete with China in matching with their investments or so-called deep pockets but it should maneuver dexterously through the effective use of diplomacy, focus on developing its "soft power" capabilities through cultural exchange, people-to-people contact, film tourism, air connectivity, provide assistance in infrastructural developments, open opportunities for its expanding demographic dividend in particular the skilled-labor/technicians and defense cooperation with Central Asian Republics bilaterally as well as multilaterally.

Pakistan may bring up the issue of Kashmir on SCO platform seeking a role for Russia and China to mediate. Being a bilateral issue, India can refuse to entertain a third party involvement and that will be in conformity with the SCO's mandate, which does not extend to solving bilateral disputes between member-states. Over the last 17 years of its existence, SCO has refrained from dealing with disputes between its members. For instance, conflicts and disagreements on water, boundaries and territory between Uzbekistan, Kazakhstan, Kyrgyzstan and Tajikistan have not been on the agenda of the SCO.[109]

In strategic circles, it was also being discussed that by providing membership to India in SCO, China will seek a reciprocal membership in the South Asian Association for Regional Cooperation (SAARC) or Bay of Bengal Initiative for Multi-Sectoral Technical and Economic Cooperation (BIMSTEC), with a view to dilute India's influence in the region. It may well be appreciated that Indian government will have inbuilt mechanism in the sphere of diplomacy and statesmanship to anticipate such situations and deal with it appropriately.

AREAS OF COMPETITION

Energy: From Competition to Cooperation

Energy is the basic requirement for the economic growth and prosperity of a nation. Thus the consumption of energy resources is directly related to the development of a nation. Rapidly growing populations with massive infrastructure and construction projects have accelerated the energy demands in China and India at astonishing pace. But their indigenous energy resources are limited to support their economic growth. At the 2011 level of extraction, China and India's proven oil reserves would be depleted within a decade.[110] China's proven oil reserves stand at 18 billion barrels compared to 5 billion barrels in India.[111] Some experts estimate that as India industrializes and urbanizes, its oil and gas imports will grow at a faster rate than that of China.[112]

Energy security becomes an inseparable component of a state's foreign policy, if the state is dependent upon external sources to fulfill its energy needs. China is the world's largest consumer of oil, importing nearly 40-50 percent of its oil, while India is world's sixth largest consumer of energy, importing 70 percent of its oil and 50 percent of gas requirements. Procuring the energy resources, transporting the same through vital international sea lanes, fluctuations in price and uncertainties about free and secured flow of energy due to multifarious reasons, have compelled India and China to treat energy security as a foreign policy as well as a strategic priority. India's former Prime Minister, Dr. Manmohan Singh had stated that it was India's vital national interest to pursue a sound energy security strategy and he said, "*By energy security, I refer not merely to the assurance of the supply of energy in ample quantity. Real energy security implies assured supply of good quality energy at affordable prices*".[113] The assured access to energy is the principal driver that is generating continued competition between India and China. Energy security considerations have been motivating China and India to purchase equity stakes in energy fields and obtain exploration rights, resulting in to intense competition. Some of the examples are:

- The exit of Western oil majors from Venezuela following "re-nationalization" policies in 2006 presented an opportunity for Indian and Chinese companies to move in.[114] Indian companies became participants in the Venezuelan petroleum sector, having secured two exploration projects between 2008 to 2010 and had also signed contracts with Petroleos de Venezuela, S.A. (PDVSA) to purchase oil through Venezuela for Reliance and other Indian refineries. By end

2013, the potential participation by India expanded significantly due to increased interactions and signing of multiple agreements between the oil companies of the two countries but Indian companies have actually committed very little real money.[115] China had been more aggressive and their role in Venezuela involved: loans to the Venezuelan government; direct investments to quantify, develop and exploit oil blocks; loans to PDVSA to cover its share of petroleum joint ventures; augmentation of Venezuelan refinery capacity; and the sale of major assets for future petroleum deliveries, including oil tankers and drilling rigs. Although the presence of Chinese companies in Venezuela's oil industry dates back to 1997, it is the 2008 agreement with CNPC to develop Junin-4 (formalized in 2010), which grabbed more attention.[116] China has been one of Venezuela's biggest creditors, providing it loans, cash and investment totaling more than US$65 billion between 2007 and 2016, primarily through oil-for-loan deals.[117] The International Monetary Fund's forecast of 2,349 percent inflation for Venezuela in 2018, up from an estimated 2,069 percent in 2017, is a rude reminder for China – the Latin American country's key foreign creditor – about the risks of overseas investment. As Venezuela slides into bankruptcy, and economic and social conditions worsen over there, Beijing is growing impatient since it has little leverage to protect its interests.[118] Further, there used to be 400,000 ethnic Chinese living in Venezuela but tens of thousands have returned to China in the past three years as its economy has imploded and violent protests have taken over the streets.[119] Conditions in Venezuela should be a reminder to China that it has to be more careful with its outbound investment and it must study a country's risks carefully and make proper plans before investing there.

- Indian and Chinese companies were also competing in Brazil, the site of the world's largest offshore oil discoveries. In 2013, India's ONGC Videsh Limited (OVL), the overseas arm of state-owned Oil and Natural Gas Corporation along with Royal Dutch Shell Plc. jointly acquired Brazil's Petroleo Brasileiro SA's (Petrobras) 35 percent stake in the Brazilian Offshore oil field, BC-10 block in the Campos Basin for around $1.54 billion (around Rs.9,440 crore) by preempting Sinochem, China's largest chemical producer.[120]

- Myanmar's energy sector has emerged as an important destination for the growing rivalry between China and India, with both countries keen to secure new hydrocarbon reserves. Prior to the construction of the pipelines, intense bidding war occurred between the two nations over gaining exclusive rights to the lucrative A1 and A3 blocks in the Shwe gas fields. Exploration began off the Rakhine Coast, Myanmar in 2000 and huge natural gas deposits were discovered in 2003. The new find in block A-1 off the Rakhine state contained 'a world-class commercial-scale gas deposit' estimated to hold 4.2–5.8 trillion cubic feet of gas, with a potential of 14 trillion cubic feet. The gas field in Shwe-1, block A-1 is located in the northernmost point of the Rakhine offshore area, making it easier to export gas to India. The Korean firm Daewoo International operates and owns 60 percent of Myanmar's gas-rich A-1 block, in which India's Oil and Natural Gas Corporation (ONGC) holds 20 percent stake, and the Gas Authority of India Limited (GAIL) and the Korea Gas Corporation each holds 10 percent. The GAIL has been appointed by Myanmar as the agency responsible for marketing gas from A-1 block. Another block, A-3 lying close to A-1, owned fully by Daewoo, is estimated to hold 6.0 trillion cubic feet of recoverable gas. The Myanmar Ministry of Energy decided against imposing any duty on export of oil and natural gas and gave concession to GAIL to export 90 percent of any gas produced from fields in the A-1 block.[121]

  According to evaluations by Daewoo, the discovered gas could be exported to the Indian market through one of three pipeline routes. Two overland possibilities would have carried gas directly from Myanmar or via Bangladesh, while the third option was to be a sub-sea link in the Bay of Bengal. Given the geographical location, overland pipelines transiting through Bangladesh were the most cost-effective way of getting gas from Myanmar to India. The 800-km Myanmar–Bangladesh–India pipeline was estimated to cost about US$5 billion (approximately Rs 12,000 crore) and the gas was to be delivered from 2009. GAIL also proposed a 1573 km pipeline from Sittwe port in Myanmar through Tripura/Mizoram, Assam and West Bengal to Gaya in Bihar (doubling the total pipeline length would increase the cost by another US$3 billion). Bangladesh set forth many conditions for allowing any pipeline to cross its territory. India underestimated domestic political development in Bangladesh and Myanmar had no reason to wait for. India's pipeline plans, desperately awaited to be negotiated, were finally rejected by the regime in Myanmar after China's state owned company moved ahead. China matched India's offer very aggressively and India suffered from delays in decision-making.[122] Indian President and other Indian officials also conducted state visits to lobby the deal but their efforts went into vein. This deal gave advantage to China to get the entire stock from A-1 and A-3 blocks in the Rakhine offshore area. This move came immediately after China became successful in signing a contract with Junta government to construct a hydroelectric dam worth $150 million in the country. China's Natural Development Reform Commission approved plans in April 2006 with Myanmar government for a construction of 1100 km pipeline after Acting Prime Minister of Myanmar, Thein Sein, made a five-day visit to Beijing and Yunnan. The construction of pipeline was finally given a green signal in June 2009 and it was decided to build oil and gas pipeline from deep water port of Kyaukpyu on the West coast of Myanmar to Ruili in Yunnan province.[123] (Both gas and oil pipelines are covered in detail in Chapter 2 under Myanmar). China agreed to pay an annual transit fee of $150 million for 30 years for the pipeline's 990 km stretch in Myanmar. Though, in mean time, Indian state owned company ONGC acquired three offshore deep water exploration Blocks i.e. AD-2, AD-3 and AD-9 on 23 September 2007 on the ground of mutual understanding and cooperation.[124] But China was able to outmaneuver India through its sheer financial clout and greater experience in the global energy industry.[125] In a second onshore licensing round in January 2013, Myanmar had offered 18 onshore areas. Industry sources said 59 companies, including Sinopec of China were originally pre-qualified to bid for these 18 blocks. OVL won two onshore blocks: B2 (Zebyutaung-Nandaw) having an area of 16,995 sq. km, is located in Northern Myanmar, bordering the state of Manipur in India, and EP-3 (Thegon-Shwegu), having an area of 1,650 sq. km, is located in Central Myanmar. Sinopec did not figure in the final allotment.[126] This was followed by an offshore bidding round for 30 oil and gas blocks (11 shallow water and 19 deep sea), wherein Reliance and Oil India Limited with Oil Max and Mercator were able to win two blocks each in March 2014.[127]

- Backed by diplomatic efforts, Indian energy companies have been aggressively pursuing a share in the world's most prolific oil and gas fields. According to the ONGC official website, ONGC Videsh Limited has stakes in 38 oil and gas projects in 17 Countries.[128] ONGC Videsh Limited produced a record 12.57 million tonnes of crude oil and equivalent gas from its assets abroad in 2016-17. For 2017-18, the company's target was 14.37 million tonnes of oil and oil equivalent gas production. It has so far invested USD 27.23 billion in overseas projects; the highest by any Indian company.[129] In addition to OVL, there are other Indian public and private sector oil and gas companies, which are acquiring assets abroad: Indian Oil has nine overseas active assets in eight countries; Oil India Ltd has joint venture and alliances in eight countries; and Bharat Petro Resources, a wholly-owned subsidiary of Bharat Petroleum Corp. Ltd. has 17 blocks worldwide across six countries.[130]

Purchase of equity stakes in energy fields and resulting competitions are increasingly being supported by military capabilities leading to the potential for heightened tensions and even conflict.[131] For instance, in 2011, China had objected to India's ONGC Videsh Ltd's plans of exploring two offshore oil blocks that Vietnam claimed to be in its Exclusive Economic Zone in the South China Sea. Prior to that an Indian Battleship INS Airavat was also challenged on radio by the Chinese Navy.[132] During Vietnamese Prime Minister Nguyen Tan Dung's two-day visit to New Delhi, on 28 October 2014 India secured oil exploration rights from Hanoi in parts of the contentious South China Sea, for which China warned India against meddling in its dispute with Vietnam over islands in the South China Sea.[133] Despite growing number of pipeline projects, China will remain dependent on sea transfers of energy from suppliers in the Middle East. Hence the maritime security concerns have provided the rationale to China and India for development of blue-water naval capabilities, to protect critical economic assets and secure access to energy resources.[134]

It is apparent that both nations want to be energy independent but in an increasingly interconnected and globalized world, neither India nor China is appreciated to have the financial or political capital to unilaterally and effectively develop energy resources across all energy markets.[135] Being latecomers in the international energy environment, most of the good oil and gas assets in stable countries are unavailable because they were already owned by national companies in the producer countries or Western oil countries. China and India have to depend on destabilizing countries like those in Africa and Latin America.[136] It is ideal to take a consortium approach, which would help in mitigating the risks such as what happened in Venezuela recently. In 2006, India's ONGC and the China's CNPC had signed a pact for bilateral oil cooperation and possible joint crude purchases, which enabled exploration and production (E&P) operations in Myanmar, Sudan, and Syria.[137] For example in Sudan both countries work together – India drills the oil and China provides the infrastructure by building the pipelines.[138] Yet, these agreements did not result in joint bidding or policy cooperation. On 19 June 2012, both the companies signed a Memorandum of Understanding (MoU) with a view to strengthen existing E&P operations in Myanmar, Sudan, and Syria, and look ahead for making joint bids on foreign oil and gas fields and jointly invest in infrastructure development in the future. With the signing of the MoU, more safeguards are likely to be adopted to ensure that bidding should not get out of hand, and prices to stay reasonable.[139] This approach will ensure greater energy security for both the countries and mitigate the risk on individual firms and countries. This is the right step to reduce competition and strengthen greater energy cooperation between India and China.

China and India both are in the process of adopting other sources of clean and renewable energy such as wind and solar. According to an article in the Global Times "*China is ahead of India in energy technologies including wind and solar technology as well as equipment manufacturing. China also has huge funding resources. In contrast, India has an edge in energy information management and wind energy, and also has a large energy market. In addition, Indian firms are more internationalized. Their complementarities offer great opportunities for the two countries to jointly invest in the energy sector.*"[140] In the wind energy sector, for example, Chinese turbine maker Goldwind Science & Technology Co. Ltd. and Indian turbine maker Suzlon Energy Ltd. are competing with leading Western companies such as General Electric. In addition, China's second-largest manufacturer of wind turbines, Ming Yang Wind Power Group Ltd. is aggressively expanding into the Indian market.[141] There is scope for the two countries to move together in solar photovoltaic industry through joint ventures and technology sharing to capture the expanding solar energy market.

Trade Competition in Southeast Asia

The Association of South East Asian Nations (ASEAN), which was formed in 1967, currently consists of 10 countries: Singapore, Malaysia, Thailand, Indonesia, Philippines, Brunei, Vietnam, Cambodia, Laos and Myanmar. Located at the center of the Indo-Pacific, ASEAN region had a combined GDP of about US$2.55 trillion in 2016.[142] With an estimated population of about 639 million people,[143] it is the world's third largest consumer market in population terms, behind only China and India. More importantly, the populations in the ASEAN countries tend to be young along with a low dependency ratio. Presently, there are 213 million youth (15-34 years) in ASEAN countries, constituting the largest ever cohort of ASEAN youth. The peak population of just over 220 million is expected in 2038.[144] In recent years the labor force in Southeast Asia has been growing twice as fast as China's and even more critical is that their labor costs are generally below those of China. The average monthly wage rate in China is more than $600, whereas among the ASEAN, Thailand's monthly wage of about $400 is the highest and Indonesia's monthly wage of approximately $200 is the lowest.[145] In fact, it is ASEAN's competitive cost of labor – coupled with policies that facilitate industrial clustering – that it has become an attractive destination for trade and investment by multinationals as also other nations. Rising production costs in China already have been driving the momentum of manufacturing and production location decisions toward ASEAN countries. The formal establishment of the ASEAN Economic Community (AEC) on 31 December 2015 has intensified the attraction. The AEC seeks to achieve greater regional integration, as it aims to consolidate Southeast Asia's diverse economies into a single market.[146] FDI inflows to the ASEAN region increased to US$136.2 billion in 2014, which actually overtook China for the first time since 1993.[147]

China's trade and investment ties with ASEAN far exceed India's. The total value of trade between the ASEAN region and China reached a record $514.8 billion in 2017, more than six times the value of trade between ASEAN and India, which stood at $81.3 billion in the same year. In 2017, China had a trade surplus of $43.4 billion with ASEAN, whereas India had a trade deficit of $12.9 billion.[148] China's Outward Foreign Direct Investment (OFDI) in ASEAN region is much more compared to India ($ 9.21 Billion vs. $1.04 billion in 2016).[149]

Unbalanced trade with China has led to retaliation, mostly in the form of non-tariff barriers such as national standard certifications and mandatory local content requirements. Besides various other factors, trade imbalance is the major source of concern among ASEAN decision makers about the region's continued economic dependence on China. Business associations, politicians and academics have been calling for a review of the ASEAN-China Free Trade Agreement since 2012. Further, Chinese funds often come with strings attached, such as requirements that Chinese labor, materials and finance be used. Politicians in the region have used this to stir up public fears about Chinese encroachment, particularly when temperatures are running high over territorial disputes.[150]

Undesirable economic dependency on China combined with its territorial disputes with members of the ASEAN in the South China Sea offers an opportunity to India for a reinvigorated push into the region. India had initiated the "Look East" Policy in the early 1990s, following the end of the Cold War and liberalization of the Indian economy. The aim was to strengthen relations with the booming economies of Southeast Asia through improved land and sea connections but it was foiled by the Asian financial crisis. The "Look East" Policy was reinitiated in 2002, wherein India attempted to widen its scope by including China, Japan, South Korea, Australia and New Zealand.[151] An important milestone in India's "Look East" Policy was the India-ASEAN Free Trade Agreement (FTA), which was signed in 2009. India's FTA provided for gradual elimination of tariffs based on timelines and is far more limited than China's as it is starting from a much lower base.[152] China-ASEAN FTA provided zero tariff for more than 90 percent of the products exchanged between China and ASEAN. The significant reduction in tariff provided a strong impetus to the fast growth of bilateral trade between China and ASEAN. In fact, after signing of the FTA with ASEAN, India has been experiencing a negative trade balance with the regional grouping. Its trade deficit with ASEAN has almost doubled from $6.7 billion in 2010 to $12.9 billion in 2017. This is mainly due to India facing competition from Southeast Asian countries in the manufacturing and plantations sectors. The initial agreement being only for goods, India managed to get a similar agreement for services in 2012 but that is still awaiting ratification by some of the members of ASEAN.[153]

In the present circumstances, it is unlikely that India will be able to change the trade balance with ASEAN on the basis of merchandise goods. Hence, the other option is to make increased investments in the region, knowing fully well the availability of abundant resources, human as well as material and a flourishing middle-class market, which is expected to touch 400 million by 2020, thereby offering huge potential on the supply side. The Southeast Asian region has been receiving huge investments from abroad – US$ 1,252 billion in FDI from 2003 to 2016.[154] India has invested only US$ 39.72 billion from 2007 to 2016.[155] Another aspect is that base salaries among emerging economies like CLMV (Cambodia, Laos, Myanmar, Vietnam) in the ASEAN are substantially lower than those in India, and thus these countries are winning in terms of labor-cost competitiveness. The most pertinent case is in respect of export of readymade garments to the US, where countries like Cambodia, Indonesia and Vietnam are increasingly overtaking India. Vietnam has a 10 percent share in this US$ 104 billion market, as compared to India's six percent, followed by Indonesia with five percent share, and Cambodia, two percent. Facing stiff competition from its Asian peers, India's textile exports to the world have almost halved from 24.26 percent in 2001 to 13.71 percent in 2016. Hence Indian textile firms, amongst other stakeholders, should proactively seek to explore the ASEAN market to take advantage of the economies of scale, and protect itself from losing revenue.[156]

Under the leadership of Prime Minister Narendra Modi, in 2014, the "Look East" Policy has been rechristened as "Act East" Policy, providing fresh impetus to India's efforts to reenergize the multidimensional aspects of its relations with the ASEAN region. India is focusing on connectivity, commerce and culture as foundation towards a stronger relation with the region and for greater regional integration. More significantly, India's Northeastern region will reap rich dividends through greater connectivity between India and Southeast Asia, hence Northeast becomes a natural partner in India's Act East Policy vis-à-vis the ASEAN.[157] Efforts are on to boost connectivity with the region, particularly with ASEAN countries in the Greater Mekong sub-region – Laos, Cambodia, Myanmar, Vietnam and Thailand. India's Minister of State for Commerce and Industry, C R Chaudhary said at the ASEAN-India Business and Investment Meet and Expo held at New Delhi in January 2018, "*Connectivity and infrastructure are major challenges to further push the trade ties between India and the ASEAN.*" The long-delayed flagship project such as the1400 km India-Myanmar-Thailand Trilateral Highway, which was initiated in 2002, has already missed its completion date. According to the Minister considerable progress has been made in the construction of trilateral highway. This highway begins from Moreh in Manipur and ends in Bangkok, going through Myanmar (See Annexure 12). The project's completion now hinges on the National Highway Authority of India (NHAI) developing a 121-km two-lane highway between Yagyi and Kalewa in Myanmar, with the External

Affairs Ministry providing Rs 1,117 crore for this section. The section in Myanmar is expected to be finished in May 2019 and the overall project is scheduled to be completed by 2021.[158] There are talks to extend the project to Cambodia, Laos and Vietnam and the proposed route from India to Vietnam will be known as the East-West Economic Corridor (EWEC). Kaladan Multi Modal Transit Transport Project (KMTTP) is also under implementation. The project aims to improve connectivity between Indian ports on the Eastern seaboard and Sittwe port in Myanmar and then from Myanmar to Mizoram by road transport. There is also a proposal to establish rail link between India and Vietnam. There is Rih-Tedim project in Myanmar, which aims to establish connectivity between Eastern Mizoram and Western Mizoram.[159] A consensus on finalizing the proposed protocol of the India-Myanmar-Thailand Motor Vehicle Agreement (IMT MVA) has been reached in 2013. This agreement will have a critical role in realizing seamless movement of passenger, personal and cargo vehicles along roads linking India, Myanmar and Thailand; thus enhancing the flow of trade and people-to-people contact.[160]

Giving momentum to his "Act East" Policy, Prime Minister hosted the heads of all 10 ASEAN countries as chief guests on the occasion of India's 69th Republic Day celebrations on 26 January 2018. In 2017, India and ASEAN had observed 25 years of their dialogue partnership, 15 years of summit level interaction and five years of strategic partnership, which culminated on 25 January 2018 in the Commemorative Summit whose theme was "Shared values, Common Destiny".[161] Prime Minister Narendra Modi assured the leaders of the ASEAN, at the end of the two-day summit in New Delhi, that India would "exert efforts" so that the Regional Comprehensive Economic Partnership (RCEP) can be signed as planned in November. Negotiations to create the RCEP began in November 2012, during an ASEAN summit in Cambodia.[162]

Regional Comprehensive Economic Partnership (RCEP)

RCEP is an ASEAN-centered, pan-Asian trade pact comprising its 10-member countries and its six free trade agreement (FTA) partners – India, China, Japan, South Korea, Australia and New Zealand. The RCEP has been viewed as an alternative to the Trans-Pacific Partnership (TPP), a trade agreement that had been spearheaded by the US under President Barack Obama's administration. The TPP included some of the countries that fall into the proposed RCEP – Australia, New Zealand, Singapore, Vietnam, Brunei, Japan and Malaysia –

India, China, Japan and South Korea. It is estimated to cover over one-third of the world's GDP with a collective market consisting of 48 percent of the world's population.[163] It covers a wide range of issues including trade in goods, trade in services, investment, intellectual property rights, competition policy, dispute settlement and economic and technical cooperation.[164]

India has a vital interest in seeking greater liberalization of trade in the information technology (IT) and IT-enabled services (ITES) due to its globally competitive IT sector while it has lesser interests in manufactured goods (except pharmaceuticals and textiles) and agriculture commodities. In contrast, RCEP countries like China, South Korea and Japan are export powerhouses in manufactured goods and are actively seeking the goods market of India. Likewise, Australia and New Zealand are pressing for lower tariffs to gain greater market access in India's food, wine and dairy sectors.[165]

India has so far resisted pressures to dismantle tariff barriers on several agricultural and industrial products during RCEP negotiations, claiming it needs to protect these sectors and the people working in them. The ASEAN countries collectively want a removal of customs duties on at least 90 percent of all traded commodities; some members, such as Australia, have pressed for an even higher proportion of duties to be eliminated. Indian manufacturers are apprehensive that once the tariff and non-tariff trade barriers are removed under the RCEP, Indian markets will be flooded with cheaper Chinese goods. It would also significantly diminish the effectiveness of the 'Make in India' initiative set to boost domestic manufacturing.[166] It has been argued that the RCEP also fails to address India's concerns on services, especially in terms of allowing India's world class professional workers to undertake short-term work in member countries. While India has done well in services in Europe, the United States (US), the United Kingdom (UK) and Australia, the Asia-Pacific market has accounted for only about 8 to 12 percent of the total business of Indian IT companies. The bulk of this business is in IT, business process outsourcing (BPO) and consulting services. Services are inherently more difficult to execute and are not profitable in ASEAN to the extent they are in the US and the UK.[167]

Economic prudence demands that India should engage with RCEP and other FTAs on its own terms. The real economic costs and benefits should be the basis rather than elusive geo-political gains. To remain part of the substantial economic growth that Asia is likely to witness in the near future, India needs to stay interconnected with its regional trading partners through formalized and coordinated regional trade pacts. For example, despite the US pulling out of the TPP, the other 11 countries have agreed to proceed with it and even American President Donald Trump alluded recently at the World Economic Forum in Davos to reconsider the US re-joining the TPP with a few modifications.[168] With number of issues yet to be resolved, signing of the RCEP agreement at the end of this year may not be advisable. India needs to assess its own choices and weigh the impact on its whole trade space vis-a-vis the narrow base of the advantages that RCEP may offer. There are ways and means to address India's concerns of Chinese imports flooding the Indian market through the RCEP route. In the current RCEP negotiations, it is possible for India to allow selected Chinese industrial goods to enter the Indian market duty free only at a later date, say five or ten years, to enable Indian industries to adjust. As Chinese costs are also rising fast, it would be fair to permit Chinese goods after a lapse of five or ten years. Such a move may also serve to attract small-medium Chinese enterprises to establish their commercial presence in India – these enterprises are currently relocating their operations to Southeast Asian countries such as Vietnam and Thailand due to rising cost in China. From a trade perspective, this foreign direct investment from Chinese companies may also reduce India's perennial trade deficit with China as an alternative to focusing on increasing exports to China.[169]

After all, it is believed that the final game plan is to have both RCEP and TPP subsumed into a larger Free Trade Area of the Asia-Pacific (FTAAP) planned under the auspices of the APEC. Hence, India needs to develop a comprehensive new approach towards FTAs combining long-term vision with a short-and medium-term strategy that can easily adapt to changing global economic conditions.[170]

Sino-Indian Trade Rivalry in South Asia

The formation of South Asian Association for Regional Cooperation (SAARC) in 1985 was the first institutionalized effort to forge multilateral cooperation among the countries of the region. SAARC includes Afghanistan, Bangladesh, Bhutan, India, the Maldives, Nepal, Pakistan and Sri Lanka; and with a population of over 1.76 billion, it is one of the largest regional organizations in the world.[171] China entered into SAARC as an observer at the Dacca summit meeting in 2005 supported by Pakistan, Nepal and Bangladesh but resisted by India, Bhutan, Afghanistan and Maldives.[172] In fact SAARC is probably one of the only regional organization in the world that has more observers than its member states – apart from China, there are eight observers in SAARC: the United States, European Union, Australia, Japan, South Korea, Iran, Myanmar and Mauritius.[173]

South Asia provides economic opportunity and strategic benefits to China as it is seeking a greater role in the Indian Ocean. Thus, China has been developing economic and political links with SAARC member states. China follows its ancient strategy of "*hexiao kongda*" (Cooperate with the small countries to counter the big) in South Asia to counter India.[174]

China has been pushing for a permanent membership of the SAARC while India is opposed to it as it considers South Asia within its sphere of influence. Further, implications of full membership in SAARC are crucial as it carries the weightage of a veto. After all, in other fora like the Asian Development Bank, Beijing had vetoed some Indian projects for political reasons.[175]

During the 18th SAARC Summit at Kathmandu in November 2014, China expressed its interest in joining the regional bloc as a full-member state, supported by Pakistan, Nepal and Sri Lanka but as happened in the past, reluctance from India kept the proposal from moving forward.[176]

Though India might have succeeded in preventing China from becoming a permanent member of the SAARC, China has reached out to South Asian states in a major way. China's delegation to the SAARC summit was led by Vice Foreign Minister Liu Zhenmin. Liu pledged that China would seek deeper ties with South Asia, especially on the economic front. He said, "*China has put forward a series of initiatives – promising to increase trade between South Asia and China to US$150 billion and investment of $ 30 billion in infrastructure development in the next five years.*" Besides this, China is giving 10,000 scholarships for South Asian students, apart from providing skills training to thousands of others.[177]

In principle, China and India share common goals for SAARC: increasing regional integration through infrastructure connections and enhance trade and investments. In reality, this is leading to a power struggle between China and India in the strategic landscape of South Asia, where smaller countries in the region are befriending China to balance against the pre-dominance of India. Over the last decade, China has become a significant economic player in the region, developing strong ties with smaller states through trade, aid, investment and diplomacy.

Trade in South Asia

India's global trade was worth $ 768.9 billion in 2017-2018, of which only about $ 26 billion was with the SAARC partners. The country wise trade details are given in Annexure 13. In contrast, China's trade with the SAARC countries (less India) during the same period was about $ 37.2 billion.[178]

In spite of having arrived at trade agreements viz., South Asian Preferential Trading Arrangement (SAPTA) in 1995 followed by South Asian Free Trade Agreement (SAFTA) in 2004 (signed in 2004 and implemented in 2006),[179] trade barriers within the region have not been broken because each nation has its own policies, approaches and vulnerabilities. SAFTA sought to create a free trade zone, in which it laid down a framework for eliminating customs duties on all traded goods by 2016. But according to most observers, SAFTA has not taken off the way it had been envisaged. Most countries still have only a limited number of items in the trade basket.

Pakistan and India have 1,209 items on the "negative list" – bilateral trade is prohibited in these goods and commodities. India has been exploring the possibility of permitting import of more items at a lower duty from Pakistan but deep-seated animosity between India and Pakistan, punctuated by four wars, on-going ceasefire violations, border intrusions and its waging of proxy war by providing support to terrorist organizations for indulging in violence in the State of Jammu & Kashmir and elsewhere in the country, have stood in the way of broader regional trade expansion. India has already given the Most Favored Nation (MFN) status to Pakistan. If Pakistan also gives India the same status, this will provide a big boost to the export of textiles, cotton, vegetables, coffee, tea and spices from India. It is an irony of relations that despite having an integrated check point on the Wagah-Attari border, trucks or load-carriers of one country are not allowed to cross over to other country but the goods are transshipped to other trucks, leading to wastage of time, energy and loss through breakage etc.[180] Whereas China shares an extensive strategic and economic relationship with Pakistan calling it 'Iron Brother" and 'All Weather Friend'.[181] Pakistan-China volume of trade, which was $ 4 billion in 2006-2007, reached $13.77 billion in 2015-16,[182] whereas India-Pakistan trade volume reached a paltry $ 2.4 billion in 2017-18.

China overtook India as Bangladesh's top trading partner somewhere around 2005. China displaced many Indian goods in Bangladesh, offering cheaper Chinese products, especially cotton and other fabrics central to the garment industry, without the visa, transport and customs challenges that had limited trade between India and Bangladesh.[183]

It is believed that poor infrastructure, especially roads, and complex procedures are also major obstacles in improving trade relations within the SAARC. Infrastructure in Bangladesh is reported to be better than India – as there are custom landing stations in India with no roads. Therefore, traders prefer to take the illegal route to escape the procedural bottlenecks that add to costs in India. According to a World Bank report, nearly three-fourths of India's total trade with Bangladesh is carried out illegally.[184]

As regards garments, China's population is in need of inexpensive manufactured goods as the China's workforce is aging and becoming more expensive. Bangladesh was wise enough and took timely decision to take away large chunks of China's textiles manufacturing capacity. In 2013, there were approximately 5,000 garment factories in Bangladesh, employing about four million people, mostly women, all part of Bangladesh's US $ 19 billion-a-year industry, export-oriented ready-made garment (RMG) industry. Bangladesh is second only to China, the world's second-largest apparel exporter of Western brands.[185] China has been negotiating a Free Trade Agreement with Bangladesh – indicating the importance China is giving to trade ties with members of the SAARC.

China's trade with Sri Lanka lags behind India's but the gap is narrowing. In 2016, Chinese exports to Sri Lanka reached $ 4billion, coming closer to Indian exports at $ 4.36 billion.[186] India already has preferential trade relations with Sri Lanka through their mutual SAARC membership as well as Indo-Sri Lanka Free Trade Agreement (ISFTA), which covers over 4,000 products and came into full effect in 2008.[187] China is in the process of negotiating the FTA with Sri Lanka. But the talks between China and Sri Lanka for FTA have reportedly hit major hurdles as Colombo was insisting on a right to review the free trade pact after 10 years but China was not ready to agree. Another contentious issue was that China wanted zero tariffs on 90 percent of goods, the two countries sold to each other as soon as an agreement is signed while Colombo would rather have it started with zero tariffs only on half of the products concerned and to be expanded gradually over 20 years.[188]

Nepal attracts significant attention from both China and India because of its strategic location. A 1996 trade agreement between India and Nepal increased bilateral trade volume, which now accounts for almost seventy percent of Nepal's total trade (In 2016, Nepal had a total trade of $ 7.20 billion, out of which India's share was $ 4.9 billion). Nepal had imports worth $ 863 million from China against $ 4.52 billion from India in 2016.[189] However,

China will exploit every available opportunity to dominate the strategic space of Nepal. In October 2015, at the height of the protests by the Madhesi, China opened the border crossing point at Jilung, which links Tibet and Nepal. It was used to transport petroleum products and other essential items. From 10 November to 10 December, China exported nearly 6,000 tons of cargo, valued at $ 43.5 million, to Nepal.[190]

Aid and Investment

To establish its footprint in South Asia, India follows the aid route, whereas China focuses on a more capitalist approach through development assistance and government investment programs, particularly for large infrastructure projects.[191] As defined by the OECD, Overseas development assistance is concessional in character and requires a "grant element of at least 25 percent";[192] further, the debt-servicing conditions on Chinese loans often fall outside of OECD standards. As per their laid down terms and conditions, projects funded by Chinese concessional loans are required to be awarded to Chinese companies and to source Chinese goods, linking Chinese aid to its government investment activities. A realistic comparison between 'aid and investment' provided by China and India cannot be carried out due to lack of transparency: India releases its figures publicly, whereas China provides only outlines.[193]

To counter China's aggressive investments in South Asia (see Annexure 14), India has enhanced its aid to its neighbors and is concentrating on speedy and effective implementation of its own development projects. In the financial year 2018-19, India has increased its aid to Nepal to Rs 650 crore, a 73 percent increase from the previous year. Bhutan remains the priority with the largest allocation of Rs 1813 crore, demonstrating the special economic relationship that India and Bhutan share.[194] India's aid to its South Asian neighbors in 2017-18 and 2018-19 is illustrated in Annexure 15.

Remittances from Migrant Workers

India has much stronger economic and cultural linkages among South Asian countries as compared to China, which are reflected by the labor migration from the two countries. The remittances provided by such migration represent the weightage of economic ties. In the financial year 2017-18, around four million South Asian migrant workers in India sent about $ 5.6 billion in remittances back to their home countries, while in case of China around thirty nine thousand workers sent $ 122 million (including to India) according to the World Bank data. More than 80 percent of labor in India is from Bangladesh and remittances from India infused the Bangladeshi economy with more than \$ 4 billion, nearly six times the value of the \$ 685 million of Bangladeshi goods imported by India in the same year. Thus remittances have become a vital economic component of the relationship.

On the other hand, Chinese and Indian workers in South Asian countries also sent significant remittances home. India received almost \$ 4.7 billion from migrant workers in South Asia in 2017-18, while China received about \$ 1.2 billion in the same year. Interestingly, \$ 992 million (i.e., 84 percent of the total) of China's remittances from South Asia came from Bangladesh, which has established extensive trade ties with China.[195] Countries wise details of migrant labor and remittances are illustrated in Annexure 16.

Infrastructure in South Asia

The South Asian region is one of the least economically integrated regions in the world. Besides the protectionist policies and political compulsions, the major hindrance is the lack of connectivity leading to high transportation costs and unacceptable time delays. The core of China's "One Belt and One Road" strategy is interconnectivity, and the premise is the infrastructure connection. The implementation of "One Belt and One Road" strategy needs a variety of transport corridor including highway, railway, port and airport as the important cohesive arrangement to promote business exchanges and cooperation. On the other hand, the convenience of transportation can reduce the cost of trade. China has long since increased infrastructure investments in parts of South Asia, especially harbor construction such as: Gwadar harbor in Pakistan, Hambantota port in Sri Lanka and Chittagong port in Bangladesh.[196]

Pakistan is the main entrance for China to enter the Indian Ocean, the Arabian Sea and the Persian Gulf and other regions. Its special geographical position could be an important fulcrum to connect the "Silk Road Economic Belt" with "21st Century Maritime Silk Road". Therefore, China-Pakistan Economic Corridor (CPEC) is the "flagship project" of "One Belt and One Road". Sri Lanka has a significant strategic position in South Asia and is a key hub of sea communications. Its advantage in transport, transit and supply is obvious. Bangladesh is located at the intersection of China, India and ASEAN and is expected to become an important commercial hub. Historically, India is at the most important meeting point of the North Silk Route, the South Silk Route and Maritime Silk Road.[197]

Thus South Asia has a vital strategic significance in the smooth implementation of "One Belt and One Road". All the countries of South Asia have supported and joined China's "One Belt and One Road" except India because of the contentious CPEC, which passes through Pakistan Occupied Kashmir and hence India's opposition to it. Irrespective of the above, China's and India's efforts in South Asia can overlap, such as in the development of Bangladesh-China-India-Myanmar economic corridor, opening up new opportunities for constructive cooperation.[198]

Greater connectivity will enable both China and India to tap further into Asian markets through trade and investment, although India will be hard-pressed to compete against cheaper Chinese products in the short-term till the Indian manufacturing sector takes off.

Soft Power

The concept of using soft power has been known to China and India since ancient history and dates back to their philosopher-strategist Lao Tsu and Kautilya respectively. In the modern context, the term was first coined by Harvard Professor Joseph S. Nye, Jr. in the late 1980s and he defined "soft power" *as "the ability of a country to persuade others to do what it wants without force or coercion."*[199] It excluded the more traditional forms of influence such as investment and aid or payment. According to him, a country's soft power can come from three primary sources: its culture, its political values and its foreign policies.[200] However, the term's usage has been broadened by China; visualizing that country's attractiveness can be conveyed through various means including culture, diplomacy, participation in the multinational organizations, businesses' action abroad, and the gravitational pull of a nation's economic strength.[201] China has incorporated soft power as a fundamental component of its comprehensive national power. Soft power has become an essential aspect of its diplomacy as it would enable China's rise palatable to the world and may create healthy respect and ultimately support for China's political model and policies.[202]

The United States proclaims itself to be the world leader in soft power based on the strength of its democracy, human rights ideals and above all the concept of Universal harmony. Notwithstanding the fact that concept of Harmony is a traditional Chinese concept expounded by Confucius (551 B.C. to 479 B.C.), who said that the Universe existed only because it was in a state of harmony,[203] though in modern context, "Harmonious Society" ("*hexie shehui*") as a concept was introduced by Hu Jintao after his succession to power in 2002.[204] Similarly, ancient India had "*Vasudhaiva Kutumbakam*" a Sanskrit phrase that means "*the whole world is one single family*" taking its origin from the Vedic Scripture "*Maha Upanishad*" (Chapter 6, Verse 72).[205]

Both countries have different models for attaining soft power supremacy in the same global space. The Chinese model is straightforward – exchange between money and diplomatic influence in return for unhindered access to natural resources or even territory. For example in Africa, in return for building roads, railways, power plants, football stadiums, writing off loans and removing tariffs, China is getting loads of oil, timber, copper and raw materials. Whereas India's presence in Africa was more of an inspiration such as India's freedom struggle, subsequent commercial success of Indian Diaspora in Africa and non-aligned movement etc. According to senior Indian officials, the difference between the two models can be summarized as "*China's is resource-based investment, whereas Indian investment concentrates on capacity building*".[206]

Jonathan McClory developed the world's first composite index for measuring the soft power of countries, which was published as "The Soft Power 30: A Global Ranking of Soft Power" in July 2015. This maiden work was the result of a research collaboration between Portland, Facebook, and ComRes.[207] However in its latest version of 2017, Portland established a new partnership with the University of South California's Center on Public Diplomacy.[208] China finished last in the Soft Power 30 rankings despite the fact that China had launched a soft power blitz following a directive from the Chinese President Hu Jintao at the 17th Party Congress in 2007.[209] China's investment in soft power has since been both significant and rapid – spending almost $ 10 billion a year over the last decade. This is more than the combined government spends of the US, UK, France, Germany, and Japan on soft power.[210]

However, China could not achieve much of a return on its investment as determined by the results of this composite index. In Portland's 2016 report on soft power, it moved up to 28th and in 2017 it further attained 25th ranking out of 30 (according to Monocle also, China remained 20th out of 25 countries in soft power).[211] India does not figure anywhere in this index. It may be appreciated that one of the biggest challenges in measuring soft power accurately is its inherently subjective nature. Rather than attempt to design against subjectivity, the Soft Power 30 index embraces it. The report is based on polling surveys from public in 25 different nations, represented by a total of 11,000 persons in 2017 report.[212]

Since there are no well-defined metrics to measure the potential of soft power resources and, India and China follow different approaches to attain soft power, it will be logical to assess their strengths and weaknesses and then see the impact created by them in various regions of the world.

China's Soft Power: Strengths and Weaknesses

China's strengths lie in its cultural pursuits and it is home to the second largest number of UNESCO World Heritage Sites. China has made significant investments in developing its soft power over recent years, with the opening of over 500 Confucius Institutes.[213] These institutes are teaching Mandarin and the CPC's version of history to more than 100 million foreigners; Beijing aims to have 1,000 institutes up and running by 2020.[214] China's universities have also seen an influx of foreign students from various countries as Chinese language and cultural studies have skyrocketed in popularity. As of 2016, over 4,43,000 overseas students studied in China.[215] China bears a special cultural magnetism for worldwide tourists as 139 million foreign tourists travelled to China in 2017, up 0.8 percent from 138 million in 2106, bringing in a revenue of £8.9 billion. Further, consumption created by foreign travelers in China on things such as hotels and restaurants amounted to £50.13 billion. The number of inbound visits is predicted to reach 140 million in 2018, with foreign exchange earnings expected to reach a total of £91.6 billion, according to a report by China's National Tourism Administration.[216]

A few cultural symbols of China, promoting its soft power: Chinese novelist Gao Xingjian won China's first Nobel Prize for Literature in 2000 and the Chinese film "Crouching Tiger, Hidden Dragon" became the highest grossing non-English film. Yao Ming, the Chinese star of the U.S. National Basket Ball Association's Houston Rockets, is rapidly becoming a household name.[217] In 2010, China produced a promotional film, featuring such celebrities as Basket ball star Yao Ming and Hong Kong businessman Li Ka-shing to polish its image. Chinese writings on soft power also promote *'The Great Wall, Peking Opera, pandas, martial arts and movie star Zhang Ziyi'*.[218]

The information and communication technologies (ICT) have the great potential to leverage discrete soft power efforts. China has been exploiting this information-dominated environment to influence the foreign publics through a number of means such as internationally orienting its state-owned media entities like China Central Television (CCTV) and Xinhua and increasing Chinese cultural exports like films and music. The CCTV had launched the China Global Television Network (CGTN) in six languages.[219] CCTV has been aggressively promoting itself as "Your Window on China and the World" to international audiences while presenting its insider view on Asia as a direct counterpart to Western media.[220] Further, Xinhua, the states news agency, had launched 24 hour Chinese and English language channels. The state-sanctioned competition between CCTV and Xinhua is intentional, and there were news reports that each had received approximately $ 1.5 billion to expand abroad.[221] There were reports that in 2009-2010, Beijing invested $ 8.9 billion in external publicity work, including 24-hour cable news channel.[222]

The elaborately staged 2008 Beijing Olympics enhanced China's reputation abroad and the 2010 Shanghai Expo was a great success, having attracted more than 70 million visitors giving a further boost to China's global brand. But it was followed by the jailing of activist and Nobel Peace Laureate Liu Xiaobo, arrest of artist Ai Weiwei, the domestic crackdown on human rights activists, and building the largest program of censorship, have all undercut China's soft power gains.[223]

Despite massive investment, China's soft power still lags far behind that of Western powers, which was admitted by China's former President Hu Jintao himself in an article in January 2012, "*The overall strength of Chinese culture and its international influence is not commensurate with China's international status. The international culture of the West is strong while we are weak.*"[224] Many reasons for China's relative weakness in soft power despite its huge spending have been identified:

- The first and foremost is the contradiction between China's desire to enhance its soft power abroad while refusing to allow its own people rights and freedom, which affects China's position even in its own backyard. Repression of major segments of civil society such as handling of large-scale student-led protest for democracy in Hong Kong in September 2014, referred, as "Umbrella Revolution" is a case in point.[225]
- Second, China remains resolutely unwelcoming to the soft power of others. Xi Jinping recently urged Chinese universities to limit the impact of Western scholarship on their teaching, including preventing

the use of imported textbooks or blocking Facebook, Twitter, Google, and Instagram. China wants to be welcome abroad but is much less welcoming at home.[226]

- Third, the party is far more concerned about its soft power within China than it is with its influence outside. Ultimately, its public diplomacy efforts are directed toward retaining and justifying its position internally.[227]
- Fourth, there is a huge cultural trade deficit: far more foreign culture products are imported than the cultural products that China exports. The Japanese Kung fu and American Hollywood movies, and even Hyundai and other Korean products and cultural products are so popular in China.[228]
- Lastly, soft power by definition results from civil society e.g., American culture is reflected by products such as Coca-Cola, McDonald, Blue jeans and Hollywood movies, none of which are government creations. China is out of sync with much of the rest of the world. It rejected the universal values of the West, such as democracy and human rights but had nothing to offer, other than appeal to traditional Confucian values.[229]

Concerned over China's negative image abroad, President Xi Jinping has vowed to use its cultural soft power to project the Communist giant as a responsible nation. He intends to deepen the reform in its cultural system, promote social core values and push forward the cultural industry.[230] Xi Jinping stated in an address: "*We should increase China's soft power, give a good Chinese narrative, and better communicate China's message to the world.*"[231]

With his strategic vision, political will and after having ensured the availability of financial capital, Xi Jinping has launched his ambitious Belt and Road Initiative. Huge sums of money committed to infrastructure projects is anticipated to open new corridors of trade, development and prosperity. It is probably first time in the contemporary era that China has managed to combine the hard power of its economic muscle with the soft power of a cooperative, inclusive narrative that emphasizes shared prosperity and regional development.[232]

India's Strengths in Soft Power

Earlier India's soft power abroad was being projected by the Indian Council for Cultural Relations (ICCR). ICCR has a total of 36 foreign cultural centers, with the aim to promote artistic and cultural traditions through a range of activities such as Festivals of India abroad.[233] Comparing this with over 500 Confucius institutes of China and still counting, it appears that India's soft power lags far behind that of China's. However, the comparison is unfair because India is pursuing its soft power on a different plane and with Prime Minister Narendra Modi as the torch bearer of India's soft power, it has made great strides.

Modi's Brand of Soft Power. Most importantly, Narendra Modi has adopted soft power as an inalienable part of his foreign policy. His foreign policy doctrine is labeled as ***Panchamrit,*** whose five pillars are: dignity, dialogue, shared prosperity, regional and global security, and cultural and civilizational links. While the previous governments had also used soft power to support foreign policy, their efforts were comparatively adhoc and were not based on a structured and consistent approach.[234] Modi's policy to use soft power is different from his predecessors in many ways. Some of the innovative methods, which distinguish Modi from his predecessors, are: First, ensuring to address Indian Diaspora during foreign visits, and frequently alluding to Indian culture and tradition in his speeches. During the visit of an Indian prime minister, Indian embassies organized formal receptions with a few prominent overseas Indians. It was more of an opportunity of *darshan* than dialogue on issues of the community. Prime Minister Modi started a new concept – courting and strengthening the Diaspora. About 30 million people of Indian origin form the global Indian Diaspora and that is Prime Minister Modi's 'soft power'.[235] During his first official visit to the United States in September 2014, Modi addressed more than 18,000-strong American Indian crowd at Madison Square Garden, New York. The venue was fully packed and those unable to find a place preferred to watch Modi and listen to his speech outside on the big screens. Accompanied by 30 US lawmakers, Modi delivered his speech in Sanskritised Hindi, punctuated with shlokas and he received a 'Rockstar welcome'. Striking feature about Modi is his choice of communicating in Hindi and reminding his audience about the cultural value of Ancient India. For example in his speech at the Council on Foreign Relations in New York he recited the Sanskrit Shloka "*Sarve Bhavantu Sukhina...*".[236] Through his choice of Hindi as against other rival politicians, who adhere to English as if to impress their erstwhile colonial masters about their mastery of the language, Modi has established his Indianness and asserted India's great power status. He attracted 70,000 UK-settled Indians at Wembley Stadium in London and 50,000 overseas Indians at the International Cricket Stadium in Dubai. Wherever the Indians are present, Modi has addressed them.[237] On the occasion of the birth anniversary of Mahatma Gandhi on 2 October 2016, Modi inaugurated Pravasi Bharatiya Kendra (Indian Diaspora Center) in New Delhi and said, "*Let us view our Diaspora not only in terms of Sankhya (number) but let us see it as Shakti (power)*".[238] Because of Modi's outreach initiatives, Indian Diaspora feel "connected and relevant". Modi's initiatives prompted many to visit India frequently than earlier, invest and "do their part to promote India's interests even while residing outside India".[239]

Second, Modi evolved an ingenious approach to showcase India's soft power assets to foreign leaders – One, during their India visits, he organized official talks at different cities of India, which were related to its culture or history rather than following the usual practice of having in the capital, New Delhi e.g., Modi invited Chinese President Xi Jinping during his visit to India in September 2014, to Ahmadabad and together they visited the Gandhi Ashram, founded by Mahatma Gandhi. Similarly in December 2015, Japanese Prime Minister Shinzo Abe was invited to Indian religious city of Varanasi, famous for holding religious sites of Hinduism as well as Buddhism (Sarnath) and together they attended the famous Hindu religious ritual of *Aarti* in the evening, performed on the banks of River Ganga;[240] Two, mementos presented by Modi during his engagements with world leaders were selected with great forethought – representing not only India's diversity and rich cultural heritage but also the relationship between the two countries, e.g., he gifted a reproduction of 'Khamsa-i-Khusrau' by the 13th Century Sufi poet Amir Khusrau, to Islam Karimov, the Uzbek dictator, gold-plated replica of Kerala's Cheraman Juma Masjid to Saudi King Salman bin Abdulaziz, a rare 7th Century manuscript of the Holy Quran written in Kufic script to Iran's President Rouhani, a specially handcrafted pair of bookends with inscriptions from the Bhagavad Gita for the UK Prime Minister David Cameron.[241]

Modi Government's Soft Power Initiatives. Modi government has developed a cohesive, strategic and institutionalized approach for the use of soft power. The significant soft power initiatives are related to India's culture and civilization and are described in succeeding paragraphs.

- **Buddhism.** Buddhism is being employed by the Modi government for two key foreign policy goals: strategically to offset Chinese soft power and economically to stimulate religious tourism in India. The government's Buddhism focus is apparent in some of the official government initiatives. On 4 May 2015, India initiated and hosted International Buddha Purnima Diwas to celebrate the birth of Lord Buddha. While China has taken steps to build and preserve Buddhist monasteries in Myanmar, Cambodia and Thailand, Modi's strategy is to visit monasteries during his trips to East Asia and present countries with saplings from the sacred Bodhi tree in Bihar. Of late, there appears to be an ongoing cultural appropriation rivalry between India and China. The Chinese government views Lumbini in Nepal (Buddha's birth place) as the focal point of religious tourism[242] and a China backed foundation has proposed to spend $3 billion to convert Lumbini into a 'cultural zone'.[243] Whereas, the Indian government asserts that Bodh Gaya in Bihar is much more important since that is the place where Buddha attained enlightenment, and is actively marketing the destination. The Indian Ministry of Tourism and Culture in collaboration with the World Bank is planning to develop a fast track Buddhist Tourist Circuit.[244]

  Prime Minister Modi has very skillfully employed the charm of Buddhism in India's immediate neighborhood. His Buddhist connect was most pronounced in Sri Lanka: He made a strategic choice to visit Sri Lanka's first Capital and the Jaya Sri Mahabodhi at Anuradhapura, which still symbolizes the hallowed memory of Sri Lanka's ancient historic link with India. He inaugurated the India funded Jaffna Cultural Center and paid a visit to Colombo's Mahabodhi temple.[245] Modi was the Chief guest at International Vesak Day celebrations held at Colombo, Sri Lanka on 12 May 2017. In the opening remarks during his speech he said, "*On this auspicious occasion, I also bring with me the greetings of 1.25 billion people from the land of the Samyaksambuddha, the perfectly self-awakened one.*" He announced that from "*August this year, Air India will operate direct flights between Colombo and Varanasi. This will ease travel to the land of Buddha for my brothers and sisters from Sri Lanka, and help you directly visit Sravasti, Kusinagar, Sankasa, Kaushambi and Sarnath.*"[246] Through the message of Buddhism, Modi has steered the India-Sri Lanka relationship away from old baggage of Tamil politics and brought it within the ambit of cultural unity. Apart from Buddhism, the pragmatic Modi government is using other religions to underline strong ties with countries. While interacting with Central Asian Republics, Modi reminded them about the shared Islamic heritage between India and Central Asia that gave birth to Sufi traditions of peace and tolerance.[247] In addition; it also reflected Modi's efforts to project India's soft power by way of proposing closer ties between trans-international cities and states/provinces to forge greater partnership. Modi established similar sister-city agreements with other countries such as Kyoto-Varanasi (Japan), Chennai-Chongqing, Hyderabad-Qingdao, Aurangabad-Dunhuang (China), Hyderabad-Brisbane (Australia) and proposed that relationship between countries can prosper fully "*only if we bring our states and cities together*". As regards China, a sister-state / province relationship has been established between Karnataka and Sichuan.[248]

- **Yoga.** Yoga is a valuable soft power resource available to India, which Prime Minister Modi has employed very effectively as part of his cultural diplomacy. Through intense networking with a large number of nations and successful lobbying at the United Nations General Assembly, Modi managed to obtain United Nations' approval of 21 June as 'International Yoga Day', the first of which was celebrated in 2015. While addressing the 69th session of the United Nations General Assembly, Prime Minister Modi stated, "*Yoga is an invaluable gift from our ancient tradition, yoga embodies unity of mind and body, thought and action...a holistic approach [that] is valuable to our health and well-being.*"[249] Modi celebrated the first 'International Yoga Day' in 2015 on the Rajpath, with 35,985 people belonging to 84 nationalities, doing 21 yoga postures – earning two Guinness World Record titles for "largest yoga session" and "most nationalities in a yoga session."[250] Internationally, about 125 million people practice yoga. In 2016, on the International Yoga Day at Dubai, led by Baba Ramdev, Indian yoga guru, 1,00,000 people participated creating Guinness Book of World's Record. Sri Sri Ravi Shankar, founder of 'Art of Living Foundation' and a strong proponent of yoga, applies yoga to realize peace and reconciliation among warring parties in conflict situations around the world. His foundation has travelled and created impact not only in the nooks and corners of India but also in other countries such as Iraq, Cote d' Ivoire, Cameron and Sri Lanka.[251]

- **Ayurveda.** Ayurveda, an ancient Indian practice is another soft power resource. At present, there are about 2000 Ayurvedic Retreat Centers around the world, and out of these about 100 centers are based in the United States.[252] In November 2014, Modi government set up a separate ministry called AYUSH (Ayurveda, Yoga, Unani, Siddha and Homeopathy) to institutionalize India's ancient heritage endowment as also to enable Ayurveda to attain the same exalted status as Traditional Chinese Medicine (TCM) through better packaging and promotion.[253] Ayurveda is virtually the only competition to TCM as there is a $40 billion herbal market in the world. India has been sending experts to teach Ayurveda in American Medical Colleges. Ayurveda is quite popular in the West, while TCM, a traditional market leader in East and South-east Asia is jostling for same space.[254]

- **Bollywood.** Bollywood has been one of India's biggest cultural exports. Movies not only depict the social life, living style, culture and human values of a country but strengthen people-to-people connect in countries located far away. Bollywood does not appear to be official soft power tool in India's foreign policy.[255] However, its planned usage may deliver the appropriate results; as according to Professor Joseph Nye in an Information Age, the best propaganda comes from a source, which is not meant to be propaganda, thereby increasing its credibility.[256] Bollywood is the producer of highest number of films in the world, surpassing Hollywood with an annual output of over 1000 movies.[257] It is popular in Afghanistan, Pakistan, Central Asia, the Middle East, South East Asia and even in Europe and the United States. Even during the peak of violence in Afghanistan in 1990s, people never failed to watch Indian TV soap serial – "*Kyunki Saas Bhi Kabhi Bahu Thih*" (of course dubbed in Dari).[258] When NATO ousted the Talibans in Afghanistan, one of the first things local people did was to bring out their hidden collections of Bollywood songs. Recognizing the craze of Bollywood movies among Afghanis, in 2007, the United States had requested India to send some Bollywood stars to Afghanistan to speak about urgent social issues.[259]

Pakistan, though India's traditional rival, its people's love for Bollywood movies is well known. There was a prolonged official ban on screening of Bollywood movies, which was lifted in 2008 but Pakistan is still managed to watch pirated copies of Indian movies. Indian blockbuster 'Sholay' was released in Pakistan on 23 March 2015 in theatres, 40 years after its release in India and yet movie theatres were fully booked.[260] It is believed that it was the 2015 movie 'Bajrangi Bhaijan' – in which the hero helped a mute Pakistani girl return home, overcoming multiple obstacles – that stimulated the Pakistani government to let Geeta, a deaf and mute Indian girl, stranded in Pakistan for 13 years, finally return to India and be reunited with her family.[261]

As regards Myanmar, the India-Myanmar relations are popularly signified by 5B's, which are Buddhism, Business, Bollywood, Bharatanatyam and Burma teak, but it is the taste for Bollywood that has contributed immensely in fostering the friendship and mutual understanding between the two neighbors.[262]

In Syria during the regime of Hafez-al-Assad, the life size portrait of the then Bollywood superstar, Amitabh Bachchan, was as big as of al-Assad.[263] During the Cold War era, Raj Kapoor and his films like 'Awara' and 'Mera Naam Joker' were extremely popular in Soviet Union. In the United States, Hindi films are increasingly playing in multiplexes to satisfy demands of increasing Indian diaspora.[264] Bollywood movies are making their mark in East European countries like Poland and Lithuania as well as in Russia. Shah Rukh Khan is extremely popular in Poland, where a number of Shah Rukh Khan Movie festivals have been held.[265]

Prime Minister Modi has employed the soft power of Bollywood with great finesse. Three days before his arrival in Xian, Bollywood star Aamir Khan landed in China on his maiden visit, for the commercial release of his blockbuster film PK. His previous movie '3 Idiots' was very well received in China.[266] Aamir Khan is affectionately called "*Mi Shu*" or "*Uncle Mi*" in China and is probably India's biggest cultural export. The timings of his arrival implied that he was meant to prepare the Chinese public for Modi's visit and to some extent, ensure that Narendra Modi got a warm welcome.

Some of China's attempts to project cultural influence have stumbled. Despite having made huge investments to build up its film industry, China has struggled to produce a big cross over hit since Ang Lee's "Crouching Tiger, Hidden Dragon" in 2000. Even Zhang Yimou's "The Great Wall", supposedly China's best shot in recent years, aspiring to become a global blockbuster, flopped miserably at box offices outside China.[267] Recently, Alibaba Picture's special effects – heavy fantasy film "Asura", made with a budget of 750 million yuan ($113.5 million) – the most expensive Chinese film ever made – opened on Friday, 13 July 2018 but became a flop of historic proportions –collecting a paltry $7.3 million on its opening weekend and pulled out from theatres. The estimated loss of $106 million would make it the fifth-biggest flop in movie history worldwide. Six years in the making, the film was made to promote traditional Chinese culture but it was heavy on expensive visuals, featuring 2,400 scenes with special effects in its run-time of just 141 minutes.[268] Many Chinese are expressing concerns that their film industry – in its quest to catch up with Hollywood – has become too narrowly focused on profit and entertainment over quality and substance.

On the contrary, the mammoth bookings for Aamir Khan's 'Dangal' and 'Secret Superstar' had shown that Indian films had toppled not only Hollywood but even China's domestic films. 'Dangal' was India's first big hit at the Chinese box office- collecting more than $194 million in two months, making it one of the 20 highest-grossing films of all time in China. Runaway success of 'Dangal' has prompted Chinese production companies to turn their gaze from West to East.[269] Suddenly, Chinese companies are racing to collaborate with Bollywood. 'Secret Superstar' rampaged the Chinese foreign box office, making almost Rs 450 crore plus in 10 days toppling 'Star Wars: Last Jedi' and 'The Maze Runner', followed by 'Bajrangi Bhaijan' and then 'Hindi Medium'. This is a creditable achievement despite the fact that Chinese market just accepts four Indian films a year compared to 38 of Hollywood.[270]

Interestingly, during a meeting between Prime Minister Narendra Modi and President Xi Jinping on the sidelines of the Shanghai Cooperation Organization in Astana (June 2017), Xi Jinping told Modi how much he had appreciated 'Dangal'.[271] With a view to reinforce Sino-Indian cultural bonding, a film on the life of Xuanzang was jointly produced by India's Eros Group and China Film Group, consequent to the signing of Memorandum of Understanding by Modi in Shanghai for approval of this film production, which had a star cast from both the countries. Kung Fu Yoga is another jointly produced, cross-cultural and multi-lingual movie with shooting having taken place in both the countries.[272]

With a view to reduce differences and reconcile people on either side, particularly after Doklam, Indian ambassador Gautam Bambawale recently told the Global Times, "*China must import more Bollywood films to understand India better.*"[273]

- **Sanskrit.** Sanskrit played an important role in developing the identity of India and its soft power. With a view to propagate the ancient language globally, Minister of External Affairs, Mrs Sushma Swaraj announced $20,000 International Sanskrit Award to scholars contributing significantly to the language. While addressing Sanskrit Conference in Bangkok in June 2015, Mrs Swaraj emphasized the importance of mastering Sanskrit to solve some of the biggest problems plaguing the world such as poverty, global warming and terrorism.[274] Sanskrit can be used to strengthen India's relationship with countries like Indonesia, the biggest and most powerful ASEAN member whose language has been influenced by Sanskrit as well as Mongolia, whose rulers even in present times, prefer to have their names written in Sanskrit, rather than in their own language.[275]

- **Connection Between Science and Religion.** India traces the origin of science in its ancient scriptures like 'Vedas' and gives due credit to its ancient saints-cum-philosophers-cum-scientists. Aryabhata, Bhaskara I, Brahmagupta, Varahamihira contributed to mathematics and astronomy in the ancient period.[276] India decided to sponsor an "*International Conference of Zero*" and gifted a bronze bust of Aryabhata to the UNESCO Headquarters to showcase its age-old intellectual tradition and contributions.[277] Though some of our own home grown scientists or so-called academic intellectuals mock at Modi government's attempts to eulogize linkage of science to ancient scriptures. The 2015 Hollywood movie "The Man Who Knew

Infinity", based on the life of the famous Indian mathematician, Srinivasa Ramanujan, displays the connection between science and religion, a characteristic trait of Indian culture and identity.[278]

- **Indian Cuisines.** Indian food has become increasingly popular in various parts of the world. Indian spices have captured the popular imagination by featuring in films like 'Mistress of Spices' and 'Today's Special' and a whole host of television shows like Outsourced and The Big Bang Theory. Indian foods like Samosa, Chaat, Chicken Tikka masala, Biryani, Masala Dosa, Kebabs and curries have become immensely popular the world over and one can easily find these in UK, Canada, Europe, the United States, the Middle East and even China. This reflects the soft power that India has brought abroad through its food.[279] According to a report of 2003, there were about 9,000 Indian curry houses in the United Kingdom, employing about 70,000 staff. The Indian food industry in the United Kingdom is worth £3.2 billion and accounts for two-thirds of all eating out. In London, there are more Indian restaurants than in Mumbai and Delhi, and Indian restaurants in Britain serve about 2.5 million customers every week. According to a report of 2007, more than 1,200 Indian food products were introduced in the United States since 2000. Though the Indian food has entered in the West recently, its spread to countries of South East Asia, Middle East, Central Asia and Caribbean Islands could be traced to at least few centuries. In the ancient and medieval periods, India had a strong naval trade with Eastern Coast of Africa through the Arabian Sea, and with the countries of South East Asia through the Bay of Bengal and Indian Ocean, and land route with China, Central Asia and Persia using the Silk Road, through which not only spices but a whole lot of goods, ideas, knowledge and skills were transported.[280]

- **Digital Diplomacy.** Harnessing the power of the digital media to cultivate and project soft power is the corner stone of Prime Minister Modi's policy initiatives. Modi's use of digital tools has been central to his success as both a politician and a global advocate for India.[281] Modi's use of Facebook, Twitter and other platforms around his official state visits has been particularly effective and provides an excellent example of digital diplomacy. Modi is also active on YouTube, Tumblr, LinkedIn, Pinterest, and StumbleUpon; in November 2014, he shared his first photo on Instagram (it was from the 25thASEAN Summit in Myanmar and generated 32,000 "likes").[282] At present Prime Minister Modi has 44.9 million followers on Twitter and he has made 21,800 tweets (as on 27 December 2018).[283] His Foreign Minister Sushma Swaraj has 12 million followers and 6,040 tweets till 27 December 2018.[284] The tweet on International Day of Yoga from the Prime Minister's office was followed by 20 million people worldwide.[285] He had skillfully used Twitter to demonstrate his close friendship with Japanese Prime Minister Shinzo Abe as well as to extend public invitation to President Obama for India's Republic Day Celebrations in 2015.[286]

- **Democracy.** An attractive, functioning and free political system like democracy is definitely a draw to international audiences and is a useful source of soft power as against communism or dictatorship. Beside, joining in a number of multilateral democracy promotion forums, in 2000, India became a founding member of the Communities of Democracies. In 2005, India joined the UN Democracy Fund and became its second major donor (contributing $25 million) after the United States ($38 million).[287] Being the largest democracy in the world, India is emerging as a leading global power with the fastest economic growth, setting an example for other countries to emulate its political system. Except for a brief period of emergency from 1975 to 1977, regular elections have been held in India. During the 2014 nation-wide elections, there were about 814 million eligible voters (100 million more than the last elections in 2009) and there were 930,000 polling stations to exercise their voting rights.[288]

- **Comparison of China's and India's Developmental Aid / Investment to Various Countries.** Having observed as to how China has been influencing the developing countries through liberal grant of aid and developmental packages, Modi has adopted the policy of foreign aid and line of credits or soft loans to promote India's policies in these countries. Modi government is in the process of creating its own foreign aid agency named the India Agency for Partnership in

Development (IAPD), which would be able to spend an estimated $ 11.3 billion in the next 5-7 years. Presumably, it is on the lines of U.S. agency for International Development.[289] In terms of visible gains, China is clearly ahead of India in this field. However, if one closely monitors the impact of aids/grants on the local populace, things are not as simple to be compared merely in terms of quantum of investment made. Africa is strategically important to both the countries as India and China both are intensely competing for African energy supplies, especially crude oil and minerals.

In 2004, India had lost out to China on a huge oil bid in Angola because compared to $ 2 billion grant by China, India offered a paltry $ 200 million to develop Angola's railways. Same story was repeated in Latin America, when during the 2007 World Cup India constructed one stadium in Barbados but China built six and it doesn't even play cricket. By 2007, African public started protesting against Chinese presence. Zambia was the first to start, after a Chinese-owned copper mine blew up. The Zambian opposition launched riots led by their fiery leader Michael Sata, to the extent that Chinese President Hu Jintao took the Chambishi copper belt off his itinerary when he visited Zambia in February 2007. Chinese investment brought with it Chinese labor (many reportedly from prison camps) depriving the locals job opportunities. There was a lurking fear that China might be invading Africa silently.[290] India has taken a different path. Indian investments are largely private sector, supported by the government with the lines of credit. Intent on keeping costs down, Indian companies found it easier to employ locals. In the process, locals ended up with a greater stake in the Indian projects. For example Indian IT giant TCS has a presence in Brazil, Uruguay and Chile – and all with local talent. Latin America is looking at Indian companies, as 'partners' not out to rob them of jobs and resources as the Chinese are now believed to be doing.[291]

Interestingly, both India and China have learnt from each other in this sphere. At the China-Africa summit in Beijing in September 2006, Hu Jintao pledged hospitals and schools to prevent his country from being branded as the new marauders of African continent. Following into the footsteps of China, India also held its first India-Africa Forum summit at New Delhi in April 2008, the second one at Addis Ababa in May 2011 and third one again from 26 to 29 October 2015 at New Delhi. While participating in the third India-Africa Forum summit (IAFS-III), attended by 41 Heads of State and Government and officials from 54 African countries, Modi offered Africa a concessional credit of $ 10 billion over five years and a grant assistance of $ 600 million. Besides other development activities, the assistance also included 50,000 scholarships in India to Africans. Modi's aid packages are much bigger than the ones offered in previous years, in terms of amount and scope and cover a large number of countries.[292]

Development of a 'Soft Power Matrix'. The Modi government is developing a "soft power matrix" with the aim of calibrating the effectiveness of India's soft power outreach in dealings with neighboring countries. The outreach efforts being calibrated include propagation of Gandhian values and philosophy, the strength of Bollywood, educational scholarships extended by the Ministry of External Affairs, humanitarian assistance and disaster relief and so on. It is expected that once this matrix is in place, it would help foster better diplomatic traction in India's immediate neighborhood and beyond.[293]

How China is utilizing its colossal economic strength to entice developing nations of Asia, Africa and Latin America in the garb of grants and developmental aid, is now an open secret. However, lately the two Asian giants are competing to project their soft power in the field of 'cultural influence'. Jiang Jingkui, Director of the Southeast Asian Research Institute at Peking University said, "*China's development has been very comprehensive in terms of politics, economics and military but in terms of soft power, India has done better than China.*" He further said, "*Although India's economy is not as developed, they have put a huge emphasis on promoting their culture, including things like Buddhists traditions and yoga.*"[294] New York Times had reported, "*'Dangal' has revived concerns in China that it is falling behind.*"[295] China's soft power tools like the Belt and Road Initiative have failed to convince India, as its hidden agenda is known to the whole world. However, soft diplomacy has played an important role even during heightened tensions such as Doklam Standoff.[296]

Rather than competing, both the countries should exploit the constructive role of soft power for mutual benefit and prosperity of people. Efforts should be made to enhance cultural and people-to-people linkages through encouraging tourism, making bi-lingual films jointly, increasing exchanges between students, enlarging the scope of sister-city or sister-province concepts and so on.

Competition for Space Superiority

In the Cold War era, the United States and the Soviet Union were competing with each other to attain superiority in the space. The race ended with the demise of the Soviet Union and the global space order appeared to have shifted. As the events indicate, there is an emerging competition for space superiority between China and India as both the countries place greater emphasis on space related achievements and using the same as a means of increasing regional prestige and bolstering national capabilities: For example, when China had announced that it would send a human into orbit in 2003, a few days later, the then Prime Minister of India, Atal Behari Vajpayee publicly urged his nation's scientists to land a man on the Moon. Accordingly, India's space budget had increased by double-digit percentages.[297]

Though China considers herself to be in competition with the United States as it is apparent from the statement of Wu Yanhua, Vice Administrator of the China National Space Administration, who stated in mid-2016 that his organization aimed *to "rank among the world's top three (alongside the U.S. and Russia) by around 2030*"[298] but experts regarded this ambition to be fanciful and China's space program is decades behind that of NASA. The United States has been the dominant space power for decades and is way ahead in technological advancements. Based on spending levels, the position is unlikely to change for at least next several years. According to OECD figures for 2013, the United States had the biggest annual budget for space exploration at $ 39.3 billion, followed by China at $ 6.1 billion, Russia at $ 5.26 billion and India at 8th position with $ 1.16 billion.[299]

Major Achievements: China

Success in space is used by the Communist Party to generate nationalist pride as also to justify its own legitimacy to power. China considers leadership in outer space as a stepping-stone to greater global leadership as well as a cohesive force for the unity of the Chinese people in order to rejuvenate China.[300]

China's space program was launched around 1960 and it was driven by military objectives. In 1993, China National Space Administration (CNSA) was set up to coordinate the country's space activities. Its first major achievement was the launch of Shenzhou (Divine Vessel)-1, an unmanned craft in 1999. In 2003, the first Chinese *taikonaut* entered space and thus China became the third country in the world to achieve this feat. Since then, China has launched six manned space missions. In 2011, CNSA launched a space lab, Tiangong

(Heavenly Palace)-1 and followed that up with two robotic and two manned dockings with it. CNSA reportedly lost control over Tiangong-1 in 2016 but it had been able to launch another space station, the Tiangong-2, a few months later on 15 September 2016. In April 2017, China launched its first unmanned cargo spacecraft.[301]

The Chinese space station will be composed of three modules, including a core module and two experiment modules. The first core module (20 ton) of the space station (60 ton) will be launched in 2019, followed by two experiment modules. The space station will enable astronauts to stay in space for up to six months. China is likely to open its space station to scientists worldwide after the station is completed around 2022. China has reportedly drafted a strategic framework with United Nations Office for Outer Space Affairs to offer opportunities on the application of Chinese space station to members of United Nations.[302]

On 21 May 2018, China launched its relay satellite Queqiao (meaning "Magpie Bridge" taken from a Chinese folk story, in which an arc formed by birds reunites two lovers separated by the heavens), which will act as a bridge between ground stations and the lunar probe. With Queqiao, having entered the moon's orbit, China has planned to send a lunar probe to the side of the moon that never faces the Earth. No space program has ever reached that part of the lunar surface because of communications difficulties. According to Zhang Lihua, Manager of the relay satellite project, "*The launch is a key step for China to realize its goal of being the first country to send a probe to soft-land and probe the far side of the moon.*" Keeping in tune with the plan, China launched its Chang'e-4 moon mission successfully on 07 December 2018, sending the Lander and Rover in to lunar transfer orbit. Before even having completed less than a month in the orbit, on 03 January 2019 the Lander and Rover have landed in the Von Karman Crater in the South Pole-Aitken Basin, the part that is never visible from the earth – an important milestone in China's rapidly developing space program. In 2013, China became the third country to make a soft landing on the moon, employing Chang'e-3 craft with the Yutu (literally Jade Rabbit) rover. The Chang'e-4 moon mission is part of a larger Chinese program of lunar exploration – carrying eight payloads and will conduct low-frequency radio astronomical observation, survey the terrain, detect the mineral composition and shallow lunar surface structure and measure the neutron radiation and neutral atoms to study the environment. The first and second Chang'e missions were designed to gather data from orbit, while the third and fourth were built for surface operations. Chang'e-5 and 6 are sample return missions, delivering lunar rock and soil to laboratories on Earth.[303]

China is seeking to become the first country to conduct joint orbital and surface exploration of Mars in a single mission. Planning its ambitious mission to Mars in 2020, the probe will be made up of three parts: Orbiter, Lander and Rover. According to State News Agency Xinhua, "*The Lander will separate from the orbiter at the end of a journey of around seven months and touchdown in a low altitude area in the Northern hemisphere of Mars where the rover will explore the surface.*" There will be 13 payloads in the mission including "six rovers". The probe is planned to be launched on a Long March-5 carrier rocket. China is also reportedly planning to send probes to Jupiter in 2036 and Uranus in 2046. Beijing's space exploration program is highly ambitious – The former Soviet Union, the United States, European Space Agency and India have all sent probes to Mars, but only NASA has successfully deployed a rover on the surface.[304]

Having seen China's ability to develop and launch manned space vehicles of Shenzhou kind or a similarly sized space lab, China has the potential to develop space weapons platform. To date all of the unmanned and manned Shenzhou flights have performed military missions. Both a shuttle or space plane could be equipped with missiles or nano-satellites that could serve as "space mines" or they could be equipped with High-Power Microwave (HPM) or laser weapons to destroy a range of targets in Earth orbit. Such spacecraft might also be equipped to deploy hypersonic projectiles to targets on Earth.[305]

Major Achievements: India

India has been pursuing space technology since 1962 but its space program was driven by development applications of space technology. The program driven by the government policy body Indian Space Research Organization (ISRO) focused mainly on satellites for communication, weather forecasting and resource surveys.[306] In the initial years, Indian programs, like China, benefited from cooperation with the Soviet Union and later the Russian Federation. Many of India's earlier achievements in space exploration were due to Soviet's help such as launch of India's first satellite Aryabhata by a Soviet Cosmos-3M vehicle in 1975, and the first Indian (Sqn Ldr Rakesh Sharma) to fly into space did so onboard a Soviet spacecraft in 1984.[307]

It was India's successful mission to the Moon in 2008 that caught the world's attention – Chandrayaan-1, India's first unmanned lunar probe was launched on 22 October 2008. Though it operated for 312 days as opposed to the intended two years but the mission achieved 95 percent of its planned objectives. Among its many achievements was the discovery of widespread presence of water molecules in lunar soil. Using data collected by India's Chandrayaan-1 mission, NASA detected magmatic water locked under the surface of the moon.[308] Chandrayaan-2 is the follow-on to India's first planetary mission and was originally scheduled for launch in 2013 but was postponed due to failure of Russia's Phobos-Grunt Mission and now India is going alone.[309] As part of this mission, ISRO is planning to send an orbiter, a lander and a six-wheeled 20 kg rover to carry out a soft-landing on the moon. If successful, it will make India the fourth nation to soft-land a spacecraft on the moon after the US, Soviet Union and China. ISRO plans to launch the mission atop a Geosynchronous Satellite Launch Vehicle (GSLV) Mk III.[310] ISRO suffered setbacks in the recent past –the PSLV-C39 launch failure of August 2017 and the loss of communications with the GSAT-6A satellite in April 2018, hence for the process of checking and re-checking the satellites, GSAT-11 was called back from its Guyana launch port in late April due to doubts that the problem, which inflicted GSAT-6A could be there on GSAT-11 also. India needs more time to conduct additional tests, in order to minimize the risk of potential failure and according to ISRO Chairman K Sivan "*Chandrayaan-2 mission will be launched successfully by the year-end.*" However, later he amended himself and informed that Chandrayaan-2 mission would be launched during early 2019 – anytime between 3 January and 14 February 2019. In the past, 47 lunar landings have happened, out of which 27 failed, pegging the success rate at less than 50 percent.[311]

In 2011, a Chinese attempt to send a spacecraft named Yinghou-1 to Mars was aborted because of a technical problem. The ISRO then fast-tracked its Mars mission called Mangalyaan, successfully launching it on 05 Nov 2013, with in just 15 months. After a 300-day flight and covering a distance of nearly 680 million km, when the Mars Orbiter Mission (MOM) Spacecraft entered the red planet's orbit on 24 Sep 2014, India became the first country to do so in its maiden attempt. India had not only stolen a march over China but it also became the fourth space power after the US, Europe and Russia to have successfully sent a spacecraft to Mars. It is the cheapest Mars mission to date. At around $ 74 million, it cost less than Hollywood space thriller "Gravity" ($ 100 Million) and roughly a 10th of NASA's $ 671 million MAVEN (Mars Atmosphere and Volatile Evolution Mission) that entered Mars orbit two days before MOM.[312] Mangalyaan had been named among the best inventions of 2014 by Time magazine, which described it as a technological feat that will allow India to flex its "interplanetary muscles".[313] The Mangalyaan now has pride of place on India's new 2,000-rupee currency note. For the sake of records,

India had launched Chandrayaan-1 at an estimated value of $ 83 million. According to ISRO's Dr. K Sivan, at Rs 800 crore, Chandrayaan-2 is much cheaper than 'Interstellar', Christopher Nolan's mega sci-fi Hollywood movie (made at the cost of Rs 1,062 crore).[314]

India has established its credibility as a space power and has translated into tangible economic benefits when it comes to the big business of satellite launches –India can reportedly put a satellite into space at a price that is 60 to 70 percent lower than other countries. Up to 2016, India had launched 79 satellites from 21 countries, including satellites from big companies like Google and Airbus, earning at least $157 million. In 2016, India launched 20 satellites in one go but on 15 February 2017, ISRO successfully launched 104 satellites from a single rocket, a record feat, which broke the earlier record of 37 satellites by Russia in 2014: three were Indian satellites and remainder 101 foreign satellites were from six countries – the US, Kazakhstan, Israel, the Netherlands, Switzerland and UAE.[315]

As of end 2018, India has 49 satellites in space and the nation's need is for another 41.[316] Manned mission was not a priority earlier but in 2016, India had tested a scale model of a Reusable Launch Vehicle, which resembled the US space shuttle. In 2014, it also successfully tested the capabilities of a crew module to re-enter the Earth's atmosphere.[317] The Union Cabinet has approved Rs 10,000 crore ($ 1.4 billion) in end-December 2019 for "GaganyaanProgram" that envisages two unmanned flights and one manned flight with a three-member crew to the space by 2022. The spacecraft will be launched to the low earth orbit for a duration ranging from one orbital period to a maximum of seven days.[318]

Areas of Competition: China vs. India

The Satellite navigation system has emerged as an embodiment of a nation's comprehensive strength, core competitiveness and technological ability. As of April 2013, the United States NAVSTAR Global Positioning System (GPS) with 24 satellites and the Russian Global'naya Navigatsionnaya Sputnikovaya Sistema (GLObal NAvigation Satellite System or GLONASS) were the only operational global navigation satellite systems (GNSSs). After more than 20 years of efforts by the Chinese space scientists, its *BeiDou* (or **Big Dipper**) satellite navigation system achieved the regional status in 2011 and it is planned to be expanded into a global navigation system by 2020, a program that has been called **Compass**. The Compass system is proposed to consist of five geostationary satellites and 30 non-geostationarysatellites.[319] With that aim, China has started extending its *BeiDou* Navigation Satellite System (BDS) to Thailand and Sri Lanka, and then to the entire Southeast Asia. It had established the first batch of three overseas Continuously Operating Reference Stations (CORS) and its networking for BDS in Thailand in December 2013 and is now planning to establish at least 10 CORS in Sri Lanka. With the establishment of CORS in Thailand and Sri Lanka, BDS coverage will be extended to a minimum of 3000 km more towards Southeast Asia and South Asia. By the end of 2016, BDS already had a constellation of 32 satellites and it has offered its services to all countries participating in its One Belt, One Road infrastructure plan.[320]

India has developed its own system – Indian Regional Navigation Satellite System (IRNSS), comprising a total of seven satellites. The set-up was completed with the launch of seventh and final satellite on 28 April 2016. It will be called NAVIC (Navigation with Indian Constellation) as announced by Prime Minister Narendra Modi after the launch – naming it after Indian mariners (*'naviks'*) and dedicating the system to them.[321]

However, the first Indian navigation satellite in the IRNSS fleet – IRNSS 1A has been stricken with three onboard failed atomic clocks (Rubidium clocks came from the same vendor as several clocks that have failed on Europe's Galileo Navigation satellites), eliminating its ability to transmit precise position data to users on the ground and it was to be replaced by IRNSS-1H. IRNSS-1H was launched atop PSLV on 31 August 2017 but it failed to separate from the launcher despite having reached the orbit.[322] Reportedly, four other satellites have also developed faults in one of their three atomic clocks. According to ISRO Chairman, added efforts were on to revive the IRNSS 1A clocks. ISRO has catered for backup satellites for such contingencies and has planned to launch the IRNSS-1I, as a replacement satellite to complete India's navigation constellation, so as to have an experimental service by end-2018. There is a plan to have 11 satellites in the cluster, including the replacements for malfunctioning satellites so that there is built in redundancy against a possible failure in future/hostile action.[323] Accordingly, IRNSS-1I was successfully launched on 12 April 2018. Further, IRNSS-1J has been planned for launch in 2019 and it will carry an indigenous atomic clock.[324]

In response to China's BDS extension, India has resorted to space diplomacy to influence its neighbors and allies in East Asia. In Vietnam, India will set up a satellite tracking and imaging center that will give Hanoi access to pictures from Indian earth observation satellites that cover the region, including China and the South China Sea. India has 11earth observation satellites in orbit, offering pictures with differing resolutions and areas. Unlike other overseas stations, the facility will enable Vietnam to receive Indian Remote Sensing (IRS) pictures directly and in return granting India the tracking site. The cost of facility is estimated to be around $23 million, which will be borne by the ISRO.[325] On 5 May 2017, India made its biggest space diplomatic push in South Asia by successfully launching the GSAT-09 or the "South Asia" satellite. The satellite will provide different communication applications in Ku-band and its data will be shared with Nepal, Bhutan, Maldives, Bangladesh and Sri Lanka. Pakistan had turned down the offer. Having costed Rs 450 crore to ISRO, the satellite has a life span of more than 12 years.[326] The satellite is an attempt not only to strengthen India's ties with its immediate neighbors and promote India-led regional cooperation but also to contain increasing Chinese influence in the region and countering its space cooperation with these countries.[327]

China's space program is significantly ahead of India's in several areas: China has superior space launch vehicle capabilities; It has bigger and more powerful rockets; more satellite tracking stations and launch stations, contributing to CNSA's large and growing number of orbital launch missions. In 2016, China and the United States attempted 22 orbital launches each, followed by Russia with 19, European Union with nine and ISRO with seven.[328] Further, China's robotic lunar exploration program is technologically and programmatically superior to India's lunar and Mars missions.

It is appreciated that India is fast catching up with China in space arena, particularly with the development of its GSLV and the reusable launch vehicle program. India's big advantage in the satellite launch business is "*its reliable and cost-effective launches especially for launching small satellites in the low earth orbit*". A launch by Ariane-5, the most successful commercial rocket in use right now, costs more than $100 million, while that by Space X's Falcon 9 costs around $62 million. In comparison, a PSLV launch costs $15 million. There is a great demand for PSLV launches and according to ISRO's former Chairman A.S. Kiran Kumar "At the moment we are doing 4-5 a year. By 2020, we are hoping to get to 18 launches a year".[329] ISRO had managed seven launches in 2018. ISRO's new Chairman Dr. K Sivan has raised the bar further; according to him the space agency is planning to carry out 32 missions in 2019.[330] India's successful launch of a record-breaking 104 satellites into orbit and its cost-effective space program have served as a wake-up call for

China's commercial space industry. Global Times said, "*Competition with India for commercial space launches may be inevitable, and the most urgent action needed for China to expand its market share is to reduce the cost of putting satellites in to orbit*".[331] However, it is to be remembered that roughly 80 percent of the revenue has historically come from the launch of heavy satellites in geosynchronous orbit. According to Professor Zong Qiugang, a researcher with the Institute of Space Physics and Applied Technology at Peking University, the space program in China "*is probably the most expensive in the world.*" For example, in 2007, China and Japan each sent an orbiter to the Moon. China's Chang'e probe cost 1.4 billion yuan and Japans' Selene 32 billion yen. Adjusted for purchasing power parity at the time, the actual cost of Chang'e was a third higher than the Japanese spacecraft.[332] If CNSA is able to reduce the cost of satellite launch substantially in the long-run then Sino-Indian competition for share of the global space launch market, especially for small and micro-satellites will increase dramatically. This competition is beyond diplomacy and economic competition as the space dominance has direct influence on military component.

From a capability perspective, India's greatest shortfall is its lack of long-range radars and laser ranging systems that can track space objects – this infrastructure is "extremely limited if not non-existent". These systems are crucial to protecting space-based assets, as they allow space agencies to detect inactive satellites and space debris, which might collide with sophisticated and costly equipment in orbit. These systems also enable a nation to track anti-satellite weapons, and are thus critical to defense capabilities and monitoring of other space powers.[333] If the U.S. involvement in India's program takes the shape of technology sharing, India could rapidly develop its tracking technologies.

In respect of anti-satellite capabilities, although China's oft-stated policy is to "not enter into an arms race" and to "ban weapons" in space but its successful test of a direct-ascent anti-satellite (ASAT) interceptor on 11 January 2007, revealed China's intention to build a credible military space combat capability. As a follow-up to the January 2007 test, China conducted space launches on 13 May 2013 and 23 July 2014, which were inconsistent with China's public statements about the use of space for peaceful purposes.[334] While in 2007, Chinese military had launched a KT-1 rocket to destroy a redundant weather satellite in Low Earth Orbit (LEO), approximately 800 km above the Earth, in 2013 China launched its new ASAT missile, the Dong Neng-2 or DN-2, assessed to be a "ground-based, high earth-orbit attack missile."[335]

Not to be left behind, in 2012 Dr. V.K. Saraswat, the then Chief of the Defense Research and Development Organization (DRDO) had stated during an interview with 'India Today' that "*India has all the building blocks for an anti-satellite system in place.*" He further added, "*We don't want to weaponize space but the building blocks should be in place. Today... all the building blocks (for an ASAT weapon) are in place.*" A little fine-tuning is required to be done electronically and physical test will be avoided because of the risk of space debris affecting other satellites.[336]

India-Japan Cooperation in Space Exploration

China's growing space capabilities have brought India and Japan closer, leading to greater cooperation between them in space exploration. During the visit of Japanese Prime Minister Shinzo Abe to India from 13 to 14 September 2017, both the Prime Ministers acknowledged that outer space is an ever-expanding frontier of human endeavor and welcomed the "*deepening of cooperation between the space agencies of the two countries in the field of earth observation, satellite based navigation, space sciences and lunar exploration.*" They welcomed establishment of the ISRO – Japan Aerospace Exploration Agency (JAXA).[337] Working under the space cooperation Memorandum of Understanding signed in November 2016, the newest chapter in their friendship saga is reportedly a joint mission to the Moon by ISRO and JAXA in which their Lander and rover mission (still in its preliminary stages) will bring back surface samples from the planet. Interestingly, Japan and India have each had their successful lunar missions in the past: JAXA's lunar orbiter spacecraft 'Selene' landed on the moon in 2009 after successfully orbiting it for a year and eight months; whereas India's first moon probe, Chandrayaan-1 was launched in 2008. Beside the worthy-sounding scientific aims, it appears that there is a political dimension also to this joint mission i.e., jointly challenging China's audacious moves into space exploration.[338]

Top leadership of China or India will not ever declare about the existence of a space competition between the two countries but timings of space-related developments in concert with each other indicate that a space race indeed is occurring. Failure of one nation gives an advantage to other to either catch up or advance ahead such as Chinese aborted attempt to Mars in 2011motivated India to fast-track its Mangalyaan in 2013; Similarly, the failure of China's Long March 5 rocket in 2017, on one hand is a rare setback to the highly successful space program of China in delaying some missions but at the same time providing an opportunity to rival India to move ahead in the space.

The value of crossover technologies is another important reality for China and India. Upwards of 90 percent of technologies developed during a space program have applications in other fields as through these, nations can improve domestic quality of life, sharpen military capabilities and produce technologies to compete in a global environment.

4

India's Strategic Initiatives

CHINA having attained an impressive economic and military might over the past four decades; Xi Jinping thought that it was high time to shed the Deng Xiaoping's strategy of "*Hide our capacities and bide our time; be good at maintaining a low profile; and never claim leadership*"[1] and to claim predominance in Asia and at least an equal status with the United States in global arena. On the economic front, Xi Jinping launched his flagship Belt and Road Initiative with the vision of rebalancing the slowing down of Chinese economy through – utilizing China's excessive and surplus capacities to develop Asian infrastructure; streamline foreign trade; ensure stable energy supplies; and consolidate Beijing's regional influence. Such a network would also provide an opportunity to expand the international use of Chinese currency, 'Yuan', in transactions throughout the region, while new infrastructure could "*break the bottleneck in Asian connectivity*", according to Xi.[2] In the field of military power, Xi Jinping had launched a comprehensive reforms and restructuring of People's Liberation Army (PLA) combined with a massive military modernization program. Though the current reform efforts are scheduled for completion by the end of 2020, the military modernization would essentially complete by 2035 – an acceleration, shortening the original schedule by 15 years from 2049 to 2035.[3] The aggressive behavior of China is most visible in the South China Sea, where it has not only created massive new islands through land reclamation, stretching hundreds of miles South and East from its most southerly province of Hainan but also militarized these on an unprecedented scale. In fact, US Defense Secretary James Mattis during his address at Shangri La Dialogue, Singapore on 02 June 2018 pointed out, "*China's militarization of artificial features in the South China Sea includes the deployment of anti-ship missiles, surface-to-air missiles, electronic jammers and, more recently, the landing of bomber aircraft at Woody Island.*" In May, the Chinese military landed nuclear-capable bombers on its artificial islands for the first time. Mattis further added, "*The placement of these weapon systems is tied directly to military use for the purposes of intimidation and coercion.*" He said, "*Make no mistakes: America is in the Indo-Pacific to stay. This is our priority theater.*"[4]

It is generally believed now that China has probably acted a bit too early to assert its power while the United States may have also reacted too late; allowing China enough time and strategic space to challenge the United States. The United States has realized that "*China seeks to displace the United States in the Indo-Pacific region, expand the reaches of its state-driven economic model, and reorder the region in its favor.*" The United States had been supporting China's rise in the belief that its integration in to the post-war international order would liberalize China. On the contrary, China expanded its power at the expense of the sovereignty of others.[5]

As the events have unfolded since the end of the Cold War, "*the Indo-Pacific region has emerged as the world's most dynamic geopolitical zone. Shifting balances of power there are reshaping international perceptions*", according to former US Ambassador Chas W. freeman, Jr.[6]

Indo-Pacific and the Growing Importance of India

Indo-Pacific in itself is not a new term. It has a long-standing acceptance as a distinct bio-geographic region in the realm of marine science.[7] The current usage of this term in geo-political sense occurred in the first decade of 21st Century. In fact, it is a rediscovery of what German strategist Major Karl Ernst Haushofer once called the *Indopazifischen Raum* "Indo-Pacific region/ space" in his geopolitical ruminations in the 1920s and 1930s.[8] Interestingly, Admiral Alfred Thayer Mahan had also described the Indian and Pacific Oceans as future 'hinges of the world's geopolitical destiny', because control of this region could enable a nation to influence geo-political developments in Eurasia.[9] The post-World War II period experienced a surge in the economic fortunes of the countries in the region, particularly Japan and Australia. It is these countries, which promoted the term 'Asia-Pacific' in the 1970s and 1980s to bring themselves closer to the United States and the rapidly growing economies of the East Asia.[10] With the world's center of economic and strategic gravity having been shifted to Asia, particularly India and China, once again it was Japan, whose Prime Minister took the lead in underlining the importance of Indian and Pacific Oceans. During a speech delivered by Shinzo Abe, Prime Minister of Japan to the Indian Parliament on 22 August 2007, he quoted from the book titled "Confluence of the Two Seas", authored by the Mughal Prince Dara Shikoh in 1655, "*The Pacific and the Indian Oceans are now bringing about a dynamic coupling as seas of freedom and of prosperity.*"[11] Later in October 2010, former US Secretary of State, Hillary Clinton in a speech at Honolulu, used the phrase 'Indo-Pacific' to describe a newly emerged and integrated theater. She emphasized the importance of 'Indo-Pacific' to global trade and commerce and brought out that "*this is an explicit and significant reflection of the growing strategic convergence between the two countries (i.e., the US and India) with respect to the region*".[12] In June 2012, Australia's Defense Minister Stephen Smith, at the Shangri La Dialogue, stressed the importance of 'Indo-Pacific' by stating that, "*It has risen as a region of global strategic significance...and is emerging as a single strategic system.*"[13] In Australia, the policy establishment moved further and with a defense white paper in the beginning 2013, it became the first country formally to name its region the 'Indo-Pacific', which suits its two ocean geography. Japan has its own poetic formulation: the "Confluence of two seas" (*futatsu no umi no majiwari*). Indonesia also added 'Indo-Pacific' to its vocabulary.[14]

In the year 2017, 'Indo-Pacific' became a buzz-word in various forums, where it was used extensively by Japan, Australia, India and ultimately it was officially adopted by the United States in its National Security Strategy, December 2017; Wherein 'Indo-Pacific' is defined as "*the region, which stretches from the West coast of India to the Western shores of the United States, representing the most populous and economically dynamic part of the world.*"[15] India has not formally defined it but if one constructs a geo-political definition of 'Indo-Pacific' from Prime Minister Modi's keynote address at Shangri La on 01 June 2018, then the region "*extends from the shores of Africa to that of the Americas...and Southeast Asia is at its center.*"[16] Though Modi's speech at Shangri La was well-guarded and carefully worded to avoid upsetting the present bonhomie established between him and Xi Jinping, US Defense Secretary Jim Mattis made direct references to China in conveying stinging rebukes during his speech next day.

The centrality of India in region and its importance has been clearly recognized by the United States and, therefore, it has re-named the US Pacific

Command as the 'Indo-Pacific Command'. James Mattis, while answering a question by The Sunday Guardian replied, "*We won't change the name of the Command if it won't reflect what actually its focus is. We are looking right now at the role of the Indian Ocean, with the largest democracy in the world coming into its own with economic progress – that's India. We need to recognize the growing significance of the Indian Ocean, the Indian subcontinent and India itself. So, I wanted to make certain that the title reflected the reality.*"[17] Interestingly before coming to address the Shangri La Dialogue, James Mattis had announced in Hawaii on 31 May, "*In recognition of the increasing connectivity between the Indian and Pacific Oceans, today we rename the US Pacific Command to US Indo-Pacific Command.*"[18] In its National Security Strategy, the United States has re-affirmed its support for India, "*We will deepen our strategic partnership with India and support its leadership role in Indian Ocean security and throughout the broader region.*"[19]

As regards China, its disliking toward 'Indo-Pacific' nomenclature is understandable. The Chinese foreign policy establishment took very long to embrace the Asia-Pacific label, a concept evolved to signify the role of the United States in a region, which Beijing would have preferred to simply refer as Asia. China considers the idea of 'Indo-Pacific' as a ploy to dilute its importance by equating the region with yet another substantial power i.e., India.[20] Outwardly, the roots of new 'Indo-Pacific' are embedded in economics but these are intertwined with deep political and strategic implications.

Modi's Vision of 'Indo-Pacific' Region

'Indo-Pacific' carries different connotation for different countries of the region, to suit their own national interests. The official adoption of 'Indo-Pacific' by India has also gathered steam over a period of one year. In the inaugural address at Second Raisina Dialogue, New Delhi on 17 January 2017, Prime Minister Narendra Modi generally adhered to the term 'Asia-Pacific' and used 'Indo-Pacific' only once by stating "*We believe that respecting Freedom of Navigation and adhering to international norms is essential for peace and economic growth in the larger and inter-linked marine geography of the Indo-Pacific.*"[21] Modi articulated India's vision for 'Indo-Pacific' region and underlined the role of India as a 'strategic autonomy' during his keynote address at Shangri La Dialogue, Singapore in June 2018, which can be condensed as under:

- For India, the Indo-Pacific is a natural region. With Southeast Asia at its center, its ten countries connect the two great oceans in both the geographical and civilizational sense. Inclusiveness, openness and ASEAN centrality and unity, therefore, lie at the heart of the new Indo-Pacific. India does not see the Indo-Pacific Region as a strategy or as a club of limited members. Nor as a grouping that seeks to dominate. And by no means do we consider it as directed against any country.

- India stands for a free, open, inclusive region, which embraces us all in a common pursuit of progress and prosperity. It includes all nations in this geography as also others beyond who have a stake in it. We should all have equal access as a right under international law to the use of common spaces on sea and in the air that would require freedom of navigation, unimpeded commerce and peaceful settlement of disputes in accordance with international law.[22]

Through his vision for the 'Indo-Pacific', Modi not only reassured and reinforced the centrality of ASEAN and its unity, which was continuously getting undermined by Chinese influence but through a veiled message directed his concern at China about its predatory economic policies being adopted to subdue the small nations of the region through heavy debt burden.[23] He elaborated "*Connectivity is vital. It does more than enhance trade and prosperity... There are many connectivity initiatives in the region. If these have to succeed, we must not only build infrastructure, we must also build bridges of trust. And for that, these initiatives must be based on respect for sovereignty and territorial integrity, consultation, good governance, transparency, viability and sustainability. They must empower nations, not only place them under impossible debt burden. They must promote trade, not strategic competition.*"[24]

Before coming to Singapore, to deliver his keynote address at Shangri La Dialogue, Prime Minister Narendra Modi toured through ASEAN, beginning with Indonesia (30 May), followed by a pit-stop in Malaysia and then ending at Singapore (1 June), thereby establishing the centrality and importance of ASEAN in the 'Indo-Pacific' region. As it is, the ASEAN nations are feeling uncomfortable with China's aggressiveness in the South China Sea, but they are not in a position to denounce it in public because of their economic/trade-dependency on Beijing. Most of the ASEAN nations have been looking up to major powers to obtain some kind of support, which can restrain China and Prime Minister Modi provided it in a very subtle manner in his Indonesian visit.[25] The joint statement issued at the end of the visit underscores the guiding principles for operating in the Indo-Pacific region, "*Both leaders reiterated the importance of achieving a peaceful and prosperous Indo-Pacific Region where sovereignty, international law, freedom of navigation and overflight, sustainable development and an open and fair trade and investment system are respected.*"[26]

India's Role Aspirations

The attainment of a desired role by a country in the international system is often influenced by its elites' perception and aspirations. All nations, of course, like to think of themselves as special and India is no exception to this. It is not that Modi's predecessor was in any way less enthusiastic or ambitious in thinking of India as a Great Power but owing his position to someone else and guided by narrowly defined self-interest, he was constrained to exercise his independent thinking and was comfortable with the status quo. Prime Minister Narendra Modi's aspiration is to make India a 'leading power', rather than just a balancing power.[27] In Modi's vision, a leading power is essentially a great power. According to renowned strategic thinker Ashley J. Tellis, for India to become a great power will depend on "*its ability to achieve multi-dimensional success in terms of improving its economic performance and wider regional integration, acquiring effective military capabilities for power projection coupled with wise policies for their use, and sustaining its democracy successfully by accommodating the diverse ambitions of its people.*"[28] Modi's foreign policy vision is driven by a desire to make India a major economic and strategic player in shaping the new Asian century and also to place New Delhi at high table.[29] His foreign policy involves befriending technologically advanced countries like the United States, France and Israel to obtain a wide array of technologies that will advance India's growth.

Ashley J. Tellis in his seminal work "India as a Leading Power" has inferred from a 2012 Pricewater Cooper (PwC) study that "*Contemporary projections of global growth out to 2050 suggest that India will become a true pole by then.*"[30] It may be remembered that these are all linear projections, which do not take in to account intangible factors, which can set the nation on a wholly new course irrespective of whether up or down e.g., arrival of a dynamic new leader, demographic upheaval, and invention of new revolutionary scientific techniques not thought of earlier and so on. For instance, Zheng Bijian, Chairman of the China Reform Forum, who propounded the concept of "peaceful rise" for China, had elucidated that China would require 45 years "*before it can be called a modernized, medium-level developed country.*" Zheng had divided this period into three stages: in the first (from 2000 to 2010),

China would seek to double its GDP; in the second (from 2010 to 2020), Beijing would aim to repeat this feat, bringing per capita incomes to approximately $ 3000 (per annum); over the following thirty years, (from 2020 to 2050) "*China will continue to advance until it becomes a prosperous, democratic and civilized socialist country.*"[31] But China had risen inexorably along the developmental track and what Zheng had anticipated to happen by 2020, had already been accomplished in half of its time. According to the World Bank's statistical record, China's GDP in year 2000 was $ 1198.5 billion and by 2010, its GDP at $5878.6 billion[32] was almost five times. As far as per capita income was concerned, China had attained the figure of $3414 by year 2008.[33] China's meteoric rise became a matter of debate among the economists.

According to the PwC February 2017 report titled "The World in 2050" India's GDP would surpass US GDP in purchasing power parity (PPP) terms by 2040 (In 2040, GDP in PPP US $ trillion – China 47.4; India 30; US 28.3). However, in terms of Market Exchange Rates (MER) India will be a distant third behind the United States with China leading (2040, GDP in MER, US $ trillion – China 36.6; US 28.3; India 15.3). PwC prediction is based on the premise that India's economy will grow by about 4.9 percent per year from 2016 to 2050, with only 0.7 percent of that growth caused by population growth. With this growth, India's economy would go from accounting for 7 percent of world GDP (PPP) to 15 percent by 2050, whereas China's share will only grow from present 18 percent (2016 IMF estimates) to 20 percent, whereas the US share of 16 percent will come down to 12 percent.[34]

Fourth Industrial Revolution

The President of the World Economic Forum (WEF), Borge Brende, firmly believes that Fourth Industrial Revolution can help India leapfrog traditional phases of development and accelerate its transition to a developed nation. Brende wrote a blog post on Prime Minister Narendra Modi's website (10 April 2018), stating that "*The impact of technological revolution on economies and society is not preordained and can be shaped by policies at the local, national and global levels. In order to optimally leverage the Fourth Industrial Revolution for our collective progress and prosperity, we need governance frame works, protocols and policy systems that ensure inclusive and equitable benefits.*"[35] He deeply appreciated the initiatives taken by Prime Minister Narendra Modi for bringing in necessary structural reforms and promoting an entrepreneurial ecosystem and said, "*India is well positioned to enhance its global leadership in a post Fourth Industrial Revolution era.*"[36] Realizing the country's potential to lead in and influence the Fourth Industrial Revolution, the World Economic Forum has partnered with Mukesh Ambani owned Reliance Industries Ltd (RIL) to set up the Center for Fourth Industrial Revolution in the Silicon Valley at San Francisco and in India, it is going to be its first center outside of Silicon Valley.[37]

Prime Minister Narendra Modi, while addressing the plenary session of the 10th BRICS Summit at Johannesburg on 26 July 2018 said that India would work with other member states of the BRICS economic bloc to prepare for the Fourth Industrial Revolution. He said, "*New systems and products will open new roads for economic development*". He further said, "*When digital platforms, e-commerce and market places will get linked with such technologies, a new kind of industry and business leaders will surface.*"[38] For Prime Minister Narendra Modi, it is a national mission to make the best use of the Fourth Industrial Revolution technologies for taking India on a path of high economic growth.

Strategic Autonomy

Until recently, the concept of autonomy was, in the political and strategic discourse, engulfed in the broad paradigmatic concept of non-alignment. In fact, Howard B. Schaffer, a leading South Asia specialist and his wife Teresita, a rare diplomatic couple in their book "India at the Global High Table: The Quest for Regional Primacy and Strategic Autonomy" had considered India's 'strategic autonomy' as the direct intellectual heir of non-alignment in the post-Cold War era and the two shared a core characteristic, namely, maximizing freedom of action.[39] Strategic Autonomy can be defined as a set of discourses and strategies aiming to safeguard the independence in both the foreign policy decision-making process and its implementation as well as independence in the use of strategic military assets. In the field of foreign policy, strategic autonomy is associated with a set of discourses / practices aiming to promote a multi-faceted diplomacy, to avoid alliance-like structures and to favor 'selective partnerships'. At a technological and military level, it is more a set of strategies aiming to provide India with self-sufficiency / self-reliance and thus reduce dependency on the developed countries by different concrete policies. In both cases, the main objective is to create or to keep a sufficient strategic space in order to maintain autonomous rooms (in terms of technical and economic self-sufficiency) to maneuver in national decisions.[40]

From a practical perspective, 'strategic autonomy' is about expanding one's room for maneuver by engaging all potential partners. It allows keeping decision-making power with ourselves, avoiding alliances, and building our capabilities while working with others when it is in India's interest to do so.[41] As one of the world's largest economies and as a rising power, Modi is advocating that India needs more intensive partnerships with all great powers, including the United States and China.[42] While addressing the Shangri La Dialogue in June 2018, Prime Minister Narendra Modi affirmed that India seeks robust partnership with all major powers viz., the United States, Russia, China, Japan and ASEAN nations. He stated, "*It is a measure of our 'strategic autonomy' that India's strategic partnership with Russia, has matured to be special and privileged.*" While recalling his informal summit at Sochi with President Putin he said that both shared their views on the need for a "*a strong multi-polar world order for dealing with challenges of our times.*" India's global strategic partnership with the United States was described by Modi as the one which "*has overcome the hesitation of history and continues to deepen across the extraordinary breadth of our relationship.*" Regarding China, he stated, "*No other relationship of India has as many layers as our relations with China.*" Having displayed maturity and wisdom in ensuring a peaceful border by both nations, Modi said, "*I firmly believe that Asia and the world will have a better future when India and China work together in trust and confidence, sensitive to each other's interests.*" India's ties with Japan have been completely transformed from economic to strategic. With ASEAN, from dialogue partner, India has become strategic partner over the course of 25 years and with each Southeast Asian country, it has growing political, economic and defense ties.[43]

However, India's strategic autonomy is constrained by two major factors. First, in this world of economic interdependence, its operationalisation presents a challenge, especially when the country is running a persistent trade deficit. Second, despite Modi government's quest for "Make in India", India is heavily dependent on imports for most of its major military inventory. The indigenous defense manufacturing, a goal of every Indian government since Independence has remained a distant dream.[44] Thus, the gap between the aspiration and reality need to be patched if strategic autonomy is to be exercised in totality.

India's Strategic Initiatives

First and foremost, Prime Minister Narendra Modi has very timely valued the long history of India as a maritime nation and visualized that the arc of influence of Indian Ocean extends far beyond its littoral limits – its water touching the shores of over 40 countries.[45] Open and secure seas ensure connectivity between nations, irrespective of being small or large, which in turn leads to prosperity for all. The economic prosperity through oceans is one of the main objectives of Modi government to transform India. He has provided his personal vigor to the maritime influence of the country and within first year of assuming the charge of his office, introduced and advocated the concept of 'SAGAR', though literally translated as ocean in Hindi, but stands for 'Security and Growth for All in the Region'. Other strategic initiatives evolved under his patronage are 'Mausam', speeding up the North-South Transport Corridor, Asia-Africa Growth Corridor and so on.

'SAGAR'

In March 2015, during his visit to Mauritius, Prime Minister Modi had described his vision for the Indian Ocean in one word – SAGAR. The initiative of SAGAR is not just limited to safeguarding India's mainland and islands. It encompasses all efforts to deepen economic and security cooperation in India's maritime relationships. Modi has highlighted that "*convergence, cooperation, and collective action will advance economic activity and peace in our maritime region.*" India does not follow an exclusive approach but rather the government considers that responsibility for peace, prosperity and security in the Indian Ocean should rest with all those who live in this region and it is aiming to bring all countries together on the basis of respect for international law.[46] While India's modern and multi-dimensional Navy is instrumental in establishing linkages and coordination with regional navies for exercise of freedom of navigation and adhering to international norms in the Indian Ocean, quest for economic prosperity through oceans is part of Modi government's larger efforts to transform India. An important part of India's transformation is Modi's vision of "Blue Economy", which involves: building new pillars of economic activity in the coastal areas and in linked hinterlands through sustainable tapping of oceanic resources; strengthening marine research; development of eco-friendly, marine industrial and technology base, and fisheries.[47] Modi's 'Act East' policy also falls under the broader umbrella of 'SAGAR', wherein India's East and North-east are being connected with its land and maritime partners to the East.[48] India's foreign policy in the Indian Ocean Region (IOR) has been given a fresh impetus by setting up of a separate IOR Division under the Ministry of External Affairs in January 2016.[49]

SAGAR is being pursued vigorously by the Modi government through both regional and national initiatives/projects:

- **Indian Ocean Naval Symposium (IONS).** The IONS is a regional forum of Indian Ocean littoral states launched by Indian Navy in February 2008. It is a voluntary initiative that seeks to increase maritime cooperation among navies of the littoral states of the IOR by providing an open and inclusive forum for discussion of regionally relevant maritime issues. In the process, it endeavors to generate a flow of information between naval professionals that would lead to common understanding and possibly cooperative solutions on the way ahead. There are 32 (23 members and 9 observers) Navies of the IONS, which have been geographically grouped into four sub-regions. With a view to promote collective security in the region, the forum has working groups on HADR, Information Security and Interoperability (IS&I) and maritime security (anti-piracy).[50]

- **Indian Ocean Rim Association (IORA).** The vision for IORA originated during a visit by late President Nelson Mandela of South Africa to India in 1995, wherein he propelled the concept of an Indian Ocean Rim for "socio-economic cooperation". His sentiments and rationale stimulated the formation of Indian Ocean Rim Initiative in March 1995. Two years later in March 1997, it led to the creation of Indian Ocean Rim Association for Regional Cooperation (IOR-ARC), now simply called the Indian Ocean Rim Association (IORA).[51] IORA's apex body is the Council of Foreign Ministers (COM), which meets annually. IORA comprises 21 member states and 7 dialogue partners. Indian Ocean Research Group and the Indian Ocean Tourism Organization have observer status. The organization collectively aims at enhancing economic cooperation for sustained development and balanced economic growth of its members. During his visit to Mauritius on 12 March 2015, Prime Minister Narendra Modi emphasized the importance of IORA by linking it with SAGAR. He said, "*Our Indian Ocean Rim Association can be an important instrument for pursuing our vision for a sustainable and prosperous future in the region... We will pursue this with new vigor in the years ahead.*"[52] The first ever IORA Leaders' Summit was held on 7 March 2017 at Jakarta, Indonesia commemorating the 20th Anniversary of the Association, which took it to new heights, especially in terms of defining its goals. With the chair of IORA passing on to South Africa in 2018, it is keen to address the key challenge to build on cooperation in six priority areas.[53] Undoubtedly, India has been taking a pivotal role in the association in tandem with the PM's strategic vision for engagements in the IOR as defined by SAGAR.[54]

- **Sagarmala Project.** The Sagarmala is a national program aimed at accelerating economic development in the country by harnessing the potential of India's coastline and inland waterways. Sagarmala was articulated by the then Prime Minister Shri Atal Bihari Vajpayee in 2003 and announced by Prime Minister Narendra Modi in 2014. It was approved by the Union Cabinet on 25 March 2015.[55]

  India is located along key international trade routes in the Indian Ocean and has a long coastline of 7500 km and 14,500 km of potentially navigable waterways. Twelve major and 200 non-major ports located along the Western and Eastern coastlines have so far been responsible for 90 percent of India's trade by volume.[56] Yet, capacity constraints and lack of modern facilities at Indian ports cause extensive time delays in shipping the goods in and out of the country and has held back India's share in world trade. For example, Turnaround time (TAT) at major ports was approximately 4 days in 2014-15 as against the global average benchmark of 1-2 days. Some of the private sector ports in India like Mundra and Gangavaram, have been able to achieve a turnaround time of around 2 days. Secondly, last mile connectivity to ports is one of the major constraints in smooth movement of cargo to/from the hinterland. Around 87 percent of Indian freight uses either road or rail for transportation of goods. Water-borne transport is much safer, cheaper and cleaner, compared to other modes of transportation but it accounts for less than 6 percent of India's modal split; Whereas in case of China, coastal and inland water transportation form 47 percent of China's freight modal mix, for Japan and the US, this share is 34 percent and 12.4 percent respectively. The constraints on connectivity and sub-optimal modal mix results in higher logistics cost thereby affecting the manufacturing sector and export competitiveness.[57]

As part of the program, a National Perspective Plan (NPP) for the comprehensive development of India's coastline and maritime sector had been prepared and it was released by the Prime Minister on 14 April 2016 at the Maritime India Summit 2016. As per the NPP, 415 projects have been identified across India to attain the four objectives:

- ✓ One, Port modernization and new port development – Under the Sagarmala initiative, the Government plans to develop six new ports across five coastal states of India. 189 projects with a projected cost of US$ 21 billion have been identified. Currently, 42 projects worth around US$ 3.6 billion are under implementation.
- ✓ Two, Port connectivity enhancement –Considering that improved port connectivity can provide the much needed boost to internal trade as well as Export and Import, 170 port connectivity enhancement projects have been identified as a part of Sagarmala at a projected cost of US$ 35 billion. In addition, the new National Waterways Act, 2016 aims to facilitate the use of 111 inland waterways across 24 states as sustainable mode of transport. With the law's enactment, several inland waterways would become National Waterways and come under the stipulated regulations for development. Government projects such as inland container depots, Jal Marg Vikas Project, Dedicated Freight Corridors (DFCs), Bharatmala initiative and the plan for pipeline expansion will provide a boost to development of multi-modal transport hubs, helping reduce the cost of freight transportation.
- ✓ Three, Port-linked industrialization – 33 port-linked industrialization projects at a project cost of US$ 65 billion, anchored by the Sagarmala Project will complement the 'Make in India' vision. Coastal Economic Zones (CEZs) have been proposed as economic regions hosting industrial clusters and will become a focal point of Port-linked industrialization. They have the potential to create direct and indirect employment of 4 million and 6 million respectively. They will also be aligned to industrial corridors such as the Delhi-Mumbai Industrial Corridor and Chennai-Bangalore Industrial Corridor. India targets boosting exports from US$ 465 billion in 2014-15 to US$ 900 billion by 2020 through Port-linked industrialization. Under the Sagarmala Program 14 CEZs

with an investment potential of Rs 15 trillion have been identified.

✓ Four, Coastal community development – With 72 coastal districts hosting 18 percent population of India, the development of these communities has become an integral aspect of Sagarmala. 23 projects have been identified so far under this aspect of the initiative. US $ 648 million have been projected as costs related to skill development, cold chain development, fisheries, aquaculture, local tourism and recreational facilities. The projects are to be implemented in phases at a projected cost of US $ 123 billion over 10 years from 2015 to 2025[58] (See Map of Sagarmala at Annexure 17).

The project is promising. If one goes by the example of Shenzhen in China since 1978, it helped created an estimated 7 million jobs and the city's GDP grew 50 times to $180 billion after the development of ports.[59] In case of India also, if everything goes as per plan, there will be a logistics cost savings of close to $ 5.3–6.1 billion per year and it is expected that Sagarmala could boost India's merchandise exports to $110 billion by 2025. Sagarmala Project seems to be progressing well as the project timeline has been reduced from 10 to just 5 years.[60]

'Mausam'

Project 'Mausam', a foreign policy initiative of the Modi government is often referred to as an answer to China's 'Maritime Silk Road'.[61] The project derives its title from the reliance on Monsoon winds by Indian sailors in ancient times for maritime trade. To start with, on 20 June 2014, 'Mausam' was presented as a Ministry of Culture project by Shri Ravindra Singh to an international audience at the 38th session of the World Heritage Committee at Doha, Qatar. One of the main deliverables of this project was the proposal to nominate maritime cultural landscapes across the Indian Ocean as a trans-national property on the World Heritage List of UNESCO. Director General UNESCO, who was present at the launch function, had expressed a great interest in this project. The endeavor of Project 'Mausam'- Mausam: Maritime Routes and Cultural Landscapes, is to position itself at two levels: first, at the macro level, it aims to re-connect and re-establish communications between countries of the Indian Ocean world, which would lead to an enhanced understanding of cultural values and concerns; second, at the micro level, the focus is on understanding national cultures in their regional maritime milieu.[62]

India has identified 39 countries for the project, which include Bahrain, Bangladesh, Cambodia, China, Pakistan, Sri Lanka, Syria, UAE, South Africa and Vietnam.[63] Apparently, Project 'Mausam' is essentially an initiative propounded by Ministry of Culture but if executed properly, it will enhance India's diplomatic outreach with the IOR nations. Contrary to the China's BRI strategy of impinging upon sovereign decision making powers of the countries by burdening them with heavy debt, focus of Project 'Mausam' is to gain the trust of the nations involved through sharing the knowledge systems / ideas by strengthening cultural linkages and develop equitable economic partnerships. Further, formation of people to people linkages will enable India to leverage its soft power.[64]

China has stalled India's efforts to get a transnational heritage status for the project from UNESCO by claiming that it will affect its proposal of reviving the maritime silk route. If India gets the heritage status, no other project can interfere with the designated area.[65] That is the significance of this project!

Project 'Mausam' would allow India to re-establish its ties with its ancient trade partners and re-establish an "Indian Ocean World" along the littoral of the Indian Ocean. This world would stretch from East Africa, along the Arabian Peninsula, past Southern Iran to the major countries of South Asia and thence to Sri Lanka and Southeast Asia[66] (See Mausam Map at Annexure 18).

International North-South Transport Corridor (INSTC)

In September 2000, Russia, Iran and India had signed an agreement in St. Petersburg laying out a vision for INSTC. In May 2002, after all three countries had ratified the agreement; the three transport ministers officially launched the INSTC project.[67]

The North-South Transport Corridor is an ancient route that connected South Asia with North Europe for centuries. The modern day 7200 km INSTC has been envisaged as a multi-modal transportation route linking Mumbai (India) to Bandar Abbas (Iran) by sea, from Bandar Abbas to Bandar-e-Anzali (an Iranian port on the Caspian Sea) by road, and then from Bandar-e-Anzali to Astrakhan (a Caspian port in the Russian Federation) by ship, and thereafter from Astrakhan to other regions of the Russian Federation and further into Europe by Russian railways (See Route Map of INSTC at Annexure 19). The INSTC later expanded to include eleven new members. The revised route is expected to offer both quicker and cheaper transportation than the primary alternative – the shipment of goods from South Asia through the Mediterranean and Suez Canal and then into the Atlantic and North Sea to Baltic ports.[68]

In the past, the development on this project had been slow and not much progress could me made till 2012. A meeting of the INSTC member countries was held in New Delhi on 18 January 2012 to discuss modalities for moving forward on the INSTC project, wherein support of countries like Turkmenistan, Uzbekistan, Kyrgyzstan and Turkey was considered essential to complete the missing links in the INSTC.[69] To understand the problem areas and to assess the full potential of the corridor, dry run was carried out with two 20 ft containers on two different routes of INSTC in August 2014 by the Federation of Freight Forwarders' Associations in India (FFFAI). Two routes used were:

- *Route 1.* NhavaSheva (India) – Bandar Abbas / Iran (By Sea) – Astara / Iran – Astara / Azerbaijan – Baku / Azerbaijan (By Road), total distance: 1265nm and 2250 km.
- *Route 2.* NhavaSheva (India) – Bandar Abbas / Iran (By Sea) 1265 nm – Amirabad / Iran (By Road) 1500 km –Astarakhan (Russia) (By Sea) 1000nm.

From the dry run, it emerged that the successful activation of the INSTC will help connect India to Russia within 17-20 days at competitive freight rates, leading to development of trade on the INSTC as against 30 days on the current route (or even six weeks by sea). As regards the cost, cost of shipment would be reduced by 2500 USD per 15 tons of cargo – meaning a price improvement of USD 166 per ton. India could beat Pakistan / Europe trade into CIS / Russia with this and look forward to realizing their full export potential in agro trade.[70]

Another freight test run was carried out under the aegis of Russian Railways Logistics in October 2016 by sending out the first shipment of industrial radiators from Mumbai to the Freyt Villadzh Vorsino transport and logistics complex in Kaluga Oblast. The transit time was 22 days. It was confirmed that the new route reduced delivery times in half and offered shipping rates 20 percent lower than on the rail route through Turkmenistan and Kazakhstan.[71] Participants brought out the continuing difficulties in implementing the INSTC project. The 150 km railway section in Iran, from Rasht to Astara was reported to be the missing link. A total of 164 km in length, currently 162 km had already been completed and because of this, journey times between Mumbai and Moscow will be reduced further to 14 days. Test runs have already been carried out and it was expected to be launched in 2018.[72] There are also purely logistical difficulties: One, differences in the range of goods offered for shipment from North to South and vice versa – there will be problem with the containers, empty containers will pile up at one end of the route, while at the other end, there will be short supply; two, difficulties in customs clearances such as moving from India to Russia, via Iran and Azerbaijan, the cargo has to cross state borders three times and if the goods are destined for Europe, then it is altogether a different issue. Ideally, there should be a single transport document for cargo when it arrives at Bandar Abbas port to destination stations in Russia. The importance of the INSTC was stressed during Russian President Vladimir Putin's visit to India in October 2016 as it can become a key factor in the deepening of economic integration in the region. Hence, the small technical and bureaucratic problems need to be resolved urgently.[73]

Further, according to Russian logistics experts, the main obstacle to the development of the project is the lack of awareness among shippers about the possibilities this service offers and as a consequence, their lack of confidence in this route. To develop the transport corridor, a regular shipping service needs to be established between the sea ports of Mumbai and Bandar Abbas and demand is to be created in the market. Shippers will need time to adapt to the new route.[74]

The potential of INSTC will be tremendous for India if linked with the Southeast Asian countries. This will boost trade between Europe and Southeast Asia as well. Undeterred by the US sanctions against Iran, the partner countries have not only shown their commitment toward the project in words, but in actions also. India's External Affairs Minister Mrs. Sushma Swaraj during her visit to Astana, Kazakhstan on 3 August 2018 said, "*The INSTC is gaining momentum and the member states are working together to popularize the corridor.*"[75]

Asia-Africa Growth Corridor (AAGC)

The initial idea of the AAGC was born during the discussion between Prime Ministers Narendra Modi and Shinzo Abe at the India-Japan annual summit meeting in Tokyo in November 2016. At the end of this meeting Indo-Japan Joint Statement was released on 11 November 2016 wherein the Prime Ministers expressed their intentions to work jointly and promote "*the development of industrial corridors and industrial network in Asia and Africa.*"[76]

As a follow up to this, the Research and Information System for Developing Countries (RIS), New Delhi, the Economic Research Institute for ASEAN and East Asia (ERIA), Jakarta, and Institute of Developing Economies-Japan External Trade Organization (IDE-JETRO), Tokyo, developed the Vision Document based on consultations with Asian and African think tanks. Officially named the "Asia-Africa Growth Corridor: Partnership for Sustainable and Innovative Development" – this Vision document was unveiled by the Indian and Japanese government officials in the 52nd Annual Meeting of the African Development Bank (AfDB) on 25 May 2017 in Gandhinagar, India. Prior to that on 23 May 2017, in his inaugural address of the meeting, Prime Minister Narendra Modi announced the proposal of AAGC and stated, "*The idea is that India and Japan, with other willing partners, would explore joint initiatives in skills, health, infrastructure, manufacturing and connectivity.*"[77] It may be of interest to note that this announcement was made in the backdrop of China's Belt and Road Forum (BRF) meeting held in Beijing on 14-15 May 2017.

India has a long history of development cooperation in Africa and it has unique distinction in providing affordable, appropriate and adaptable technology. However, being a developing country itself, India's development partnerships in Africa get constrained due to resource limitations. Japan, on the other hand, is in a position to play a major complementary role to overcome these constraints. Japan has also contributed in improving social and economic conditions in Africa mainly through aid, grants and technical assistance since 1993.[78] India and Japan can synergize their expertise to meet the developmental needs of Africa in a holistic manner. With this as a premise, the AAGC has been planned to be raised on four pillars: one, Development and Cooperation Projects; two, Quality Infrastructure and Institutional Connectivity; three, Enhancing Capacities and Skills; and four, People-to-People partnership.[79]

The centrality of people to people partnership would be the unique feature of this initiative. The strengths of AAGC will be aligned with the development priorities of different countries and sub-regions of Africa, taking advantage of simultaneous homogeneity and heterogeneity among them. This would be undertaken to improve growth and interconnectivity between and within Asia and Africa for realizing a free and open Indo-Pacific region.[80]

The AAGC is an endeavor to create a 'free and open Indo-Pacific Region' by rediscovering ancient sea-routes and creating new sea corridors that will link the African continent with India and countries in South Asia and Southeast

Asia. The project stakeholders hope the sea corridors will be "low-cost" and have "less carbon foot print" as compared to a land corridor. For example, under the AAGC, there is a plan to connect ports in Jamnagar (Gujarat) with Djibouti in the Gulf of Eden. Similarly, ports of Mombasa and Zanzibar will be connected to ports near Madurai; Kolkata will be linked to Sittwe port in Myanmar. India is developing ports under the Sagarmala Project specifically for this purpose. Besides developing sea corridors, the AAGC also proposes to build robust institutional, industrial and transport infrastructure in the countries of Asia and Africa. The whole purpose is to enable economies of Asia and Africa to integrate further and collectively emerge as a globally competitive economic bloc. Japan will contribute through its state-of-the-art technology and ability to build quality infrastructure, while India will bring in its expertise of working in Africa. The private sector of both countries are expected to come together to form joint ventures and consortiums, for building infrastructure, power or agriculture oriented projects in Africa.[81]

Chinese strategists have responded critically to the announcement of AAGC by Prime Minister Modi at the 52nd Annual Meeting of the African Development Bank and said that in actuality, it was a duplication of the "freedom corridor" designed by his Japanese counterpart Shinzo Abe during his Japan visit last November. It is further stated in the Global Times, "*In the eyes of Indian Media outlets, this Asia-Africa connectivity initiative is a counter to China's Belt and road.*"[82] However, the AAGC is conceptually different from China's BRI and it is qualitatively superior and people friendly as compared to the BRI: first, Unlike BRI which entails development of a land and sea corridor both, AAGC will essentially be a sea corridor linking Africa with India and other countries of Southeast Asia and Oceania; second, AAGC will be based on a consultative process, which will be profitable and bankable unlike the "government-funded model" of BRI; third, Centrality of people in Africa will be of prime consideration, rather than excessive emphasis on trade and economic relations alone.[83]

The AAGC is focused on capacity-building and expanding the manufacturing base and trade between Africa and Asia. The overall aim is to transform the region into a growth corridor that will embed the development processes and value chains in Africa and Asia. It will enable the connected economies to further integrate and emerge as a globally competitive economic region. The AAGC will bring out the economic gains for Africa through its integration with India, South Asia, Southeast Asia, East Asia and Oceania.[84]

In totality, working closely with the international community, the AAGC will be instrumental in realizing a 'free and open Indo-Pacific Region' through convergence of Japan's Expanded Partnership for Quality Infrastructure (EPQI) with India's 'Act East' Policy.[85]

Revival of the Bay of Bengal Initiative for Multi-Sectoral Technical and Economic Cooperation (BIMSTEC) as Alternative to SAARC

On 06 June 1997, Bangladesh, India, Sri Lanka and Thailand formed BIST-EC (where BIST denotes the first letter of each country and EC stood for economic cooperation) in Bangkok and its foundation document was called the 'Bangkok Declaration'. Myanmar joined the organization six months later and its name was changed to BIMST-EC (where M stood for Myanmar) on 22 December 1997. Nepal was granted observer status in 1998 and thereafter Nepal and Bhutan were granted full membership in 2004.[86] The organization remained dormant for a long time and it took seven years for the member states to organize its first Summit in Bangkok on 31 July 2004, where it was rechristened to the modern day nomenclature of BIMSTEC or the Bay of Bengal Initiative for Multi-Sectoral Technical and Economic Cooperation. It took another decade to establish its permanent Secretariat at Dhaka in 2014.[87] Second summit was held in India in 2008 and the third in Myanmar in 2014. All this shows that so far BIMSTEC had remained neglected and sidelined.[88]

But now the economic and strategic significance of the Bay of Bengal is growing rapidly with the re-emergence of the idea of the 'Indo-Pacific' region. The Bay is evolving as the center of the 'Indo-Pacific' region again. With five members from South Asia (Bangladesh, Bhutan, India, Nepal and Sri Lanka) and two from Southeast Asia (Myanmar and Thailand), the Bay of Bengal or in particular BIMSTEC has the huge potential to leverage its unique position as a bridge linking South and Southeast Asia.[89] Further, because of Pakistan's continuing support for and export of terrorist groups as part of its state policy and its intransigent attitude, the 19th SAARC Summit scheduled in Islamabad in November 2016 could not be held as India, Bangladesh, Afghanistan, Bhutan and Sri Lanka decided to pull out from it. Following this, India decided to raise the profile of BIMSTEC, which pointedly excludes Pakistan, to overcome Islamabad's policy of blocking all regional cooperation. Islamabad had blocked a regional connectivity project at the last SAARC Summit in Kathmandu. India's Foreign Secretary S Jaishankar had stated, "*Problem with SAARC is that some basic sorts of standards of regional cooperation have to apply. If you say that I will be a regional member but will not allow regional trade, I will not allow regional connectivity, will not allow regional motorways, I will not allow regional railways, then, what is it about.*" He added that if these countries found their initiatives blocked as desired under SAARC, they would look to other regional groupings such as the BIMSTEC to meet these needs.[90]

India took the initiative and organized a BRICS-BIMSTEC Outreach Summit and BIMSTEC leaders retreat in Goa in October 2016. The leaders agreed to an 'Agenda for Action'. Since then, several steps have been taken to inject urgency in the organization. BIMSTEC has 14 priority areas. Every country is assigned a lead role for particular subjects.[91] The fourth BIMSTEC summit was held in Kathmandu on 30-31 August 2018, in which substantial progress was made with regard to regional connectivity via land and sea and achieved what SAARC could not achieve in defining cross-border terrorism.[92]

Connectivity is the key driver for BIMSTEC as India's Northeast and Myanmar connect the South with Southeast Asia. Sooner this physical proximity is converted into real connectivity, dividends will flow enormously from this sub-region, otherwise afflicted by poor infrastructure and insurgent groups.[93] At Kathmandu Summit, Prime Minister Narendra Modi emphasized that connectivity should include connectivity in trade, transport, digital networks and people-to-people connect.[94] In terms of physical connectivity, BIMSTEC has at least three major projects awaiting completion: Kaladan Multimodal project to link India's East / Northeast with Myanmar – 1360 km (framework agreement signed between India and Myanmar in 2008); Asian Trilateral Highway connecting India and Thailand through Myanmar (Moreh in Manipur to Mae Sot in Thailand via Myanmar , likely to be completed by 2021);[95] and Bangladesh, Bhutan, India and Nepal (BBIN) Motor Vehicle Agreement (MVA) for movement of goods and vehicles among them (signed on 15 June 2015 in Thimpu, Bhutan) – Bhutan has not yet ratified the pact but pending ratification, Bhutan has given its consent for the BBIN MVA to come into force amongst the other three countries i.e. Bangladesh, India and Nepal, who have already ratified it. Trial movement of cargo vehicles will continue to be conducted along scheduled routes from April 2018 onwards, before finalizing the protocol for cargo vehicular movement.[96]

India's grand connectivity plans require considerable funding, an area where it cannot match China. Further, it has to keep countries leaning toward China, such as Nepal in check through diplomatic maneuvering as they are capable of creating hurdles at the last moment; such as Nepal within a week of hosting the BIMSTEC Summit tried to play SAARC card ostensibly at the behest of China/ Pakistan and made progress in BIMSTEC conditional on reviving

SAARC and it considered BIMSTEC and SAARC as complementary to each other. Later, after having confirmed its participation in the first-ever joint military week-long exercise of BIMSTEC states being held in Pune, India from September 10th, Nepal government did not allow Nepalese Army to participate in the drill.[97]

India-ASEAN Ties: Move Beyond Commerce to Cultural and People Connectivity

Besides 'Act East' Policy, Modi government has devised Three Cs (Commerce, Culture and Connectivity) formula for strengthening engagement with ASEAN.[98] While the commerce and land connectivity between India and ASEAN nations have been deliberated upon earlier in Chapter 3, it is the culture and air as well as digital connectivity, which will facilitate people-to-people contact in a shorter timeframe and thereby establish a long-lasting tie between India and ASEAN nations. India's relations with Southeast Asia date back to more than 2000 years. According to Singapore Prime Minister Lee Hsien Loong, "*Southeast Asian cultures, traditions and languages have been profoundly influenced by these early linkages. We see Indic Hindu-Buddhist influences in historical sites such as the Angkor Temple Complex near Siem Reap in Cambodia, the Borobudor and Prambanan temples near Yogyakarta in Indonesia, and the ancient candis in Kedah in Malaysia. The Ramayana is embedded in many Southeast Asian cultures, including in Indonesia, Myanmar and Thailand. Singapore's Malay name is Singapura, derived from Sanskrit and meaning 'lion city'.*"[99] In spite of such longstanding and intimate cultural links between India and Southeast Asia, people-to-people relations remain sparse, which need to be revived through cultural tourism. There is a glaring imbalance in terms of air connectivity to member nations of ASEAN: There are about 484 flights a week between 16 Indian cities and Singapore. The figure is 200 flights a week each in respect of Malaysia and Thailand. In comparison, there are no direct flights between India and Indonesia, the largest and most important country in the ASEAN. Similarly, there are regular shipping links between Indian ports and Singapore and Klang (Malaysia) but few or none at all with other ports in the region.[100] Enhanced air and sea connectivity will not only boost tourism but will also add to commerce of both India and ASEAN nations.

India, being a pioneer in the field of Information & Communication Technology (ICT), there is a great scope for nations to work together to expand digital connectivity in the region. During the retreat meeting of ASEAN Heads of State / Governments with Indian Prime Minister in New Delhi in January 2018, both sides reaffirmed their commitment to enhance physical and digital connectivity in line with the Master Plan on Asean Connectivity 2025 and the Asean ICT Master Plan (AIM) 2020 by availing the $ 1 billion line of credit announced by India.[101] According to a previous statement by Union telecom minister Manoj Sinha, "*the digital connectivity projects are of strategic importance and can have a transformative impact on the economy and cooperation between ASEAN and India.*"[102]

Without getting involved into great power rivalry, whether it is US-China or China-India, ASEAN nations would welcome an enhanced Indian maritime presence in the South China Sea as a hedge against China but at the same time they will not like to annoy China. They will focus on strengthening their maritime capabilities for which they need more maritime information sharing and maritime domain awareness from India and Japan. India will have to balance its security cooperation within the ASEAN region rather than being selective.[103]

QUAD: Is it Enough to Revive the Quadrilateral Security Dialogue of 2007 or 'QUAD' Concept Needs to be Progressed Differently

The United States, Japan, India and Australia came together as the "Core Group" to provide urgent humanitarian assistance in the aftermath of the 2004 Indian Ocean Tsunami disaster. In 2006, Japanese Prime Ministerial candidate Shinzo Abe suggested a value-based foreign policy and closer ties with Australia and India. Abe won the election and the same got included in the new government's foreign policy. The U.S. Vice President Dick Cheney endorsed the idea of quadrilateral involving Australia, Japan, the United States and India.[104] They then met formally just once as the Quadrilateral Security Dialogue in 2007 before newly elected Australian Prime Minister Kevin Rudd directed foreign minister Stephen Smith to withdraw from the nascent dialogue as China expressed concern at that time, considering it as an attempt or an exercise at containment.[105] However, Australia wanted to continue with the trilateral dialogue between Japan, Australia and the United States. Requests by subsequent Australian governments to take part in multilateral exercises (Ex Malabar) with India were declined by the latter over apprehensions that it would unnecessarily create diplomatic tensions with China.[106]

On the sidelines of the November 2017 East Asia Summit in Manila, the

Philippines, officials from the United States, Japan, India and Australia met once again to reestablish and re-conceptualize the Quadrilateral Security Dialogue (or QUAD). China's expanding maritime strategy and the increasing assertiveness of its land reclamation and territorial claims in disputed areas in the South and East China Seas over the past decade have been proclaimed as a key driver of a strengthening alignment among the Quad members.[107] China's maritime strategy has two components: One, the visible economic component, which is propagated through Xi's ambitious and much advertised 'One Belt and One Road'; and the second one is the military – Chinese Military Strategy White Paper, released in May 2015, declared that People's Liberation Army Navy (PLAN) would "*gradually shift its focus from 'offshore waters defense' to the combination of 'offshore waters defense' with 'open seas protection',*"[108] implying the requirement of power-projection capabilities and these are already evident through increased presence of PLAN's surface vessels and submarines in the Indian Ocean. This will impact the member nations of the QUAD differently and will vary according to their individual strategic interests / concerns:

- **India.** Through Belt and Road Initiative (BRI), China is extending its strategic influence deep into India's own maritime neighborhood. Both components of the BRI, the maritime and overland routes, are being perceived as attempts to 'encircle' India – as these involve massive investments in both economic and security-related infrastructure in India's neighborhood. China's predatory lending practices that feed corruption and impose heavy debt burden on the government of these countries have been thoroughly exposed such as in Sri Lanka, Pakistan and the Maldives. Further, construction of CPEC through Indian claimed territory of POK violates the sovereignty and territorial integrity of India. Chinese development of the Gwadar Port, a deep sea port in Baluchistan, is not only intended as a natural link between the overland and maritime components of the China's BRI for commercial purposes but will support increased Chinese military presence in the Indian Ocean.[109]
- **The United States.** The United States has to find a way to counteract growing Chinese influence in the 'Indo-Pacific' region, particularly in the vacuum left by its withdrawal from the Trans-Pacific Partnership (TPP).[110]
- **Japan.** Japan imports around 90 percent of its energy, which passes through the Straits of Malacca. Japan is wary about China's BRI as it could be employed to limit or block energy shipments to East Asia.[111]

- **Australia.** While Australia lies outside the direct route of the Maritime Silk Road, it is concerned by Chinese interference in domestic politics and about China's increasing project aid in the Pacific Islands to Australia's near North, fearing it could undermine governance and render fragile states more vulnerable to coercion.[112]

The first Quad meeting on 12 November 2017 addressed seven core themes: the rules-based order in Asia; freedom of navigation and over flight in the maritime commons; respect for international law; enhancing connectivity; maritime security; the North Korean Threat and nonproliferation; and terrorism.[113] There was no joint statement at the end but each country issued the official read outs of the meeting, which differed in contents and emphasis. Only the statements from Australia and the United States made a reference to the term "quadrilateral".[114]

The second consultative meeting of the so-called 'Quadrilateral' or 'Quad' group of countries was held among the officials of the United States, Japan, India and Australia in Singapore on 07 June 2018, on the sidelines of an ASEAN senior officials meeting. Like the first meeting, each of the four countries released a statement on the four-way consultations, without making any reference to the arrangement being a "quadrilateral". In spite of some variations in their statements, each country supported a free, open, prosperous and inclusive 'Indo-Pacific' region. The latest meeting came just days after the Shangri La Dialogue in Singapore where Indian Prime Minister Narendra Modi and the US Defense Secretary James Mattis delivered the keynote addresses but none of them made any reference to Quad. However, Indian statement on this second 'Quad' meeting made reference to "India's vision for the 'Indo-Pacific' region as outlined in the Prime Minister's keynote address at Shangri La Dialogue and taking a cue from Modi's address included 'maritime cooperation' in it.[115]

In principle, the Quad has already done the job its proponents want it to do: sending a warning to China.[116] There may be euphemism of showing 'strength in numbers' but unless the strategic intent is supported by real substance, Quad 2.0 may fizzle out. Though President Trump's National Security Strategy is categorical by affirming that the United States would seek to 'increase quadrilateral cooperation' with Japan, Australia and India,[117] while the others may not be forthright. During his recent summit in Tokyo with Japanese Prime Minister Shinzo Abe in January 2018, the Australian Prime Minister Malcolm Turnbull did not mention the Quad at all.[118] In an interview with the Australian Financial Review, Shinzo Abe was asked "Could the Quad evolve into closer military cooperation that, for example, would require Australia and Japan to come to each other's aid?" He stated, "*Ensuring the Indo-Pacific remains a free and open public good will require the cooperation of four countries... While maintaining cooperation, we will be contributing to the foundation of the region's prosperity, that is, the peace and stability of the region... This does not mean engaging in any military activities.*" He further added, "*We should raise our voice about the importance of cooperation as well as the rule of law. We have to have freedom of navigation. So by raising our voices and engaging in concrete activities we wish to accomplish what I want.*" In the same vein, he told that "*For the stability of this region it is very important that the Japan's self defense force, the Australian Navy, the American Navy, and the Indian Navy cooperate to contribute to stability.*" According to Abe, "*idea is not to contain China, not to stand against [a] rising China. If China agrees with this concept... we will work on them coming into the group.*"[119]

If 'Quad' is just a forum to raise their voice and the last two dialogue meetings were attended by only bureaucrats, then for it to fructify as a 'Security Alliance' to implement what has been envisaged for the 'Indo-Pacific' region, then there must be a real convergence of strategic interests. The mere rhetoric of commonalities and shared values will fall flat when it comes to respective national interests of each country – that too when dealing with China.

- **Why not to launch 'QUAD' as 'Economic Initiative' First.** The United States is the sole military and technological super power and will continue to remain so for the coming decades. If there is competition, then it is in the field of economy where China is racing ahead to dislodge the United States from Number One position. Shift in the balance of economic power is emerging from the 'Indo-Pacific' region. By a significant margin, almost every Asian country now has China rather than the United States as its largest trading partner, and China's share continues to grow. In the case of Japan, trade with China is now a little over 20 percent of the total, while the United States accounts for just 12.5 percent. In the case of India, China's trade is 16 percent and U.S. trade is around 6 percent of the total. South Korea's trade with China is equal to the total of its trade with both the United States and Japan. Indonesia's trade is 14 percent with Japan, 12.5 percent with China and 7 percent with the United States. Total U.S. trade with greater China – including Hong Kong and Taiwan – is now greater than U.S. trade with Canada.[120] Asian prosperity has therefore come to depend more on continued Chinese success than that of the United States, even though the American market powered the initial Asian lift-off. The result is an increasingly integrated economic region, which is now Sino-centric. Further, China's massive and expanding "Belt and Road" trade infrastructure project will envelop many countries of this region in a debt trap, making them subservient to Chinese masters. The 'QUAD' can become an effective multilateral partnership (as India is wary of entering into an alliance) if the member countries have converging economic goals – the United States wants to regain its economic dominance in the Indo-Pacific; India wants to become a secure and prosperous nation by taking advantage of its demographic dividend and fastest growing economy; Japan wants to overcome its recession by properly investing its accumulated yens; Australia wants to be part of rapid economic growth in South, Northeast and Southeast Asia – all these nations are democracies, respecting rule of law, believing in open and transparent business, sharing prosperity and having common interests in maritime security and secure sea lines of communication. India needs to identify projects in the 'Indo-Pacific' region, which could be taken up for development by a consortium-based approach – initially may be started as a bilateral venture between say India and Japan but visualizing their future scope and benefits, could be expanded to include the United States (Triad) and Australia (Quad). India can contribute its skilled manpower and other countries bringing in funds and technology. ***The shared prosperity amongst the nations will lead to shared security as a natural phenomenon.***

'Neighborhood First': Strengthen Strategic Leverages

Any ingress made by China in India's immediate neighborhood or in the Indian Ocean littoral, by strengthening its footprint either in the form of economic gains or political upheaval is regarded by analysts as part of China's 'String of Pearls' strategy or 'strategic encirclement' of India. And it is celebrated by vested media as loss of one more citadel by India to China on the geographical chessboard. Whereas in geo-strategic space, immediate events do not govern the strategic loss or gain but have long-term implications thereby allowing the opponent enough time and space to launch his own initiatives or undertake countermeasures. India's close proximity to its neighboring countries offers it certain distinct advantages, which if taken into account while developing its strategic leverages, cannot be easily neutralized by China despite having so-called deep pockets. The present Indian government rightly recognizes this aspect and in a recent meeting (on 3rd July 2018) with India's ambassadors, External Affairs Minister Mrs. Sushma Swaraj laid out a three-pronged approach to deal with China's increasing engagement in the South Asian and Indian Ocean neighborhood: First, track Beijing's activities carefully; Second, pursue our own projects and commitments with full vigor; and Third, educate and advise neighbors on the negative consequences of engaging with China.[121] Peculiarities of India's neighbors, i.e. their strengths and vulnerabilities, which offer them significant advantages are being discussed in subsequent paragraphs.

- **Nepal**

No two countries in the world are as closely placed, geographically, culturally and strategically, as India and Nepal. India is where Nepalese go to study, find jobs, plan marriages, invest in a second home and undertake pilgrimages.[122] When the relations are so intimate, the expectations become very high from both sides and even small defiance irrespective of the past bonhomie becomes a source of irritation, ready to be exploited by an envious neighbor. This is particularly true in case of India-Nepal relations. Recognizing the sensitivity of relations, and strategic importance of Nepal, Narendra Modi was the first Indian Prime Minister to visit Nepal after a gap of 17 years in August 2014. When a devastating 7.8 magnitude earthquake struck Nepal on 25 April 2015, India's assistance reached Nepal within six hours and it included 16 National Disaster Response Force (NDRF) teams and 39 IAF aircraft sorties with 571 tons of relief material. Total Indian relief assistance to Nepal amounted to approximately US$ 67 million followed by a post-earthquake reconstruction package of US$ 1 billion (US$ 250 million grant and US$ 750 million concessional Line of Credit).[123] But, thereafter India-Nepal relations hit a low over the promulgation of the constitution and the Madhesi agitation. New Delhi was accused of enforcing a nearly five-month long 'blockade' between end 2015 and early 2016, in support of Madhesis. Except for supporting the cause of Madhesis, Indian government did not officially declare any blockade of Nepal. Coming just months after an earthquake, this caused unprecedented hardship to Nepal's people, generating strong anti-India sentiments among the country's hill communities. It also brought back memories of a year-long blockade by India in 1989 for buying military hardware from China. During the Madhesi blockade, Chinese cleverly used the supposedly symbolic train to Gyirong and land route to carry fuel (1.3 million liters of petroleum) during this period to convey to the Kathmandu-elite that geographical distance between them was easily surmountable.[124] After nearly five months, the blockade began to be slowly lifted in February 2016 as Nepal agreed to a few minor changes in the constitution. Nepalese Prime Minister Khadga Prasad Sharma Oli visited China the very next month and sealed a number of major pacts including a transit agreement allowing Nepal access to Chinese seaports and Chinese loans to build an international airport in the tourist town of Pokhara.[125]

Following up the agreement signed during Oli's visit to China in March 2016, China and Nepal have finalized a transit protocol on 07 September 2018 that will give Kathmandu access to four Chinese seaports of Tianjin, Shenzhen, Lianyungang and Zhanjiang and three land ports of Lanzhou, Lhasa and Xigaste. The protocol is expected to be signed when Chinese President Xi Jinping visits Nepal in 2019 and thereafter the arrangements will come into effect.[126] This is being projected as of historic significance as it would end Nepal's dependence on India for trade with other countries, which could only be carried out via Indian ports. By all means, Nepal being an independent country should have flexibility in conducting its trade and need to have alternative options. But these agreements are higher on symbolism and away from ground reality, which is dictated by terrain configuration and geographical proximity between Nepal and India vis-à-vis China. These aspects need to be highlighted:

- ✓ Being a landlocked country sandwiched between India and China, Nepal is dependent upon its neighbors for international trade and access to the sea. The terrain between India and Nepal is more hospitable – comprising of mountains with heights ranging from 600 to 2200 meters, valleys and plains; in contrast its terrain with China is mountainous with average heights of 6,100 meters. Most of the passes between China and Nepal remain snow-bound throughout the year. Hence, travel and transport through the Indian plains is a much convenient and practical option.
- ✓ While the 1,868 km of Nepal's border with India, bordering the states of Uttarakhand, UP, Bihar, West Bengal and Sikkim is an open border,

its 1415 km border with China is topographically a harsh terrain. Population flow between Nepal and India has always been "continuous and unrestricted".[127]

- ✓ Around 5.4 lakh Nepalese migrants work in India (in contrast, there were only 2,400 of them in China in 2017-18), whose remittances form a significant component of the Nepal's GDP. Around 4.4 lakh Indians worked in Nepal during the same period.[128]
- ✓ Deep linguistic and cultural similarity, religious affinity, historical ties, geographical proximity and family connections between Nepal and India cannot be overwhelmed by trade or economic ties with China, which will prove unsustainable in the long-term. Further, the Nepalese enjoy equal rights to Indian citizens. They can travel freely to each other's countries, live and work there, engage in business and own property.
- ✓ The nearest Chinese seaport, Tianjin is situated more than 3,000 km away from the Nepalese border, as against 704 and 800 km from the Kolkata and Haldia ports respectively, in India currently being used by Nepal. Nepal's infrastructure in its Northern region to connect with the proposed Tianjin port is not in place, and will take tremendous efforts and investment to be operational. Undoubtedly, this will be an alternative available to Nepal in case of blockade of routes from India to Nepal but in this situation, carrying perishable and essential items like foodstuffs, and petroleum products will cost Nepal heavily in terms of time and money.[129]
- ✓ Nepal has been allowed to conduct export-import trade to and from third countries through Visakhapatnam port in Andhra Pradesh since February 2016 but Nepali importers still prefer Kolkata port. Vizag port is 1436 km far from Birgunj (Nepal) whereas Kolkata is only 704 km from Birgunj.[130] In fact, Nepal wants another high-sea port of India, which is at a shorter distance from Nepal as compared to Vizag. It is Dhamra port in Odisha, which is 1,028 km from Birgunj.[131]
- ✓ As regards, rail connection from Tibet to Nepal, the proposal was first accepted in 2008 and promises were made to establish rail connectivity by 2013 but it did not happen. The Lhasa rail line has been brought up to Xigaste. Only by 2020, as per the current Chinese plans, this line will be brought nearer the Nepal border within Tibet (i.e., up to

Kyirong). There is no firm commitment as to how it will then be extended within Nepal, linking Kathmandu with Pokhara and Lumbini as proposed by the Nepali side.[132] A recent technical report prepared by the Chinese side has indicated that it will take around nine years to construct a railway link from Kyirong to Kathmandu at an estimated cost of nearly US$ 2.5 billion.[133] Construction of railway track through 6000 meter high mountains, either through tunnels or winding channels involve stupendous costs and efforts and estimated time of completion can be widely varied. Therefore, there are different estimates by different agencies. The degree of difficulty can be assessed from the fact that a simple fiber optic link for internet connection from Kathmandu to Tibet region, which could have been established in December 2014, was launched in January 2018 – a delay of three years, first due to devastating earthquake and later due to working conditions of high altitude.[134] It may be apt to quote Hou Yanqi, the Deputy Head of Asia Division in China's Foreign Ministry, who said that while China would work on rail link from Xigaste to Gyirong within Tibet, its "extension in to Nepal is a long-term plan, at a point far off in future."[135]

✓ Besides the cost, as the Nepalese government will have to do the cost-benefit analyses before choosing projects under the BRI, lest they not fall in to debt trap like Sri Lanka. Further, rail connectivity between Tibet and Nepal is a politically sensitive issue for the Chinese authorities. The proposed rail will not only bring Nepalese and other foreigners in to Tibet but also facilitate the flight of disaffected Tibetans in to Nepal and then to India. China will have to decide on the extent to which Tibet can be opened to the outside world through land route.[136]

✓ There are practical difficulties in getting fuel from China. Even if Nepal Oil Corporation and Petro China Company Limited were to sign an agreement, the issue of dual taxation in Tibet, which raises the cost of fuel – remains unresolved. While the Indian refinery of Barauni is only 374 km away, the nearest Chinese refinery is more than 2,000 km from Nepal. Assuming China finds no reason for a massive oil subsidy to Nepal, this distance alone will make Chinese fuel much more expensive than Indian.[137] Higher transportation costs make Sino-Nepal trade economically unviable. Nepal's turn to China to meet its long-term fuel requirements is unrealistic. China is not in a position yet to match India in supplying fuel to Nepal. Nepal's annual purchase of fuel from India reached 1.37 billion liters. China's supply of 1.3 million liters of gasoline to Nepal – though it might make a great impression – can realistically only meet Nepal's needs for a much lesser period.[138]

✓ Already, the complaints are emerging that the Pokhara Airport, which the Chinese are building is vastly overpriced. It was estimated to cost about $140 million but was contracted to a Chinese company at US$ 216 million with loans from the Chinese EXIM Bank. As in Sri Lanka, the extra cash has allegedly been used to fill up politicians' coffers. Prime Minister now faces Rajapaksa moment. There are similar complaints about the way Maoist leader Dahal hurriedly cleared the Budhi Gandak dam deal with the Chinese in his last days as Prime Minister.[139]

Prime Minister Oli, widely viewed as pro-Beijing in his outlook, has been relatively cautious in trying to maintain a balance in Nepal's ties with India and China. When he became the Prime Minister for the second time in February 2018, Oli made his first foreign tour to India in April. Prime Minister Modi reciprocated immediately by paying a two-day visit to Nepal in the second week of May. It seems that Indo-Nepal relations have been placed back on a sound footing. Modi's emphasis on culture, democracy and development was aimed at reaching out to the Nepalese people as well as politicians, underlining the vast commonalities between the two countries.[140] He declared, "*As Nepal enters a new era of consolidating gains of democracy and achieving rapid economic growth and development, India will continue to remain a steadfast partner of government of Nepal to implement its vision of samriddha Nepal, sukhi Nepali (prosperous Nepal, happy Nepali)*."[141]

On the development front, both the prime ministers launched the $1.4 billion, 900 Megawatts Arun III hydropower project and agreed on a timeline by which to implement key projects, including the construction of a 130 km rail link between Kathmandu and Raxaul in Eastern Bihar, for smoother movement of passengers and cargo. The two prime ministers also launched a bus service from Janakpur, the birthplace of Goddess Sita, to Ayodhya, the birthplace of Hindu God Ram – connecting the so-called Ramayana circuit. Most significantly, perhaps, Modi promised to resolve all pending issues in

India-Nepal ties by September 19, Nepal's Constitution Day. These include the trade deficit in favor of India, the exchange of demonetized Indian currency in Nepal and lack of progress in India funded projects in Nepal.[142] Some analysts also suspect a Chinese hand behind Nepal's thaw in relations with India. Beijing can connect Kathmandu by rail from the Northern border but the Belt and Road will be incomplete, if not unviable, until India grants connectivity.[143] The gains that robust trade with Nepal promises are unlikely to compensate for the losses that China would incur by provoking India with a population of 1.3 billion and a growing consumer market.

There is a definite acceleration of Indian projects. There is a definite acceleration of Indian projects. India has been able to deliver on 16 of the 21 points raised by Nepal Prime Minister K P Sharma Oli during his visit to India in April 2018, with Prime Minister Modi personally keeping a track on progress of these. The remaining five issues are reportedly concerning infrastructure projects, where Kathmandu has to act on issues like land acquisition etc.[144] Survey for the electric rail network between Raxaul and Kathmandu has been completed by the Indian team. Further, India has already started building five cross-border railway lines between Nepal and India; Out of these one line from Jayanagar to Janakpur-Kurtha and second between Jogbani and Biratnagar have been finished.[145] On 28 September 2018, India has agreed to extend the Motihari-Amlekhgunj oil pipeline, currently being built to Chitwan, Just 100 km South of Kathmandu along with an LPG pipeline. With the construction of these dedicated oil and gas pipelines, it will be easier for Nepal to import petroleum products from India.[146]

Nepal can draw tremendous economic benefits from the rapidly growing economy of India because of its geographical proximity to India vis-à-vis China. Four aspects, which will bring proximity to Nepal are: India as an energy market, India as a job market, India as a global market of products and India as a source of FDI and foreign currency.[147] India lacks skilled manpower to meet the demand of its industries. According to government report of India, around 119 million additional skilled laborers will be required by 24 sectors such as construction, retail, transportation, logistics, automobile and handloom by 2022.[148] Around 50,000 Nepalese are presently working in the Indian Army as a part of Gorkha Regiment[149] and they retire very young, and would still be in need of re-employment. They should be imparted skilled training before retirement and given the option to join industry. Having observed ups and downs in Indo-Nepal relations, it is evident that the relations at the people's level are little influenced by relations at the political level. Now it will be up to the ruling government in Nepal to decide whether to draw benefits from its close neighbor, India, in a transparent manner or fall in to the debt trap of a distant neighbor in the name of development. The previous Nepalese government led by Sher Bahadur Deuba had scrapped a $2.5 billion deal with China's state-owned Gezhouba Group to build a hydropower facility in the West of the country. Reportedly, under Chinese pressure, the present government has reversed its previous government's cancellation of the $2.5 billion Budhi Gandak Dam project. China bagged the project without competitive bidding and inflated the project cost. This will leave Nepal struggling to repay the Chinese debt.

However, to counter China's ingress in to Nepal, India will have to act speedily and improve its connectivity with Nepal, complete the promised projects on priority and sharpen its diplomacy with Nepal.

- **Bangladesh**

Bangladesh would have been the most reliable and natural partner of India because its creation is owed to the direct involvement and initiative of India. In fact, it will not be an exaggeration to say that Bangladesh-India bilateral cooperation had begun in the battlefield of 1971.[150] But after the assassination of its founder president Sheikh Mujibur Rehman, the subsequent governments, which came in to power, were inimical to the interests of India. With assumption of power for the second time in 2009 by Prime Minister Sheikh Hasina (Mujibur Rehman's daughter), India-Bangladesh relations have substantially improved. As an appreciative gesture from Bangladesh in recognizing the supreme sacrifices made by 1,661 Indian soldiers for the liberation of Bangladesh, a special Sommanona ceremony was jointly organized by the Governments of India and Bangladesh during Sheikh Hasina's visit to India on 27 April 2017 in Manekshaw Center, Delhi Cantonment.[151]

Security issue had bedeviled Indo-Bangladesh ties in the past as insurgency in Northeast India was sheltered by Bangladesh and supported by China.[152] Hasina, since assumption of power, has firmly controlled the situation and did not allow any terrorist activities, or any terrorist group to use Bangladesh's soil to launch an attack against India or any neighboring country.[153]

Similarly, Prime Minister Narendra Modi, after assumption of office in May 2014, has taken the India-Bangladesh relations to newer heights. According to Modi, "*Relations between India and Bangladesh have entered a golden phase... complicated issues related to land boundary and coastal boundary, which seemed impossible to solve at one point, were finally resolved.*"[154] Forty-one years after the conclusion of the Indira-Mujib Border Accord of 1974, the Land Boundary Agreement (LBA) between the two countries was concluded and ratified during Modi's visit to Bangladesh in June 2015.[155]

The bilateral relationships between India and Bangladesh are now well beyond the 'strategic partnership' and encompass every important sector, viz., security, trade, connectivity, energy, civil nuclear agreement, defense, and introduction of new bus and train services, etc.

- **Enhanced Connectivity.** South Asia is the least connected region in the world. Currently, both countries are working to extend road, rail and coastal shipping links, as these would expand the regional economy. Building a bridge over Feni River, the establishment of rail connectivity between Akhaura and Agartala and the development of Ramgarh-Subroom will be 'game-changer' when these will directly connect the Northeast Indian States with the Chittagong port.[156] The Bangladesh's approval for transit of food grains to Tripura, using the Ashuganj river port was a good beginning.[157] The two sides signed a pact to allow Indian cargo ships to use Bangladesh's Mongla and Chittagong ports. Indian goods at present have been travelling via Singapore to reach Bangladesh in three weeks; now they would go directly to Bangladesh in a week.[158] Another protocol had been signed on inland water transit and trade that would allow the use of the river of two countries to promote trade among Northeastern states and adjoining parts of Bangladesh. The water transit protocol is for a period of five years.[159] Both governments are currently working on the restoration of eight railway links between West Bengal and the Northeast India with Bangladesh, which were snapped during the 1965 Indo-Pakistan War.[160] For boosting people-to-people contact, two new inter-country bus routes were inaugurated during Modi's visit in June 2015: Dhaka-Shillong-Guwahati and Kolkata-Dhaka-Agartala. Transit through Bangladesh drastically reduces travel time to India's Northeast; for instance, the current road distance between Agartala and Kolkata is 1,650 km but via Bangladesh it is only 350 km.[161]

- **Energy Cooperation.** Bangladesh has laid down a goal of achieving an installed capacity of 24,000 MW of power generation by 2021 and

Prime Minister Modi has agreed to provide his full support for the same.[162] India has been supplying 660 MW of power through Bheramara-Bahrampur and Tripura-Comilla inter-connection[163] and India has agreed to increase it to 1000 MW. Private sectors have also made their valuable contribution: Reliance Power Ltd. signed a deal with the state-run Bangladesh Power Development Board to set up an LNG-fuelled 3000 MW power plant at a cost of $ 3 billion and Adani Power Ltd. will set up two coal-fired plants with a total capacity of 1,600 MW that will cost more than $ 1.5 billion.[164] Both countries have also started cooperation on renewable energy and nuclear power. India will be providing Bangladesh technical assistance for the construction of the 2,400 MW Rooppur Nuclear Power Plant in Pabna. Another coal-based plant namely Maitree Super Thermal Power Project of 1,320 MW at Rampal, Bagerhat of Bangladesh by Bangladesh-India Friendship Power Plant Company (Pvt) Ltd. is progressing well.[165]

- **Trade.** India exported goods worth US$ 8.6 billion and imported US$ 685 million in 2017-18. India has trade surplus with Bangladesh in tune of US$ 7.9 billion.[166] Though India offered duty-free and quota free entry to Bangladesh goods under the SAFTA agreement in 2011, Dhaka was slow in taking advantage of the facility, concentrating primarily on ready-made garments.[167] Endeavors are being made by both sides to improve the trade balance. The most practical way is that Bangladesh will establish two special economic zones that would allow Indian companies to set up base to manufacture and export goods to India. This will create masses of jobs for Bangladeshis and at the same time help Bangladesh in reducing its huge trade deficit. In turn, it will benefit India as per capita income of Bangladesh will rise, as a consequence its buying capacity, which in turn will make Bangladesh a bigger and more attractive market for India.[168] It will be a win-win situation for both the countries. To this end, several Indian mega-companies like Hero Motor Corp., Tata group and CEAT have set up such projects in Bangladesh.[169] In 2010, India provided US$ 1 billion soft loan to Bangladesh and it was the largest ever credit package offered by India to any nation at that time. Commending Bangladesh for full utilization of this line of credit, Prime Minister Modi had announced a second line of credit worth US$ 2 billion during his visit in June 2015,[170] which is under various stages of utilization. In 2017, India announced the third line of credit for US$ 5 billion to Bangladesh with US$ 500 million set aside for defense purchases from India.[171] Further, Bangladesh could sell natural gas to India from its colossal gas reserves to reduce its trade deficit.

- **Water.** Bangladesh and India share 54 common rivers and the issue of water sharing during the lean season has been a sensitive and delicate issue as it has a direct impact on food production and quality of life of hundreds of millions of people in both countries. Ganges water sharing agreement was signed during Sheikh Hasina's first term. For Teesta water sharing, the two countries had worked out a solution for an interim water sharing agreement in 2011 but it could not be concluded due to last minute objection raised by the West Bengal Government. Prime Minister Narendra Modi has assured that India would be able to deliver on the Teesta water sharing agreement.[172] He emphasized that water was not a political issue but a humanitarian one, and he would work to seal the deal.[173] Sooner that happens, greater will be the bonding between the two nations.

Further to counter China, India should join Japan to develop the deep seaport at Matarbari. With a view to develop its blue economy, Bangladesh wants to gradually transform Payra port in to a deep seaport, where it has constructed primary infrastructure from its own funds. It is expected to handle 75,000 containers a year once it becomes fully operational – a capacity five times more than the existing seaports. There is a plan to develop a link between the Payra port and India's Northeast. Reportedly, Bangladesh had signed two MoUs worth US$ 600 million with two Chinese companies for setting up two of the 19 components of the Payra port project. The whole project is estimated to be of US$ 20 billion, out of which dredging itself would constitute 35 percent according to the study report. India Ports Global has agreed to design, fund and build Payra deep-seaport on its own. There is a strong possibility that India Ports Global would be selected to develop the port. If this initiative by India materializes, bilateral ties between the two countries will be taken to new heights.[174]

The geographical proximity and cultural affinity between India and

Bangladesh need to be leveraged through optimum application of soft power, economic and energy interdependence, tourism and people-to-people contacts. Greater the contact between the people of the two countries and once the two economies get intertwined, the populace of the two countries will enjoy the fruits of development, following the Indian Prime Minister's motto of *'Sab ka Saath, Sab ka Vikas'*. This will make the close cooperation between the two countries immune to political uncertainties. The contentious issues inhibiting the full growth of their relationship need to be resolved to mutual benefit of both the countries and prevent this strategic space be encroached upon by China.

• Sri Lanka

Unnerved by growing Chinese influence in Sri Lanka, India is endeavoring to strengthen ties with the Colombo government through – economic cooperation, reconstruction efforts in Northern Sri Lanka enabling the people to rebuild and restart their lives in the erstwhile LTTE strong holds, promotion of cultural linkages and enhancing people-to-people connect and tourism.

India provided finances for the construction of the Northern Railway in Sri Lanka and has planned to develop Kankesanthurai harbor and Palaly airport, both of which were heavily damaged in the war with the LTTE guerillas. India helped to demine acres of thickly forested land in Mullaitiva.[175]

With the election of Maithripala Sirisena as Sri Lankan President in January 2015, relations between the two countries were set to improve. He made it a point to make India as his first visit to a foreign country, and during that visit, signed four agreements, which are expected to strengthen bilateral cooperation: civilian nuclear cooperation; cooperation in the fields of agriculture and culture; agreement to expand defense; and security cooperation.[176] With an aim to reassert New Delhi's influence over Colombo after its drift towards China and bring a paradigm shift in the bilateral relations, Prime Minister Narendra Modi was prompt in reciprocating the visit. In the last 28 years, he was the first Indian Prime Minister to have visited Sri Lanka for a bilateral meeting. In Colombo, Prime Minister Modi announced a slew of measures to boost bilateral ties: issuing visa on arrival to Sri Lankan tourists from 14 April 2015 (the Sinhala and Tamil New Year); India's cooperation in developing a Ramayana Trail in Sri Lanka and a Buddhist Circuit in India; setting up of a Joint Task Force on Ocean Economy to tap the vast oceans that hold enormous promise for both countries; and a fresh line of credit of up to US$ 318 million for Sri Lankan railways.[177] Modi became the first Indian and second world leader to visit Tamil heartland Jaffna ravaged by war. He handed over 27,000 new homes to Tamils who had become homeless during the civil war.[178] During his stay, Modi flagged-off train services at Talaimannar, built with India's assistance in the post-war period.[179]

During his election campaign, Sirisena had promised to scrap infrastructure contracts with China, including the port city project off Colombo. But Sri Lanka cannot afford to antagonize China as the latter has already invested huge amounts in projects. The commercial value of some of the infrastructure projects has been questioned, while Chinese loans have contributed to the country's huge national debt of US$ 64.9 billion or 76 percent of GDP. After coming to power, Sirisena suspended projects that he said were badly priced and financed on onerous terms. But eventually, with the country's economic crisis worsening, he allowed them to go ahead – China had been asked to resume work at the US$ 1.4 billion Colombo project in October 2016. Although a deal to increase the commercial viability of the loss-making Hambantota facility and also help Sri Lanka generate much needed funds has been held up.[180]

Chinese loans are given with extremely high interest rates. For the Hambantota port project, Sri Lanka borrowed US$ 301 million from China with an interest rate of 6.3 percent, while the interest rates on soft loans from the World Bank and Asian Development Bank are only 0.25-3 percent. Interest rates of India's line of credit to the neighboring countries are as low as 1 percent, or even less in some cases.[181] Further, China not only protects the interests of Chinese investors but also ensures huge job creation for its own people such as port project would have created 85,000 jobs for China.

Moreover, Sri Lankan government investigators had discovered that US$ 2 billion were secretly transferred to Dubai accounts by people close to the Rajapaksa government. The total amount of foreign exchange reportedly ferreted out by the Rajapaksa family and cronies were more than US$ 10 billion. Sri Lankan media had earlier reported bribes paid by Chinese companies to the Rajapaksa family members and their close associates.[182]

India's importance to Sri Lanka is beyond question: It is the island's largest trading partner and has provided over US$ 2.5 billion worth of development assistance. Over 70 percent of the cargo handled in Colombo port is transshipment cargo to and from India.[183] The two countries are keen to upgrade their existing FTA by signing a new trade pact called the Economic and Technology Cooperation Agreement (ECTA), which will lay the foundation for Sri Lankan exports and investments to benefit more from the rapidly growing Indian market.[184] This would enhance commercial ties between Sri Lanka and India's fast growing Southern states.

Japan and India are considering building a port and industrial zone at Trincomalee to compete with China's recent takeover of the Hambantota deep seaport and corresponding economic zone.[185] *For India Trincomalee has a strong strategic value.*

Not to be left behind, China wanted to build houses and roads in Sri Lanka's North and East, in a bid to expand its influence beyond the island's South. In April 2018, state-run China Railway Beijing Engineering Group Co Ltd. won a more than US$ 300 million project to build 40,000 houses in the Northern district of Jaffna. China's EXIM bank was to provide the finances. But the project has been halted after residents demanded brick houses instead of the concrete structures planned by the Chinese firm, saying they preferred their traditional dwellings. This has given an opportunity for India to step in as India has already built 44,000 houses in the North in the first phase of reconstruction through a grant to Sri Lanka. Reportedly, Sri Lankan authorities have opened negotiations with India for the housing project.[186]

China will leave no stone unturned to enlarge its footprint in Sri Lanka. In June 2018, The New York Times reported that China Harbour Engineering Company gave US$ 7.6 million for Rajapaksa's reelection bid, which he lost to Sirisena in early 2015.[187] While presiding over a ceremony marking the start of construction of a Chinese-funded kidney hospital in his home constituency of Polonnaruwa, 230 km from Colombo, President Sirisena announced that he had been gifted 2 billion Yuan (US$ 295 million) by China's President Xi Jinping to be utilized for any project of his wish.[188] It is evident that China will try its level best to influence the ruling government in Sri Lanka, irrespective of whosoever is in power.

Knowing fully well, India's sensitivities to Chinese naval influence in its neighborhood, in May 2017 Sri Lanka had rejected Chinese request to dock a submarine on its port. Having been emboldened after the Doklam standoff, Sri Lanka is trying to balance China with India. Reportedly, Sri Lanka is attempting to work out a business plan with the Airport Authority of India for operating the country's loss-making Mattala Rajapaksa International Airport in Southern Hambantota.[189] Three rounds of official negotiations have been completed but the agreement is yet to be finalized. The governments after detailed negotiations have reportedly agreed that India with a 70 percent stake in the joint venture, will contribute US$ 225 million to revamp and run the airport while the Sri Lankan side will invest the balance. As per the draft agreement, India will operate the airport on a 40-year lease.[190]

Sri Lankan government clearly sees benefit from cultivating ties with both the countries as a means of transforming the island in to a regional commercial hub. Having lost Hambantota port to China for 99-year lease, Sri Lanka has to be extremely cautious while accepting loans or grants from China to avoid falling in to 'debt trap' again.

• Myanmar

Sensitive to its location between the two Asian giants, Myanmar is keen to leverage the growth potential of both the nations to its advantage by maintaining good relations with the both. But it is also wary of its economic dependence on China. Myanmar might be heading towards a debt crisis similar to Sri Lanka as China was reportedly forcing Myanmar to hand over majority stake (70-85 percent) in its deep sea strategic port Kyaukpyu. The US$ 7.3 billion project is funded by China and Myanmar on 85:15 ratio based on the agreement struck by the former military-backed government of President Thein Sein. The economic zone faced opposition from activists and residents who criticized the tender process stating that the development would have a negative impact on local people.[191] To avoid the Chinese debt trap, project size has now been tremendously scaled down and the revised cost would be around US$ 1.3 billion, something that is much more practicable for Myanmar's use. The original plan was to develop about 10 berths at the 25-meter deep seaport to accommodate bigger oil tankers, but the size will now be revised to only two berths.[192] China is expected to take controlling stakes, as high as 85 percent, in many Chinese-funded projects in Myanmar, although initial agreement for some of them was on a 50/50 basis.[193]

Myanmar would welcome closer economic ties with India to balance and offset its domineering ties with China.[194] Fundamentals of India's bilateral relationship with Myanmar are based on: the substantive development partnership, trade and revival of cultural and people-to-people ties. Defense relations too have been growing steadily, especially between the two armies and navies.

Prime Minister Narendra Modi had visited Myanmar earlier in 2014 to attend the ASEAN-India Summit while the Myanmarese President and Suu Kyi visited India in 2016. His first bilateral visit on 5-7 September 2017 came at a time when the Myanmarese government was facing international pressure over the flight of 125,000 Rohingya Muslims in to Bangladesh in just two weeks after Myanmar's military launched a crack down in the Rakhine state. Modi said that India shared Myanmar's concern over "extremist violence" in the Rakhine state, especially the loss of innocent lives of the people and the security personnel.[195] According to Foreign Secretary S Jaishankar, "*India is committed for assistance to the Rakhine state development program because we (India) really believe that the medium way of addressing problems in the Rakhine area is really to look at development aspects.*"[196]

After Modi-Suu Kyi talks, 11 agreements were signed between the two sides. He also announced grant of gratis (no-cost) visa to Myanmarese citizens who wish to visit the country. Prime Minister Modi highlighted the development initiatives India has taken in Myanmar, especially in capacity building of institutions.[197] For instance, in the health care sector, India has upgraded three hospitals in Myanmar and is building a hospital in Nay Pyi Taw.[198] He informed that the Paletwa Inland Waterways Terminal and Sittwe port under the Kaladan project have been completed. Both sides will be responsible for the operation and maintenance of the port. The final component of the project, the road from Paletwa to Zorinpui is still under construction. The construction work is scheduled to begin shortly on reconstruction of bridges on the Tamu-Kyigone-Kalewa Road and on the Kalewa-Yargyi Sector of the Trilateral Highway. He further added that the high-speed diesel from India has started coming through trucks to meet the needs of Upper Myanmar. Forty percent of Myanmar's daily consumption of 200,000 barrels of high-speed diesel is in Mandalay and other parts of Northern Myanmar. Myanmar requires some 5 million tonnes of diesel annually and this demand can be easily met from Assam. The feasibility of laying oil pipeline from Numaligarh refinery to Myanmar can be explored. On the other hand, Myanmar is rich in gas (4 to 6 trillion cubic feet of gas reserves were discovered in Myanmar recently), which can be supplied to India through a pipeline.[199] He said in future India would take up projects that will be according to the needs and priorities of Myanmar.[200]

It was agreed that enhanced air connectivity between the two countries would boost people-to-people contacts as well as promote greater tourism, trade and investment flows. India will provide complete financial and technical assistance to Myanmar for development of Pakokku Airport or Kalay Airport. Feasibility of construction of a rail link between Tamu and Mandalay is also being explored. The two sides acknowledged the importance of pulses in the bilateral trade basket, and the implications this trade has for the Myanmar farmers and Indian consumers. Modi paid a visit to the famed heritage city of Bagan, where the Archaeological Survey of India has done a "stellar work" in renovating the Ananda Temple after a 2016 earthquake.[201]

India is Myanmar's fifth largest trading partner and tenth largest source of foreign investments. India contributes only 1.36 percent of Myanmar's total foreign direct investment. By the end of June 2017, India's investment in Myanmar stood at US$ 740.64 million.[202] India-Myanmar bilateral trade saw a decline from US$ 2.16 billion in 2016-17 to US$ 1.60 billion in 2017-18.[203] India-Myanmar bilateral trade is expected to reach US$ 10 billion by the end of 2020 but that will require tremendous efforts from both the sides.[204]

• Maldives

The Maldives, with its 1,192 coral islands, is one of the world's most geographically dispersed countries, as well as the smallest Asian country by both land area and population, with around 3,85,000 inhabitants.[205] It is of key importance to India as it sits astride critical sea lanes of communication through which much of India's shipping passes. With the surprise defeat of autocratic President Abdulla Yameen in 23 September elections and the victory of opposition candidate Ibrahim Mohamed Solih of Maldivian Democratic Party (MDP), it is very much expected that India will likely regain its influence in the Maldivian Archipelago. However, India must learn from its experience with Sri Lanka where even after the defeat of President Mahinda Rajapaksa in 2015 elections, China has regained its influence over the new incumbent despite some initial hiccups because Sri Lanka's economy was under heavy Chinese debt. Maldives is also under similar situation – as a result of the infrastructure development plans signed by the two countries during Yameen's tenure, Maldives is now under huge Chinese debt – somewhere between US$ 1.3 and 3 billion – a figure that represents almost half of the country's GDP.[206] Morally and politically, the outcome of Maldivian elections represents the triumph of Indian patience[207] and its policy of non-intervention. In the hindsight one could visualize, had India intervened militarily in the Maldives, emulating the precedence of 1988, it would have antagonized the local populace – stirring their nationalistic sentiments and strengthening Islamic fundamentalists in the country that has produced hundreds of young jihadi fighters who had gone to join the Islamic State in Iraq and Syria (ISIS) – reportedly over 200 Maldivians and shockingly most of them were ex-military men of Maldives National Defense Force (MNDF).[208] Coordinating with the US, UK and the European Union and probably it was the intervention threat in being if the voting were not free and fair, India aided the electoral outcome.

Since November 1988, having crushed a coup attempt by mercenaries, India has been providing considerable economic assistance and training in the fields of health, civil society development, infrastructure development, disaster relief and telecommunications to Maldives. In 2008, following the first direct presidential elections in the Maldives, India committed to supporting and strengthening electoral systems and democratic structures. It was after the change in government in Male during the February 2012 "soft coup" that the new government started cozying up with China.[209] With China having made deep inroads in to what India once considered its natural sphere of influence, the strategic equation has now become different. Though within hours of the political upheaval, Mr. Solih had spoken to Indian Prime Minister Narendra Modi and publicly declared that India was the Maldives' "closest ally",[210] India has to tread cautiously while once again reasserting its influence in the Maldives.

Because of its closer geographical proximity to India vis-à-vis China, its vulnerability to natural disasters, for sustenance of its population, Maldives has to depend on India. Some of these peculiarities are:

- Sea distance from Male to China is in the range of 4301 to 4963 nautical miles (Mawei Port and Jiujang Port respectively), which will take 18 to 21 days for a ship to reach at 10-knot speed. Whereas in case of India, Port of Cochin is just 493 nautical miles while Mumbai is 934 nautical miles from Male – taking two to maximum four days by ship. Air distance from India to Maldives is 2142 km whereas in case of China it is 5838 km. A non-stop flight from Shanghai to Male takes 7 hrs 55 minutes while from India it takes only 2.38 hrs.
- Male city, with almost 38 percent of the total resident population of Maldives (129,381 persons in September 2014),[211] is located on a low-lying island in the Indian Ocean, has no natural water source and is entirely dependent on treated sea water. On 4 December 2014, a major fire had broken out in the city's lone water treatment plant,

causing extensive damage to the cabling of the generator resulting in disconnection of water supply. Left with no tap water safe for human consumption in Male, Maldives declared a state of crisis and appealed for aid from India, Sri Lanka, the United States and China. India had been the swiftest to respond: India's foreign ministry was contacted at night 4th December and the first Indian aircraft (IL-76) arrived in Male at 1315 hrs on the very next day with a large consignment of bottled water, followed by four more aircraft – IL-76 and C-17 carrying water later in the day. Indian Navy's patrol vessel INS Sukanya, carrying 35 tonnes of fresh water and two Reverse Osmosis (RO) plants on board capable of producing 20 tonnes of fresh water per day, arrived in Male at night. A large tanker vessel INS Deepak carrying 900 tonnes of fresh water was dispatched from Mumbai. India also dispatched spare parts and mechanics to assist in fixing the damaged machinery. While China could send water assistance via commercial flights on 06 December followed by a military vessel carrying 960 tonnes of fresh water to the Maldives (Obviously, considering the ship distance it would have arrived after the crisis was over).[212] In fact, it demonstrated India's capacity to serve as the Indian Ocean's "first responder" in times of crisis.

- There are over 5,000 expatriates (by an unofficial account almost 40,000) from the Maldives who live in India, in what is recorded as the second largest population of Maldivians living abroad after Sri Lanka.[213] India is a preferred destination for Maldivians for education, medical treatment, recreation and business. According to Indian Ministry of External Affairs, more and more Maldivians are seeking long-term visa for pursuing higher studies / medical treatment in India.[214] On the contrary, approximately 29,000 Indians live and work in Maldives and almost 22,000 of them live in Male. People from Kerala and Tamil Nadu have historically been in close contact with the Maldives through trade, which continues till today where Indian professionals and workers contribute to the Maldivian economy and society.[215] Indian tourists also account for close to 6 percent of tourists Maldives receives every year. There is no Maldivian presence in China. On the other hand, Chinese constitute one-third of the tourists coming to Maldives.

It may be remembered that one nation's vulnerability or weakness can become other nation's strength depending upon the relations they want to pursue. India and Maldives are socially, economically and geographically inter-linked. If they work together, it will be mutually beneficial to both nations, leading to a "win-win" arrangement.

With Mohamed Solih declaration of "India first" policy, the bilateral relations between the two countries appeared to be back on the course. Prime Minister Narendra Modi was the only head of state or government to be invited and was present during the swearing-in ceremony of the president-elect.[216] PM Modi will have to take the lead in strengthening relations, particularly in the fields of security, trade and development partnership:

- ✓ First, to reassert India's primacy of security in the Indian Ocean Region. India has planned to set up a network of coastal surveillance radars (CSR) from Sri Lanka down to the middle of the Indian Ocean in Mauritius. Cleared in 2011, this Rs 600 crore project was part of New Delhi's plans to enhance maritime domain awareness in the wake of the 26/11 Mumbai attack in which terrorists exploited the sea route.[217] While CSRs have been set up in Sri Lanka (6), Mauritius (8) and Seychelles (1), the first batch of 10 radars that were to come up in Maldives got delayed due to some minor differences. In 2009, India and Maldives had signed an agreement to set up radars on all 26 atolls. The Maldives radar chain was to be networked with the Indian coastal radar system, with a control center in India. The control center called Integrated Management and Analysis Center (IMAC) is already functional at Gurugram and gets a live feed from 50 coastal radar stations across the nation as well as systems in Sri Lanka, Mauritius and Seychelles.[218] The issue would have been resolved during Prime Minister Modi's planned visit in March 2015, which got curtailed. With the changed scenario now, the issue should be resolved with the new Maldivian government on priority and radars should be deployed to cover the gaps in surveillance.
- ✓ On 08 July 2013, India, Sri Lanka and the Maldives had signed a tripartite agreement on maritime cooperation to secure sea routes in the Indian Ocean Region.[219] This needs to be followed vigorously.
- ✓ India had signed a preferential trade agreement with Maldives in 1981, according to which, India supplies all essential commodities, aggregates

and river sand to Maldives, while the Maldives could sell anything it manufactured to India, without restrictions. Since the Maldives had tuna to export, it worked out well. But Maldives having signed FTA with China, it will open floodgates for cheap Chinese goods in to the Maldives. The 1981 agreement allowed Maldives unrestricted access to India but it had no space for third country re-exports. FTA is assessed by Indian officials as China's way of accessing the Indian market through its neighbors. In Sri Lanka too, the new SEZ in Hambantota is actually aimed at the Indian market.[220] This issue has to be taken care off with the new ruling dispensation in the Maldives. As the signs appear, the Maldives' new government is likely to pull out of FTA with China. Mohamed Nasheed, the Chief of the Maldivian Democratic Party, which leads the ruling federal alliance said, "*The trade imbalance between China and the Maldives is so huge that nobody would think of an FTA between such parties.*" He further added, "*China is not buying anything from us. It is a one-way treaty.*" He said that parliament would not pass the law changes required for the zero tariffs agreement to come in to force.[221]

- ✓ Total trade volume between the two countries has almost doubled from US$ 128.65 million in 2012-13 to US$ 222.68 million in 2017-18. However, while Indian exports have increased substantially from US$ 122.36 million to US$ 217.00 million, Maldivian exports to India have decreased leaving a trade deficit of almost US$ 211 million in 2017-18.[222] India's current exports to Maldives are four times as large as Chinese exports to the Maldives.

While China's strategy is focused on acquisition of military bases through infrastructure development based on debt trap, the Indian solution should be to enhance its bilateral trade, strengthen its cultural and historical relations with Maldivians by promoting tourism and, boost its defense and maritime security cooperation through capacity building, training, information sharing and joint exercises.

Though Solih's party has previously said that it would review Chinese investments but given the scale of Chinese debt one should not depend on such rhetoric. Rather, India should find a way out in collaboration with other friendly countries to provide soft loan to Maldives for refinancing Chinese debt. Responding to the Maldives' "India first" policy, Prime Minister

Narendra Modi announced a $1.4 billion package for the Maldives on the occasion of the visit of President Ibrahim Solih to India in December 2018. The package is in addition to a loan of $25 million that India gave during a visit by Maldives' new Foreign Minister Abdullah Shahid in November 2018. However, President Solih,while speaking to press about his state visit to India made it clear that the $1.4 billion financial assistance offered by India would not be used to repay its debt to China. Solih emphasized that the assistance would be solely utilized to develop the country's infrastructure and ease budgetary constraints. Regarding massive debt from China, President Solih said that they would talk to China for reducing interest rates and maybe extending repayment periods on those loans.[223]

- **Mauritius**

With some 70 percent of Mauritius population being of Indian origin, the bilateral relationships between the two countries have always been driven by the deep cultural ties. For decades, India has been the major contributor of military equipment and training to Mauritius. The head of Mauritius' navy and the Mauritian national security advisor are Indian officers. Beijing is aspiring to maintain a permanent presence in the island nations of the Indian Ocean region. Prime Minister Narendra Modi took a very timely initiative to visit Mauritius in March 2015. During his visit, Indian government signed an agreement for the development of infrastructure on Agalega Island. It was reportedly announced that India would upgrade airfield and port facilities at North Agalega Island, located some 1100 km Northeast of Madagascar, which is spread over 70 sq km and is closer to India's Southern coast. These facilities will enhance the capabilities of the Mauritian Defense Forces in safeguarding their interests in the Outer Island. Agalega could be used as a staging point for Indian Navy and will substantially help India's maritime reconnaissance efforts throughout the Western Indian Ocean.[224] Modi commissioned the US$ 50.8 million, 1300-ton India-built warship Barracuda in to the Mauritian National Coast Guard on the country's national day on 12 March 2015. This was the first of such sales to this strategic island nation, while the Indian government cleared export of 13 more warships to Mauritius.[225] India extended a US$ 500 million concessional credit line to Mauritius and promised to build petroleum storage and bunking facility, as also a second cyber city. Most important aspect in the strategic context is the recognition and encouragement given to Mauritius to play a stellar role in the IORA with its secretariat located in Mauritius.[226] Indian President Ram Nath Kovind visited Mauritius and Madagascar in mid-March 2018 when India announced a new US$ 100 million line of credit for defense procurement by Mauritius and a defense cooperation agreement with Madagascar is also being planned.[227] Mauritius also hosts the World Hindi Secretariat. In this respect, India has a great edge over China and this advantage should not be allowed to be diluted.

• Seychelles

Currently, India and Seychelles share close military ties as New Delhi helps the island nation secure its EEZ by presenting it surveillance aircraft and patrolling ships. Prime Minister Narendra Modi's visit to Seychelles on 10-11 March 2015 was the first visit by an Indian Prime Minister in 33 years. An agreement was signed between India and Seychelles during Modi's visit for the development of infrastructure on the uninhabited Assumption Island that is near the Northern end of the Mozambique Channel. Along with the Suez Canal, the Channel is the main route for shipping between the Atlantic and Pacific Oceans. Control over this and other so-called Indian Ocean 'choke points' has long been a key objective of the Indian Navy. This deal will allow the Indian Navy access to these facilities. Interestingly, in the 1960s the US had also planned to build a base on an island near Assumption before it settled on Diego Garcia.[228] Later, there was political opposition to this move in Seychelles, when Seychelles President Danny Faure was quoted as saying by local media in June 2018 that the country would develop military facilities at the island on its own and that the project with India "will not move forward". However, the issue got resolved during President Faure's visit to New Delhi on 25 June 2018, and both countries agreed to work together on a project to develop the naval base at the Assumption Island, keeping each other's concerns in mind. India also announced US$ 100 million credit to Seychelles for augmenting its defense capabilities. India had gifted one Dornier Maritime Patrol aircraft to Seychelles in 2013 and the second one, promised during Modi's visit in 2015, was presented on 26 June so that it could reach Seychelles before its National Day on 29 June 2018.[229] Prime Minister Modi's visit was concluded with signing of four bilateral agreements and he emphasized the importance of jointly developing marine ecology and marine resources, the so-called "Blue Economy".[230] An expansion of the India-Sri Lanka-Maldives trilateral maritime security arrangement to include Mauritius and Seychelles is very much on the cards.[231]

• Vietnam

Vietnam is a proven barrier to Chinese expansionism, as is evident from their stance against China in South China Sea. India and Vietnam had signed a defense agreement way back in 1994. India has been providing submarine training to Vietnamese sailors at Navy's submarine school INS Satavahana in Visakhapatnam since October 2013 and it is likely to train Vietnam Air Force pilots in flying Sukhoi fighters as well. During President Pranab Mukherjee's visit to Vietnam in September 2014, India offered a US$ 100 million concessional line of credit, under which India is transferring four naval offshore patrol boats to Vietnam.[232] The two countries signed a vision statement for next five years in 2015 and a MoU on cooperation between the coast guards of the two countries. Prime Minister Modi's visit to Vietnam in September 2016 was the first in the last 15 years by an Indian Prime Minister, where he announced a new defense credit line of US$ 500 million and elevated the strategic partnership to the comprehensive strategic partnership, signifying India's deep commitment to help Vietnam to build its defense capabilities.[233] India is now willing to sell the BrahMos supersonic cruise missiles to Vietnam, a long-standing demand by Hanoi. The previous Indian government was little hesitant, citing reservations by Russia, being a co-developer but Russia has now given its consent. India has agreed to provide civil nuclear cooperation to Vietnam and it has started the process to sell its small 220 MW nuclear reactors to Vietnam.[234] Vietnam has also granted the Indian Navy basing rights at the NhaTrang Port, which is situated close to Cam Ranh Bay, extensively used by the Americans earlier. This will allow Indian warships to make regular port calls and get a foothold in the South China Sea.[235] Indian and Vietnamese leaders have agreed to work with Japan in a trilateral format to coordinate positions on security and economic policies, a step, which will have big implications for the balance of power in Asia.[236]

Bilateral trade between the two countries has reached US$ 12.83 billion in 2017-18.[237] Vietnamese Prime Minister Nguyen Xuan Phuc has expressed the hope that two-way trade between the two countries would reach the targeted US$ 15 billion by 2020 by bolstering investment ties in areas of India's strength and Vietnam's demand, while minimizing and removing trade obstacles.[238] During Modi's visit, an agreement was signed between the two countries under which Larsen & Toubro would design and build vessels for the Vietnam Coast Guard, and to transfer ship building technologies to Vietnam. Energy is another area of cooperation between India and Vietnam – while India's ONGC Videsh has been working with Vietnam in oil exploration activities, India's Tata Power was awarded a US$ 1.8 billion thermal power project in Vietnam's SocTrang Province – further strengthening their energy relations.[239]

In spite of Vietnam and China having territorial disputes in the South China Sea, their economic relations are robust with the volume of their bilateral trade having already surpassed US$ 100 billion mark in 2016.[240] Thus it is highly unlikely that Vietnam will do anything to jeopardize its economic interests with China. While India's relations with Vietnam in the field of defense and security cooperation are robust and dynamic but to make a mark in economic field, India has to undertake transformational measures.

• Mongolia

Narendra Modi became the first Indian Prime Minister to visit Mongolia, 60 years after both countries formally established diplomatic relations on 24 December 1955. India had played an important role in getting Mongolia membership to key international forums including the United Nations (UN), despite strong opposition from China and Taiwan. Mongolia was finally admitted to the UN in 1961. In a reciprocal gesture, Mongolia co-sponsored a 1972 UN resolution with India and Bhutan for the recognition of the newly liberated Bangladesh.[241]

Sandwiched between Russia to the North and China on the other three sides, Mongolia has evolved the concept of the "third neighbor". While it strikes a balance between the two geographic neighbors and avoids domination by either, it seeks out friends or "virtual neighbors" in other regions, both in the West and in Asia.[242] Post the Sino-Soviet split, Mongolia sided with the Soviet Union and relations between Mongolia and China remained tense primarily due to China's claims of lost territory and fears of encroachment in the country. Post-1984, their relations took a turn and today China is Mongolia's biggest trading partner.[243] However, China will always put constraints on its independent foreign policy. For instance, in December 2016 China hiked transit tariffs on Mongolian trucks, as part of its action to protest Dalai Lama's visit to Mongolia.[244]

India-Mongolian bilateral ties have been growing to counter the influence of China. In the recent past, relations between the two countries have been largely centered around increased bilateral cooperation in areas like defense and security, trade, and civilian nuclear energy. In 2009, Mongolia was among the first to sign a Uranium deal with India. Joint India-Mongolia military exercise 'Nomadic Elephant' was held for the first time in 2004 and its 12th iteration was held at Vairengte, Mizoram for two weeks in April 2017. India is also an active participant in annual week-long joint training exercise called the 'Khaan Quest' hosted by Mongolia.[245]

Incorporating Mongolia as an integral part of India's 'Act East' Policy, Prime Minister Modi announced on 17 May 2015 in Ulan Bator, a US$ 1 billion line of credit to support expansion of Mongolia's economic capacity and infrastructure. The two Prime Ministers agreed to deepen defense cooperation and upgraded the comprehensive partnership to "Strategic Partnership".[246] While India has positioned radar systems in Mongolia, able to monitor Chinese missile tests, it is also having a quiet discussion over basing rights.[247] India will help Mongolia to develop its dairy sector based on the Amul model of cooperatives.[248]

India has had deep historical and cultural linkages of over 2600 years with Mongolia, a Buddhist majority nation. Buddhism was spread in Mongolia by Emperor Ashoka and his disciples. People from Mongolia often travel to India to visit the Buddhist sites. A large number of Indian literary works like Panchtantra and Ramayana have been published in Mongolian language. Hindi films are very popular in Mongolia and the TV serial Mahabharata dubbed in Mongolian had been telecast on Ulaanbaatar TV.[249] There is a huge potential for enhancing two-way ties based on Buddhism and historical links, which Indian Prime Minister highlighted during his address to Mongolian Parlaiment.[250]

• Bhutan

Bhutan has been India's time-tested and all-weather friend in the region. Unlike Nepal, it has never adopted a balance-India policy by engaging China. It has denied space to the Indian insurgents operating in the Northeast to the extent that in 2003, the then King Jigme Singye Wangchuck personally led the offensive by the Royal Bhutan army to cleanse anti-India insurgents from the Bhutanese soil.[251]

It is not a secret that China has been trying to reduce India's influence in Bhutan by endeavoring to establish full-fledged diplomatic relations, as they have offered to open a consulate in Thimpu. But India's major concern is the way China wants to resolve its border dispute with Bhutan. Bhutan has dispute on 4,500 sq km of land with China in its Northern and Western parts (almost

10 percent of the total area of the country). In 2012, China had offered to exchange 495 sq km of area of Bayul Pasamlung and Jakarlung Valleys in Bhutan's North (Bumthag) for Sinchulumpa Dramana and Shaktoe with a total area of 269 km in the West (adjacent to Sikkim and Siliguri in the tri-junction area of India, Bhutan and China). Bhutan's first elected Prime Minister Jigmi Y Thinley had given his consent to Chinese Premier Wen Jiabao in Rio de Janeiro during their meeting on 21 June 2012. However, this deal was aborted following the humiliating defeat of Thinley and his party in 2013 general elections in Bhutan.[252] This deal could have proven detrimental to India's strategic interests as China was likely to have access to the most sensitive Chicken Neck belt of India. China has also been laying claim to Doklam Plateau, which ultimately led to Doklam Stand-off in June 2017. These are important areas of concern for India's own boundary talks with China. The short-sighted policy of cutting fuel subsidy, just before the elections in Bhutan, did more harm than any good to India's age-old relations with Bhutan.[253]

Narendra Modi's decision to make Bhutan as his first foreign destination after becoming Prime Minister signaled a significant shift in India's neighborhood policy. Modi's visit to Bhutan was not solely guided by economic interests but reflected a synergy that took an entire gamut of relations, i.e. foreign policy, security and economic cooperation. Bhutan has been central to India's two major strategic policies – the 'Neighborhood First Policy' and the 'Act East Policy'.[254] It was in fitness of this strategic synergy that Modi's visit to Bhutan was signified and encompassed various initiatives: He laid the foundation stone for the development of 600 MW Kholongchu hydroelectric power station,[255] a joint venture between India and Bhutan; inaugurated the Supreme Court building constructed by India; doubled the amount of scholarships being provided to Bhutanese students in India, which will now be worth Rs two crore; promised to assist Bhutan in setting up a digital library which will provide access to Bhutanese youth to two million books and periodicals. Modi described his vision for bilateral relations as "*Bharat to Bhutan (B2B)*" i.e. "Bharat should stand for Bhutan and Bhutan for Bharat".[256]

For Bhutan's 11th Five Year Plan (2013-2018), whose key objectives included self-reliance and inclusive green socio-economic development, India's contribution of Rs 4,500 crore represented 68 percent of total external assistance received by the country. In addition, India committed assistance of Rs 500 crore under an economic stimulus plan.[257] Recently, a sum of Rs 2,650 crore from the Ministry of External Affairs (MEA) budget has been kept aside for Bhutan (among other countries in the neighborhood) as an aid for technical and economic development such as the hydro-electric power projects.[258] Governed by the India-Bhutan Trade and Transit Agreement of 1972, the total bilateral trade between the two countries stood at Rs 8,723 crore in 2016 with total imports being Rs 5528.5 crore (82 percent of Bhutan's total imports) and exports recorded as Rs 3205.2 crore including electricity (90 percent of Bhutan's total exports).[259] Government of India also reimburses the excise duty paid by Bhutan to buy manufactured goods from India. Bhutan also enjoys duty free transit of its exports to third countries.[260]

Bhutan has the potential to generate 24,000 MW of hydropower. India has pledged to assist Bhutan in developing at least 10,000 MW of hydropower and import the surplus electricity to India by 2020, according to the 2006 India-Bhutan agreement on hydropower, with an additional protocol in 2009. Under this model, Bhutan not only gets electricity for its own use, but also exports the surplus power to India, earning much needed revenue and foreign exchange. India gets relatively cheap power. Hydropower exports contribute around 40 percent to Bhutan's revenue and 25 percent of its GDP.[261]

In the recently held elections in October 2018, the Druk Nyamrup Tshogpa (DNT) was able to convincingly defeat the left-leaning Druk Phuensum Tshogpa (DPT). DNT won 30 seats in the 47-seat Bhutanese parliament. Its leader Lotay Tshering, a Dhaka University educated MBBS, has made it clear that he would be guided by the King in conducting foreign policy and ties with India are non-negotiable. DNT's manifesto, with its slogan 'Narrowing the Gap' promised social and economic development, striving to transform Bhutan to a developed country by 2045.[262]

Though India and Bhutan share an exemplary bond but China will make all the efforts to lure Bhutan in to its own sphere of influence by offering greater economic incentives, through influx of greater number of tourists and even influencing the younger generation of Bhutan through internet and social media. Cracks are often visible in India-Bhutan friendship because there are certain issues, which may appear to be trivial but require timely intervention to build a successful bilateral relationship:

- The over-dependence of Bhutan on imports from India has led to the neglect of an important sector like agriculture, which could have otherwise provided substitutes for many products imported from India. The share of the agriculture sector in GDP declined from 24 percent in 2004 to 16 percent in 2013. The decrease in the share of agriculture in GDP is attributed to structural changes from an agrarian economy to a hydropower and service dominated one. Though the latter has led to higher GDP growth rates but it has a narrow employment base. According to the Asian Development Bank (ADB) report "Since the development of the hydropower subsector began in the 1980s, the share of agriculture in GDP has been steadily displaced".[263] The share of agriculture sector in Bhutan's GDP was approximately 55 percent in 1985.[264] The ADB has recommended to improve agriculture sector to help achieve more balanced and inclusive growth.

- Bhutan's geographically disadvantaged location has made its economy hugely dependent on India. Over 60 percent of Bhutan's expenditure is on imports from India; 90-95 percent of what Bhutan borrows from India finds its way back to India. This is not only detrimental to Bhutan's sustainable growth but also unsuitable for a healthy bilateral relationship with India.[265] The fact that the money borrowed is not a significant investment in Bhutan is a complaint that should be addressed by Indian policy makers well in time before this view gets proliferated uncontrollably in the future. According to views prevalent amongst Bhutan's business community, Bhutanese are not actively participating in economic activities; for example, most of the important sectors – like mining and construction – are in Indian hands. Even non-competent sectors, not needing specific skills, such as that of crushing stones are given to Indian contractors, which is being resented by Bhutanese. Even the fundamentals of hydropower industry are being questioned by some Bhutanese on account of the massive Indian influence and accompanying economic participation.[266]
- India's assistance in the area of hydropower is also being viewed with suspicion. Critics have argued that the economic benefits from collaboration in hydropower have declined. Not only the commissioning of the projects have been delayed but their costs have escalated massively – almost two to three times. Initial financing terms, where India would finance the entire project costs with a 60 percent grant component and 40 percent loan have been reversed with 60-70 percent as loan component and interest rates also higher. Economic analysis has revealed that the net profit per unit of electricity sold has fallen sharply since 2007 and the hydropower has contributed to steep rise in Bhutan's debt. Not only the hydropower projects are having massive environmental impacts, these have failed to build local

capacities, with most of the contracts going to Indian companies.[267] The high growth rates of Bhutan's economy have been driven by the hydropower sector but without a commensurate increase in gainful employment for a rapidly growing and educated labor force, which poses significant economic challenges.[268]

- India's subsidized exports to Bhutan comprising of almost all essential goods have hurt the growth of domestic sectors within Bhutan while helping India exercise its hold on Bhutanese market. India's stranglehold over Bhutan's economy along with unfair business practices often leads to economic crisis such as the debt and the rupee crunch.[269]

Of late, the Bhutanese government is also willing to have a deeper engagement with China in areas of tourism, education, culture and agriculture etc. Though it may be too early to predict that China can hurt India's stake in Bhutan but it is a forewarning that India may not continue to enjoy the leverage it always had with Bhutan, if China is allowed to penetrate into India's sphere of influence in Bhutan. Bhutan is on its way to democratization therefore the aspirations of large number of stakeholders and particularly the youth have to be addressed by India in a pragmatic manner, rather than focusing on ruling dispensation only. Domestic economic activity in Bhutan must be encouraged. Indian companies should provide technological and managerial expertise with greater participation by locals who should be imparted requisite skill training.

Accelerate Policy Implementation

Modi government has enunciated excellent policies to make India a great power such as "Make in India", "Swacchh Bharat" or "Clean India", "Digital India", "Skill India", "Clean Ganga" and so on but implementation has either been inordinately delayed or it has been poor except in case of "Digital India". The blame should lie at the bureaucracy for: their lack of will to implement, lack of energy, lack of expertise, their habit of taking circuitous route to approach and resolve any problem, i.e., the so-called red-tapism. Otherwise, it should not take four and half years to implement what has been planned in the first year. In military's parlance, if one intentionally fails to implement the orders of his leader, it is regarded as disloyalty or otherwise it is gross inefficiency and in both the cases he ought to be removed from that position. It was an excellent idea propounded by the present government to appoint officers from different fields as joint secretaries in selected ministries.[270] Only the experts can produce "out-of-the-box" solutions to certain problems. For example, the trade imbalance between India and China cannot be rectified just by increasing the export of home-produced raw material because the enough may not be available in the country to satisfy their demand. Similarly, India's manufacturing sector will take time to come up and produce items at globally competitive rates. Only a commerce expert with deep knowledge of global trade can resolve these dilemmas.

As regards foreign policy, strength of India's diplomatic corps is miniscule compared to its counterparts in the United States, China and even Brazil. According to the Ministry of External Affairs, India's diplomatic corps consists of around 1,750 officers (750 IFS Grade-A officers, 250 IFS Grade-B personnel, military attaches and other officers).[271] According to Naresh Chandra Task Force Report of 2012, "*The Ministry of External Affairs does not have enough diplomats to anticipate, analyze and act on contemporary challenges*".[272] According to former foreign secretary Shyam Saran, "*You cannot run an expansive foreign policy of an emerging great power with less than a thousand diplomats and a budget that treats the Ministry of External Affairs as a side show*". He further adds, "*There is also the issue of quality that can only be improved through better recruitment and capacity building*".[273] Further having been selected through a tough competitive examination, the IAS/IFS cadre considers itself to be a "Know All" and something superior than the remainder class, without having an institutionalized system to carry out timely training for handling higher appointments or developing subject expertise. All these factors lead to failure in monitoring the pulse of people in the friendly foreign countries, their attitude toward India, and persistent delay in delivery of projects promised by Indian leaders, particularly in neighboring countries. This allows Indian areas of influence being encroached upon by China, resulting in crisis management to win back those countries in to our fold but at the same time it results in loss of face, undermining our international credibility. Mr Shyam Saran has suggested creation of an effective, efficient and autonomous development agency to overcome the shortcomings and ensure delivery of projects in time.[274] This is a short-term and adhoc measure. The sole responsibility for implementation of policies/projects enunciated by the Political leader of the country, whether within the country or on foreign shores should be that of the bureaucratic cadre, the purpose for which it has been created and they should be geared up for the task accordingly.

Enhance Investment in Building Up and Modernizing India's Defense Forces

Investment in a country's defense is like insurance, which if taken well in time then it acts like a safeguard against any unforeseen eventualities but it cannot be purchased after a disaster had already struck. Thus nations spent money on their armed forces during peace time in anticipation that they will protect the nation in case of a surprise attack by an enemy. With a share of 1.56 percent of the estimated GDP of 2017-18 and in the following year also 1.58 percent of the GDP for 2018-19, the defense budget of India is the lowest since 1956-57 despite the fact that there is a huge void in India's defense preparedness and the armed forces have grave shortages in many areas ranging from ammunition, assault rifles, bullet-proof jackets, night-fighting devices to howitzers, missiles, helicopters, fighters and warships. The allocation is not in consonance with India's security challenges and threats along the Western and Northern borders.[275] Major General B C Khanduri (Retd), Chairman of the Standing Committee on Defense, who posed uncomfortable questions to the government about the critical low stock of armaments and 68 percent of equipment with armed forces being of vintage category, was removed on 18 September 2018.[276]

Just by celebrating Deepawali with troops at Siachen Glacier during his first year or emulating the United States by asking people to welcome the soldiers in uniform at railway stations or airports with clapping, Prime Minister Narendra Modi may be trying to impress the common public about his respect or love for the Indian armed forces but ground reality is that he has proven himself no different than the previous government leaders, who have systematically ignored and downgraded the armed forces. Addressing Combined Army Commanders' Conference and projecting his desire for "jointness" and "integration" carries no meaning unless a serious modernization drive for armed forces is set in motion. The incremental addition of few aircraft, ships or guns will not make India a great power. Prime Minister Narendra Modi has the charisma and the will to take the nation forward therefore he needs to have personal indulgence for restoring the glory of the Indian Military, both in terms of material and morale of its men. One cannot lower his guard by considering the friendly stance of his opponent. If capability is there, a nation can change its intentions overnight based on its national interests. Therefore, follow the Army's famous dictum "*More you sweat in peace, Less you bleed in war*".

5

Conclusion

"As our (India and China) relations are deepening and our regional and international role evolving, there are expectations from our two countries to lead Asia and usher in an Asian Century."

—Sushma Swaraj, India's Minister of External Affairs

"China and India, two great ancient civilizations, have great potentials in terms of people-to-people exchanges."

—Wang Yi, China's State Councilor and Foreign Minister

THE geographical heart of the global economy is now located in the 'Indo-Pacific' Region, wherein almost every Asian country has China rather than the United States as its largest trading partner and China's share is continuing to grow. China's rapid economic growth and industrialization has led to a tremendous increase in its energy requirements. Interestingly, China is dependent upon sea-transportation for 90 percent of its foreign trade and 82 percent of its energy needs in the form of oil and gas, which pass through the Sea lanes of communication of the Indian Ocean but more importantly via the Malacca Straits.[1] Bypassing the Indonesian archipelago via pipelines across Myanmar and Pakistan is not a viable option for China as it would meet only a fraction of its energy requirements. Therefore, Chinese leadership is fully aware that to become a world power, it is necessary to become a maritime power, which is capable of defending its interests in the farseas.[2] It may be too farfetched for China to challenge the American military supremacy on the high seas for a decade or even more. Hence, China has devised a strategy to expand its strategic space in the South China Sea by creating and militarizing the artificial islands to restrict the freedom of maneuver of the US Navy and extend its reach in to the Indian Ocean by getting bases and increasing the presence of its naval vessels. Further, China has visualized that to alter the Asian balance of power, it does not have to match America's military strength. Therefore, simultaneously, it has developed asymmetric capabilities like Anti-access/Area-denial (A2/AD) capabilities, which can significantly restrict America's ability to dominate its land and maritime peripheries. Thus, there is a common maritime challenge from China faced by India in the Indian Ocean and by the United States in the Pacific Ocean, or in other words, there has emerged a common Indo-Pacific strategic challenge leading to significant US-India naval convergence.[3]

Somewhere around 1980s, China and India were roughly equal in terms of aggregate economic size and per capita income. But a delayed decision by more than a decade by Indian leadership to liberalize its economy has left it far behind China – China's economy is 4.7 times larger than India's and it also spends nearly four times as much on defense as India. China's real GDP growth peaked in 2007 at 14.2 percent but starting 2010, its economic growth was on downward spiral dropping to 6.8 percent in 2017[4] while India has emerged as the fastest growing economy in the world.

India sees herself as co-equal of China and is not willing to settle for a secondary place in the Asian Balance of power and in the International system where Beijing intends to play a larger role in setting and enforcing rules. If China is not prepared to accommodate India's geopolitical interests and keep playing power games in India's immediate neighborhood then India will not be left with any other alternative but to balance China.[5] In international politics, increases in power, especially a rival's growing strength can be checked by countervailing power. The means of accomplishing this are internal balancing and external balancing.[6] Internal balancing involves building up economic and military resources to achieve a measure of strategic parity if not strict equality. External balancing is achieved through alliances and partnerships.[7]

China has been building its strategic capabilities comprehensively and has undertaken reforms, restructuring and modernization of its armed forces in a time bound manner – ranging from transforming the border infrastructure to cyber warfare capabilities – so as to form a modern military force by 2035. Whereas India's efforts in internal balancing are albeit slow and not commensurate with its ambition to become a great power – whether it is construction of border infrastructure, modernization of its armed forces, developing an indigenous defense industrial base or even enhancing its manufacturing capabilities under "Make in India". Upgrading its human resource potential through National Skill development mission so that its demographic dividend can be gainfully exploited has left much to be desired.

In respect of External balancing, Indian government under the leadership of Prime Minister Narendra Modi has not only strengthened the strategic partnership with the United States, Japan, Russia, Vietnam, Indonesia and other nations but has taken it to new heights. India's stated official policy is to maintain 'Strategic Autonomy' and it will avoid being drawn in to an alliance type of relationship[8] but as it is evident from the past history; India is not alien to balance of power strategies. Its defacto alliance with the Soviet Union during the 1970s was a classic balancing act against Sino-U.S. rapprochement[9] and its practical utility was demonstrated to the whole world in December 1971 when President Nixon had dispatched the US Seventh Fleet's Task Force 74, led by the nuclear powered aircraft carrier Enterprise to the Bay of Bengal with sinister designs but was neutralized due to prompt action by Soviet nuclear-armed flotilla on the sea and movement of land forces against the Chinese.[10] Considering the present international environment of uncertainty when the United States wants to stay as a sole superpower while China is challenging its supremacy and other emerging powers are seeking multi-polarity, it requires great political skills to deftly maneuver through the current turbulence. In other words, without courting conflict with China, the partnership with the United States has to be strengthened and without antagonizing the United States, India's time-tested strategic relationship with Russia should not be diluted. At the same time, technological and economic strength of Japan should be co-opted to build connectivity and infrastructure in India's immediate neighborhood as also in the extended neighborhood to strengthen democratic forces in these countries, lest they become victims of Chinese debt trap. All these are being achieved by Prime Minister Narendra Modi with great finesse through what foreign affairs analysts describe as a diplomatic balancing act, unmatched by many of his predecessors. For instance, despite the threat of the so-called U.S. Law, Countering America's Adversaries Through Sanctions Act (CAATSA) and knowing fully well its implications, Modi government has gone ahead in signing the US$ 4.5 billion deal with Russia for supply of S-400 Air Defense System. The United States will continue to pursue what it considers its national interest and the challenge for India is to safeguard its own national interests. Acquisition of S-400 Air Defense System is being considered as a strategic necessity as its both the Western and Eastern neighbors are nuclear armed and the former is posing the threat of battlefield tactical nuclear weapons. Further, India and Russia are likely to sign a logistic supply agreement soon that will allow their military forces to share each other's facilities on similar lines as with the United States. Leasing of another Akula Class nuclear-powered attack submarine from Russia is in talks as the 10 years lease of INS Chakra is coming to an end this year.[11] Moreover, India's share of arms acquisition from Russia had come down and not only India has been increasingly acquiring American equipment but is cooperating with the United States on several critical strategic interests.[12] The U.S. Deputy Secretary of State, William Burns had noted that, "*India's strong presence across the Indian and Pacific Oceans is a source of comfort [for the United States] and affirms its potential as a net security provider in the maritime domain. Towards this end, the United States is interested in working with India... as we explore future maritime security cooperation.*"[13] Recently, the signing of the Communications, Compatibility and Security Agreement (COMCASA) in September 2018 between the two countries, which was a follow-up to the earlier U.S.-India Logistics Exchange Memorandum of Agreement (LEMOA) in 2016 has significantly deepened India's military relationship with the United States, particularly in the maritime sphere.[14] The United States needs India more than India needs the United States, not only to balance China but it has several interests in India: Defense sales, vibrant market and convergent perspectives on the Indo-Pacific, which it would not like to sacrifice.[15] As a logical conclusion, according to the provisions in the 2019 US defense budget, the US President should exercise his powers to waive the sanctions against India in respect of Russia. Beside giving temporary waivers from sanctions for India and seven other countries for import of Iranian crude oil, the US government has provided for an exception from the imposition of certain sanctions with respect to Iranian port of Chabahar that India has developed and will be used for logistics support to Afghanistan. That is an encouraging step, further strengthening the US-India relationship.

China has reached a stage that given its economic might and kind of investment it is making to attain technological prowess in emerging fields like Artificial Intelligence, Robotics and cyber space that the United States will find it difficult to counter China without support from countries like India and Japan. Only sale of military equipment may not be adequate unless the United States makes a serious effort for technology transfer to India so that the latter can develop its own defense industrial base. Further, trade war alone cannot prevent China from indulging in intellectual property thefts and unfair trade practices to attain its target of becoming a "world manufacturing power" by 2025 – the state-driven "Made in China 2025" (MIC2025) plan unveiled in 2015 that aimed to lift the country's industries to take on the Western tech giants in cutting-edge technologies.[16] Interestingly, in August 2018, a little-known mainland Chinese start-up proudly announced it had "broken the American monopoly" with the development of an original web browser – Redcore. But Beijing-based Redcore's claim to fame was short-lived – its software was quickly found to have traces of Google's Chrome. Redcore was forced into a swift public climb-down, an incident that not only confirmed Beijing's strong-arm tactics for technology transfers and intellectual property theft but it was also a reality check for China on the gap it faces with the US in its quest to become a technical superpower.[17]

It is because the Western companies moved manufacturing to China for making use of its cheap labor and shifted supply chains for assembling of high-end ICT products (like Apple) that China's economy grew tremendously. The United States can help India to boost its manufacturing sector by shifting some of its companies to India or even utilize Indian IT companies to assist the United States in designing new America-based value chains and factories.[18] Indian IT companies will not only earn revenue for India but will help create jobs for Americans – a "win-win" situation for both.

Finally, the influence of conflict, competition and cooperation on China-India relations will continue to produce a somewhat unbalanced power dynamic. The outright conflict may be unlikely as both countries want peace and tranquility for economic prosperity but friction between the two powers will remain until the basic causes of conflict are removed. The current Chinese and Indian leadership should be given the credit for pursuing mutual cooperation despite their litany of differences. The buzz words like 'competitive cooperation' or 'competition plus cooperation' between China and India are away from ground reality. China is far more economically dynamic than India and the former will always assert its economic influence over India's neighbors to draw them in to its own sphere by manipulating their leaders such as in Sri Lanka, Nepal and the Maldives. There is going to be more competition than cooperation between the two countries. However, India must focus on long-term relationships with its neighboring countries, which should be based on enhancing people-to-people contact, strengthening common bond of religion and culture, developing their infrastructure in a time bound manner, building up institutions and most importantly respecting the opinion of their people to reinforce the democratic process.

NOTES

Chapter 1: Introduction

1. Enrico Marelli and Marcello Signorelli, "China and India: Openness, Trade and Effects on Economic Growth", *The European Journal of Comparative Economics*, Vol.8, n.1, p.131, available at http://www.academia.edu/5941663/China_and_India_Openness_Trade_and_Effects_on_Economic_Growth
2. "Historical Statistics for the World Economy 1 - 2003 AD", available at www.ggdc.net/maddison/historical_statistics/horizontal-file_03-2007.xls (China with a population of 138 million had annual GDP of $82.8 billion (1990 "international" dollars), constituting 22.3% share of world GDP, whereas India with a population of 165 million people had annual GDP of $90.8 billion, forming 24.4% share of world GDP)
3. The World Fact Book, Central Intelligence Agency (US), available at https://www.cia.gov/library/publications/resources/the-world-factbook/geos/ch.html; and https://www.cia.gov/library/publications/resources/the-world-factbook/geos/in.html (China's GDP in FY 2017 at US $11.94 Trillion in terms of Official Exchange Rate was 4.89 times larger than India's GDP of US $2.439 Trillion in the same year. According to Chinese Envoy Luo Zhaohui, China's GDP in 2017 was US $12.3 Trillion. However, in terms of Purchasing Power Parity [PPP], China's GDP was US $ 23.12 Trillion in 2017, which became 2.4 times larger than India's GDP of US $ 9.447 Trillion at PPP.)
4. "Full text of Xi Jinping's report at 19th CPC National Congress", *China Daily*, 04 November 2017, available at http://www.chinadaily.com.cn/china/19thcpcnationalcongress/2017-11/04/content_34115212.htm
5. Brigadier (Dr.) Rajeev Bhutani, "Rise of China: 2030 and Its Strategic Implications", Pentagon Press, New Delhi, 2015, p.278.
6. "National Security Strategy of the United States of America", December 2017, pp. 45-46.
7. Rup Narayan Das, "India-China Relations – A New Paradigm", Institute for Defence Studies &Analyses (IDSA) Monograph Series No.19, May 2013, New Delhi, pp. 30-31; and "Text of the Prime Minister's Letter to US President Bill Clinton", Embassy of India, Washington DC, 13 May 1998, available at http://www.indianembassy.org/industrel/pmletter.htm; and "China is Enemy No 1: George", Indian Express, 3 May 1998.
8. The quintessence of human wisdom regarding civil authority is found in the 'Shanti Parva' and 'Anushasana Parva' of the Mahabharata. In these sections of the epic, Bhishma's description of the essentials of statesmanship comprises one of the finest portions of this sacred text, available at https://www.revolvy.com/page/Shanti-Parva?
9. "World has enough space for growth ambitions of India, China", *Zee News*, 27 October 2010, available at http://zeenews.india.com/news/nation/world-has-enough-space-for-growth-

ambitions-of-india-china_664081.html

10. Michael Ignatieff, "Enemies vs. Adversaries", *The New York Times*, 16 October 2013, available at http://www.nytimes.com/2013/10/17/opinion/enemies-vs-adversaries.html
11. Nirupama Rao, "China May Be an Adversary, But Making It an Enemy Will Not Serve India", The Wire, 06 October 2017, available at https://thewire.in/184678/india-china-relations-adversary-enemy/
12. Global Trends 2030: Alternative Worlds", US National Intelligence Council, p.25.
13. N.K. Singh, "With tectonic changes, 21st Century is India's", *Hindustan Times*, New Delhi, Wednesday, 22 November 2017.
14. Samuel Sherraden, "Putting China's Low Household Consumption in Perspective", New America Foundation's World Economic Roundtable, 15 March 2011, pp1-3. Available at http://roundtable.newamerica.net/blogposts/2011/
15. N.K. Singh, op.cit.
16. Hu Weijia, "India could compete with China by using an appropriate economic growth model", *Global Times*, 05 March 2018, available at www.globaltimes.cn/content/1091910.html
17. H.E. Luo Zhaohui, "Turn the page to a new chapter", The Hindu, 22 September 2017, available at https://www.thehindu.com/todays-paper/tp-opinion/turn-the-page-to-a-new-chapter/article19731914.ece
18. "Remarks by Ambassador Luo Zhaohui at CII Seminar on China-India Relations", 03 January 2018, Claridges Hotel, New Delhi, available at in.china-embassy.org/eng/gdxw/t1524943.htm
19. Shubhajit Roy, "In breaking of ice, Foreign Secretary Vijay Gokhale visits China; Pakistan on Table", *The Indian Express*, New Delhi, 25 February 2018, available at https://indianexpress.com/article/india/in-breaking-of-ice-foreign-secy-vijay-gokhale-visits-china-pakistan-on-table-doklam-crisis-5077047/
20. Sutirtho Patranobis, "Indo-China ties improve, but doubts remain", *Hindustan Times*, New Delhi, 17 July 2018, available at https://www.hindustantimes.com/india-news/india-china-ties-improve-but-doubts-remain/story-GbwJKIs2JplhktTQpLUcpM.html
21. Ibid.
22. "PM Modi meets Chinese President Xi Jinping on sidelines of BRICS Summit", The Hindu, 27 July 2018, available at https://www.thehindu.com/news/national/pm-modi-meets-chinese-president-xi-jinping-on-sidelines-of-brics-summit/article24528356.ece#!
23. "At G20 meetings, Modi bats for multilateralism", *Hindustan Times*, New Delhi, Saturday, 01 December 2018.
24. "Text of Prime Minister's Keynote Address at Shangri La Dialogue", Press Information Bureau, Government of India, Prime Minister's Office, 01 June 2018, p.6, available at http://pib.nic.in/newsite/PrintRelease.aspx?relid=179711

Chapter 2: Sino-Indian Relations: Sources of Conflict

1. Debates of Provisional Parliament, December 04, 1947, Column 1255.
2. Shao Chuan Leng, "India and China", Far Eastern Survey, vol.21, no.8, 21 May 1952, pp. 73-78.
3. Nirupama Rao "China May Be an Adversary, But Making It an Enemy Will Not Serve India", The Wire, 06 October 2017, pp 2-3, available at https://thewire.in/184678/india-china-relations-adversary-enemy/
4. Department of Defence (DoD), United States of America, "Annual Report to Congress: Military and Security Developments Involving the People's Republic of China 2013", p.22.

available at www.defense.gov/pubs/2013_China_Report_FINAL.pdf

5. Lt Gen Vinod Bhatia, PVSM, AVSM, SM (Retd), "The Dragon Dares The Elephant Once Again", South Asia Defence Strategic Review, Vol. II, Issue 2, May-June 2017, p.16.
6. Nirupama Rao, op.cit., p.3.
7. Rup Narayan Das, "India-China Relations – A New Paradigm", Institute for Defence Studies &Analyses(IDSA) Monograph Series No.19, May 2013, New Delhi, p.30.
8. Nirupama Rao, op.cit., p.4.
9. John W. Garver, "Protracted Contest: Sino-Indian Rivalry in the Twentieth Century (Seattle, WA: University of Washington Press, 2001), p.5.
10. Sreedhar, "China Becoming a Superpower and India's Options", Strategic Analysis Vol. XX, No.4, July 1997, p.534.
11. Brahma Chellaney, "Differential equations", *Hindustan Times*, New Delhi, Wednesday, February 13, 2008.
12. Sreedhar, op. cit., pp. 534-535.
13. Sreedhar, op. cit., p. 537 and Rup Narayan Das, op. cit., pp. 26-27.
14. JayadevaRanade, "It Takes Two to Tango", *The Times of India*, New Delhi, Thursday, 16 July 2009.
15. Rup Narayan Das, op. cit., pp. 30-31; and "Text of the Prime Minister's Letter to US President Bill Clinton", Embassy of India, Washington DC, 13 May 1998, available at http://www.indianembassy.org/industrel/pmletter.htm; and "China is Enemy No 1: George", Indian Express, 3 May 1998; and Waheguru Pal Singh Sidhu and Jing-dong Yuan, "China and India: Cooperation or Conflict?" (Boulder, CO: Lynne Rienner, 2003), p.32.
16. Manoj Joshi, "China, sweet and sour", *Hindustan Times*, New Delhi, Wednesday, 31 May, 2006.
17. Rup Narayan Das, op. cit., p.30.
18. G. Parthasarathy, "Need for measured responses to Chinese assertiveness", Northern Indian Patrika, Allahabad, Monday, 20 September 2010.
19. NayanChanda, "Stapled Visas A Step Forward", *The Times of India*, New Delhi, Saturday, 26 October 2013.
20. G. Parthasarathy, "Games Neighbours Play", *The Times of India*, Allahabad, Monday, 29 June 2009.
21. Harsh V. Pant, "It'll Take Hard Work", *The Times of India*, New Delhi, Tuesday, 14 December 2010.
22. Lt Gen Vinod Bhatia, PVSM, AVSM, SM (Retd), op.cit., p.17.
23. Kanti Bajpai, "India and China: softly, softly", *The Times of India*, New Delhi, Saturday, 27 April 2013.
24. Rajat Pandit & Deeptiman Tiwary, "Indian soldiers made tactical retreat at one point in Chumar", *The Times of India*, Tuesday, 23 September 2014 and Rajat Pandit, "China troops thin out in Chumar", *The Times of India*, Thursday, 25 September 2014.
25. "President Xi stresses military headquaters' loyalty to Party", Xinhua, 23 September 2014 available at http://africa.chinadaily.com.cn/china/2014-09/23/content_18643491.htm
26. Jayadeva Ranade, "China is placing key generals on India border near Ladakh", The Sunday Guardian, 31 January 2015, available at http://www.sunday-guardian.com/investigation/china-is-placing-key-generals-on-india-border-near-ladakh
27. Ministry of Foreign Affairs, Royal Government of Bhutan, "Press Release", 29 June 2017, available at http://www.mfa.gov.bt/press-releases/press-release-272.html
28. Oriana Skylar Mastro and Arzan Tarapore, "Countering Chinese Coercion: The Case of

Doklam", War on the Rocks, 29 August 2017, available at https://warontherocks.com/2017/08/countering-chinese-coercion-the-case-of-doklam/

29. "Doklam Phase II will test India more than Phase I", Live Mint, 23 January 2018, available at http://www.livemint.com/Opinion/5ZTEKWGtdv0M6A0BWM7g1L/Doklam-phase-II-will-test-India-more-than-phase-I.html
30. Keith Johnson, "China Tops U.S. as Biggest Oil Importer", Foreign Policy, 11 May 2015 available at foreignpolicy.com/2015/05/11/china-tops-u-s-as-biggest-oil-importer-middle-east-opec-sloc/ (According to *Reuters*, in April China imported a record 7.4 million barrels of oil a day, just nipping the 7.2 million barrels a day imported by the United States. In fact by other measures, including net imports of all petroleum products, China had already elbowed its way into first place in late 2013.)
31. Brigadier (Dr.) Rajeev Bhutani, "Rise of China: 2030 and Its Strategic Implications", Pentagon Press, New Delhi, 2015, p.345.
32. Shen Dingli, "Don't shun the idea of setting up overseas military bases", China.org.cn, 28 January 2010, available at http://www.china.org.cn/opinion/2010-01/28/content_19324522_2.htm
33. "Chinese navy to actively maintain peace and stability of Indian Ocean", *Global Times*, 17 December 2012, available at http://www.globaltimes.cn/content/750602.shtml
34. "China's Military Strategy (full text)", Xinhua, 27 May 2015, available at http://english.gov.cn/archive/white_paper/2015/05/27/content_281475115610833.htm
35. Jeff M. Smith, "China-India Relations in the Modi-Xi Era", US-China Economic and Security Review Commission, 10 March 2016, p.5., available at https://www.uscc.gov/sites/default/files/SMITH_Remarks%20031016.pdf
36. Matthew Southerland, Iacob Koch-Weser and Angela Zhang, "China-India Relations: Tensions Persist Despite Growing Cooperation", U.S.-China Economic and Security Review Commission Staff Report, 22 December 2014, p.5., available at https://www.uscc.gov/sites/default/files/Research/Staff%20Report_China-India%20Relations—Tensions%20Persist%20Despite%20Growing%20Cooperation_12%2022%202014.pdf
37. US DoD Annual Report to Congress, "Military and Security Developments Involving the People's Republic of China 2015", pp19-24, to be referred later as US DoD "MSDC2015", available at www.defense.gov/pubs/2015_China_Military_Power_Report.pdf
38. Matthew Southerland, Iacob Koch-Weser and Angela Zhang, op.cit.p.5.
39. "The Military Balance 2013", International Institute of Strategic Studies, London, pp. 252-253.
40. "China builds up strategic sea lanes", *The Washington Times*, 17 January 2005, available at https://www.washingtontimes.com/news/2005/jan/17/20050117-115550-1929r/
41. Ananth Krishnan, "Maldives for deeper ties with China", The Hindu, 12 December 2012, available at http://www.thehindu.com/news/international/maldives-for-deeper-ties-with-china/article4188735.ece.
42. Ben Blanchard, "China formally opens first overseas military base in Djibouti", *Reuters*, 1 August 2017, available at https://www.reuters.com/article/us-china-djibouti/china-formally-opens-first-overseas-military-base-in-djibouti-idUSKBN1AH3E3
43. Joseph Braude and Tyler Jiang, "Why China and Saudi Arabia Are Building Bases in Djibouti", The World Post, available at https://www.huffingtonpost.com/joseph-braude/why-china-and-saudi-arabi_b_12194702.html
44. Steven Hoffmann, "Perception and China Policy", in Frankel and Harding (eds.), "The India-China Relationship", p.48.

45. Christopher J. Pehrson's "String of Pearls: Meeting the Challenge of China's Rising power across the Asian Littoral"(Covers "String of Pearls" in adequate detail).
46. John W. Garver, op.cit., p.188.
47. Lisa Curtis, "China's Military and Security Relationship with Pakistan", 'Testimony before the U.S.–China Economic and Security Review Commission on May 20, 2009', available at https://www.heritage.org/testimony/chinas-military-and-security-relationship-pakistan
48. "Agni effect: Is China, Pakistan mulling to scale up defence cooperation to counter India's ballistic missile progress", PTI, 17 March 2017 available at http://www.firstpost.com/world/agni-effect-is-china-pakistan-mulling-to-scale-up-defence-cooperation-to-counter-indias-ballistic-missile-progress-3340200.html ; and Franz-StefanGady, "China, Pakistan Hold Defense Talks", *The Diplomat*, 15 June 2017, available at https://thediplomat.com/2017/06/china-pakistan-hold-defense-talks/
49. Mahendra Ved, "Feverish Pak-China Militarisation", *Asia Defence News*, January 2010,p.18; G. Parthasarathy, Northern Indian Patrika, Allahabad, Monday, 20 September, 2010, op. cit., & Senthil Periasamy, "Foreign Policy of China - Strategy of String of Pearls", Civil Services Chronicle, September, 2010, p.32.
50. "China-Pakistan Relations Enter New Phase" available at https;//www.strategic-culture.org/news/2017/04/03/china-pakistan-relations-enter-new-phase.html; and Franz-Stefan Gady, op.cit.
51. Study by the Centre for Non-Proliferation Studies at the Monterey Institute of International Studies cited in *Hindustan Times*, New Delhi, 06 September 2000.
52. Lisa Curtis, op.cit.
53. K Subrahmanyam, "Another Rogue State", *The Times of India*, New Delhi, Tuesday, October 17, 2006.
54. Brigadier (Dr.) Rajeev Bhutani, "RISE OF CHINA: 2030 and Its Strategic Implications", Pentagon Press, New Delhi, 2015, p.280.
55. Zofeen T Ebrahim, "What's Happening at Pakistan's Gwadar Port?", *The Diplomat*, 17 June 2017, available at https://thediplomat.com/2017/06/whats-happening-at-pakistans-gwadar-port/ ; and Lisa Curtis, op.cit.
56. Adnan Aamir, "Will Gwadar go the way of Hambantota? Why Chinese loans to Pakistan are sparking takeover fears along the economic corridor", *South China Morning Post*, 27 December 2017, available at http://www.scmp.com/comment/insight-opinion/article/2125783/will-gwadar-go-way-hambantota-why-chinese-loans-pakistan-are
57. Zofeen T Ebrahim, op.cit.
58. "China Turning Pakistan Port Into Regional Giant", available at https://www.voanews.com/a/pakistan-china-gwadar-port/4084175.html; and "China-Pakistan Relations Enter New Phase", op.cit.
59. Imtiaz Ahmad, "Pakistan to pay China $40 bn for CPEC projects", Hindustan Times, Thursday, 27 December 2018.
60. Chidanand Rajghatta, "Pak has ceded control of Gilgit in PoK to Beijing", *The Times of India*, Allahabad, Saturday, 11 September 2010.
61. "Expert: China Gilgit gambit is strategic", *Hindustan Times*, Lucknow, Friday, 03 September 2010.
62. Brahma Chellaney, "Dragon Designs", *Hindustan Times*, New Delhi, Thursday, 22 June 2006.
63. Amal Jayasinghe, AFP, "Modi to steer Sri Lanka away from China on landmark trip", Business Insider, 13 March 2015 available at www.businessinsider.com/afp-modi-to-steer-sri-lanka-

away-from-china-on-landmark-trip-2015-3?IR=T

64. Ramtanu Maitra, "Modi strengthens ties with Indian Ocean neighbours", Vijayvaani.com, 21 March 2015, vijayvaani.com/ArticleDisplay.aspx?aid=3528
65. Peter Fuhrman, "China's ambitions for sleepy Hambantota could shift world trade routes", *The Financial Times*, 26 September 2017 available at https://www.ft.com/content/f0d88070-9f99-11e7-9a86-4d5a475ba4c5
66. Uditha Jayasinghe, "Struggling port forces Sri Lanka closer to China", 27 October 2017, available at https://www.chinadialogue.net/article/show/single/en/10173-Struggling-port-forces-Sri-Lanka-closer-to-China
67. Peter Fuhrman, op. cit.
68. Uditha Jayasinghe, op. cit.
69. Freddie Kleiner, "China's role in Sri Lankan development sparks fears over sovereignty, local economy", *South China Morning Post*, 23 January 2018, available at http://www.scmp.com/comment/insight-opinion/article/2130047/worries-build-sri-lanka-over-chinas-financing-development
70. Yigal Chazan, "India and China's Tug of War Over Sri Lanka", *The Diplomat*, 23 May 2017, available at https://thediplomat.com/2017/05/india-and-chinas-tug-of-war-over-sri-lanka/
71. Peter Fuhrman, op.cit.
72. P.K. Balachandran, "China Overtakes India as Sri Lanka's Largest Trading Partner", The Citizen, 14 December 2017, p.2. available at http://www.thecitizen.in/index.php/en/newsdetail/index/5/12511/china-overtakes-india-as-sri-lankas-largest-trading-partner
73. Uditha Jayasinghe, op.cit.
74. "India takes on China at another battlefront: A Sri Lankan airport", *ET* Online, 14 October 2017, available ateconomictimes.indiatimes.com/articleshow/61079813.cms?utm_source=contentofinterest&utm_medium=text&utm_campaign=cppst
75. Dr Sudha Ramachandran, "A New Era for India-Sri Lanka Relations?", *The Diplomat*, 26 February 2015 in https://thuppahi.wordpress.com/2015/02/28/sri-lankas-balancing-act-between-india-and-china/#more-15882
76. P.K. Balachandran, op.cit., p.1.
77. Kinling Lo, "A Chinese flag flies over Sri Lanka as China extends its reach into India's backyard", *South China Morning Post*, 05 January 2018, available at http://www.scmp.com/news/china/diplomacy-defence/article/2126897/chinese-flag-flies-over-sri-lanka-china-extends-its
78. Brahma Chellaney, "Counter China's Designs", *The Times of India*, New Delhi, Wednesday, January 16, 2008.
79. Nayan Chanda, "Winds of Change in Myanmar," *The Times of India*, New Delhi, Saturday, 26 November 2011.
80. Brigadier (Dr.) Rajeev Bhutani, op. cit., p.283.
81. "China Opens Delayed Myanmar Oil Pipeline to Get Mideast Crude Faster", *Bloomberg News*, April 11, 2017, available at https://www.bloomberg.com/news/articles/2017-04-11/china-opens-delayed-myanmar-oil-link-to-get-mideast-crude-faster;SaibalDasgupta, "China-Myanmar gas pipeline operational", *The Times of India*, New Delhi, Monday, 21 October 2013; "Gas pipeline links China and Myanmar," *The Times of India*, New Delhi, Tuesday, 30 July 2013 and US DoD "MSDC 2015", op. cit., p.24.
82. "Chinese Puzzle over Burma's SIGINT Base," JanesDefence Weekly (London), 29 January 1994.
83. Brigadier (Dr.) Rajeev Bhutani, op.cit., p.283.
84. Tridivesh Singh Maini and Sandeep Sachdeva, "China Faces Increasing Competition in

Myanmar", *The Diplomat*, 14 November 2017, available at https://thediplomat.com/2017/11/china-faces-increasing-competition-in-myanmar/

85. Nayan Chanda, op.cit.
86. Brigadier (Dr.) Rajeev Bhutani, op.cit., p.284.
87. Tridivesh Singh Maini and Sandeep Sachdeva, op. cit.
88. Jeff Opperman, "Following Dam Cancellation, Myanmar Can Lead On Sustainable Energy", Forbes.com, 25 January 2018, available at https://www.forbes.com/sites/jeffopperman/2018/01/25/following-dam-cancellation-myanmar-can-lead-on-sustainable-energy/#7e833a112fbe; and "Pakistan, Nepal, Myanmar Cancel Chinese Projects", 5 December 2017, available at https://learningenglish.voanews.com/a/pakistan-nepal-myanmar-cancel-chinese-projects/4150396.html
89. "Bangladesh's Strategic Relations with China", Chapter- IV, pp. 123-125, available at http://shodhganga.inflibnet.ac.in/bitstream/10603/120035/9/09_chapter%204.pdf
90. Subhash Kapila, "Bangladesh-China Defence Cooperation Agreement's Strategic Implications: An Analysis," South Asia Analysis Group, 14January 2003, available at www.southasiaanalysis.org/paper582
91. en.wikipedia.org/wiki/Bangladesh-China-relations.
92. M. Jashim Uddinand Mahbubur Rashid Bhuiyan, "Sino-Bangladesh Relations: An Appraisal", *BIISS Journal*, Vol. 32, No. 1, January 2011: 1-24, p.11, available at www.biiss.org/biiss_journal/january_2011.pdf
93. Wikipedia, op.cit.
94. Shannon Tiezzi, "China, Bangladesh Pledge Deeper Military Cooperation", *The Diplomat*, 04 December 2015, available at https://thediplomat.com/2015/12/china-bangladesh-pledge-deeper-military-cooperation/
95. Dhaka Tribune, 18 March 2014 as cited in Sudha Ramachandran, "China's Sinking Port Plans in Bangladesh", China Brief, Volume: 16, Issue: 10, 21 June 2016 available at https://jamestown.org/program/chinas-sinking-port-plans-in-bangladesh/
96. "Defense Update Bangladesh" available at https://defenseupdatebangladesh.wordpress.com/category/bangladesh-china-defence-relations/
97. Aziz Tarak, "Ming Class Attack Submarine in Bangladesh Navy", Bd newsnet.com, 25 January 2017, available at http://bdnewsnet.com/2017/01/25/defense/ming-class-submarine-bangladesh-navy/
98. Commodore Gopal Suri, "Chinese Submarines for The Bangladesh Navy An Assessment", VIF, 13 April 2016, available at http://www.vifindia.org/article/2016/april/13/chinese-submarines-for-the-bangladesh-navy-an-assessment
99. "Defense Update Bangladesh", op.cit.
100. Asma Masood, "India-Bangladesh-China Relations: A Complex Triangle", Myanmar Business Today, Vol. 3, Issue 13, 30 March 2015, available at https://www.mmbiztoday.com/articles/india-bangladesh-china-relations-complex-triangle
101. M Shahidul Islam, "Xi Jinping's visit: Implications for Bangladesh-China relations", *The Daily Star*, 14 October 2016, available at http://www.thedailystar.net/op-ed/economics/implications-bangladesh-china-relations-1298533
102. Muhammad Hasan, "Bangladesh-China economic military and diplomatic relations", International Affairs, 20 October 2016, available at http://internationalaffairsbd.com/bangladesh-china-economic-military-diplomatic-relations/#_ftn1
103. Shannon Tiezzi, op.cit.
104. Sudha Ramachandran, "China's Sinking Port Plans in Bangladesh", China Brief, Vol. 16, Issue 10, 21 June 2016 available at https://jamestown.org/program/chinas-sinking-port-plans-

in-bangladesh/

105. "China's Xi elevates ties with Bangladesh to strategic partnership as two countries ink deals worth billions", *Straits Times*, 14 October 2016, available at http://www.straitstimes.com/asia/south-asia/chinas-xi-elevates-ties-with-bangladesh-to-strategic-partnership-as-two-countries
106. Nurul Islam Hasib, "What is meant by a strategic partnership between Bangladesh and China?", bdnews24.com, 14 October 2016, available at https://bdnews24.com/bangladesh/2016/10/14/what-is-meant-by-a-strategic-partnership-between-bangladesh-and-china
107. Rajeev Ahmed, "So, which of the favours of China would Bangladesh deny?", *Dhaka Tribune*, 28 October2017,http://www.dhakatribune.com/opinion/op-ed/2017/10/27/which-favours-china-bangladesh/
108. Annabelle Heugas, "The geopolitics of Rakhine", Mizzima, 31 October 2017, available at http://www.mizzima.com/news-opinion/geopolitics-rakhine
109. Sudha Ramachandran, "Rohingya Crisis: Will China's Mediation Succeed?", China Brief, Vol. 17, Issue 15, 22 November 2017, available at https://jamestown.org/program/rohingya-crisis-will-chinas-mediation-succeed/
110. Ibid.
111. Jigme Yeshe Lama, "China & Its Peripheries: Securing Nepal in South Asia," IPCS Issue Brief available at www.ipcs.org/issue-brief/south-asia/china-and-its-peripheries-securing-nepal-in-south-asia-232.html.
112. Uma Shankar Prasad, "Study of Nepal's Economic relations with China", *The Journal of Development and Administrative Studies* (JODAS), Vol. 23(1-2), p.26, downloaded as file:///Users/rajeevbhutani/Downloads/15446-51802-1-PB.pdf
113. Saransh Sehgal, "China Expands into Himalayan Neighbour Nepal", The International Relations and Security Network (ISN), ETH Zurich, 15 January 2014, available at www.isn.ethz.ch/Digital-Library/Articles/Detail/?id=175398
114. Jigme Yeshe Lama, op. cit.
115. Nihar R Nayak, "China's Growing Military Ties with Nepal", IDSA, 31 March 2017, available at https://idsa.in/idsacomments/china-growing-military-ties-with-nepal_nrnayak_310317
116. "First ever joint military training: landmark on China-Nepal defense cooperation", Nepal Foreign Affairs, 17 April 2017, available at http://nepalforeignaffairs.com/first-ever-joint-military-training-landmark-on-china-nepal-defense-cooperation/
117. Dr. Geeta Kochhar, "Nepal-China Closeness: What India Loses?", Chennai Centre for China Studies, C3S paper No:1135, 24 April 2013, available at https://www.c3sindia.org/society-politics/nepal-china-closenesswhat-india-loses/
118. Uma Shankar Prasad, op. cit., pp. 27-28.
119. Dr. Geeta Kochhar, op. cit.
120. iasscore.in/national-issues/growing-proximity-between-nepal-and-china-an-analysis
121. Ananth Krishnan, "China is largest FDI source for Nepal, overtakes India", *The Hindu*, 26 January 2014, available at http://www.thehindu.com/news/international/world/china-is-largest-fdi-source-for-nepal-overtakes-india/article5618081.ece
122. "China tops in FDI pledges to Nepal in first half of FY 2017-18", Xinhua, 27 January 2018, available at http://www.xinhuanet.com/english/2018-01/27/c_136927876.htm
123. Dr. Geeta Kochhar, op. cit.
124. Sanjeev Giri, "Nepal, China sign deal on OBOR", *The Kathmandu Post*, 12 May 2017, available at http://kathmandupost.ekantipur.com/news/2017-05-12/nepal-china-sign-framework-deal-on-obor.html

125. "New strategic rail network to Tibet's borders endangers environment, raises regional security concerns (Updated)", International Campaign For Tibet, 17April 2015, available at https://www.savetibet.org/new-strategic-rail-network-to-tibets-borders-endangers-environment-raises-regional-security-concerns/#2
126. "Nepal in talks with China to build $8 billion cross-border rail link: finance ministry official", *Reuters*, 14 May 2017, available at https://www.reuters.com/article/us-china-silkroad-nepal/nepal-in-talks-with-china-to-build-8-billion-cross-border-rail-link-finance-ministry-official-idUSKBN18A05F
127. "China Nepal Railway - Lhasa to Kathmandu Train in Future", Tibet Discovery.com, 26 January 2018, available at http://www.tibetdiscovery.com/train-to-tibet/china-nepal-railway/
128. "New strategic rail network to Tibet's borders endangers environment, raises regional security concerns (Updated)", op.cit.
129. Jigme Yeshe Lama, op. cit.
130. Brigadier (Dr.) Rajeev Bhutani, op. cit., p.286.
131. Liu Zhen, "Nepal looks to China for internet access after years of depending on India", *South China Morning Post*, 12 January 2018, available at http://www.scmp.com/news/china/diplomacy-defence/article/2128054/nepal-looks-china-internet-access-after-years-depending
132. defence.pk/threads/china-acquires-a-base-in-maldives-against-india-with-some-help-from-pakistan.8165/
133. Sudha Ramachandran, "Maldives: Tiny Islands, big intrigue, "Pakistan Defence, 27 July 2001 (updated Nov 10, 2007).
134. Darshana M. Baruah, "Modi's Trip and China's islands: The Battle for the Indian Ocean", *The Diplomat*, 11 March 2015 available at thediplomat.com/2015/03/modis-trip-and-chinas-islands-the-battle-for-the-indian-ocean/
135. S Y Surendra Kumar, "China's Footprints in Maldives: Concern for India?", p.20., downloaded as file:///C:/Users/CENJOWS/Downloads/1570-1-3089-1-10-20171115.pdf
136. B Raman, "Maldives' Relations with India & China", South Asia Analysis Group, Paper No 5327, 14 December 2012, available at www.southasia analysis.org/node/1092; and Harsh V. Pant, "Islands Nations Play China, India," Yale Global, 9 January 2013-yaleglobal.yale.edu/content/island-nations-play-china-india
137. Asma Masood, "India-Maldives-China: Strategic Relations", C S Chennai Centre for China Studies, C3S Paper No 0003/2015, 7 January 2015, available at www.c3sindia.org/uncategorized/4753
138. Namaste Ni Hao, "The Maldives Crisis: What Is At Stake For China And India?", *Swarajya Mag*, 17 February 2018, available at https://swarajyamag.com/world/the-maldives-crisis-what-is-at-stake-for-china-and-india
139. Chang Yong, Huang Haimin, "Interview: China-Maldives relations to grow in leaps through Trade Investment, says president", available at news.xinhuanet.com/english/china/2014-08/15/c-133559638.htm
140. Jhinuk Chowdhury, "Can China's Inroads Into The Maldives Displace India?", *Huffington Post*, 18 December 2015, available at https://www.huffingtonpost.in/jhinuk-chowdhury/maldives-helping-china-co_b_8695656.html
141. Rajat Pandit, "Chinese moves in Maldives worry India", *The Times of India*, New Delhi, Monday, 10 October 2011.
142. S Y Surendra Kumar, op.cit., p.18.
143. "Maldives President Calls India 'Closest Friend and Ally', But Defends Restrictions on Diplomats", The Wire, 26 December 2017, available at https://thewire.in/208186/maldives-

india-relations-china-fta/

144. D.S. Rajan, "Indian Ocean: China-India-US Jostling for Power; cases of Sri Lanka and Maldives", South Asia analysis Group, Paper No. 5878, Dated 23 February 2015, www.southasiaanalysis.org/node/1718
145. Jhinuk Chowdhury, op.cit.
146. "China's ocean observatory in Maldives sparks fresh security concerns", *The Times of India*,26 February 2018, available at https://timesofindia.indiatimes.com/chinas-ocean-observatory-in-maldives-sparks-fresh-security-fear/articleshowprint/63072040.cms
147. Sudha Ramachandran, "India and the Maldives Emergency", *The Diplomat*, 08 February 2018, available at https://thediplomat.com/2018/02/india-and-the-maldives-emergency/
148. Saibal Dasgupta, "China gains where India lost, bags Male airport deal", *The Times of India*, New Delhi, Thursday, 18 September 2014.
149. Asma Masood, op.cit.
150. S Y Surendra Kumar, op. cit., p.19.; and N Manoharan, "India-Maldives Relations: A Tale Of Two Concerns – Analysis", *Maldives Times*, 29 June 2017, available at https://maldivestimes.com/india-maldives-relations-a-tale-of-two-concerns-analysis/
151. Namaste Ni Hao, op.cit.
152. Mujib Mashal, "Maldives Crisis Could Stir Trouble Between China and India", *New York Times*, 14 February 2018, https://www.nytimes.com/2018/02/14/world/asia/maldives-china-india.html
153. Saibal Dasgupta & Agencies, "Chinese military bases in Indian Ocean?", *The Times of India*, New Delhi, Tuesday, December 13, 2011.
154. Harsh V. Pant, op.cit.
155. Ramtanu Maitra, op.cit.
156. Robert D. Kaplan, "Monsoon: The Indian Ocean and the Future of American Power", Random House, New York, 2010, p.11.
157. Wade Shepard, "Why China Just Added the Belt and Road Initiative to its Constitution", *Forbes*, 25 October 2017, available at https://www.forbes.com/sites/wadeshepard/2017/10/25/why-china-just-added-the-belt-and-road-initiative-to-its-constitution/#3d46ec8f42ab
158. Raghu Dayal, "China's One Belt, One Road Gamble", *The Hindu*, 11 May 2017, available at https://www.thehindubusinessline.com/opinion/chinas-one-belt-one-road-gamble/article9693579.ece
159. Ibid.; Brahma Chellaney, "Dragon designs," op.cit.; and Vikram Sood, "Caught in the middle", *Hindustan Times*, New Delhi, Wednesday, 05 September 2007; and "141st Report of the Rajya Sabha Committee on Petitions Praying for Development of Railway Network in Uttarakhand, Himachal Pradesh and other Himalayan States presented on December 19, 2011" cited in Rup Narayan Das, op. cit., p.35.
160. www.freetibet.org/resources
161. Brahma Chellaney, "Dragon designs", op.cit.
162. Herbert Wulf, "China, India and the three Cs", 6 March 2014, available at https://www.sipri.org/commentary/blog/2014/china-india-and-three-cs
163. Central Tibetan Administration, http://tibet.net/about-cta/
164. John Garver, "China's Decision for War with India in 1962", in 'New Approaches to the Study of Chinese Foreign Policy' Robert S. Ross and Alastair Iain Johnston, Stanford University Press, 2005 as cited in Matthew Southerland, Iacob Koch-Weser and Angela Zhang, op.cit., p.17.
165. Ben Blanchard, "China tells Dalai Lama again to respect reincarnation", *Reuters*, 10 December

2014, available at https://www.reuters.com/article/us-china-tibet/china-tells-dalai-lama-again-to-respect-reincarnation-idUSKBN0H50ST20140910

166. Sandeep Unnithan, "Process to select the 15th Dalai Lama to begin in next one or two years: Dalai Lama", *India Today*, 11 August 2017, available at https://www.indiatoday.in/india/story/dalai-lama-15th-dalai-lama-dalai-lama-institution-rajendra-mathur-memorial-lecture-china-india-tibet-1029110-2017-08-11
167. "Not my business to decide on successor: Dalai Lama", Interview with Shishir Gupta, *Hindustan Times*, New Delhi, Tuesday, 25 December 2018.
168. Sunil Kataria, "Dalai Lama says Tibetan people should decide on his succession", *Reuters*, 12 April 2017, available at https://www.reuters.com/article/india-dalai-lama-reincarnation-copy/dalai-lama-says-tibetan-people-should-decide-on-his-succession-idUSKBN17B07B
169. Sebastian BIBA, "New Concerns, More Cooperation? How Non-Traditional Security Issues Affect Sino-Indian Relations", *Journal of Current Chinese Affairs*, 45, 3, 3-30, p.13, available at https://journals.sub.uni-hamburg.de/giga/jcca/article/download/995/1002
170. "Dalai Lama event in Delhi cancelled, 'Thank You India' programme shifted to Dharamsala, here is why", FE Online, 6 March 2018, available at http://www.financialexpress.com/india-news/dalai-lama-event-in-delhi-cancelled-thank-you-india-programme-shifted-to-dharamsala-here-is-why-india-china-tibet/1088630/
171. John W. Garver, "Protracted Contest", (Seattle, WA: University of Washington Press, 2001), op.cit., p.75.
172. Hemanta Mishra, "The Global Significance of the Tibetan Plateau: Strategic Options to Address Environmental Security in the Region", Presentation, 5 June 2009, pp. 18-20, available at https://hcss.nl/sites/default/files/files/reports/Water_on_the_Tibetan_Plateau_ Ecological _and_Strategic_Implications_for_the_Region_-_030909.pdf
173. Brahma Chellaney, "Averting Water Wars", Presentation, 5 June 2009, p.51.available at https://hcss.nl/sites/default/files/files/reports/Water_on_the_Tibetan_Plateau_Ecological_and_Strategic_ Implications_for_the_Region_-_030909.pdf
174. Ibid., p.50.
175. "Tibet: An Environmental Challenge Why Tibet Lies at the Heart of the Great Development Challenges of the Asian Century", Australia Tibet Council 2016, p.6. available at http://docplayer.net/25200961-Tibet-an-environmental-challenge-why-tibet-lies-at-the-heart-of-the-great-development-challenges-of-the-asian-century.html
176. Syed Iqbal Hasnain, "River Runs Through It", *The Times of India*, New Delhi, Tuesday, 17 August 2010.
177. "Tibet: An Environmental Challenge", op.cit., p.7.
178. Brahma Chellaney, "Ominous rise of a thirsty dragon", *The Times of India*, New Delhi, 07 August 2011.
179. Colonel (Dr.) P K Vasudeva, "China Begins Construction of Tibet's Biggest Dam: Suwalong Project", *Indian Defence Review*, 17 May 2016 available at http://www.indiandefencereview.com/news/china-begins-construction-of-tibets-biggest-dam-suwalong-project/ ;Brahma Chellaney, "Ties and Troubled Waters", *The Times of India*, New Delhi, Tuesday, 29 June 2010; and Saibal Dasgupta, "China opens huge Brahmaputra dam", *The Times of India*, New Delhi, Wednesday, 14 October 2015.
180. "China for more dams on Tibetan rivers instead of Brahmaputra", *The Times of India*, 23 November 2017, available at https://timesofindia.indiatimes.com/world/china/china-for-more-dams-on-tibetan-rivers-instead-of-brahmaputra/articleshow/61765625.cms; and Colonel (Dr.) P K Vasudeva, op. cit.

181. "Why India is worried about China's dam projects on the Brahmaputra river", *Economic Times*, 5 October 2016, available at https://economictimes.indiatimes.com/news/politics-and-nation/why-india-is-worried-about-chinas-dam-projects-on-the-brahmaputra-river/articles
182. Syed Iqbal Hasnain, op.cit. and "Tibet: An Environmental Challenge", op.cit., p.7. (citing Michael Buckley 2014 'Meltdown in Tibet: China's Reckless Destruction of ecosystems from the highlands of Tibet to the deltas of Asia')
183. HTC and Guardian, "China Planning world's biggest dam on Brahmaputra", *Hindustan Times*, Lucknow, Wednesday, 26 May 2010
184. Syed Iqbal Hasnain, op.cit.
185. Beth Walker, "China plans more dams and mega infrastructure in Tibet", 21 March 2016, available at https://www.thethirdpole.net/2016/03/21/china-plans-more-hydro-projects-and-mega-infrastructure-in-tibet/
186. Ibid.
187. Satyendra Tripathi, "China's Dam-Building In The Brahmaputra Could Spell Crisis For India", 12 October 2016, available at https://www.huffingtonpost.in/satyendra-tripathi/china-s-dam-building-in-the-brahmaputra-could-spell-crisis-for-i_a_21580587/
188. "Tibet: An Environmental Challenge", op. cit., pp.7-8.
189. Satyendra Tripathi, op.cit.
190. "Tibet: An Environmental Challenge", op. cit., p.8.
191. Satyendra Tripathi, op.cit.
192. "Why India is worried about China's dam projects on the Brahmaputra river", *Economic Times*, op. cit.
193. Brahma Chellaney, "Ties and Troubled Waters", op.cit.
194. "The Global Significance of the Tibetan Plateau: Strategic Options to Address Environmental Security in the Region", op. cit., pp 72-73.
195. Govt. of India, Ministry of Commerce & Industry site available at http://commerce-app.gov.in/eidb/default.asp (updated 23 April 2018) (accessed on 02 June 2018).
196. P R Chari, "Sino- Indian Relations: The Mahbubani Thesis", IITM CSC Article # 69, 13 February 2014.
197. Anilesh S. Mahajan, "Great Wall of India", Business Today, 31 December 2017, available at https://www.businesstoday.in/magazine/the-hub/india-china-chinese-imports-china-pakistan-economic-corridor-import-export-trade-india-china-relation/story/265720.html
198. Indrani Bagchi, "India decides to fight back aggressive China", *The Times of India*, New Delhi, Saturday, 29 Dec 2012.
199. Govt. of India, Ministry of Commerce & Industry site, op. cit.
200. Chaitanya Mallapur, "India's Trade Deficit With China Up Twofold In A Decade To 2016-17; Can India Benefit From U.S.-China Trade War?", Bloomberg, 16 April 2018, available at https://www.bloombergquint.com/global-economics/2018/04/16/indias-trade-deficit-with-china-up-twofold-in-a-decade-to-2016-17-can-india-benefit-from-us-china-trade-war
201. V Rishi Kumar, "India achieves 20 GW of installed solar capacity within eight year", The Hindu, 30 January 2018, available at https://www.thehindubusinessline.com/economy/india-achieves-20-gw-of-installed-solar-capacity-within-eight-years/article22591953.ece
202. Anilesh S. Mahajan, op. cit.
203. Malini Goyal, "How China beats India hollow in Trade and dominates Indian homes, markets and economy", *The Economic Times*, 16 July 2017, available at https://economictimes.indiatimes.com/news/economy/foreign-trade/china-dominates-indian-homes-markets-and-

economy-as-trade-deficit-widens/articleshow/59611452.cms

204. "Trade between India and China", Lok Sabha Unstarred Question No. 450 to be Answered on 18th December, 2017, available at http://164.100.47.190/loksabhaquestions/annex/13/AU450.pdf (In FY 2017-2018, India imported Electronic components worth $ 3.02 billion as against $ 4.4 billion and Telecom instruments for $ 9.01 billion as against $ 11.3 billion during the last fiscal year. See ser 126 and 128 at p.10. Annex II); and "Why India must take China's warning of a trade war seriously", *The Economic Times*, 17 August 2017, available at https://economictimes.indiatimes.com/news/economy/foreign-trade/why-india-must-take-chinas-warning-of-a-trade-war-seriously/articleshow/60101196.cms; and
205. Malini Goyal, op. cit.
206. Anilesh S. Mahajan, op. cit.
207. "Trade between India and China", Lok Sabha Unstarred Question No. 450 to be Answered on 18th December, 2017, op.cit.
208. Malini Goyal, op. cit.
209. K. S. Venkatachalam, "How To Fix India-China Trade", *The Diplomat*, 31 August 2017, available at https://thediplomat.com/2017/08/how-to-fix-india-china-trade/
210. *The Economic Times*, 17 August 2017, op.cit.
211. K. S. Venkatachalam, op.cit.
212. Malini Goyal, op.cit.
213. Kiran Sharma, op.cit. Kiran Sharma, "Is India-China trade war looming?", *Nikkei Asian Review*, 19 August 2017, available at https://asia.nikkei.com/Economy/Is-India-China-trade-war-looming
214. "Why India must take China's warning of a trade war seriously", *The Economic Times*, 17 August 2017, op.cit.
215. Rajendra Jadhav, "Tariffs on U.S. may help India treble cotton exports to China", *Reuters*, 5 April 2018, available at https://in.reuters.com/article/usa-trade-china-cotton/tariffs-on-u-s-may-help-india-treble-cotton-exports-to-china-idINKCN1HC1EL
216. Govt. of India, Ministry of Commerce & Industry site, op. cit.
217. Chaitanya Mallapur, op.cit.
218. Madhvi Sally, "US-China trade war: Scope for Indian oilseed meal, cotton, maize", *The Economic Times*, 05 April 2018, available at https://economictimes.indiatimes.com/news/economy/agriculture/us-china-trade-war-scope-for-indian-oilseed-meal-cotton-maize/articleshow
219. Rajendra Jadhav, op. cit.
220. Josephine Mason and Hallie Gu, "China deploys soybeans in trade war, but may hit own foot", *Reuters*, 4 April 2018, available at https://www.reuters.com/article/us-usa-trade-china-soybeans-explainer/china-deploys-soybeans-in-trade-war-but-may-hit-own-foot-idUSKCN1HB11V
221. Tomio Shida, "Soybeans symbolize the costs of a US-China trade war", *Nikkei Asian Review*, 24 April 2018, available at https://asia.nikkei.com/Politics/International-Relations/Soybeans-symbolize-the-costs-of-a-US-China-trade-war
222. Josephine Mason and Hallie Gu, op.cit.
223. "India pitches for soybean exports to China amid US trade spat", *The Economic Times*, 14 April 2018, available at https://economictimes.indiatimes.com/news/economy/foreign-trade/india-pitches-for-soybean-exports-to-china-amid-us-trade-spat/articleshow/63763354.cms; and Atul Aneja, "China to get a helping of soya", The Hindu, 14 April 2018 available at http://www.thehindu.com/news/international/china-to-get-a-helping-of-soya/

article23543256.ece

224. Naveen Thukral, "India soybean imports at record as domestic supply tightens: report", *Livemint*, 13 March 2018, available at https://www.livemint.com/Politics/FX2aGSiE1Dgo20PE7NUA6H/India-soybean-imports-at-record-as-domestic-supply-tightens.html
225. Dilip Kumar Jha, "Global price disparity to cut India's soymeal exports to half in 2018", *Business Standard*, 5 February 2018, available at https://www.livemint.com/Politics/FX2aGSiE1Dgo20PE7NUA6H/India-soybean-imports-at-record-as-domestic-supply-tightens.html
226. Madhvi Sally, op.cit.; "Perceptible improvement in India-China relations: Modi and Xi Jinping on G20 sidelines", DNA, 01 December 2018, available https://www.dnaindia.com/india/report-perceptible-improvement-in-india-china-relations-modi-and-xi-jinping-on-g20-sidelines-2691139; and Hallie Gu, Rajendra Jadhav, "China drops ban on rapeseed meal from India", *Reuters*, 22 October 2018, available at https://in.reuters.com/article/usa-trade-china-india/china-drops-ban-on-rapeseed-meal-from-india-idINKCN1MW17T
227. "India makes strong pitch to export Indian sugar to China following Modi-Xi summit", Money Control, 1 June 2018, available at https://www.moneycontrol.com/news/business/india-makes-strong-pitch-to-export-indian-sugar-to-china-following-modi-xi-summit-2580865.html
228. Liz Mathew, "China finally agrees to import buffalo meat from India", *The Indian Express*, 16 January 2017, available at http://indianexpress.com/article/business/business-others/china-finally-agrees-to-import-buffalo-meat-from-india-4476301/
229. Madhvi Sally, op.cit.
230. "India's textile exports to China on the decline", *The Textile Magazine*, 7 March 2018, available at http://www.indiantextilemagazine.in/global-industry-news/indias-textile-exports-to-china-on-the-decline/
231. Prashant Tomar, "China's shift towards Vietnam and Indonesia hits India's cotton yarn exports; decline by 10.2% in Apr-Sep, 2017", Indo Asian Commodities, 16 December 2017, available at https://www.indoasiancommodities.com/2017/12/16/chinas-shift-towards-vietnam-indonesia-hits-indias-cotton-yarn-exports-decline-10-2-apr-sep-2017/
232. Anilesh S. Mahajan, op. cit.
233. Chaitanya Mallapur, op. cit.
234. Atul Aneja, "China allows India to export non-Basmati rice, renews pact to share Brahmaputra water flow data", *The Hindu*, 09 June 2018, available at http://www.thehindu.com/news/international/narendra-modi-meets-xi-jinping-on-the-sidelines-of-shanghai-cooperation-organisation-summit/article24121487.ece
235. Govt of India, Ministry of Commerce & Industry site, op. cit.

Chapter 3: Areas of Cooperation Vs. Competition

1. Mohan Malik, "India-China Relations: Giants Stir, Cooperate and Compete" available at http://apcss.org/Publications/SAS/Asia Bilateral Relations/India-China Relations Malik.pdf
2. Jeff M. Smith, "India and China: The End of Cold Peace?", The National Interest, 10 February 2014, available at http://nationalinterest.org/commentary/india-china-the-end-cold-peace-9853
3. "India to become world's most populous nation around 2028: UN", *The Times of India*, 14 June 2013, available at https://timesofindia.indiatimes.com/india/India-to-become-worlds-most-populous-nation-around-2028-UN/articleshow/20586377.cms?referral=PM

4. Ajay Chhibber, "India and China need some kind of competitive cooperation rather than an open conflict", *The Economic Times*, 27 August 2017, available at https://blogs.economictimes.indiatimes.com/et-commentary/india-and-china-need-some-kind-of-competitive-cooperation-rather-than-an-open-conflict/
5. Shashi Tharoor, "Imagine What China and India Can Do Together", *South China Morning Post*, 29 July 2017, available at http://www.scmp.com/week-asia/geopolitics/article/2104347/imagine-what-china-and-india-can-do-together ; and Jeff M. Smith, op.cit.
6. Pankaj K Jha, "India and China in Southeast Asia: An Evolving Theatre of Competition?", *E International Relations*, 7 December 2015, available at https://www.e-ir.info/2015/12/07/india-and-china-in-southeast-asia-an-evolving-theatre-of-competition/
7. Sebastian BIBA, "New Concerns, More Cooperation? How Non-Traditional Security Issues Affect Sino-Indian Relations", *Journal of Current Chinese Affairs*, 45, 3, 3-30, pp. 4-15., available at https://journals.sub.uni-hamburg.de/giga/jcca/article/download/995/1002
8. Ibid., p.18.
9. "Agreement on Cooperation on Addressing Climate Change between the Government of the Republic of India and the Government of the People's Republic of China", 21 October 2009, available at http://www.moef.nic.in/sites/default/files/India-China%20Agreement%20 on%20Climate%20Change.pdf
10. Abhilash Roy Nalpathamkalam, "Cooperation without trust: India-China relations today", Heinrich Boll Stiftung India, 11 October 2012, available at https://in.boell.org/2012/10/11/cooperation-without-trust-india-china-relations-today
11. "Copenhagen deal: Key points", *BBC News*, 19 December 2009, available at http://news.bbc.co.uk/2/hi/science/nature/8422307.stm; and Guangyu Qiao, "Competition gives way to cooperation: rethinking Sino-Indian relations in climate change negotiations", *Chinese Journal of Population Resources and Environment*, 2014, Vol. 12, No. 4, 08 January 2015, pp.326-327, available at http://dx.doi.org/10.1080/10042857.2014.953770
12. Shailly Kedia, "Approaches to low carbon development in China and India", Science Direct, 1 November 2016, available at https://www.sciencedirect.com/science/article/pii/S167492781630034X
13. Chandrashekhar Dasgupta, "Here's why the India, China Statement on Climate Change is a Big Deal", *The Wire*, 17 May 2015, available at https://thewire.in/diplomacy/heres-why-the-india-china-statement-on-climate-change-is-a-big-deal
14. Guangyu Qiao, op. cit., p.327.
15. Matthew Southerland, Iacob Koch-Weser and Angela Zhang, op.cit. p.13.
16. Press Information Bureau, Government of India, Prime Minister's Office, "Joint Statement on Climate Change between India and China during Prime Minister's visit to China", 15 May 2015, available at http://pib.nic.in/newsite/PrintRelease.aspx?relid=121754
17. Transcript of Prime Minister's Interaction with Chinese media organizations, September 16, 2014, Media Briefings, Ministry of External Affairs, Government of India, available at www.mea.gov.in.
18. Shailly Kedia, op. cit.
19. Dhanashree Jayaram, "The Future of India's Climate Diplomacy: Trump, China and Other Factors", *Climate Diplomacy*, 22 December 2016, available at https://www.climate-diplomacy.org/news/future-india's-climate-diplomacy-trump-china-and-other-factors
20. Annie Gowen and Simon Denyer, "As U.S. backs away from climate pledges, India and China step up", *The Washington Post*, 1 June 2017, available at https://www.washingtonpost.com/world/asia_pacific/as-us-backs-away-from-climate-pledges-india-and-china-step-up/

2017/06/01/59ccb494-16e4-4d47-a881-c5bd0922c3db_ story.html? utm_term=.1fc51a4e 1800

21. Santosh Kumar, "Non-committal Trump may push China to work with India in fighting climate change", *India Today*, 2 December 2016, available at https://www.indiatoday.in/world/story/donald-trump-china-india-climate-change-global-times-355373-2016-12-02
22. Anil K. Joseph, "India, China to cooperate at WTO", 25 June 2003, available at http://www.rediff.com/money/2003/jun/25pmchina.htm
23. Swapan K. Bhattacharya and Biswa N. Bhattacharyay, "Free Trade Agreement between People's Republic of China and India: Likely Impact and Its Implications to Asian Economic Community", ADB Institute Discussion Paper No. 59, November 2006, pp. 8-10., available at https://www.adb.org/sites/default/files/publication/156696/adbi-dp59.pdf
24. "India China Joint Economic Group Meeting Begins Today", *News World India*, 26 March 2018, available at http://www.newsworldindia.in/business/india-china-joint-economic-group-meeting-begins-today/292885/
25. Jayshree Sengupta, "India & China: On the same side at the WTO", Observer Research Foundation, 1 August 2017, available at https://www.orfonline.org/research/india-china-on-the-same-side-at-the-wto/
26. Dilasha Seth, "India, China to push for food security agreement at World Trade Organization", *Economic Times*, 14 May 2015, available at https://economictimes.indiatimes.com/news/economy/policy/india-china-to-push-for-food-security-agreement-at-world-trade-organization/articleshow/47275131.cms
27. Jayshree Sengupta, op. cit., (detailed statistics available at http://www.oecd.org/officialdocuments/publicdisplaydocumentpdf/?cote=TAD/CA/APM/WP(2017)12/FINAL&docLanguage=En)
28. Ibid.
29. "Trade-distorting farm subsidies must go: India-China", *General Knowledge Today*, 1 September 2017, available at https://currentaffairs.gktoday.in/tags/india-china/page/3
30. Jayshree Sengupta, op. cit.
31. "WTO deadlock explained: India seeks permanent solution to food security issue, China wants investment debate", First Post, 13 December 2017, available at https://www.firstpost.com/world/wto-deadlock-explained-india-demands-permanent-solution-to-food-security-issue-china-pushes-for-investment-debate-4256231.html
32. Dilasha Seth, op. cit.
33. Katy Barnato and Nancy Hungerford, "I got 2 out of 4 countries right, 'Mr BRIC' Jim O'Neill says", *CNBC*, 19 May 2016, available at https://www.cnbc.com/2016/05/18/i-got-2-out-of-4-countries-right-mr-bric-jim-oneill-says.html; and Oscar Williams Grut, "The former Goldman Sachs star brought in to build the Northern Powerhouse just quit government", Business Insider India, 23 September 2016, available at https://www.businessinsider.in/The-former-Goldman-Sachs-star-brought-in-to-build-the-Northern-Powerhouse-just-quit-government/articleshow/54481970.cms (Lord Jim O'Neill had quit his unpaid role in the Treasury being unhappy with Prime Minister Theresa May's approach China).
34. "What is BRICS", 26 January 2017, available at https://www.brics2017.org/English/AboutBRICS/BRICS/
35. "IMF's World Economic Outlook April 2018", available at https://www.imf.org/en/Publications/WEO/Issues/2018/03/20/world-economic-outlook-april-2018; "Global gross domestic product (GDP) at current prices from 2012 to 2022 (in billion U.S. dollars)" ,

available at https://www.statista.com/statistics/268750/global-gross-domestic-product-gdp/;

36. Luo Zhaohui, "BRICS Collaboration and China-India Cooperation", China-India Dialogue, 1 September 2017, available at http://chinaindiadialogue.com/brics-collaboration-and-china-india-cooperation
37. Andrew F. Cooper, and Asif B. Farooq, "The Role of China and India in the G20 and BRICS: Commonalities or Competitive Behaviour?", *Journal of Current Chinese Affairs*, 45 (2016), 3, p.82., available at https://www.ssoar.info/ssoar/bitstream/handle/document/54530/ssoar-jcca-2016-3-farooq_et_al-The_Role_of_China_and.pdf?sequence=1
38. Ibid., pp. 81-83.
39. Ibid., p.84.
40. Ibid., pp. 84-85; and Asit Ranjan Mishra, "KV Kamath named BRICS bank chairman", *Livemint*, 12 May 2015, available at https://www.livemint.com/Politics/7AcLijq5HVrK7MsEX5GsGP/Govt-said-to-appoint-KV-Kamath-as-BRICS-bank-head.html
41. K J M Varma, "India, 20 others set up Asian Infrastructure Investment Bank", V C Circle, 24 October 2014, available at https://www.vccircle.com/india-20-others-set-asian-infrastructure-investment-bank/
42. Andrew F. Cooper, and Asif B. Farooq, op. cit., p.77 (According to a joint study by the Asian Development Bank and Asian Development Bank Institute, the infrastructure finance gap in Asia alone is somewhere in the range of USD eight trillion for the next decade. In India itself current requirement for infrastructure development was estimated to be over USD one trillion).
43. "India seeks higher funding from AIIB; infra push for the region", *Economic Times*, 27 February 2018, available at https://economictimes.indiatimes.com/news/economy/infrastructure/india-seeks-higher-funding-from-aiib-infra-push-for-the-region/articleshow/63097063.cms; and Kinling Lo, "How India became China-led development bank's main borrower", *South China Morning Post*, 19 January 2018, available at http://www.scmp.com/news/china/diplomacy-defence/article/2129686/how-india-became-china-led-development-banks-main
44. Andrew F. Cooper, and Asif B. Farooq, op. cit., p. 85.
45. Douglas Bulloch, "China Tries to Make A Friend of India at BRICS Meeting, But is it Too Late?", *Forbes.com*, 7 September 2017, available at https://www.forbes.com/sites/douglasbulloch/2017/09/07/china-opens-its-arms-to-india-at-the-brics-while-overlooking-doklam/#2fc4e5399382 (In addition to Doklam Stand off, there were other pinpricks: India and Japan's deepening engagement; and speculation about a recent shipment of India's BrahMos missiles to Vietnam, which would not have gone unnoticed in Beijing; India renewed cases against Chinese imports whom it accused of dumping).
46. Elizabeth Roche, "BRICS declaration names Pakistan-based terror groups in diplomatic victory for India", *Livemint*, 4 September 2017, available at https://www.livemint.com/Politics/qGrkGqzoC99RAMe9nmjpdP/Brics-2017-Nations-voice-concern-over-terror-groups-includ.html
47. Douglas Bulloch, op. cit.,
48. "How China was forced to abort permanent BRICS Plus plan by India, others", *Financial Express*, 31 August 2017, available at https://www.financialexpress.com/india-news/how-china-was-forced-to-abort-permanent-brics-plus-plan-by-india-others/834486/
49. Jamil Mustafa, "What is the G20 and how does it work?", *Telegraph*, 3 July 2017, available at https://www.telegraph.co.uk/business/0/what-is-the-g20-and-how-does-it-work/
50. Ashok Sajjanhar, "Modi in China: The G20 and Beyond", *The Diplomat*, 7 September 2016, available at https://thediplomat.com/2016/09/modi-in-china-the-g20-and-beyond/
51. Ibid.

52. "2018 G20 Buenos Aires Summit", available at https://www.revolvy.com/page/2018-G20-Buenos-Aires-summit
53. Jamil Mustafa, op.cit.
54. Ashok Sajjanhar, op.cit.
55. Ibid.
56. Geethanjali Nataraj, "India and G20: How India can reshape world economic and financial order", *Brookings*, 22 August 2016, available at https://www.brookings.edu/opinions/india-and-g20-how-india-can-reshape-world-economic-and-financial-order/
57. Ashok Sajjanhar, op.cit.; and Jamil Mustafa, op.cit.
58. Andrew F. Cooper, and Asif B. Farooq, op.cit., p.89.
59. "Modi, Xi discuss 'range of issues' on the sidelines of G20 summit", *Hindustan Times*, 16 July 2017, available at https://www.hindustantimes.com/india-news/pm-modi-chinese-president-xi-jinping-discuss-range-of-issues-on-the-sidelines-of-g20-summit/story-Mc0hfELhMuhXxh6LRLvxiI.html; and
60. "What does Shanghai Cooperation Organisation membership mean for India?", *The Hindu*, 08 June 2017, available at http://www.thehindu.com/news/national/what-does-shanghai-cooperation-organisation-membership-mean-for-india/article18825646.ece
61. Salvatore Babones, "Why Is Democratic India Joining Russia And China's 'Anti-Western' Club, The SCO?", *Forbes.com*, 29 November 2017, available at https://www.forbes.com/sites/salvatorebabones/2017/11/29/why-is-democratic-india-joining-russia-and-chinas-anti-western-club-the-sco/#42f2f8554cac
62. Ashok Sajjanhar, "India's prospects in China-dominated SCO", 5 June 2017, available at https://www.orfonline.org/expert-speak/india-prospects-china-dominated-sco/
63. Salvatore Babones, op.cit.
64. Stephen Blank, "The India-China Clash and the Expanded SCO", The Central Asia – Caucasus Analyst, 16 October 2017, https://www.cacianalyst.org/publications/analytical-articles/item/13476-the-india-china-clash-and-the-expanded-sco.html
65. Ashok Sajjanhar, op.cit.
66. Kanwal Sibal, "How India can use SCO membership to grow as an Asian power", *daily O*, 14 June 2017, available at https://www.dailyo.in/politics/sco-shanghai-cooperation-org-china-pakistan-india-membership/story/1/17808.html
67. Ibid.
68. Ashok Sajjanhar, op.cit.
69. The Hindu, 08 June 2017, op.cit.
70. Salvatore Babones, op.cit.
71. Kanwal Sibal, op.cit.
72. "Shanghai Cooperation Organization (SCO)", Asia Regional Integration Center, available at https://aric.adb.org/initiative/shanghai-cooperation-organization
73. Kanwal Sibal, op.cit.
74. "The World Fact Book", The Central Intelligence Agency, available at https://www.cia.gov/library/publications/the-world-factbook/
75. Sudha Mahalingam, "It Won't Be Easy for India to Log in to Central Asia's Energy Story", *The Wire*, 07 July 2015, available at https://thewire.in/energy/it-wont-be-easy-for-india-to-log-in-to-central-asias-energy-story
76. "Construction work TAPI gas pipeline project begins", 14 December 2014, available at https://currentaffairs.gktoday.in/tags/tapi-project
77. Sameer Patil, "After Modi's Visit, Is Central Asia Open for Indian Business?", *The Diplomat*,

28 July 2015, available at https://thediplomat.com/2015/07/after-modis-visit-is-central-asia-open-for-indian-business/
78. "PM Narendra Modi launches OVL oil block project in Kazakhstan", *The Economoic Times*, 07 July 2015, available at https://economictimes.indiatimes.com/industry/energy/oil-gas/pm-narendra-modi-launches-ovl-oil-block-project-in-kazakhstan/articleshow/47977848.cms
79. Sudha Mahalingam, op.cit.
80. Ibid.
81. Ibid.
82. "Central Asia falling short of power generation potential", 15 December 2017, available at http://www.eiu.com/industry/article/806239664/central-asia-falling-short-of-power-generation-potential/2017-12-15
83. Ibid.; and Sudha Mahalingam, op.cit.
84. "Uranium and Nuclear Power in Kazakhstan", updated February 2018, available at www.world-nuclear.org/information-library/country-profiles/countries-g-n/kazakhstan.aspx
85. "Kazakhstan agrees to supply uranium to India", *World Nuclear News*, 08 July 2015, available at www.world-nuclear-news.org/UF-Kazakhstan-agrees-to-supply-uranium-to-india-0807156.html
86. "Uranium in Uzbekistan", updated April 2018, available at www.world-nuclear.org/information-library/country-profiles/countries-t-z/uzbekistan.aspx
87. Anil Sasi, "India widens N-fuel base, signs up Uzbek firm for uranium supplies", *The Indian Express*, 27 August 2014, available at http://indianexpress.com/article/business/business-others/india-widens-n-fuel-base-signs-up-uzbek-firm-for-uranium-supplies/
88. Dipanjan Roy Chaudhury, "India and China new players in Central Asia's 'Great Game'", *The Economic Times*, 02 October 2017, available at https://economictimes.indiatimes.com/news/defence/india-china-new-players-in-central-asias-great-game/articleshow/60905273.cms
89. http://www.mapsofworld.com/country-profile/tajikistan-information-geography-history.html
90. Ashok Sajjanhar, "Tajikistan President visits India; gives big impetus to bilateral ties", available at https://www.orfonline.org/expert-speak/tajikistan-president-visits-india-impetus-bilateral-ties/
91. Alexander Sodiqov, "India's Relations With Tajikistan: Beyond the Airbase", *Eurasia Daily Monitor*, Vol. 8, Issue 36, 22 February 2011, available at https://jamestown.org/program/indias-relations-with-tajikistan-beyond-the-airbase/
92. Dr. Rashmini Koparkar, 6 January 2017, available at http://www.vfindia.org/article/2017/january/06/president-rahmon-s-visit-india-tajikistan-relations-reach-new-heights
93. "Dushanbe and Moscow Disagree over Russia's Use of Ayni Airbase", *Tajikistan Monitor*, 11 February 2011, available at https://tjmonitor.wordpress.com/2011/02/11/ayni/
94. Nivedita Das Kundu, "India-Tajikistan: An Enduring Relationship", Indian Council of World Affairs, Issue Brief, available at https://icwa.in/pdfs/ibindotajik.pdf
95. Dr. Rashmini Koparkar, op.cit.
96. "India airlifts military hospital to Tajikistan to strengthen geo-strategic footprint in Central Asia", *The Economic Times*, 18 April 2013, available at https://economictimes.indiatimes.com/news/politics-and-nation/india-airlifts-military-hospital-to-tajikistan-to-strengthen-geo-strategic-footprint-in-central-asia/articleshow/19609593.cms
97. Ashok Sajjanhar, op.cit.
98. Harsh V. Pant, "India can't allow Chinese to overshadow its influence in Central Asia", *Daily O*, 9 June 2017, available at https://www.dailyo.in/politics/china-central-asia-russia-shanghai-cooperation-organisation/story/1/17730.html

99. Ashok Sajjanhar, "India-Central Asia relations: Expanding vistas of partnership", *Raisina Debate*, 22 June 2016, available at https://www.orfonline.org/expert-speak/india-central-asia-relations-expanding-vistas-of-partnership/
100. Suyash Desai, "India's SCO Challenge", *The Diplomat*, 05 December 2017, available at https://thediplomat.com/2017/12/indias-sco-challenge/
101. Kanwal Sibal, op.cit.
102. Suyash Desai, op.cit.
103. "PM's opening remarks at the SCO Summit in Astana, Kazakhstan", 09 June 2017, available at https://www.narendramodi.in/pm-s-opening-remarks-at-the-sco-summit-in-astana-kazakhstan-535799
104. Ashok Sajjanhar, 05 June 2017, op.cit.
105. Sutirtho Patranobis, "Why China has stopped urging India to join BRI", The *Hindustan Times*, New Delhi, 30 April 2018.
106. Chandra Rekha, "India's ties with Russia are critical to counter China in SCO", *Daily O*, 7 December 2017, available at https://www.dailyo.in/politics/shanghai-cooperation-organisation-china-india-russia-let-jem-and-ttp-brics/story/1/20993.html
107. Dipanjan Roy Chaudhury, op.cit.
108. Sudha Mahalingam, op.cit.
109. Ashok Sajjanhar, 05 June 2017, op.cit.
110. "B.P. Statistical Review of World Energy, June 2012", available at bp.com/statistical review, pp. 6-9.
111. Namrata Panwar, "India and China competing over Myanmar Energy resources", Working draft for BISA Conference 2009, 14-16 December 2009, University of Leicester, p.4. available as file:///Users/rajeevbhutani/Downloads/BISA-Namrata_Panwar%20(2).pdf (Proven oil reserves are given to draw out a comparison between the oil resources of two countries and these are given differently by different sources and will keep varying as more discoveries are made. For example, according to *Oil & Gas Journal*, Vol. 105, No. 48 (December 24, 2007), pp. 24-25., shown at Table 4, p.32. In Energy Information Administration / International Energy Outlook 2008, as of 1 January 2008, China had 16.0 billion barrels of oil reserve [https://www.tulane.edu/~bfleury/envirobio/readings/International%20Energy%20 Outlook%2008.pdf]; Same was revised to 20.4 billion barrels as of January 2012 by *Oil & Gas Journal*, p.3. [www.eia.gov/countries/cab.cfm?fips=CH]; British Petroleum, BP Statistical Review established China's proved oil reserve at the end of 2011 at 14.7 billion barrels [n. 110. Above]
112. Matthew Southerland, Iacob Koch-Weser and Angela Zhang, op.cit.p.14.
113. "Nuke energy must to meet growing demand: PM", *The Times of India*, 21 August 2007, available at https://timesofindia.indiatimes.com/india/Nuke-energy-must-to-meet-growing-demand-PM/articleshow/2296530.cms
114. Matthew Southerland, Iacob Koch-Weser and Angela Zhang, op.cit. p.15.
115. Dr. R. Evan Ellis, "China, Russia, India, and the Venezuelan Petroleum Industry", 11 December 2013, pp. 3-4, available at www.jsg.utexas.edu/lacp/files/China-Russia-India-and-the-Venezuelan-Petroleum-Industry.pdf
116. Ibid., pp. 1-2.
117. "China's Sinopec sues Venezuelan oil firm as Beijing's patience wanes over debt crisis", *South China Morning Post*, 07 December 2017, available at http://www.scmp.com/news/china/diplomacy-defence/article/2123293/chinas-sinopec-sues-venezuelan-oil-firm-beijings
118. He Huifeng and Laura Zhou, "Why Venezuela's 2,349pc inflation is a painful lesson for

China", *South China Morning Post*, 12 October 2017, available at http://www.scmp.com/news/china/diplomacy-defence/article/2115031/why-venezuelas-2349pc-inflation-painful-lesson-china

119. He Huifeng, "As Venezuela implodes, so do the dreams of thousands of fleeing Chinese", *South China Morning Post*, 14 August 2017, available at http://www.scmp.com/news/china/economy/article/2102922/venezuela-implodes-so-do-dreams-thousands-fleeing-chinese
120. Utpal Bhaskar, "India trumps China for Brazil offshore block", *Livemint*, 15 October 2013, available at https://www.livemint.com/Companies/VdYjZFd57klkNWT7XDVaTM/ONGC-to-buy-12-of-Brazil-block-from-Petrobras-for-529-mill.html
121. Sreeradha Datta, "Bangladesh Factor in the Indo-Myanmarese Gas Deal", *Strategic Analysis*, Vol. 32, No.1, January 2008, pp. 104-106.
122. Ibid., and "Natural gas export: Yangon chooses China", The Hindu, 22 March 2007, updated 28 September 2016 available at http://www.thehindu.com/todays-paper/tp-international/Natural-gas-export-Yangon-chooses-China/article14736335.ece
123. Namrata Panwar, op.cit., pp. 14-15.
124. Ibid., p.15.
125. Michael Hart, "Myanmar: Ground Zero for China-India Energy Competition", *Geopolitical Monitor*, 31 October 2016, available at https://www.geopoliticalmonitor.com/myanmar-ground-zero-for-china-india-competition/
126. Utpal Bhaskar, op.cit.
127. "Bilateral Economic & Commercial Relations", Embassy of India, Yangon, Myanmar, available at https://embassyofindiayangon.in/pages?id...subid; and "Oil India signs contract for two oil blocks in Myanmar", *Livemint*, 13 December 2014, available at https://www.livemint.com/Industry/X41LToV7gW9LFJNLkkCa1K/Oil-India-signs-contract-for-two-oil-blocks-in-Myanmar.html
128. "Foreign assets and ventures of Indian oil companies across the world", *The Times of India*, 28 December 2017, available at https://timesofindia.indiatimes.com/business/india-business/foreign-assets-and-ventures-of-indian-oil-companies-across-the-world/articleshow/62280019.cms
129. "OVL output touches record 12.57 mntonnes in FY 17", *The Times of India*, 7 May 2017, available at https://timesofindia.indiatimes.com/business/india-business/ovl-output-touches-record-12-57-mn-tonnes-in-fy17/articleshow/58559484.cms
130. "Foreign assets and ventures of Indian oil companies across the world", *The Times of India*, 28 December 2017, op.cit.
131. "Global Trends 2025 : A Transformed World", National Intelligence Council, (Washington DC: November 2008), pp 51-63.
132. Virendra Sahai Verma, "Wrong drill?", *Sunday Times of India*, New Delhi, 25 September2011.
133. "Don't meddle in Vietnam issue: China", *The Times of India*, New Delhi, Wednesday, 29 October 2014.
134. Global Trends 2025: A Transformed World", op.cit, p.66.
135. Rosalind Reischer, "China and India Unite On Energy", *The Diplomat*, 11 July 2012, available at https://thediplomat.com/2012/07/china-and-india-unite-on-energy/
136. Susan Shirk, "China Fragile Superpower", Oxford University Press, Oxford, 2007, pp. 137-138.
137. Rosalind Reischer, op.cit.
138. Abhilash Roy Nalpathamkalam, "Cooperation without trust: India-China relations today", available at https://pdfs.semanticscholar.org/9155/ad9d91e0911a31a3daa6f212df 64e

6c687d6.pdf

139. Rosalind Reischer, op.cit.
140. "India, China should jointly bid for oil, gas fields: Beijing media", *The Economic Times*, 16 March 2017, available at https://economictimes.indiatimes.com/industry/energy/oil-gas/india-china-should-jointly-bid-for-oil-gas-fields-beijing-media/articleshow/57672357.cms
141. Matthew Southerland, Iacob Koch-Weser and Angela Zhang, op.cit. p.16.
142. "ASEAN Up", available at https://aseanup.com/asean-infographics-population-market-economy/
143. Ibid.
144. "First ASEAN Youth Development Index", July 2017, p.8., available at http://asean.org/storage/2017/10/ASEAN-UNFPA_report_web-final-05sep.pdf
145. Harry G. Broadman, "ASEAN Is Looking Like A 'China 2.0 Play'", *Forbes.com*, 25 April 2016, available at https://www.forbes.com/sites/harrybroadman/2016/04/25/asean-is-looking-like-a-china-2-0-play/#4606ad60688b
146. Jacqueline Woo, "6 things you need to know about Asean Economic Community", *The Straits Times*, 13 October 2015, available at https://www.straitstimes.com/business/6-things-you-need-to-know-about-asean-economic-community
147. "ASEAN Investment Report 2015 – Infrastructure Investment and Connectivity", The ASEAN Secretariat, United Nations Conference on Trade and Development, November 2015, p.3., available on http://asean.org/storage/2016/09/ASEAN-Investment-report-2015.pdf
148. "China-ASEAN trade volume hits record high in 2017", Xinhua, 2018-01-28 available at http://www.xinhuanet.com/english/2018-01/28/c_136931519.htm; and Government of India, Ministry of Commerce & Industry, available at http://commerce-app.gov.in/eidb/default.asp
149. "ASEAN Investment Report 2017: Foreign Direct Investment and Economic Zones in ASEAN", p.4., available at http://unctad.org/en/PublicationsLibrary/unctad_asean_air2017d1.pdf
150. "India pivots to Southeast Asia to counter China's growing clout", *Nikkie Asian Review*, 13 March 2018, available at https://asia.nikkei.com/Editor-s-Picks/FT-Confidential-Research/India-pivots-to-Southeast-Asia-to-counter-China-s-growing-clout
151. Ibid.
152. Johannes Dragsbaek Schmidt, "India China Rivalry and Competition in Southeast Asia", available at http://vbn.aau.dk/files/61143145/India_China_Rivalry_and_ Competition_ in_ Southeast_Asia_pres_in_Delhi.vbn
153. Rahul Mazumdar, "From trade to investments, re-orienting India's ASEAN strategy", *Raisina Debates*, 27 February 2017, available at https://www.orfonline.org/expert-speak/reorienting-india-asean-strategy-trade-investment/ ;andGovernment of India, Ministry of Commerce & Industry, op.cit.
154. Ibid.
155. "ASEAN-India Relations", ASEAN India, available at http://mea.gov.in/aseanindia/20-years.htm (FDI outflows from India to ASEAN countries, from April 2007 to March 2015, as per data maintained by DEA, was about US$38.672 billion.)
156. Rahul Mazumdar, op.cit.
157. Harsh V. Pant and Avantika Deb, "India-ASEAN partnership at 25", *ORF Issue Brief*, 4 July 2017, available at https://www.orfonline.org/research/india-asean-partnership-at-25/
158. "Full implementation of India, Asean FTA to boost trade", *The Economic Times*, 23 January 2018, available at https://economictimes.indiatimes.com/news/economy/foreign-trade/full-

implementation-of-india-asean-fta-to-boost-trade/articleshow/62618818.cms; Anisha Dutta and Rezaul H Laskar, "Thai envoy lays stress on motor vehicles pact", *Hindustan Times*, New Delhi, 14 December 2018.

159. Harsh V. Pant and Avantika Deb, op.cit.
160. http://mea.gov.in/aseanindia/20-years.htm, op.cit.
161. Abhijeet Pandey, "ASEAN and India face common threats, close cooperation is imperative", *Daily O*, 28 January 2018, available at https://www.dailyo.in/politics/asean-summit-chinese-aggression-narendra-modi-republic-day-terrorism-trade/story/1/22033.html
162. Samanth Subramanian, "India will help build the world's largest trade bloc with Asean", *The National*, 27 January 2018, available at https://www.thenational.ae/business/economy/india-will-help-build-the-world-s-largest-trade-bloc-with-asean-1.699280
163. Girija Pande, "The Regional Comprehensive Economic Partnership: India should join the Asian Trade Block", ISAS Brief No. 551, 7 February 2018, available at https://www.isas.nus.edu.sg/wp-content/uploads/2018/03/ISAS-Briefs-No.-551-The-Regional-Comprehensive-Economic-Partnership.pdf
164. Kavaljit Singh, "Why India Should Rethink Its Approach to RCEP Negotiations", Madhyam, 18 July 2017, available at http://www.madhyam.org.in/why-india-should-rethink-its-approach-to-rcep/
165. Ibid.
166. Samanth Subramanian, op.cit.; and Kavaljit Singh, op.cit.
167. GirijaPande, op.cit, p.2.
168. Ibid., p.3.
169. Ibid., p.4.
170. Kavaljit Singh, op.cit.
171. https://en.wikipedia.org/wiki/South_Asian_Association_for_Regional_Cooperation
172. Srikanth Kondapalli, "SAARC Summit: China's role will be keenly watched by the South Asian countries", *The Economic Times*, 26 November 2014, available at https://blogs.economictimes.indiatimes.com/et-commentary/saarc-summit-chinas-role-will-be-keenly-watched-by-the-south-asian-countries/
173. Deepak Gajurel, "China's push for SAARC membership: Anxiety for India", *Nepal Polity*, 26 November 2014, available at http://nepalpolity.com/chinas-push-for-saarc-membership-meaning-for-sa/
174. S.A.K. Madanayaka, "China, India and the Balance of Power in South Asia: with Reference to Sri Lanka's Position", Department of Economics, University of Kelaniya, available at https://www.researchgate.net/publication/315711472_China_India_and_the_Balance_of_Power_in_South_Asia_with_Reference_to_Sri_Lanka's_Position [accessed Jun 25 2018].
175. Tanvi Madan, "A Role for China in SAARC?" in 'Reinvigorating SAARC: India's Opportunities and Challenges", *Brookings Report*, 20 November 2014, available at https://www.brookings.edu/research/chinas-role-in-saarc/
176. Shannon Tiezzi, "China Makes Inroads Into India's Backyard", *The Diplomat*, 27 November 2014, available at https://thediplomat.com/2014/11/china-makes-inroads-into-indias-backyard/; and Harsh V. Pant, "India and China Slug It Out in South Asia", *The Diplomat*, 11 December 2014, available at https://thediplomat.com/2014/12/india-and-china-slug-it-out-in-south-asia/
177. Elizabeth Roche, "Pakistan, 2 others demand greater role for China in SAARC", *Livemint*, 27 November 2014, available at https://www.livemint.com/Politics/df7Jr5TNmxH9h245REpjuL/Pakistan-demands-greater-role-for-China-in-Saarc.html ;Shannon Tiezzi, op.cit., and

Harsh V. Pant, op.cit.

178. An Baijie, "Trade with South Asia to expand", *China Daily*, 15 June 2018, available at http://africa.chinadaily.com.cn/a/201806/15/WS5b22f64fa310010f8f59d111.html
179. Seekkuwa Wasam Hirantha, "From SAPTA to SAFTA: Gravity Analysis of South Asian Free Trade", available at www.etsg.org/ETSG2004/Papers/hirantha.pdf
180. Shweta Punj, "The Castaway: India is steadily losing ground to China as a trading partner of South Asian countries", *Business Today*, 22 December 2013, available at https://www.businesstoday.in/magazine/focus/india-losing-ground-as-trading-partner-south-asian-countries/story/201078.html
181. Wajahat S. Khan, "China May Soon Establish Naval Base in U.S. Ally Pakistan", *NBC News*, 19 June 2017, available at "https://www.nbcnews.com/news/china/china-may-soon-establish-naval-base-u-s-ally-pakistan-n770991
182. Aamir Saeed, "Pakistan-China trade volume reaches $13.77 billion in 2015-16: NA informed", 14 March 2017, available at http://fp.brecorder.com/2017/03/20170314153866/
183. Ashlyn Anderson and Alyssa Ayres, "Economics of Influence: China and India in South Asia, Council on Foreign Relations, 3 August 2015, available at https://www.cfr.org/expert-brief/economics-influence-china-and-india-south-asia
184. Shweta Punj, op.cit.
185. Chris Devonshire-Ellis, "China's Developing Silk Road Trade Relations with SAARC", *Asia Briefing*, 11 March 2016, available at http://www.asiabriefing.com/news/2016/03/chinaindiasaarc/
186. "OEC–Sri Lanka (LKA) Exports, Imports and Trade Partners", available at atlas.media.mit.edu/en/profile/country/lka
187. Chris Devonshire-Ellis, op.cit.
188. Shihar Aneez, "Exclusive: Free Trade Talks between China and Sri Lanka hit big hurdles", *Reuters*, 31 May 2018, available at https://in.reuters.com/
189. https://atlas.media.mit.edu/en/profile/country/npl/
190. Fahad Shah, "Nepal's Balancing Act: Walking the Tight Rope Between China and India", Foreign Affairs, 25 February 2016, available at https://www.foreignaffairs.com/articles/china/2016-02-25/nepals-balancing-act
191. "How India and China are vying for influence in South Asia", *Times of India.com*, 31 May 2018, available at https://timesofindia.indiatimes.com/india/how-india-and-china-are-vying-for-influence-in-south-asia/articleshow/63395543.cms
192. www.oecd.org/dac/stats/officialdevelopmentassistancedefinitionandcoverage.htm
193. Ashlyn Anderson and Alyssa Ayres, op.cit.
194. *Times of India.com*, 31 May 2018, op.cit.
195. "Migration and Remittances Data", The World Bank, 16 November 2017, available at http://www.worldbank.org/en/topic/migrationremittancesdiasporaissues/brief/migration-remittances-data
196. Si Xu, "China and South Asia Trade Competition and Complementary: Analysis Based on the Background of "One Belt and One Road", *Chinese Studies*, 6, 108-122, p.121. available at https://doi.org/10.4236/chnstd.2017.62010
197. Ibid., p.109.
198. Ashlyn Anderson and Alyssa Ayres, op.cit.
199. Joseph S. Nye, Jr., "Soft Power: The Means to Success in World Politics", Foreign Affairs, Capsule Review May/June 2004 Issue available at https://www.foreignaffairs.com/reviews/capsule-review/2004-05-01/soft-power-means-success-world-politics

200. Ibid. (Joseph Nye's own model for the conversion of soft power into a desired outcome comprises five steps:
Resources → Objectives → Conversion → Target Response → Outcome
One has to identify the Resources that will affect the targets in question. The process must start with a clear account of available resources and an understanding of where they will be effective).
201. Joshua Kurlantzick, "China's Charm: Implications of Chinese Soft Power", Policy Brief 47 (Washington, DC: Carnegie Endowment for International Peace, June 2006), p.1.
202. Brigadier (Dr.) Rajeev Bhutani, op.cit., p.237.
203. "Harmonious society not just utopian dream", *Global Times*, October 27, 2010 available at www.globaltimes.cn/opinion/commentary/2010-10/586744.html and "Harmonious World: China's Ancient Philosophy for New International Order", available at bw.china-embassy.org/eng/xwdt/t 367341.htm
204. Kin-man Chan, "Harmonious Society", The Chinese University of Hongkong, Hongkong China, available at www.cuhk.edu.hk/centre/ccss/publication /km-chan/CKM-14.pdf
205. "Vasudhaiva Kutumbakam - The Whole World is one family", available at vedicambassador.wordpress.com/2012/09/29/vasudhaiv-kutumbakam-the-whole-world-is-one-family.
206. Indrani Bagchi, "Who'll be the Global Soft Super power?", *Sunday Times of India*, New Delhi, 01 July 2007.
207. Jonathan McClory, "Soft Power 30: A Global Ranking of Soft Power", 2015, available at www.comresglobal.com/wp-content/uploads/2015/07/Report-Final-published.pdf, p.9.
208. Jonathan McClory, "Soft Power 30: A Global Ranking of Soft Power 2017", available at https://softpower.30.com/wp-content/uploads/2017/07/The-Soft-Power-30-Report-2017-Web-1.pdf
209. Jonathan McClory, "Soft Power 30: A Global Ranking of Soft Power", 2015, op.cit., p.27.
210. Martin Davidson, "China's soft power: A comparative failure or secret success", in "Soft Power 30: A Global Ranking of Soft Power 2017", op.cit., p.70.
211. Martin Davidson, op.cit., p.71.
212. Jonathan McClory, "Soft Power 30: A Global Ranking of Soft Power", 2015, op.cit., p.22; and Jonathan McClory, "Soft Power 30: A Global Ranking of Soft Power 2017", op.cit., p.32.
213. Jonathan McClory, "Soft Power 30: A Global Ranking of Soft Power 2017", op.cit., p.49.
214. John Lee, "Hard sell soft power" *Hindustan Times*, Lucknow, Friday, July 02, 2010.
215. "Rise in number of foreign students reflects country's bright prospects", *China Daily*, 24-10-2017, www.chinadaily.com.cn/opinion/2017-10/24/content_33637493.htm
216. Cheng Si (*China Daily*), "Tourism numbers in China see steady rise", *The Telegraph*, 13 February 2018, https://www.telegraph.co.uk/news/world/china-watch/travel/china-tourism-grows/
217. Joseph S. Nye, "The Rise of China's Soft Power", Op-Ed, *Wall Street Journal Asia*, December 29, 2005 at http://belfercenter.hks.harvard.edu/publication/1449/
218. Obja Borah Hazarika and Vivek Mishra, "Soft Power Contestation between India and China in South Asia", *Indian Foreign Affairs Journal*, Vol.11, No.2, April-June 2016, p.140.
219. Tridivesh Singh Maini, "India has an edge over China in soft power, divisive politics must not harm it", *Daily O*, 20 October 2017, available at https://www.dailyo.in/politics/soft-power-india-china-taj-mahal-sangeet-som-narendra-modi/story/1/20146.html
220. Zhang Xiaoling, "China as an Emerging Power: Winning Hearts and Minds Through

Communicating with Foreign Publics", Discussion Paper 35, The University of Nottingham, China Policy Institute; Nottingham, UK, October 2008, p.8.

221. Sophie Yu, "China's voice is about to get louder all around the World", *South China Morning Post*, October 30, 2010.
222. Joseph S. Nye Jr., "China's Soft Power Deficit", *Wall Street Journal*, May 08, 2012, p.1. available at http://online.wsj.com/news/articles/SB100014240527023044511045
223. Ibid., p.2.
224. Frank Ching, "Playing the Gentle Giant: Beijing's attempts to promote Chinese Soft power are falling short - even in Hongkong", *The Times of India*, New Delhi, Friday, 17 February 2012.
225. "Hong Kong protests: No Exit", The Economist, 04 October 2014, Hong Kong, available at http://www.economist.com/news/china/21621846-days-student-led-unrest-hong-kong-are-crisis-chinas-communist-party-no-exit [The name "Umbrella Revolution" was coined by New Yorker Adam Cotton on social media on 26 September to describe the 2014 Hong Kong protests. They had brought umbrellas to defend themselves from pepper spray and tear gas.]
226. Martin Davidson, op.cit., pp.71-72.
227. Ibid., p.72.
228. Dr Zhongying Pang, "China's Soft Power", CNAPS Visiting Fellow Presentation, The Brookings Institution, Washington, DC, October 24, 2007, p.5.
229. Frank Ching, op.cit.
230. "Concerned over negative image, China to project itself as 'cultural soft power", *The Times of India*, New Delhi, Wednesday, 01 January 2014.
231. Matthew Miller, "China's Xi strikes conciliatory note, broadens diplomatic focus", *Reuters*, 30 November 2014, available at https://www.reuters.com/article/us-china-southchinasea/chinas-xi-strikes-conciliatory-note-broadens-diplomatic-focus-idUSKCN0JE04J20141130
232. Jonathan McClory, "Soft Power 30: A Global Ranking of Soft Power 2017", op.cit., p.18.
233. Anil Sasi, "On Modi government drawing board: Tool to hardsell soft power in diplomacy", *Indian Express*, 14 February 2018, available at https://indianexpress.com/article/india/modi-diplomacy-strategic-partnership-soft-power-hard-state-india-5063098/
234. Swaroopa Lahiri, "Soft Power – A Major Tool in Modi's Foreign Policy Kit", *Journal of South Asian Studies*, 05 January 2017, p.39, available at http://www.escijournals.net/JSAS
235. Inder Singh, "Indian Diaspora is Prime Minister Narendra Modi's 'Soft Power'", India West, 31 August 2016, available at http://www.indiawest.com/blogs/indian-diaspora-is-prime-minister-narendra-modi-s-soft-power/article_794f1d86-6fcd-11e6-a407-bb0e601f843c.html
236. Rakesh Mohan Chaturvedi, "Narendra Modi taking up the issue of Cleanliness of Ganga speaking in Sanskritised Hindi in US scores with the RSS", *The Economic Times*, 3 October 2014, available at https://economictimes.indiatimes.com/news/politics-and-nation/narendra-modi-taking-up-the-issue-of-cleanliness-of-ganga-speaking-in-sanskritised-hindi-in-us-scores-with-the-rss/articleshow/44160504.cms
237. Inder Singh, op.cit.
238. "Let us view our Diaspora not only in terms of Sankhya but let us see it as Shakti", Prime Minister Narendra Modi's Speech, 02 October 2016, available at https://www.narendramodi.in/text-of-pm-s-speech-at-the-inauguration-of-pravasi-bharatiya-kendra-532559
239. Debidatta Aurobinda Mahapatra, "From a latent to a 'strong' soft power? The evolution of India's cultural diplomacy", Palgrave Communications, Vol. 2, Article number: 16091 (2016) available at https://www.nature.com/articles/palcomms201691#ref35
240. Ibid.

241. Sam Jawed, "PM Modi's Gifts For Foreign Dignitaries Will Surprise Adityanath", *The Quint,* 21 June 2017, available at https://www.thequint.com/news/india/pm-modi-gifts-foreign-dignitaries-will-surprise-yogi
242. Swaroopa Lahiri, op.cit., p.41.
243. Amit Bhandari and Chandni Jindal, "Chinese Investments in India's Neighbourhood", Gateway House Maps No. 4-9, February 2018, p.15.
244. Chandan Nandy, "For Modi Regime, Buddhism is a Soft Power Approach for Hard Power", *The Quint,* 05 May 2015, https://www.thequint.com/news/world/for-modi-regime-buddhism-is-a-soft-power-approach-for-hard-power
245. Bandu de Silva, "Emerging Cultural Emphasis In India's Foreign Policy Under Modi", *Colombo Telegraph,* 29 May 2015, available at https://www.colombotelegraph.com/index.php/emerging-cultural-emphasis-in-indias-foreign-policy-under-modi/
246. Sreemoy Talukdar, "Narendra Modi in Sri Lanka: PM is transforming India's foreign policy through soft power and cultural diplomacy", *First Post,* 12 May 2017, available at https://www.firstpost.com/world/narendra-modi-in-sri-lanka-pm-is-transforming-indias-foreign-policy-through-soft-power-and-cultural-diplomacy-3440452.html
247. Swaroopa Lahiri, op.cit.,p.41.
248. Sreemoy Talukdar, op.cit. ; and "List of Agreements signed during the visit of Prime Minister to China (May 15, 2015)", Ministry of External Affairs, Govt of India, 15 May 2015, available at http://mea.gov.in/bilateral-documents.htm?dtl/25260/List+of+Agreements+signed+during+the+visit+of+Prime+Minister+to+China+May+15+2015
249. "International Day of Yoga 21 June", available at http://www.un.org/en/events/yogaday/background.shtml
250. Abantika Ghosh, "Two New Guinness World Records; PM Modi joins in, Rajpath bends into 'Yogpath'", *Indian Express,* 22 June 2015, available at https://indianexpress.com/article/india/india-others/international-yoga-day-celebration-at-rajpath-sets-guinness-world-records/
251. Debidatta Aurobinda Mahapatra, op.cit.
252. Ibid.
253. Swaroopa Lahiri, op.cit., p.41.
254. Brigadier (Dr.) Rajeev Bhutani, op.cit., p.247.
255. Rachel Dwyer, "Why is govt neglecting Bollywood, a major source of soft power?", *Hindustan Times,* 01 July 2017, available at https://www.hindustantimes.com/opinion/why-is-govt-neglecting-bollywood-a-major-source-of-soft-power/story-7hyqWZNiXaMlB50nopoCBJ.html
256. Joseph S. Nye Jr., "China's Soft Power Deficit", *Wall Street Journal,* May 08, 2012, pp.1-2., available at http://online.wsj.com/news/articles/SB100014240527023044511045
257. Uma Sudhindra, "From Buddhism to Bollywood – The Investment in Soft Power", Vivekananda International Foundation, 08 December 2015, available at https://www.vifindia.org/article/2015/december/08/from-buddhism-to-bollywood-the-investment-in-soft-power
258. Shashi Tharoor, "India's 'Bollywood' power", *The Japan Times,* 09 January 2008, available at https://www.japantimes.co.jp/opinion/2008/01/09/commentary/world-commentary/indias-bollywood-power/#.W3UGTmQzYfF
259. Swaroopa Lahiri, op.cit., pp.43-44.
260. "Soft Power of Bollywood", The Tribune, Editorial, 14 February 2015, available at https://www.tribuneindia.com/news/editorials/soft-power-of-bollywood/41700.html
261. Pooja Pillai, "From Bajrangi Bhaijaan to Geeta: When soft power shows India and Pakistan

the way", *The Indian Express*, 26 October 2015, available at https://indianexpress.com/article/explained/from-bajrangi-bhaijaan-to-geeta-when-soft-power-shows-india-and-pakistan-the-way/

262. "India-Myanmar ties: Buddha, Bharatanatyam and Bollywood", Youth Forum on Foreign Policy", 15 January 2015, available at https://yffpindia.wordpress.com/2015/01/15/india-myanmar-ties-buddha-bharatanatyam-and-bollywood/
263. Shashi Tharoor, op.cit.
264. Debidatta Aurobinda Mahapatra, op.cit.
265. Swaroopa Lahiri, op.cit., p.44.
266. Atul Aneja, "Soft power set to define Modi's China visit", *The Hindu*, 11 May 2015, available at https://www.thehindu.com/news/international/social-media-bollywood-and-yoga-to-dominate-modis-china-visit/article7194559.ece
267. Amy Qin, "China Fears India May Be Edging It Out in Culture Battle", *New York Times*, 30 September 2017, available at https://www.nytimes.com/2017/09/30/world/asia/china-india-dangal-bollywood.html
268. "China's most expensive movie flops in first week", Agence France-Press, *Hindustan Times*, New Delhi, 18 July 2018.
269. Amy Qin, op.cit.
270. Rinku Ghosh, "Indian Soft Power Impacts China", *Daily Pioneer*, 18 April 2018, available at http://www.dailypioneer.com/columnists/edit/indian-soft-power-impacts-china.html
271. Ibid.
272. Swaroopa Lahiri, op.cit., p.44.
273. Rinku Ghosh, op.cit.
274. Swaroopa Lahiri, op.cit., p.42.
275. Bandu de Silva, op. cit.
276. Debidatta Aurobinda Mahapatra, op.cit.
277. Swaroopa Lahiri, op.cit., p.42.
278. Debidatta Aurobinda Mahapatra, op.cit.
279. Sunayana Suresh and Reza Noorani, "Indian cuisine makes a splash across the globe", *The Times of India*, 15 February 2014, available at https://timesofindia.indiatimes.com/Indian-cuisine-makes-a-splash-across-the-globe/articleshow/29822421.cms
280. Debidatta Aurobinda Mahapatra, op.cit.
281. Jonathan McClory, "Soft Power 30: A Global Ranking of Soft Power", 2015, op. cit. p.34
282. Peter Martin, "Yoga Diplomacy: Narendra Modi's Soft Power Strategy", *Foreign Affairs*, 25 January 2015, available at https://www.foreignaffairs.com/articles/india/2015-01-25/yoga-diplomacy
283. Twitter. (2016a) Narendra Modi, https://twitter.com/narendramodi?lang=en (accessed on 27 December 2018).
284. Twitter. (2016b) Sushma Swaraj, at https://twitter.com/SushmaSwaraj?ref_src=twsrc%5Egoogle%7Ctwcamp%5Eserp%77Ctwgr%5Eauthor (accessed on 27 December 2018) .
285. Debidatta Aurobinda Mahapatra, op.cit.
286. Swaroopa Lahiri, op. cit., p.44.
287. Uma Sudhindra, op. cit.
288. Vikas Pandey, "India election: World's biggest voting event explained", *BBC News*, 09 April 2014, available at https://www.bbc.com/news/world-asia-india-26847432
289. "Know Everything About How Much India Receives And Donates Foreign Aid", *The Logical Indian*, 06 November 2015, available at https://thelogicalindian.com/story-feed/exclusive/

know-everything-about-how-much-india-receives-and-donates-foreign-aid/

290. Indrani Bagchi, "Who'll be the Global Soft Super power?", *Sunday Times of India*, New Delhi, 01 July 2007.
291. Ibid.
292. Shubhajit Roy, "PM Modi offers Africa $10-bn loan, says projects to be monitored", *The Indian Express*, 25 December 2015, available at https://indianexpress.com/article/india/india-news-india/india-offers-africa-10-bn-soft-loan-seeks-stronger-ties/
293. Anil Sasi, op.cit.
294. Amy Qin, op.cit.
295. Ibid.
296. Tridivesh Singh Maini, "Can Soft Power Help Repair China-India Ties?", *The Diplomat*, 10 February 2018, available at https://thediplomat.com/2018/02/can-soft-power-help-repair-china-india-ties
297. Cameron Hickert (Class of 17), "Space Rivals: Power and Strategy in the China-India Space Race", available at https://www.schwarzmanscholars.org/news-article/space-rivals-power-strategy-china-india-space-race/
298. Ibid.
299. Emma Luxton, "Which countries spend the most on space exploration?", *World Economic Forum*, 11 January 2016, available at https://www.weforum.org/agenda/2016/01/which-countries-spend-the-most-on-space-exploration/
300. "China's Space Activities in 2006", Information Office of the State Council of the People's Republic of China, October 2006, Beijing. Ch. 1 (Aims and Principles of Development) available at www.china.org.cn/english/features/book/183672.htm.
301. Sudha Ramachandran, "Chinese and Indian Competition in Space Heats Up", *China Brief*, Vol. 17, Issue 13, 20 October 2017, available at https://jamestown.org/program/chinese-indian-competition-space-heats/
302. "China to open space station to scientists worldwide", Xinhua, 08 June 2017, available at http://www.xinhuanet.com/english/2017-06/08/c_136350379.htm
303. "China aims to land on far side of moon via launch of 'Magpie Bridge' satellite", *The Guardian*, 21 May 2018, available at https://www.theguardian.com/world/2018/may/21/china-dark-side-moon-launch-magpie-bridge-satellite; "China takes giant step toward landing on far side of moon", *New York Post*, 21 May 2018, available at https://nypost.com/2018/05/21/china-takes-giant-step-toward-landing-on-far-side-of-moon/; Paul Rincon, "Chang'e 4: China mission launches to far side of Moon", *BBC News*, 07 December 2018, available at https://www.bbc.com/news/science-environment-46471668; and Andrew Jones, "China launches Chang'e-4 spacecraft for pioneering lunar far side landing mission", *Space News*, 07 December 2018, available at https://spacenews.com/china-launches-change-4-spacecraft-for-pioneering-lunar-far-side-landing-mission/ ; and Paul Rincon, "Chang'e- 4: China mission launches to far side of Moon", *BBC News*, 07 December 2018, available at https://www.bbc.com/news/science-environment-46471668; and Sutirtho Patranobis, "In a first, China lands probe on moon's dark side", *Hindustan Times*, New Delhi, Friday, 04 January 2019.
304. Neil Connor and Christine Wei, "Beijing eyes 'robotic and human settlement' on Mars with ambitious 2020 mission", *The Telegraph*, 21 September 2017, available at https://www.telegraph.co.uk/news/2017/09/21/plans-2020-chinese-mars-probe-explore-possibility-human-settlement/
305. Brigadier (Dr.) Rajeev Bhutani, op. cit., p.193.
306. Ralph Jennings, "These Four Countries Are Racing To Compete With China in Outer Space", available at https://www.forbes.com/sites/ralphjennings/2017/10/19/meet-chinas-four-future-

asian-rivals-in-outer-space/#70ad88312c49

307. Sudha Ramachandran, op.cit.
308. "India's Chandrayaan helps NASA detect water on Moon", *Press Trust of India*, August 28, 2013 NDTV (www.ndtv.com/article/india/india-s-chandrayaan-helps-nasa-detect-water-on-moon-411525; Voice of America, "Lunar Missions Detect Water on Moon", November 02, 2009 (www.voanews.com/content/a-13-2009-09-24-voa46-68806852/362715.html;en.wikipedia.org/wiki/chandrayaan-1.
309. K.S. Jayaraman, "India Drops Russia from Chandrayaan-2 Lunar Mission", *Space News*, 15 August 2013, available at www.spacenews.com/article/civil-space/36795india-drops-russia-from-chandrayaan-2-lunar-mission.
310. Tomasz Nowakowski, "India's Chandrayaan-2 Moon Mission Slips to 2019", The Spaceflight Insider, 9 August 2018, available at http://www.spaceflightinsider.com/organizations/isro/indias-chandrayaan-2-moon-mission-slips-to-2019/
311. "India needs 45 more satellites in space", Chairman ISRO K Sivan's Interview, *Hindustan Times*, New Delhi, 12 August 2018; https://www.isro.gov.in/gslv-mk-iii-chandrayaan-2-mission; and https://www. timesofindia.indiatimes.com/india/jan-30-not-3rd-best-date-for-chandrayaan-2-review-panel/articleshow/66074297.cms
312. Pallab Ghosh, "India Mars Launch stokes Asian Space Race with China", *BBC News*, 20 October 2013, available at www.bbc.co.uk/news/science-environment -24550971; "India enters super exclusive Mars club", *The Times of India*, New Delhi, Thursday, 25 September 2014.
313. "Mangalyaan on 2014 list of top 25 inventions", *The Times of India*, New Delhi, Saturday, November 22, 2014.
314. "At Rs 800 crore, Chandrayaan-2 mission cheaper than Christopher Nolan's 'Interstellar,' says ISRO's Dr K Sivan", DNA, 20 February 2018, available at https://www.dnaindia.com/science/report-at-rs-800-crore-chandrayaan-2-mission-cheaper-than-christopher-nolan-s-interstellar-says-isro-s-dr-k-sivan-2586643
315. Katie Hunt and Medhavi Arora, "India in record satellite launch as Asia's space race heats up", *CNN*, 15 February 2017, available at https://edition.cnn.com/2017/02/13/asia/india-china-asia-space-race/index.html
316. "India needs 45 more satellites in space", op.cit. (In 2018, ISRO has launched satellites:- 12 January – 31 satellites in single flight; 29 March – GSAT-6A; 12 April – IRNSS-1I; 16 September – 2 foreign satellites; 14 November – GSAT-29; 29 November – Hys IS and 30 customer satellites; 5 December – GSAT-11, India's heaviest communication satellite launched from French Guiana atop Ariane 5; 19 December – GSAT-7A, the 39th communication satellite along with GSAT-7 & GSAT-6 will form the band of communication satellite for use of the security forces. Refer https://www.isro.gov.in/update/29-mar-2018/gslv-successfully-launches-gsat-6a-satellite)
317. Katie Hunt and Medhavi Arora, op. cit.
318. "Cabinet Approves Rs. 10,000 Crore Gaganyaan Project", Gadget 360, 28 December 2018, available at https://gadgets.ndtv.com/science/news/gaganyaan-project-approved-by-cabinet-indias-first-manned-space-mission-1969435; and "3 Indians To Spend 7 Days In Space In Rs. 10,000 Crore Gaganyaan Plan: 10 Points", NDTV, 28 December 2018, available at https://www.ndtv.com/india-news/3-indians-to-be-sent-to-space-for-7-days-by-2022-cabinet-approves-budget-1969358
319. "Beidou Satellite Navigation System to Cover Whole World in 2020", *PLA Daily*, 20 May 2010, available at eng.chinamil.com.cn/news-channels/china-military-news/2010-05/20/

content-4222569.htm

320. "China's Beidou system to expand cooperation to SE Asia", *China Daily*, 1 April 2017, available at http://www.chinadaily.com.cn/china/2017-04/01/content_28774844.htm
321. Avinash Bhat, "India's very own GPS is ready with seventh navigation satellite launch", *The Hindu*, 28 April 2016, available at https://www.thehindu.com/sci-tech/science/irnss-launch-indias-own-regional-navigation-satellite-system-takes-shape/article8531388.ece
322. Stephen Clark, "Indian navigation satellite stranded on rocket after launch", Spaceflight Now, 31 August 2017, available at https://spaceflightnow.com/2017/08/31/pslv-c39/
323. T A Johnson, "Failing clocks in space worry for India's GPS", *The Indian Express*, 26 June 2017, available at https://indianexpress.com/article/technology/science/failing-clocks-in-space-worry-for-indias-gps-4721918/
324. Chethan Kumar, "Isro aims to launch 22 missions in 2019; 50 in 3 years", *The Times of India*, 12 August 2018, available at https://timesofindia.indiatimes.com/india/isro-aims-to-launch-22-missions-in-2019-50-in-3-years/articleshow/65375131.cms
325. "India to build satellite tracking station in Vietnam that offers eye on China", *India Today*, 25 January 2016, available at https://www.indiatoday.in/world/rest-of-the-world/story/india-to-build-satellite-tracking-station-in-vietnam-that-offers-eye-on-china-305371-2016-01-25
326. "India aces space diplomacy test with Modi's satellite gift to South Asia: 14 things to know", *The Economic Times*, 5 May 2017, available at https://economictimes.indiatimes.com/news/science/india-aces-space-diplomacy-test-with-modis-satellite-gift-to-south-asia-14-things-to-know/articleshow/58534107.cms
327. Sudha Ramachandran, op.cit.
328. "2016 Space Launch Statistics", Space Flight 101.com, 31 December 2016, available at http://spaceflight101.com/2016-space-launch-statistics/
329. Rudraneil Sengupta, "India's space business is ready for lift-off", *Livemint*, 15 June 2017, available at https://www.livemint.com/Science/tWvAvnsZ7GQEiYhopKU6tM/Indias-space-business-is-ready-for-liftoff.html
330. "Chandrayaan-2 on track, 32 new missions next year: ISRO", *The New Indian Express*, 19 December 2018, available at https://www.msn.com/en-in/news/other/chandrayaan-2-on-track-32-missions-next-year-isro/ar-BBRdsjj
331. Hu Weijia, "China needs to cut commercial space costs to compete with India", *Global Times*, 20 February 2017, available at http://www.globaltimes.cn/content/1033824.shtml
332. Stephen Chen, "Space the final frontier for Chinese start-ups and venture capitalists", *South China Morning Post*, 20 May 2016, available at https://www.scmp.com/news/china/article/1947369/space-final-frontier-chinese-start-ups-and-venture-capitalists
333. Cameron Hickert (Class of 17), op.cit.
334. US DoD Annual Report to Congress, "Military and Security Developments Involving the People's Republic of China 2015", p.14 (to be referred as US DoD "MSDC 2015"), available at www.defense.gov/pubs/2015_China_Military_Power_Report.pdf
335. Harsh Vasani, "India's Anti-Satellite Weapons", *The Diplomat*, 14 June 2016, available at https://thediplomat.com/2016/06/indias-anti-satellite-weapons/
336. "India has all the building blocks for an anti-satellite capability", Dr Vijay Kumar Saraswat's Interview with Sandeep Unnithan, *India Today*, 27 April 2012, available at https://www.indiatoday.in/india/story/agni-v-drdo-chief-dr-vijay-kumar-saraswat-interview-100405-2012-04-27
337. "India-Japan Joint Statement during visit of Prime Minister of Japan to India (September 14, 2017)", Ministry of External Affairs, Government of India, September 14, 2017, available at

http://www.mea.gov.in/bilateral-documents.htm?dtl/28946/IndiaJapan

338. Leo Cendrowicz, "Step forward India, Japan and China, the new competitors in the race to explore space", *inews*, 19 January 2018, available at https://inews.co.uk/news/science/space-race-india-japan-china/

Chapter 4: India's Strategic Initiatives

1. "Deng Xiaoping's 24-Character Strategy", available at https://www.globalsecurity.org/military/world/china/24-character.htm
2. James McBride, "Building the New Silk Road", CFR Backgrounder, 22 May 2015, available at https://www.cfr.org/backgrounder/building-new-silk-road
3. Kevin McCauley, "The PLA Accelerates Modernization Plans", *China Brief*, Vol. 18, Issue 1, 12 January 2018, available at https://jamestown.org/program/pla-accelerates-modernization-plans/
4. Joshua Berlinger, "Mattis takes hardline on China in Singapore Speech", *CNN*, 02 June 2018, available at https://edition.cnn.com/2018/06/01/asia/james-mattis-singapore-shangri-la-intl/index.html
5. "National Security Strategy of the United States of America", December 2017, p.25.
6. Ambassador Chas W. Freeman, Jr. (USFS, Ret.), "Indo-Pacific Dynamics in Trans-Pacific Perspective, Middle East Policy Council, 16 April 2012, available at https://www.mepc.org/speeches/indo-pacific-dynamics-trans-pacific-perspective
7. Rory Medcalf, "A Term Whose Time Has Come: The Indo-Pacific", *The Diplomat*, 04 December 2012, available at https://thediplomat.com/2012/12/a-term-whose-time-has-come-the-indo-pacific/
8. David Scott, "The "Indo-Pacific" – New Regional Formulations and New Maritime Frameworks for US-India Strategic Convergence", *Asia-Pacific Review*, Vol. 19, No. 2, 2012 available at https://dscottcom.files.wordpress.com/2017/03/indo-pacific.pdf
9. Admiral Arun Prakash (Retd.), "Guest Column: Modi's Shangri-La moment", *India Today*, 08 June 2018, available at https://www.indiatoday.in/magazine/up-front/story/20180618-guest-column-modi-s-shangri-la-moment-1255389-2018-06-08
10. D. Gnanagurunathan, "India and the idea of the 'Indo-Pacific'", *East Asia Forum*, 20 October 2012, available at http://www.eastasiaforum.org/2012/10/20/india-and-the-idea-of-the-indo-pacific/
11. "Confluence of the Two Seas", Speech by H.E. Mr. Shinzo Abe, Prime Minister of Japan at the Parliament of the Republic of India, 22 August 2007, available at https://www.mofa.go.jp/region/asia-paci/pmv0708/speech-2.html
12. Shyam Saran, "Mapping the Indo-Pacific", *The Indian Express*, 29 October 2011, available at http://archive.indianexpress.com/news/mapping-the-indopacific/867004/2
13. Stephen Smith, "Deterrence and Regional Security", 2 June 2012 available at http://www.minister.defence.gov.au/2012/06/02/minister-for-defence-deterrence-and-regional-security-at-the-11th-international-institute-for-strategic-studies-singapore/
14. Rory Medcalf, "The Indo-Pacific: What's in a Name?", *The American Interest*, 10 October 2013 available at https://www.the-american-interest.com/2013/10/10/the-indo-pacific-whats-in-a-name/
15. "National Security Strategy of the United States of America", December 2017, p.46.
16. "Text of Prime Minister's Keynote Address at Shangri La Dialogue", *Press Information Bureau*, Government of India, Prime Minister's Office, 01 June 2018, p.6., available at http://pib.nic.in/

newsite/PrintRelease.aspx?relid=179711

17. Sheela Bhatt, "India indispensable in Indo-Pacific: James Mattis", *Sunday Guardian Live*, 02 June 2018, available at https://www.sundayguardianlive.com/news/india-indispensable-indo-pacific-james-mattis
18. Ibid.
19. "National Security Strategy of the United States of America", December 2017, p.50.
20. Rory Medcalf, op.cit.
21. "Inaugural Address by Prime Minister at Second Raisina Dialogue, New Delhi (January 17, 2017)", Ministry of External Affairs, Government of India, available at https://mea.gov.in/Speeches-Statements.htm?dtl/27948/Inaugural_Address_by_Prime_Minister_at_ Second_Raisina_Dialogue_New_Delhi_January_17_2017
22. "Prime Minister's Keynote Address at Shangri La Dialogue (June 01, 2018)", Ministry of External Affairs, Government of India, available at https://www.mea.gov.in/Speeches-Statements.htm?dtl/29943/Prime+Ministers+Keynote+Address+at+ Shangri+La+Dialogue+June+01+2018
23. Dhruva Jaishankar, "India and the Indo-Pacific Balance at Shangri La", *Hindustan Times*, New Delhi, Tuesday, 05 June 2018.
24. "Prime Minister's Keynote Address at Shangri La Dialogue (June 01, 2018)", op.cit.
25. C. Uday Bhaskar, "Modi's maritime vision is critical for Asean", *Hindustan Times*, New Delhi, Thursday, 07 June 2018.
26. "India-Indonesia Joint Statement during visit of Prime Minister to Indonesia (May 30, 2018), Ministry of External Affairs, Government of India, available at https://www.mea.gov.in/bilateral-documents.htm?dtl/29932/IndiaIndonesia+Joint+Statement+during+ visit+of+Prime+Minister+to+Indonesia+May+30+2018
27. "IISS Fullerton Lecture by Dr. S. Jaishankar, Foreign Secretary in Singapore", 20 July 2015, Ministry of External Affairs, Government of India, available at https://mea.gov.in/Speeches-Statements.htm?dtl/25493/IISS_Fullerton_Lecture_by_Foreign_Secretary_in_Singapore
28. Ashley J. Tellis, "India as a Leading Power", Carnegie Endowment for International Peace", April 2016, available at https://carnegieendowment.org/files/CP_268_Tellis_India_final1.pdf
29. Arijit Barman and Dipanjan Roy Chaudhury, "PM Narendra Modi expands on his foreign policy vision of India as a strategic global player", *The Economic Times*, 25 January 2018 available at http://js.economictimes.indiatimes.com/news/politics-and-nation/pm-narendra-modi-expands-on-his-foreign-policy-vision-of-india-as-a-strategic-global-player/articleshow/62643491.cms
30. Ashley J. Tellis, op.cit.
31. Zheng Bijian, "China's 'Peaceful Rise' to Great - Power Status", *Foreign Affairs* 84, No.5, September-October, 2005, pp. 21-24.
32. Wikipedia, World Bank WDI figures.
33. Wikipedia, "Historical GDP of the People's Republic of China", China NBS figures.
34. "The World in 2050: The Long view: how will the global economic order change by 2050?"available at https://www.pwc.com/gx/en/world-2050/assets/pwc-the-world-in-2050-full-report-feb-2017.pdf (condensed version - https://www.pwc.com/world2050)
35. Borge Brende, "India's opportunity and role in shaping the Fourth Industrial Revolution", 10 April 2018, available at https://www.narendramodi.in/reflections/india-s-opportunity-and-role-in-shaping-the-fourth-industrial-revolution-42 (First Industrial Revolution was based on advent of mechanized production from water and steam power; in the Second, electric power led to mass production and Third Industrial Revolution was due to boom in electronics and

information technology leading to automated production. Founder and Executive Chairman of the World Economic Forum, *Klaus Schwab* is credited with coining the term Fourth Industrial Revolution for having written a book by the same name. It is the fourth major industrial era since the initial industrial revolution of the 18th Century and it is characterized by a fusion of technologies that is blurring the lines between the physical, digital, and biological spheres. It is marked by emerging technology breakthrough in a number of fields including artificial intelligence, the internet of things, robotics, 3 D printing, nanotechnology, biotechnology, quantum computing, Machine learning, Block Chain and autonomous vehicles.)

36. Ibid.
37. "WEF announces establishing Center for Fourth Industrial Revolution in partnership with Reliance", *Business Standard*, 24 January 2018, available at https://www.business-standard.com/article/news-ani/wef-announces-establishing-center-for-fourth-industrial -revolution-in-partnership-with-reliance-118012400082_1.html
38. "India to work with BRICS for Fourth Industrial Revolution: Modi", *Net Indian*, 26 July 2018, available at netindian.in/news/2018/07/27/00049585/india-work-brics-fourth-industrial-revolution-modi
39. Sarang Shidore, "Higher Order", *India Today*, 15 December 2016, available at https://www.indiatoday.in/magazine/books/story/20161226-india-us-south-asia-foreign-policy-830047-2016-12-15
40. Guillem Monsonis, "India's Strategic Autonomy and Rapprochement with the US", *Strategic Analysis*, Vol. 34, No. 4, July 2010, Institute for Defence Studies and Analyses, p.612.
41. Shivshankar Menon, "India's 70-Year Pursuit of Strategic Autonomy", available at https://www.icsin.org/uploads/2017/10/07/363d3426fcb3b7d34500accd9cc4289b.pdf
42. C Raja Mohan, "Modi's American Engagement: Discarding the Defensive Mindset", *Carnegie India*, 09 April 2015, available at https://carnegieindia.org/2015/04/09/modi-s-american-engagement-discarding-defensive-mindset-pub-59733
43. "Prime Minister's Keynote Address at Shangri La Dialogue (June 01, 2018)", op.cit.
44. C. Uday Bhaskar, "Modi's strategic vision: Gap between aspiration and reality", *Economic Times*, 17 June 2018, available at https://economictimes.indiatimes.com/news/defence/modis-strategic-vision-gap-between-aspiration-and-reality/articleshow/64620961.cms; and Sarang Shidore, op.cit.
45. "Inaugural Address by Prime Minister at Second Raisina Dialogue, New Delhi (January 17, 2017)", op.cit.
46. Ibid.
47. "SAGAR stands for Security and Growth for All in the Region: PM Modi at International Fleet Review in Vishakhapatnam", 07 February 2016, available at https://www.narendramodi.in/pm-modi-at-the-international-fleet-review-2016-in-visakhapatnam-andhra-pradesh-413019
48. "Prime Minister's Keynote Address at Shangri La Dialogue (June 01, 2018)", op.cit.
49. Uttara Sahasrabuddhe and Chaitanya Mallapur, "Modi's Strategic Foreign Policy Vision: A Glass Half Full", *The Diplomat*, 17 May 2017, available at https://thediplomat.com/2017/05/modis-strategic-foreign-policy-vision-a-glass-half-full/
50. "Indian Ocean Naval Symposium (IONS 2018)", available at https://www.ionsirannavy.ir: and https://www.gktoday.in/gk/indian-ocean-naval-symposium/
51. "About IORA", available at www.iora.int/en/about/about-iora
52. "Indian Ocean Rim Association and India's Role", p.5, available at https://www.mea.gov.in/Portal/ForeignRelation/IORA_new.pdf

53. Rajiv Bhatia, "South Africa leads BRICS, IORA in 2018", Gateway House, 25 January 2018, available at https://www.gatewayhouse.in/south-africa-chairs-brics-iora/
54. "Indian Ocean Rim Association and India's Role", op.cit., p.10.
55. "SAGARMALA – Building Gateways of Growth", Ministry of Shipping, Government of India, National Perspective Plan, April 2016, p.7. available at http://sagarmala.gov.in/sites/default/files/5457695312te1.pdf
56. "Developing Ports: Sagarmala Project", available at www.makeinindia.com/article/-/v/developing-ports-sagarmala.project
57. "SAGARMALA", Ministry of Shipping, Government of India, available at www.sagarmala.gov.in/about-sagarmala/background
58. "Developing Ports: Sagarmala Project", op.cit.
59. Meera Siva, "All you wanted to know about Sagarmala", *The Hindu*, 24 May 2016, available at https://www.thehindubusinessline.com/opinion/columns/all-you-wanted-to-know-about-sagarmala/article8640858.ece
60. Ibid; and Devsena Mishra, "How Sagarmala Is Anchoring India's Port-Led Development", *Swarajya*, 22 April 2018, available at https://swarajyamag.com/infrastructure/how-sagarmala-is-anchoring-indias-port-led-development
61. Akhilesh Pillalamarri, "Project Mausam: India's Answer to China's 'Maritime Silk Road'", *The Diplomat*, 18 September 2014, available at https://thediplomat.com/2014/09/project-mausam-indias-answer-to-chinas-maritime-silk-road/
62. "Project Mausam", Ministry of Culture, Government of India, available at https://indiaculture.nic.in/project-mausam
63. "No Country Creating Obstacles In Implementation of 'Mausam'", *NDTV*, 02 August 2016, available at https://www.ndtv.com/india-news/no-country-creating-obstacles-in-implementation-of-mausam-1439060
64. Lekshmi Parameswaran, "Project Mausam to counter China's Maritime supremacy ambition", *Bharat Niti*, 16 May 2017, available at https://www.bharatniti.in/article/project-mausam-to-counter-chinas-maritime-supremacy-ambition/950
65. Ritu Sharma, "Project Mausam hits a Chinese Wall", The New Indian Express, 08 January 2017, available at http://www.newindianexpress.com/thesundaystandard/2017/jan/08/project-mausam-hits-a-chinese-wall-1557291.html
66. Akhilesh Pillalamarri, op.cit.
67. Regine A. Spector, "The North-South Transport Corridor", *Brookings*, 3 July 2002, available at https://www.brookings.edu/articles/the-north-south-transport-corridor/
68. Meena Singh Roy, "International North-South Transport Corridor: Re-energising India's Gateway to Eurasia", IDSA Issue Brief, 18 August 2015, available at https://idsa.in/issuebrief/InternationalNorthSouthTransportCorridor_msroy_180815(Other 11 members: Armenia, Azerbaijan, Belarus, Bulgaria (Observer status), Kazakhstan, Kyrgyzstan, Oman, Syria, Tajikistan, Turkey and Ukraine).
69. Ibid.
70. "International North South Transport Corridor (INSTC), Dry Run Report 2014", Government of India, Ministry of Commerce & Industry, pp. 9-10., available at http://commerce.nic.in/publications/INSTC_Dry_run_report_Final.pdf
71. Konstantin Zavrazhin, "India should be part of building the North-South Rail Corridor", *Russia Beyond*, 30 November 2016, available at https://www.rbth.com/economics/cooperation/2016/11/30/india-should-be-part-of-building-the-north-south-rail-corridor_652269
72. Majorie van Leijen, "Missing Link International North-South Transport Corridor almost

complete", *Rail Freight.com*, 24 October 2017, available at https://www.railfreight.com/corridors/2017/10/24/missing-link-international-north-south-transport-corridor-almost-complete/

73. Boris Volkhonsky, "North-South Transport Corridor begins functioning", *Russia Beyond*, 12 December 2016, available at https://www.rbth.com/blogs/the_outsiders_insight/2016/12/12/long-awaited-north-south-corridor-close-to-launch_655489
74. Konstantin Zavrazhin, op.cit.
75. "Iran Calls for Crucial Meeting on International North-South Transport Corridor", *Sputnik*, 06 August 2018, available at https://sputniknews.com/asia/201808061066997238-iran-india-north-south-corridor/
76. "India-Japan Joint Statement during the visit of Prime Minister to Japan", Ministry of External Affairs, Government of India, 11 November 2016, Paragraphs 43 & 4, available at https://www.mea.gov.in/bilateral-documents.htm?dtl/27599/IndiaJapan_Joint_Statement_ during_the_visit_of_Prime_Minister_to_Japan
77. "PM's address at the inauguration of the Annual Meeting of the African Development Bank", PM INDIA, News Updates, 23 May 2017, available at http://www.pmindia.gov.in/en/news_updates/pms-address-at-the-inauguration-of-the-annual-meeting-of-the-african-development-bank/ ; and Titli Basu, "Thinking Africa: India, Japan, and the Asia-Africa Growth Corridor", *The Diplomat*, 03 June 2017, available at https://thediplomat.com/2017/06/thinking-africa-india-japan-and-the-asia-africa-growth-corridor/
78. "Asia Africa Growth Corridor: Partnership for Sustainable and Innovative Development", A Vision Document, pp. 5-6., available at www.eria.org/Asia-Africa-Growth-Corridor-Document.pdf; "Asia-Africa growth corridor launched", *The Times of India*, 25 May 2017, available at https://timesofindia.indiatimes.com/city/ahmedabad/asia-africa-growth-corridor-launched/articleshow/58830900.cms; Dr Neha Sinha, "Asia-Africa Growth Corridor: Can It Be a Game Changer?", Vivekananda International Foundation, 05 June 2017, available at https://www.vifindia.org/article/2017/june/05/asia-africa-growth-corridor-can-it-be-a-game-changer; Jagannath Panda, "The Asia-Africa Growth Corridor: An India-Japan Arch in the Making?", Focus Asia Perspective & Analysis, No. 21, August 2017, available at http://isdp.eu/content/uploads/2017/08/2017-focus-asia-jagannath-panda.pdf
79. Sachin Chaturvedi, "Asia-Africa Growth Corridor aims for people-centric growth strategy", *Livemint*, 14 September 2017, available at https://www.livemint.com/Opinion/qTI0g1WCa8OIqRW8mKvl9H/Asia-Africa-Growth-Corridor-aims-for-peoplecentric-growth-s.html
80. "Asia Africa Growth Corridor: Partnership for Sustainable and Innovative Development", A Vision Document, Executive Summary, p.1. op.cit.
81. Avinash Nair, "To counter OBOR, India and Japan propose Asia-Africa sea corridor", *The Indian Express*, 31 May 2017, available at https://indianexpress.com/article/explained/to-counter-obor-india-and-japan-propose-asia-africa-sea-corridor-4681749/
82. Liu Zongyi, "Belt and Road remains open to India despite absence at recent forum", *Global Times*, 1 June 2017, available at www.globaltimes.cn/content/1049599.shtml
83. Avinash Nair, op.cit.
84. Anita Prakash, "The Asia-Africa Growth Corridor: Bringing together old partnerships and new initiatives", Observer Research Foundation, 25 April 2018, available at https://www.orfonline.org/research/the-asia-africa-growth-corridor-bringing-together-old-partnerships-and-new-initiatives/
85. Sachin Chaturvedi, op.cit.

86. "Bimstec: A viable alternative to SAARC", India Inc. Staff, 10 December 2016, available at https://indiaincgroup.com/bimstec-viable-alternative-saarc/
87. Dr. Sampa Kundu, "BIMSTEC: A Desirable Alternative to SAARC and An Extra Feather to India's Act East Policy", *The Kootneeti*, 12 October 2017, available at http://www.thekootneeti.com/bimstec-a-desirable-alternative-to-saarc-and-an-extra-feather-to-indias-act-east-policy/; and https://en.wikipedia.org/wiki/Bay_of_Bengal_Initiative_for_Multi-Sectoral_Technical_and-Economic_Cooperation
88. Swaran Singh, "Reviving BIMSTEC as alternative to SAARC will only stunt it", *Asia Times*, 30 August 2018, available at http://www.atimes.com/reviving-bimstec-as-alternative-to-saarc-will-only-stunt-it/
89. Rajeev Ranjan Chaturvedy, "BIMSTEC: Why It Matters – Analysis", *Eurasia Review*, 26 September 2018, available at https://www.eurasiareview.com/26092018-bimstec-why-it-matters-analysis/
90. "If SAARC fails, there's BIMSTEC: India warns Pakistan", *The Times of India*, 21 November 2016, available at https://timesofindia.indiatimes.com/india/If-SAARC-fails-theres-BIMSTEC-India-warns-Pakistan/articleshow/55545978.cms
91. Nitin Gokhale, "An Alternative to SAARC?", DNA, 08 April 2018, available at https://www.dnaindia.com/analysis/column-an-alternative-to-saarc-2602133
92. Dipanjan Roy Chaudhury, "Nepal makes BIMSTEC success conditional on SAARC revival", *The Economic Times*, 10 September 2018, https://economictimes.indiatimes.com/news/politics-and-nation/nepal-makes-bimstec-success-conditional-on-saarc-revival/articleshow/65748273.cms
93. TCA Raghavan, "What the Indo-Pacific means for New Delhi", *Hindustan Times*, New Delhi, Saturday, 31 March 2018.
94. "Bimstec can fill SAARC's space", *Hindustan Times*, New Delhi, Monday, 03 September 2018.
95. Elizabeth Roche, "Why is Bimstec so important for India?",*Livemint*, 24 October 2016, available at https://www.livemint.com/Politics/4JsOSUC4N81BK0T7zNYecK/Why-is-Bimstec-so-important-for-India.html
96. "India plans to commence BBIN motor pact with Nepal, Bangladesh", *The Economic Times*, 18 December 2017, available at https://economictimes.indiatimes.com/news/politics-and-nation/india-plans-to-commence-bbin-motor-pact-with-nepal-bangladesh/articleshow/62122790.cms; and "BBIN pact: India, Bangladesh, Nepal okay vehicle movement procedure", *Livemint*, 15 January 2018, available at https://www.livemint.com/Politics/kVaw1u3uvAq3SVugqTGkCI/BBIN-pact-India-Bangladesh-Nepal-okay-vehicle-movement-pr.html
97. Dipanjan Roy Chaudhury, op.cit.
98. Manish Chand, "Act East: India's ASEAN Journey", Ministry of External Affairs, Government of India, 10 November 2014, available at https://www.mea.gov.in/in-focus-article.htm?24216/Act+East+Indias+ASEAN+Journey
99. Ashraf Jamal, "Need to push on with ASEAN-India economic integration: Singapore PM Lee", Connected to India, 25 January 2018, available at https://www.connectedtoindia.com/need-to-push-on-with-asean-india-economic-integration-singapore-pm-lee-3510.html
100. Shyam Saran, "Beyond the hype, India-Asean ties remain a cup half full", *Hindustan Times*, New Delhi, Wednesday, 24 January 2018; and Kiran Sharma, "India's Modi courts ASEAN leaders to counter China's Belt and Road", Nikkei Asian Review, 25 January 2018, available at https://asia.nikkei.com/Politics/International-Relations/India-s-Modi-courts-ASEAN-leaders-to-counter-China-s-Belt-and-Road

101. "India, Asean to speed up work on free trade agreement, highway to Thailand", *Business Standard*, 26 January 2018, available at https://www.business-standard.com/article/economy-policy/india-asean-to-speed-up-work-on-free-trade-agreement-highway-to-thailand-118012501737_1.html
102. "India, ASEAN nations to discuss digital connectivity tomorrow", *The Indian Express*, 19 February 2017, available at https://indianexpress.com/article/technology/tech-news-technology/india-asean-nations-to-discuss-digital-connectivity-on-monday-4533291/
103. Shyam Saran, op.cit., and Preeti Saran and et al., "India, Japan, and ASEAN: Cooperation in the Indo-Pacific", Carnegie India, 22 February 2018, available at https://carnegieindia.org/2018/02/22/india-japan-and-asean-cooperation-in-indo-pacific-event-6816
104. Tanvi Madan, "The Rise, Fall, and Rebirth of the 'Quad'", War on the Rocks, 16 November 2017, available at https://warontherocks.com/2017/11/rise-fall-rebirth-quad/
105. Jesse Barker Gale, "The Quadrilateral Security Dialogue and the Maritime Silk Road Initiative", CSIS Briefs, 02 April 2018, available at https://www.csis.org/analysis/quadrilateral-security-dialogue-and-maritime-silk-road-initiative
106. Andrew Greene, "India blocks Australian bid to join Exercise Malabar naval war games", *ABC News*, 01 June 2017, available at https://www.abc.net.au/news/2017-05-31/india-rejects-australian-request-to-join-naval-war-games/8577664
107. Jesse Barker Gale, op.cit.
108. "China's Military Strategy 2015", Ch IV., available at https://jamestown.org/wp-content/uploads/2016/07/China's-Military-Strategy-2015.pdf
109. Amitendu Palit, "The Maritime Silk Road Initiative (MSRI): Why India is Worried, What China Can Do", *Global Policy*, 31 May 2017, available at https://www.globalpolicyjournal.com/blog/31/05/2017/maritime-silk-road-initiative-msri-why-india-worried-what-china-can-do; and Jesse Barker Gale, op.cit.
110. Jesse Barker Gale, op.cit.
111. Ibid.
112. Ibid.
113. Ankit Panda, "US, Japan, India, and Australia Hold Working-Level Quadrilateral Meeting on Regional Cooperation", *The Diplomat*, 13 November 2017, available at https://thediplomat.com/2017/11/us-japan-india-and-australia-hold-working-level-quadrilateral-meeting-on-regional-cooperation/
114. "India-Australia-Japan-U.S. Consultations on Indo-Pacific (November 12, 2017), Ministry of External Affairs, Government of India, 12 November 2017, available at https://mea.gov.in/press-releases.htm?dtl/29110/IndiaAustraliaJapanUS_Consultations_on_ IndoPacific_November_12_2017; "Australia-India-Japan-U.S. Consultations on the Indo-Pacific", Ministry of Foreign Affairs of Japan, available at https://www.mofa.go.jp/press/release/press4e_001789.html; "Australia-India-Japan-United States consultations on the Indo-Pacific", Australian Government, Department of Foreign Affairs and Trade, Media Release, 12 November 2017,https://dfat.gov.au/news/media/Pages/aus-india-japan-us-consultations-on-the-indo-pacific.aspx; "Australia-India-Japan-U.S. Consultations on the Indo-Pacific", U.S. Department of State, Press Statement, 12 November 2017, https://www.state.gov/r/pa/prs/ps/2017/11/275464.htm
115. Ankit Panda, "US, Japan, India, and Australia Hold Senior Official-Level Quadrilateral Meeting in Singapore", *The Diplomat*, 08 June 2018, available at https://thediplomat.com/2018/06/us-japan-india-and-australia-hold-senior-official-level-quadrilateral-meeting-in-singapore/
116. James Curran, "All shot and no powder in the Quadrilateral Security Dialogue", *East Asia*

Forum, 28 January 2018, available at http://www.eastasiaforum.org/2018/01/28/all-shot-and-no-powder-in-the-quadrilateral-security-dialogue/

117. "National Security Strategy of the United States of America", December 2017, p.46. available at nssarchive.us/wp-content/uploads/2017/12/2017.pdf
118. Peter Drysdale, "Mr Turnbull dabbles at the edge of strategic clarity in Japan", *East Asia Forum*, 23 January 2018, available at http://www.eastasiaforum.org/2018/01/23/mr-turnbull-dabbles-at-the-edge-of-strategic-clarity-in-japan/
119. "Shinzo Abe interview transcript", The Australian Financial Review, 19 January 2018, available at https://www.afr.com/news/world/asia/shinzo-abe-interview-with-the-australian-financial-review-20180118-h0kpj5
120. Ambassador Chas W. Freeman, Jr. (USFS, Ret.), op.cit.; and Govt of India, Ministry of Commerce & Industry site available at http://commerce-app.gov.in/eidb/default.asp
121. Prashant Jha, "India will adopt a three-pronged strategy to check China's influence", *Hindustan Times*, 08 July 2018, available at https://www.hindustantimes.com/india-news/india-will-adopt-a-three-pronged-strategy-to-check-china-influence/story-o3OkceE6h2URXJFL9rxiEK.html
122. Rakesh Sood, "A reset in India-Nepal relations", *East Asia Forum*, 08 June 2018, available at http://www.eastasiaforum.org/2018/06/08/a-reset-in-india-nepal-relations/
123. "India-Nepal Relations", Ministry of External Affairs, Government of India, available at http://mea.gov.in/Portal/ForeignRelation/India_Nepal_Relations_11_04_2017.pdf
124. "Dragon's embrace: As China woos it with development promises, Nepal should tread with caution", *Hardnews Magazine*, 26 August 2017, available at https://scroll.in/article/848197/dragons-embrace-as-china-woos-it-with-development-promises-nepal-should-tread-with-caution
125. Debasish Roy Chowdhury, "Driven by India Into China's Arms, Is Nepal the New Sri Lanka?", *South China Morning Post*, 25 February 2018, available at https://www.scmp.com/week-asia/geopolitics/article/2134532/driven-india-chinas-arms-nepal-new-sri-lanka
126. "Nepal to get access to Chinese ports", *Hindustan Times*, New Delhi, Saturday, 08 September 2018.
127. Sangeeta Thapliyal, "Movement of Population Between India and Nepal: Emerging Challenges", available at https://www.idsa-india.org/an-aug9-6.html
128. www.worldbank.org/en/topic/migrationremittancesdiasporaissues/brief/migration-remittances-data
129. S.D. Muni, "No zero sums in this great game", *The Hindu*, 28 March 2016, available at https://www.thehindu.com/opinion/lead/no-zero-sums-in-this-great-game/article8402444.ece
130. "Nepalese trade still prefers inefficient Kolkata port to Visakhapatnam", available at porttoport.in/headernewsdet.php?newstitle=6151
131. Pushpa Raj Acharya, "Dhamra Port an option for third-country trade", *The Himalayan Times*, 12 February 2018, available at https://thehimalayantimes.com/business/dhamra-port-option-third-country-trade/
132. S.D. Muni, op.cit.
133. Gaurab Shumsher Thapa, "Removal of mistrust in Nepal-India relations", *Asian Times*, 13 September 2018, available at http://www.atimes.com/sun-begins-to-shine-on-frosty-nepal-india-relations/
134. n.131 of Chapter 2.
135. S.D. Muni, op.cit.
136. Ibid.

137. "Growing Proximity Between Nepal and China: An Analysis", available at https://iasscore.in/national-issues/growing-proximity-between-nepal-and-china-an-analysis
138. Sudha Ramachandran, "Sino-Nepalese Relations: Handshake Across the Himalayas", *China Brief*, Vol. 15, Issue 22https://jamestown.org/program/sino-nepalese-relations-handshake-across-the-himalayas/
139. Debasish Roy Chowdhury, op.cit.
140. Elizabeth Roche, "Has Narendra Modi's visit put India-Nepal Relations back on firm footing?", *Livemint*, 14 May 2018, available at https://www.livemint.com/Politics/FgfPXFjep3yJEUesusAVfM/Has-Narendra-Modis-visit-put-India-Nepal-relations-back-on.html
141. Harsh V. Pant, "Why India needs to safeguard its ties with Nepal", Observer Research Foundation, 27 June 2018, available at https://www.orfonline.org/research/41945-why-india-needs-to-safeguard-its-ties-with-nepal/
142. Elizabeth Roche, op.cit.; and Harsh V. Pant, "India's Nepal Challenge Intensifies", *The Diplomat*, 30 June 2018, available at https://thediplomat.com/2018/07/indias-nepal-challenge-intensifies/
143. Pratim Ranjan Bose, "India-Nepal, time to turn the page", *The Hindu*, 10 May 2018, available at https://www.thehindubusinessline.com/opinion/columns/pratim-ranjan-bose/india-nepal-time-to-turn-the-page/article23840171.ece
144. Shishir Gupta, "India tries to boost Nepal ties despite China factor", Hindustan Times, Saturday, 20 October 2018.
145. "Nepal, India to expedite Raxaul-Kathmandu rail project", *The New Indian Express*, 11 July 2018, available at http://www.newindianexpress.com/nation/2018/jul/11/nepal-india-to-expedite-raxaul-kathmandu-rail-project-1841669.html; and Shishir Gupta, op.cit.
146. "India to expand LNG, petroleum pipelines to Nepal's Chitwan area", *The Hindustan Times*, New Delhi, Saturday, 29 September 2018.
147. Major Sunil Subedi, Nepal Army, "Rising Economy of India: How can Nepal Draw Economic Benefit?", Fort Leavenworth, Kansas 2016, available at www.dtic.mil/dtic/tr/fulltext/u2/1020432.pdf
148. "India will need 119 Million more Skilled Workers by 2022", *The Economic Times*, 10 April 2015, available at http://articles.economictimes.indiatimes.com/2015-04-10/news/61017912_1_sectors-skill-shortage-workforce.
149. Major Sunil Subedi, op.cit., p.10.
150. Syed Muazzam Ali, "India-Bangladesh ties: Scaling new heights", *Daily Pioneer*, Saturday, 10 March 2018, available at https://www.dailypioneer.com/2018/columnists/india-bangladesh-ties-scaling-new-heights.html
151. "Sheikh Hasina's significant visit to India", *Business Standard*, 27April 2017, available at https://www.business-standard.com/article/news-ani/sheikh-hasina-s-significant-visit-to-india-117042700997_1.html
152. Shakil Bin Mushtaq, "The Battle for Bangladesh: India vs. China", *The Diplomat*, 29 June 2018, available at https://thediplomat.com/2018/06/the-battle-for-banglades-india-vs-china/
153. Syed MuazzamAli, op.cit.
154. Santanu Chowdhury, "Indo-Bangladesh relations have entered golden phase, says PM Modi", *The Indian Express*, 26 May 2018, available at https://indianexpress.com/article/india/pm-narendra-modi-sheikh-hasina-bangladesh-bhavan-5191560/
155. Brigadier (Dr.) Rajeev Bhutani, op.cit., pp. 373-374 (For details of Land-Boundary Agreement).
156. Syed Muazzam Ali, "India-Bangladesh ties: Scaling new heights - II", Daily Pioneer, Sunday, 11 March 2018, available at https://www.dailypioneer.com/2018/sunday-edition/india-

bangladesh-ties-scaling-new-heights-ii.html

157. Varun Gandhi, "Succour To No Man's Land", *The Times of India*, New Delhi, Friday, 5 December 2014.
158. Gurcharan Das, "Modi is building on India's wondrous trading past", *Sunday Times of India*, New Delhi, 14 June 2015; and Raghav Pandey, "India-Bangladesh Ties: Scaling New Heights", available at http://www.indiafoundation.in/india-bangladesh-ties-scaling-new-heights/
159. Brigadier (Dr.) Rajeev Bhutani, op.cit., p.375.
160. Syed Muazzam Ali, op.cit.
161. Rudroneel Ghosh, "Modi's Dhaka visit can galvanise Indo-Bangla ties through Teesta and connectivity deals", *The Times of India*, New Delhi, Saturday, 30 May 2015; "Only Connect", *The Times of India*, New Delhi, Wednesday, 3 June 2015.
162. Raghav Pandey, op.cit.
163. Syed Muazzam Ali, "India-Bangladesh ties: Scaling new heights", *Daily Pioneer*, Saturday, 10 March 2018, op.cit.
164. Elizabeth Roche, "Key takeaways from Narendra Modi's Bangladesh visit", *Mint*, New Delhi, Tuesday, 9 June 2015, Vol 9, No.138.
165. Syed Muazzam Ali, "India-Bangladesh ties: Scaling new heights", *Daily Pioneer*, Saturday, 10 March 2018, op.cit.
166. Commerce-app.gov.in/eidb/default.asp(accessed on10 October2018).
167. Pratim Ranjan Bose, "India-Bangladesh trade to scale new high", *The Hindu*, 15 August 2018, available at https://www.thehindubusinessline.com/news/india-bangladesh-trade-to-scale-new-high/article24698283.ece
168. Mahfuz Anam, "Modi, hopefully, is no Manmohan", *The Daily Star*, 8 June 2015, available at www.thedailystar.net/frontpage/modi-hopefully-no-manmohan-93751; and Gurcharan Das, op.cit.
169. Syed Muazzam Ali, "India-Bangladesh ties: Scaling new heights - II", *Daily Pioneer*, Sunday, 11 March 2018, op.cit.
170. Elizabeth Roche, op.cit.
171. Shakil Bin Mushtaq, op.cit.
172. Syed Muazzam Ali, "India-Bangladesh ties: Scaling new heights - II", *Daily Pioneer*, Sunday, 11 March 2018, op.cit.
173. Indrani Bagchi, "Hasina and I think alike, says Modi", *The Times of India*, New Delhi, Monday, 8 June 2015.
174. Rupak Bhattacharjee, "Payra Port Development Will Enhance India-Bangladesh Ties – Analysis", *South Asia Monitor*, 20 January 2017, available at strategicstudyindia.blogspot.com/2017/01/payra-port-development-will-enhance.html#more
175. Indrani Bagchi, "Indian ups Lanka aid to Offset China Presence", *The Times of India*, Allahabad, Thursday, November 25, 2010.
176. Dr Sudha Ramachandran, "A New Era for India-Sri Lanka Relations?", *The Diplomat*, 26 February 2015 in https://thuppahi.wordpress.com/2015/02/28/sri-lankas-balancing-act-between-india-and-china/#more-15882
177. "Modi announces slew of steps to boost ties with Sri Lanka", *Business Standard*, 13 March 2015, www.business-standard.com/article/news-ians/modi-announces-slew-of-steps-to-boost-ties-with-sri-lanka-115031300430_1.html
178. Jagriti Kumari, "Narendra Modi's Ocean Diplomacy - Global Media Round up", *NITI CENTRAL*, 18 March 2015, www.niticentral.com/2015/03/18/narendra-modis-ocean-diplomacy-global-media-roundup-307362.html

179. Ramtanu Maitra, "Modi Strengthens Ties with Indian Ocean Neighbours", *Asian Mirror*, 22 March 2015, www.asianmirror.lk/opinion/item/7701-modi-strengthens-ties-with-indian-ocean-neighbours
180. Yigal Chazan, "India and China's Tug of War Over Sri Lanka", *The Diplomat*, 23 May 2017, available at https://thediplomat.com/2017/05/india-and-chinas-tug-of-war-over-sri-lanka/
181. "India takes on China at another battlefront: A Sri Lankan airport", *Economic Times Online*, 14 October 2017, available at https://economictimes.indiatimes.com/news/international/world-news/india-takes-on-china-at-another-battlefront-a-sri-lankan-airport/articleshow/61079813.cms
182. Bhaskar Roy, "India and the Blue Seas - Breaking from the Past", South Asia Analysis Group, Paper No. 5900, 25 March 2015, www.southasiaanalysis.org/node/1742
183. Yigal Chazan, op.cit.
184. Saman Kelegama, "India-Sri Lanka Free Trade Agreement: Sri Lanka Reaping the Benefits from Preferential Trade", *Talking Economics*, 08 August 2017, available at http://www.ips.lk/talkingeconomics/2017/08/08/india-sri-lanka-free-trade-agreement-sri-lanka-reaping-the-benefits-from-preferential-trade/
185. Wade Shepard, "China and Japan's New Great Game Intensifies in Myanmar", *Forbes.com*, 29 January 2018, available at https://www.forbes.com/sites/wadeshepard/2018/01/29/china-and-japans-new-great-game-intensifies-in-myanmar/#5c120d285ab2
186. "China is extending its sway in Sri Lanka", *Reuters*, 24 August 2018, *Hindustan Times*, New Delhi, Saturday, 25 August 2018.
187. "China's Xi offers fresh $295 million grant to Sri Lanka", Reuters, 22 July 2018, available at https://in.reuters.com/article/sri-lanka-china-grant/chinas-xi-offers-fresh-295-million-grant-to-sri-lanka-in-push-for-dominance-idINKBN1KC0CV
188. Ibid.
189. "Sri Lanka asks AAI to submit business plan on Mattala airport operation", *The Economic Times*, 19 July 2018, available at https://economictimes.indiatimes.com/industry/transportation/airlines-/-aviation/sri-lanka-asks-aai-to-submit-business-plan-on-mattala-airport-operation/articleshow/65053003.cms
190. Meera Srinivasan, "Mattala project with India is on", *The Hindu*, 03 August 2018, available at https://www.thehindu.com/news/international/mattala-project-with-india-is-on/article24595483.ece
191. Yimou Lee, Thu Thu Aung, "China to take 70 percent stake in strategic port in Myanmar – official", *Reuters*, 17 October 2017, available at https://www.reuters.com/article/china-silkroad-myanmar-port/china-to-take-70-percent-stake-in-strategic-port-in-myanmar-official-idUSL4N1MS3UB
192. "Myanmar scales back China-funded Kyauk Pyu port project in Rakhine state due to debt concerns", *South China Morning Post*, 02 August 2018, available at https://www.scmp.com/news/asia/southeast-asia/article/2158015/myanmar-scales-back-china-funded-kyauk-pyu-port-project
193. Dipanjan Roy Chaudhury, "PM Narendra Modi's visit to expand strategic and economic foot print in Myanmar", *The Economic Times*, 13 July 2018, available at https://economictimes.indiatimes.com/news/defence/pm-narendra-modis-visit-to-expand-strategic-and-economic-footprint-in-myanmar/articleshow/60298588.cms
194. Gautam Mukhopadhaya, "making up for lost time", *The Hindu*, 05 September 2017, available at https://www.thehindu.com/opinion/lead/making-up-for-lost-time/article19621257.ece
195. "India shares Myanmar's concerns over 'extremist violence' in Rakhine State: Modi", *The*

Hindu, 06 September 2017, available at https://www.thehindu.com/news/international/india-shares-myanmars-concerns-over-extremist-violence-in-rakhine-state-modi/article19630495.ece

196. "PM Modi tells Suu Kyi India is with Myanmar, but skips mention of Rohingya issue", *Hindustan Times*, 06 September 2017, available at https://www.hindustantimes.com/india-news/modi-in-myanmar-pm-praises-suu-kyi-s-leadership-vows-to-fight-terror-in-joint-statement/story-vC4Pi9WL594NnRt8Oe430J.html
197. *The Hindu*, 06 September 2017, op.cit.
198. *Hindustan Times*, 06 September 2017, op.cit.
199. "On PM Modi's Visit, Myanmar to receive first lot of diesel from India", *ET Energy World*, 02 September 2017, available at https://energy.economictimes.indiatimes.com/news/oil-and-gas/on-pm-modis-visit-myanmar-to-receive-first-lot-of-diesel-from-india/60339402?utm_source=Mailer&utm_medium=&utm_campaign=
200. "India-Myanmar Joint Statement issued on the occasion of the State Visit of Prime Minister of India to Myanmar (September 5-7, 2017)", Ministry of External Affairs, Government of India, 06 September 2017, available at https://mea.gov.in/bilateral-documents.htm?dtl/28924/
201. Bidhayak Das, "Analysis: Modi in Myanmar", *The Irrawaddy*, 04 September 2017, available at https://www.irrawaddy.com/news/analysis-modi-in-myanmar.html
202. Dr Sampa Kundu, "The Current Conundrums in India-Myanmar Bilateral trade", *Extraordinary and Plenipotentiary Diplomatist*, Vol. 6, Issue.1, January 2018, Noida, available at https://idsa.in/system/files/news/india-myanmar-skundu-diplomate.pdf
203. Commerce-app.gov.in/eidb/Icntcom.asp
204. Aye Myat, "India-Myanmar Trade to Reach $10 Billion by 2020", *Myanmar Business Today*, Vol.3, Issue 9, 25 February 2015, available at https://www.mmbiztoday.com/articles/india-myanmar-trade-reach-10-billion-2020
205. Maldives Population 2018, available at https://countrymeters.info/en/Maldives#population_2018
206. Liam Doyle, "India vs China: India wins over China as opposition takes leadership in Maldives", *Express*, 25 September 2018, available at https://www.express.co.uk/news/world/1022637/India-vs-China-Maldives-election-2018-Mohamed-Solih-India-vs-China-Belt-and-Road
207. Brahma Chellaney, "India cannot afford to rest on its oars", *Hindustan Times*, New Delhi, Tuesday, 09 October 2018.
208. Ravi Joshi, "India's stakes in Maldives' power struggle", Observer Research Foundation, 24 March 2015, www.orfonline.org/cms/sites/orfonline/modules/analysis/AnalysisDetail.html?cmaid=80394&mmacmaid=80395
209. Brigadier (Dr.) Rajeev Bhutani, op.cit., pp.379-380.
210. Amy Kazmin, "Advantage India in struggle with China over Maldives", *Financial Times*, 28 September 2018, available at https://www.ft.com/content/24b0bb54-c22d-11e8-95b1-d36dfefbb89a
211. John F. May and Fathimath Riyaza, "Maldives' Population Dynamics", 13 July 2017, available at https://www.prb.org/maldives-population-dynamics
212. Ankit Panda, "Maldives Faces Drinking Water Crisis", *The Diplomat*, 05 December 2014, available at https://thediplomat.com/2014/12/maldives-faces-drinking-water-crisis/; "India sends aircraft, vessels to resolve water crisis in Male", *Economic Times*, 05 December 2014, available at https://economictimes.indiatimes.com/news/politics-and-nation/india-sends-aircraft-vessels-to-resolve-water-crisis-in-male/articleshow/45385391.cms; Harsh V. Pant, "India and China Slug it Out in South Asia", *The Diplomat*, 11 December 2014, available at https://thediplomat.com/2014/12/india-and-china-slug-it-out-in-south-asia/

213. "Maldivians in India", https://en.m.wikipedia.org/wiki/Maldivians-in-India
214. "10 reasons why Maldives is important for India", *The Times of India,* 07 February 2018, available at https://timesofindia.indiatimes.com/india/10-reasons-why-maldives-is-important-for-india/articleshow/62814970.cms
215. "Indians in the Maldives", https://en.m.wikipedia.org/Indians-in-the-Maldives
216. "PM Modi arrives in Maldives to attend president-elect Solih's Swearing-in ceremony", *Hindustan Times,* Saturday, 17 November 2018.
217. Ankit Panda, "India Unveils New Coastal Surveillance Radar Network", *The Diplomat,* 26 March 2015, available at https://thediplomat.com/2015/03/india-unveils-new-coastal-surveillance-radar-network/
218. Manu Pubby, "India's plan to set up radar grid to monitor Indian Ocean traffic faces stumble", *The Economic Times,* 18 March 2015,https://economictimes.indiatimes.com/2015-03-18/news/60249773_1_indian-ocean-maldives-president-mohamed-nasheed
219. "India, Lanka, Maldives sign tripartite maritime security pact", *The Statesman,* 09 July 2013, available at https://www.thestatesman.com/india/india-lanka-maldives-sign-tripartite-maritime-security-pact-4712.html
220. Indrani Bagchi, "How 'India First' turned into 'China First' for Maldives", *The Times of India,* 10 February 2018, available at https://timesofindia.indiatimes.com/india/how-did-india-first-turn-into-china-first-in-the-maldives/articleshow/62864889.cms
221. Sanjeev Miglani, Mohamed Junayd, "Exclusive: Maldives set to pull out of China free trade deal, says senior law maker", *Reuters,* 19 November 2018, available at https://www.reuters.com/article/us-maldives-politics-china-exclusive/exclusive-maldives-set-to-pull-out-of-china-free-trade-deal-says-senior-lawmaker-idUSKCN1NO0ZC
222. Commerce-app.gov.in/eidb/Icntcom.asp
223. "India Announces $ 1.4 Billion Soft Loan to Maldives' Ailing Economy", *Sputnik News,* 18 December 2018, available at https://sputniknews.com/asia/201812181070763549-indias-financial-assistance-maldives/; and "India Announces $ 1.4 Bln Financial Assistance to Maldives Not to Repay China's Debt", Sputnik News, 20 December 2018, available at https://sputniknews.com/asia/201812201070863463-indias-financial-assistance-maldives/
224. David Brewster, "Modi builds India's sphere of influence in the Indian Ocean", *The Interpreter,* 17 March 2015, www.lowyinterpreter.org/post/2015/03/17/Modi-builds-Indias-sphere-of-influence-in-the-Indian-Ocean.aspx?COLLCC=3253166929& ; and Shubhajit Roy, "India to develop strategic assets in 2 Mauritius, Seychelles islands", *The Indian Express,* 12 March 2015, available at https://indianexpress.com/article/india/india-others/india-seychelles-sign-four-pacts-to-boost-security-cooperation/
225. Ramtanu Maitra, op.cit. and PranavKulkarni, "To Counter China, govt pushes naval exports to small Indian Ocean nations", *The Indian Express,* New Delhi, 04 March 2015.
226. Bhaskar Roy, "India and the Blue Seas - Breaking from the Past", South Asia Analysis Group, Paper No. 5900, 25 March 2015, www.southasiaanalysis.org/node/1742
227. Harsh V. Pant, "Why the Indian Ocean is central to our geopolitics", *Hindustan Times,* New Delhi, Tuesday, 20 March 2018.
228. David Brewster, op.cit.
229. "India, Seychelles agree to jointly develop Assumption Island naval base", *The Indian Express,* 26 June 2018, available at https://indianexpress.com/article/india/india-seychelles-agree-to-jointly-develop-assumption-island-naval-base-5233376/
230. Ramtanu Maitra, op.cit.
231. David Brewster, op.cit.

232. Rajat Pandit, "Checking China: India to train Vietnamese pilots", *The Times of India,* New Delhi, Tuesday, 28 October 2014.
233. Sumit Kumar, "India-Vietnam Relations Elevated to Comprehensive Strategic Partnership", *Indian Defence Review,* 18 September 2016, http://www.indiandefencereview.com/spotlights/india-vietnam-relations-elevated-to-comprehensive-strategic-partnership/
234. Indrani Bagchi, "India ignores China frown, offers def boost to Vietnam", *The Times of India,* New Delhi, Wednesday, 29 October 2014.
235. Indrani Bagchi, "Look East Policy: Red Carpet for Vietnam, Myanmar heads", *The Times of India,* New Delhi, Monday, October 10, 2011; and Daniel thorp, "India plans strategic encirclement of China", *Asia Times Online,* South Asia, 12 July 2012 available at www.atimes.com/atimes/South_Asia/NG12Df01.html
236. Indrani Bagchi, "New Delhi sends out a message to Beijing", *The Times of India,* New Delhi, Wednesday, 29 October 2014.
237. Commerce-app.gov.in/eidb/Icntcom.asp
238. "Vietnam, India to forge stronger investment ties", *Vietnam News,* 22 April 2017, available at https:// vietnamnews.vn/politics-laws/375173/viet-nam-india-to-forge-stronger-investment-ties.html
239. Sumit Kumar, op.cit.
240. "Vietnam-China trade may leap to US$ 100 billion this year", *Vietnam net,* 17 March 2016, available at https://english.vietnamnet.vn/fms/business/152435/vietnam-china-trade-may-leap-to-us-100-billion-this-year.html
241. Venkat Ananth, "The lesser known history India's Mongolia ties", *Livemint,* 17 May 2015, available at https://www.livemint.com/Politics/niSFjFajO6NsL5CNKIttbN/The-lesser-known-history-of-relations-between-India-and-mode.html
242. Shubha Singh, "The monk-ambassador who cemented India's relations with Mongolia", *Scroll.in,* 16 May 2015, available at https://scroll.in/article/727210/the-monk-ambassador-who-cemented-indias-relations-with-mongolia
243. Devanik Saha, "Why is Modi going to Mongolia?", *Daily O,* 18 May 2015, available at https://www.dailyo.in/politics/mongolia-china-modi-pratibha-patil-ashoka-ghenghis-khan-babur-look-east-policy-foreign-relations-trade/story/1/3759.html
244. "India, Mongolia 'cross swords'", *The Hindu,* 08 April 2017, available at https://www.thehindu.com/news/national/india-mongolia-cross-swords/article17895241.ece
245. Venkat Ananth, op.cit.
246. "India grants Mongolia $1 bn credit line to develop infra", *The Times of India,* New Delhi, Monday, 18 May 2015.
247. Daniel thorp, op.cit.
248. Prashant Rupera, "India to help Mongolia set up Amul - like diary cooperative", *Sunday Times of India,* New Delhi, 17 May 2015.
249. "India-Mongolia Relations", available at www.mea.gov.in/Portal/ForeignRelation/Mongolia_Dec2014.pdf
250. "PM Modi addresses Mongolian parliament—Times of India," timesofindia.indiatimes.com. Videos May 17, 2015
251. "India and Bhutan: Model neighbours, twinned destinies", Ministry of External Affairs, Government of India, 12 June 2014, available at https://mea.gov.in/in-focus-article.htm?23424/India+and+Bhutan+Model+neighbours+twinned+destinies
252. Prof Hari Bhans Jha, "Indian Prime Minister Narendra Modi's Visit to Bhutan: View from Nepal", South Asia Analysis Group, Paper No 5737, 30 June 2014, available at

www.southasiaanalysis.org/node/1559

253. Brigadier (Dr.) Rajeev Bhutani, op.cit., p.369.
254. Shelly Mahajan, "India-Bhutan Relations: Past, Present and Future", South Asia Program at Hudson Institute, 6 March 2018, available at http://www.southasiaathudson.org/blog/2018/3/6/india-bhutan-relations-past-present-and-future
255. Robert G. Wirsing, "Rivers run through Modi's regional agenda", *East Asia Forum*, 22 August 2014, available at www.eastasiaforum.org/2014/08/22/rivers-run-through-modis-regional-agenda/#more-43141
256. "In Bhutan, Narendra Modi vows to nurture 'B2B' ties", *The Hindu*, 15 June 2014, available at https://www.thehindu.com/news/national/in-bhutan-narendra-modi-vows-to-nurture-b2b-ties/article6116936.ece
257. Dipanjan Roy Chaudhury, "Bhutan may receive more financial assistance", *The Economic Times*, 22 October 2018, available at https://economictimes.indiatimes.com/news/politics-and-nation/bhutan-may-receive-more-financial-assistance/articleshow/66309757.cms
258. Shelly Mahajan, op.cit.
259. India-Bhutan Relations", Bilateral Brief, January 2018, available at www.mea.gov.in/Portal/ForeignRelation/Bilateral-Brief-Jan-2008.pdf
260. Shelly Mahajan, op.cit.
261. Beth Walker, "India Bhutan hydropower cooperation fraying at the edges", the third pole net, 4 October 2016, available at https://www.thethirdpole.net/en/2016/10/04/india-bhutan-hydropower-cooperation-fraying-at-the-edges/
262. Dipanjan Roy Chaudhury, *The Economic Times*, op.cit.
263. M S Subba, "ADB exhorts Bhutan to prioritise agriculture", Kuensel, 04 April 2015, available at http://www.kuenselonline.com/adb-exhorts-bhutan-to-prioritise-agriculture/
264. "Agriculture in Bhutan", available at https://www.revolvy.com/topic/Agriculture%20in%20Bhutan
265. P. Stobdan, "India's Real Problem Lies in its Bhutan Policy, Not the Border", *The Wire*, 14 July 2017, available at https://thewire.in/diplomacy/india-china-doklam-real-problem-bhutan
266. Medha Bist, "The Rupee Crunch and India-Bhutan Economic Engagement", IDSA Issue Briefs, 16 July 2012, available at https://idsa.in/issuebrief/TheRupeeCrunchandIndia Bhutan EconomicEngagement_MedhaBisht_160712
267. Beth Walker, op.cit.
268. Ibid.
269. P. Stobdan, op.cit.
270. Dipak K Dash, "Govt offers 10 posts of joint secretaries to public, private sector employees", *The Times of India*, 10 June 2018, available at https://timesofindia.indiatimes.com/india/govt-offers-10-posts-of-joint-secretaries-for-public-private-sector-employees/articleshow/64529114.cms
271. Sudha Ramachandran, "The Indian Foreign Service: Worthy of an Emerging Power?", *The Diplomat*, 12 July 2013, available at https://the diplomat.com/2013/07/the-indian-foreign-service-worthy-of-an-emerging-power/
272. Indrani Bagchi, "Staff crisis: MEA urged to hire across services", *The Times of India*, 29 July 2012, available at https://timesofindia.indiatimes.com/india/Staff-crisis-MEA-urged-to-hire-across-services/articleshow/15245651.cms?referral=PM
273. Shyam Saran, "India must focus on neighbourhood first", *Hindustan Times*, New Delhi, Tuesday, 25 September 2108.
274. Ibid.

275. Laxman K Behera, "India's Defence Budget 2017-18: An Analysis", IDSA Issue Briefs, 03 February 2017, available at https://idsa.in/issuebrief/india-defence-budget-2017-18_lkbehera_030217; and "Budget 2018: Defence budget increased by a mere 7.81% to Rs 2.95 trillion", *Livemint*, 01 February 2018, available at https://www.livemint.com/Industry/710i08pNKRjIiUBDXtpYIO/Budget-2018-Defence-budget-increased-by-a-mere-781-to-Rs2.html
276. Sobhana K. Nair, "B. C. Khanduri removed as Defence Panel Chairman", *The Hindu*, 19 September 2018, available at https://www.thehindu.com/news/national/bc-khanduri-removed-as-defence-panel-chairman/article24980589.ece

Chapter 5: Conclusion

1. Raja Menon, "India's Response to China's Naval Presence in the Indian Ocean", Asia Policy, National Bureau of Asian Research, No. 22, July 2016, p.42, available at muse.jhu.edu/article/628501/pdf
2. Ibid.
3. Jae-Hyung Lee, "China's Expanding Maritime Ambitions in the Western Pacific and the Indian Ocean", *Contemporary Southeast Asia*, Vol. 24, No. 3, 2002, pp. 549-568.
4. Yuwa Hedrick-Wong, "The Myths About China's Economic Slowdown", *Forbes*, 15 August 2018, available at https://www.forbes.com/sites/yuwahedrickwong/2018/08/15/the-myths-about-chinas-economic-slowdown/#67e4e8775d55
5. C Raja Mohan, "China's Rise, America's Pivot, and India's Asian ambiguity", p.6, available at www.india-seminar.com/2013/641/641_c_raja_mohan.htm
6. Randall L. Schweller, "The Balance of Power in World Politics", May 2016, available at http://oxfordre.com/politics/view/10.1093/acrefore/9780190228637.001.0001/acrefore-9780190228637-e-119
7. C Raja Mohan, op.cit., p.6.
8. Nirupama Rao, "Transcript of Foreign Secretary Smt. Nirupama Rao's speech at the French Institute of International Relations (IFRI), Paris", 05 May 2011, available at http://www.mea.gov.in/mystart.php?id=530117612
9. C Raja Mohan, op.cit., p.7.
10. Rakesh Krishnan Simha, "1971 War: How Russian sank Nixon's gun boat diplomacy", *Russia Beyond*, 20 December 2011 available at https://www.rbth.com/articles/2011/12/20/1971_war_how_russia_sank_nixons_gunboat_diplomacy_14041; and Rakesh Krishnan Simha, "Gunboat diplomacy: Revisiting the Enterprise incident", Russia Beyond, 14 December 2016, available at https://www.rbth.com/blogs/stranger_than_fiction/2016/12/14/gunboat-diplomacy-revisiting-the-enterprise-incident_657434

11 Sudhi Ranjan Sen, "India, Russia may get to share military facilities", *Hindustan Times*, New Delhi, Friday, 14 December 2018.

12. P S Raghavan, "India must continue to push for the US to accommodate its perspectives", *Hindustan Times*, New Delhi, Saturday, 27 October 2018.
13. William J. Burns, "U.S.-India Partnership in an Asia-Pacific Century", 16 December 2011, available at http://www.state.gov/s/d/2011/178934.htm
14. Sandeep Unnithan, "Signing COMCASA is significant milestone in cementing Indo-US ties", *India Today*, 09 September 2018, available at https://www.indiatoday.in/world/story/signing-comcasa-is-significant-milestone-in-cementing-indo-us-ties-1336178-2018-09-09; and "Seven reasons why COMCASA is so important for India", *The Economic Times*, 07

September 2018, available at https://economictimes.indiatimes.com/news/defence/seven-reasons-why-comcasa-is-so-important-for-india/articleshow/65707682.cms

15. P S Raghavan, op.cit.
16. Shannon Tiezzi, "China's Master Plan to Become a 'World Manufacturing Power'", *The Diplomat*, 20 May 2015, available at https://thediplomat.com/2015/05/chinas-master-plan-to-become-a-world-manufacturing-power/
17. Elaine Chan, "Made in China 2025': is Beijing's plan for hi-tech dominance as big a threat as the West thinks it is?", *South China Morning Post*, 10 September 2018, available at https://www.scmp.com/business/china-business/article/2163601/made-china-2025-beijings-plan-hi-tech-dominance-big-threat
18. Vivek Wadhwa, "The trade war offers us an opening", *Hindustan Times*, New Delhi, Tuesday, 23 October 2018.

ANNEXURE 1

String of Pearls

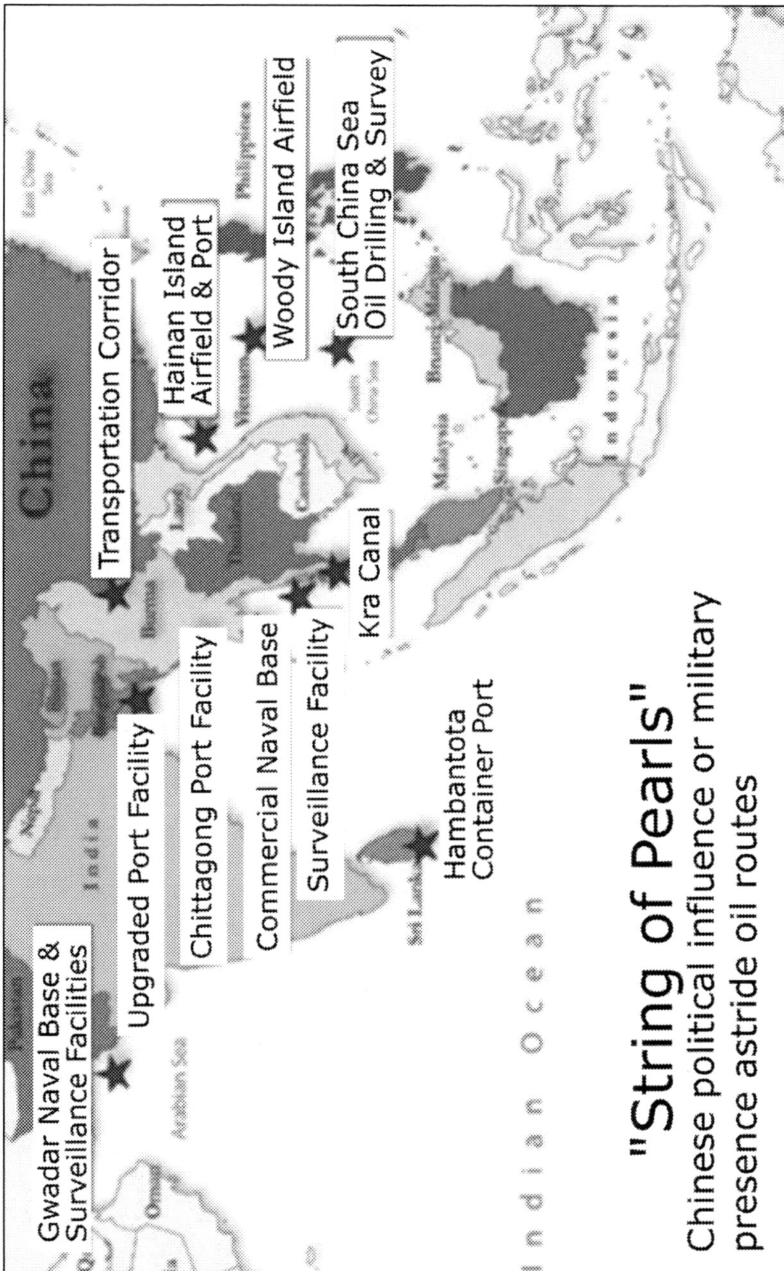

Source: U.S. Joint Forces Command (USJFCOM): JOE Report 2008 (Marinebuzz.com, 11 January 2009)

String of Pearls

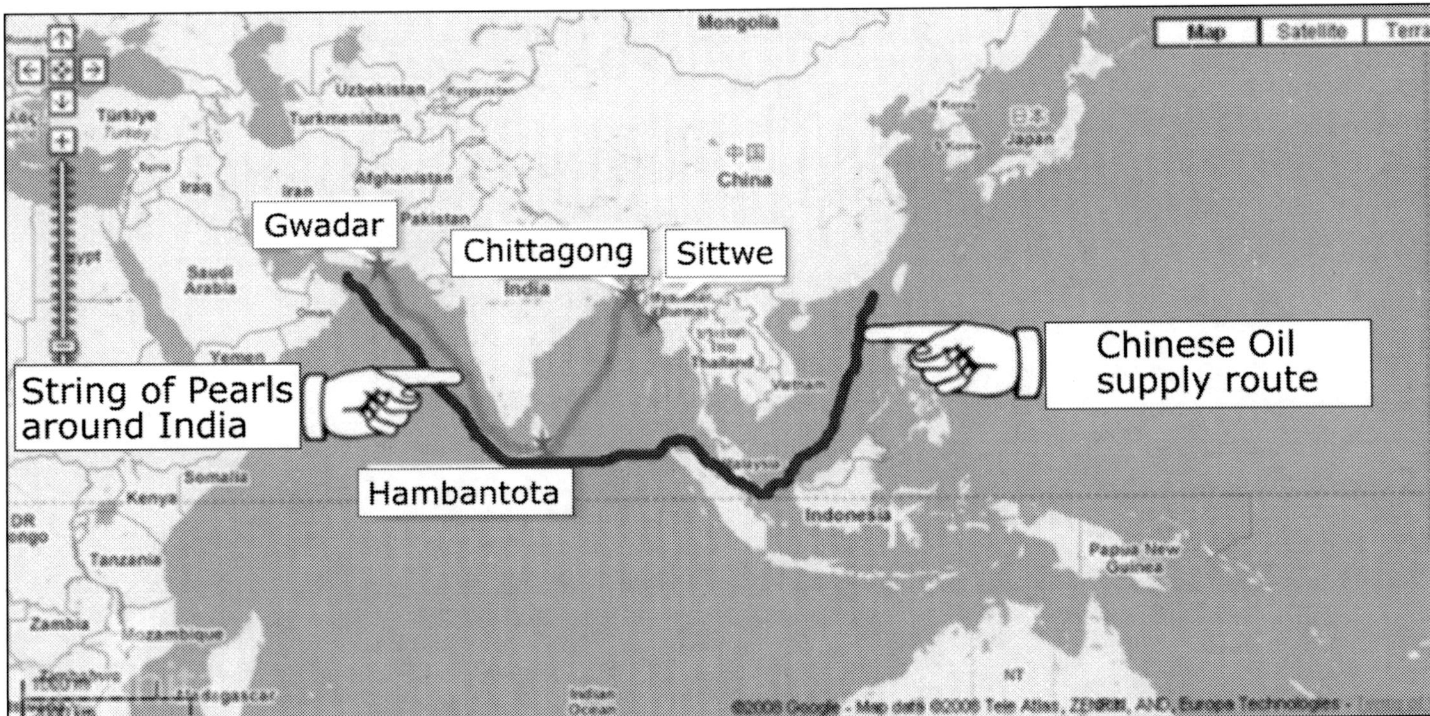

Source: Marinebuzz.com (China Garlands Indiawith String of Pearls, 23 January 2008)

ANNEXURE 2

Proposed Plan of China-Pakistan Economic Corridor (CPEC)

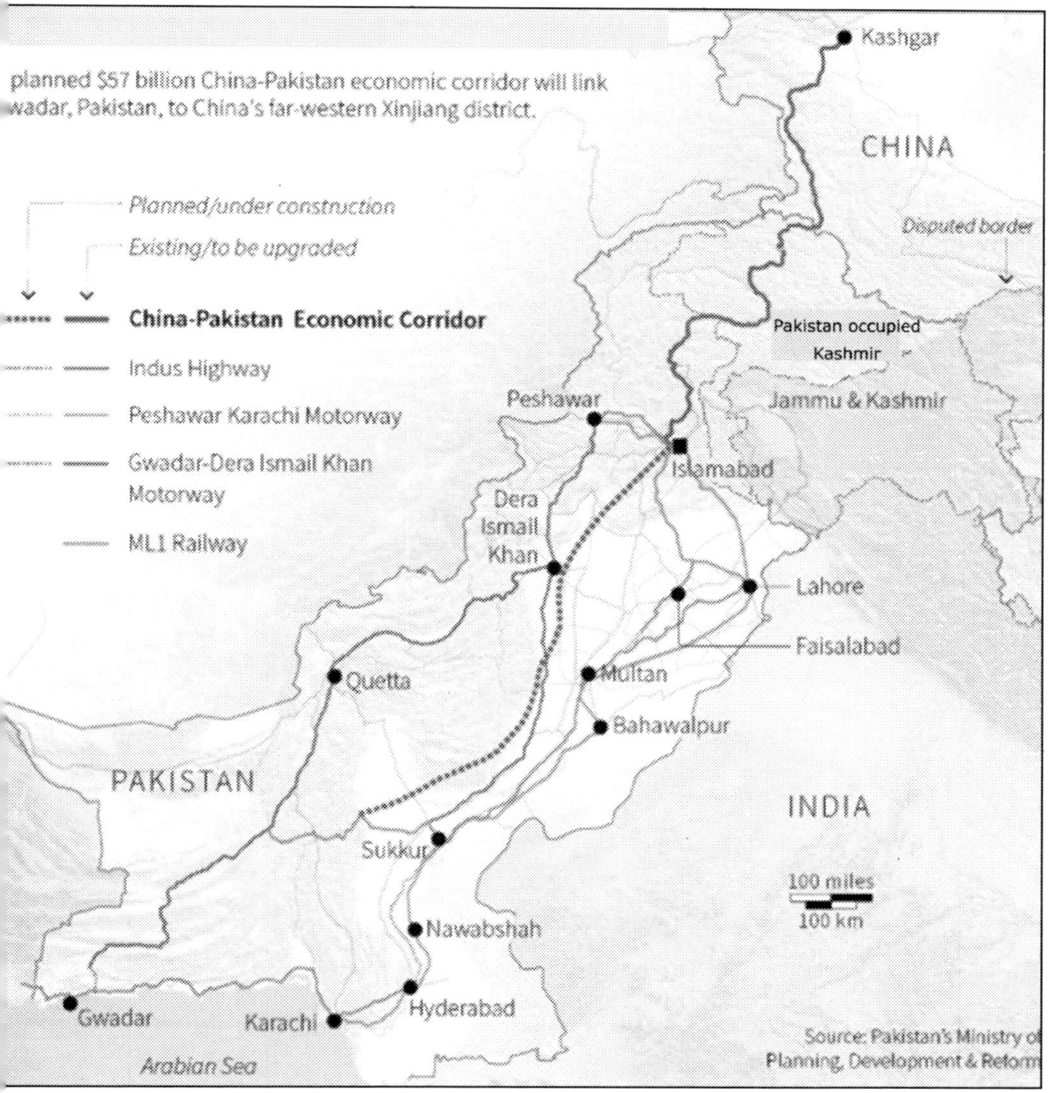

ANNEXURE 3

Bangladesh and Myanmar

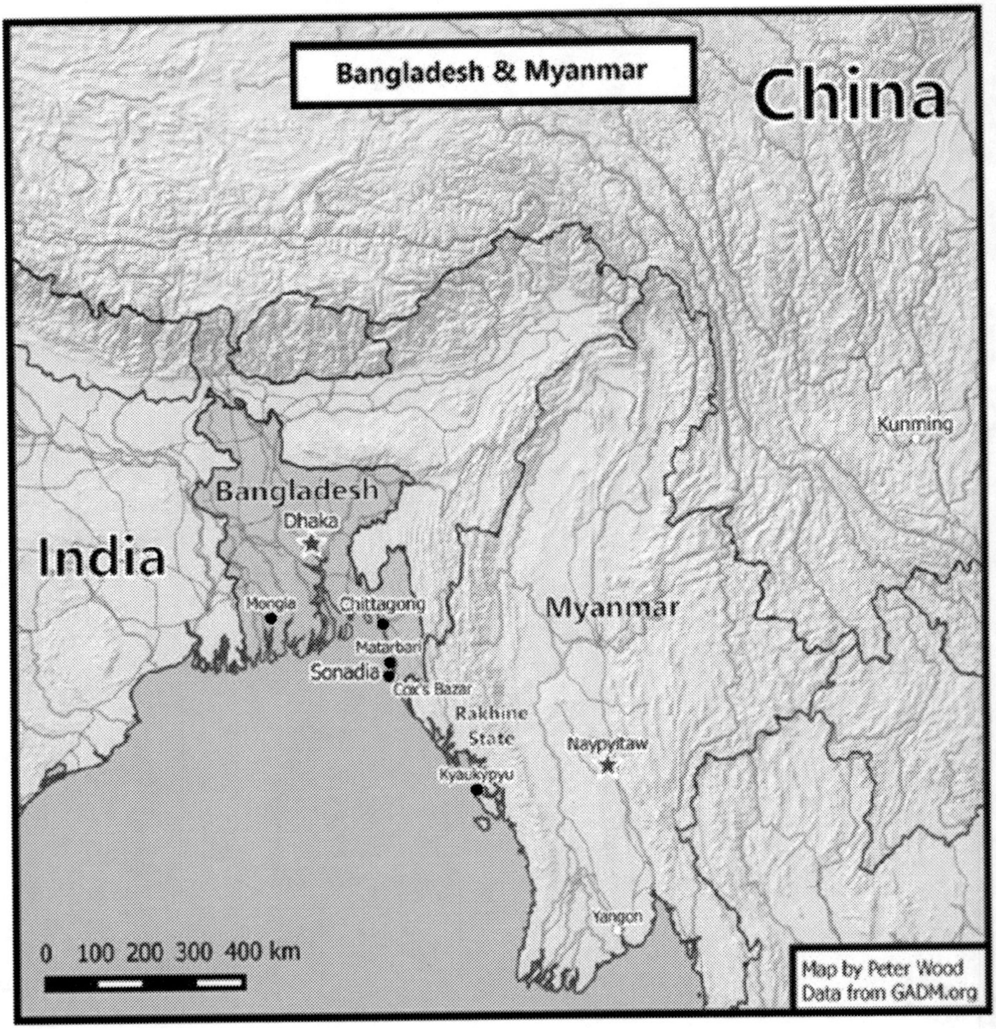

ANNEXURE 4

Outline Plan of One Belt and One Road (OBOR)

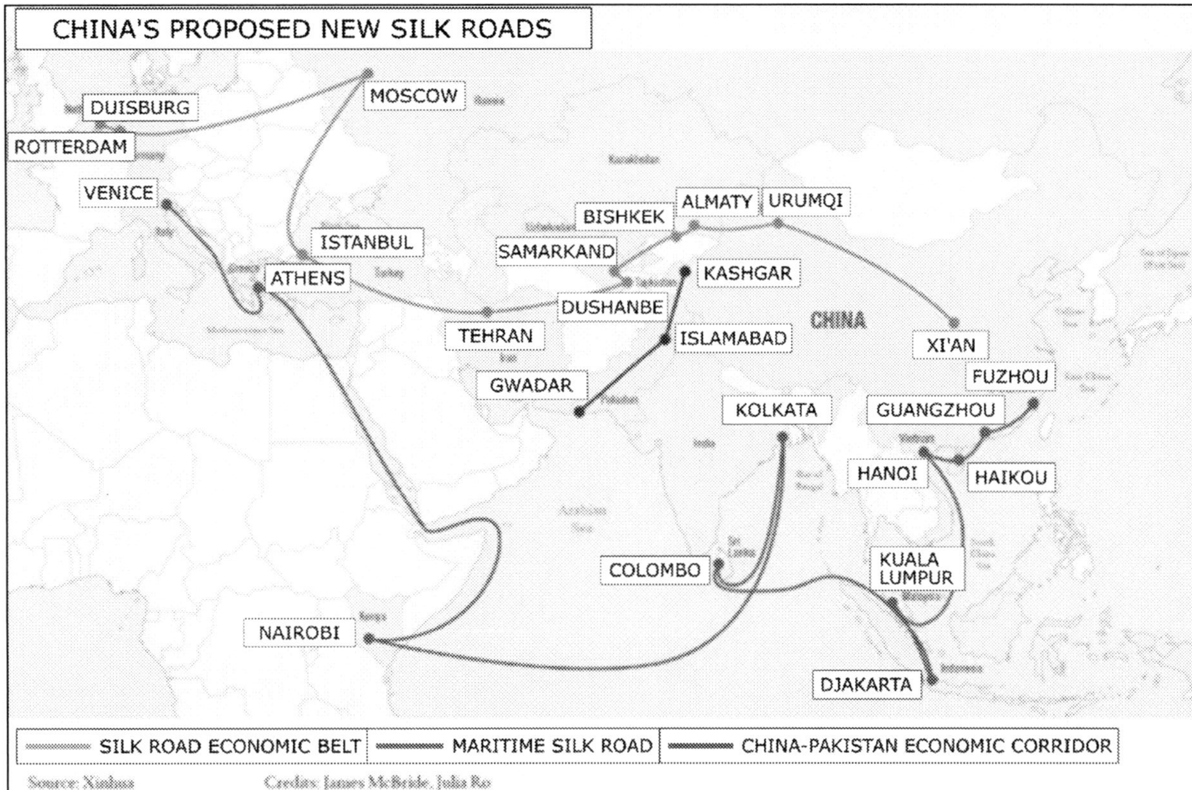

ANNEXURE 5

China's Rail-Road Network from Tibet to India's Northern Borders

Source: www.savetibet.org (12 November 2014)

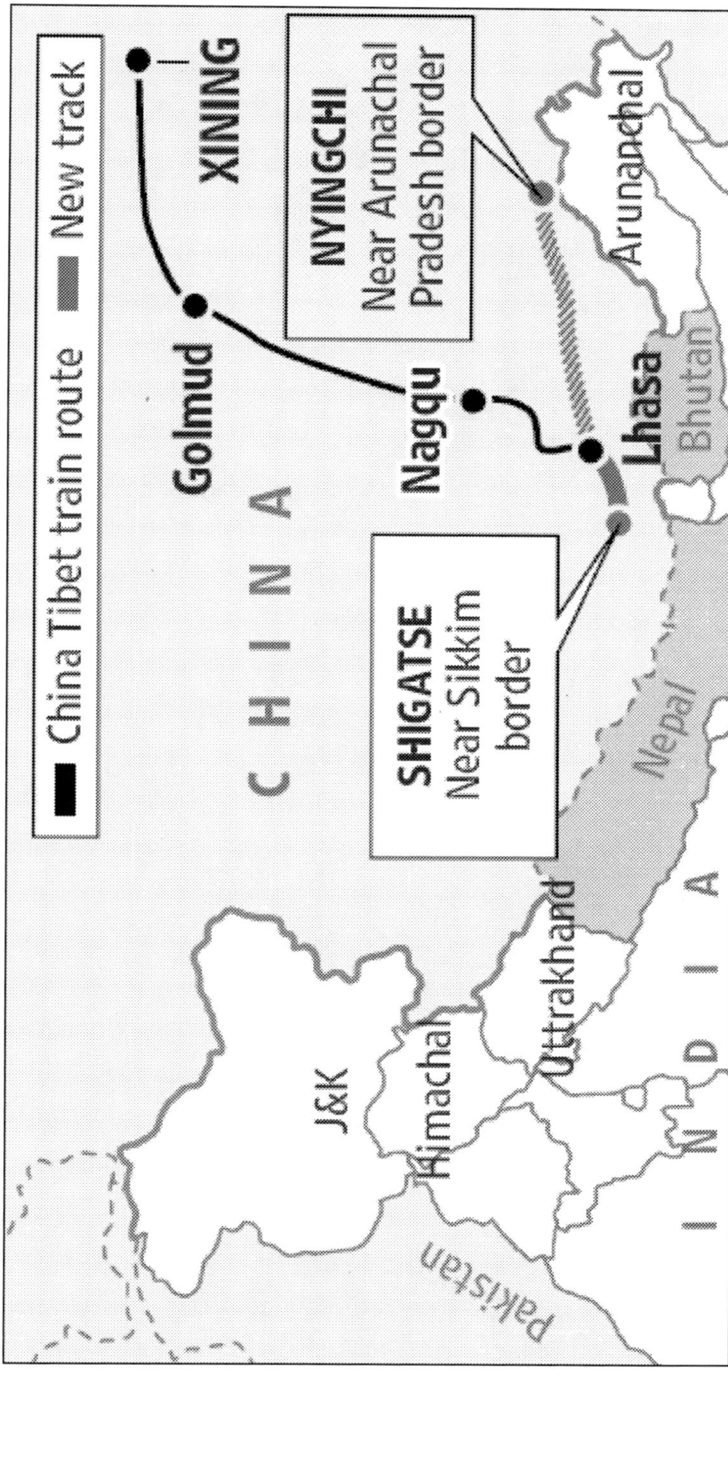

Source: www.tibetanreview.net (01 November 2014)

ANNEXURE 6

Water Diversion Plan in Tibet

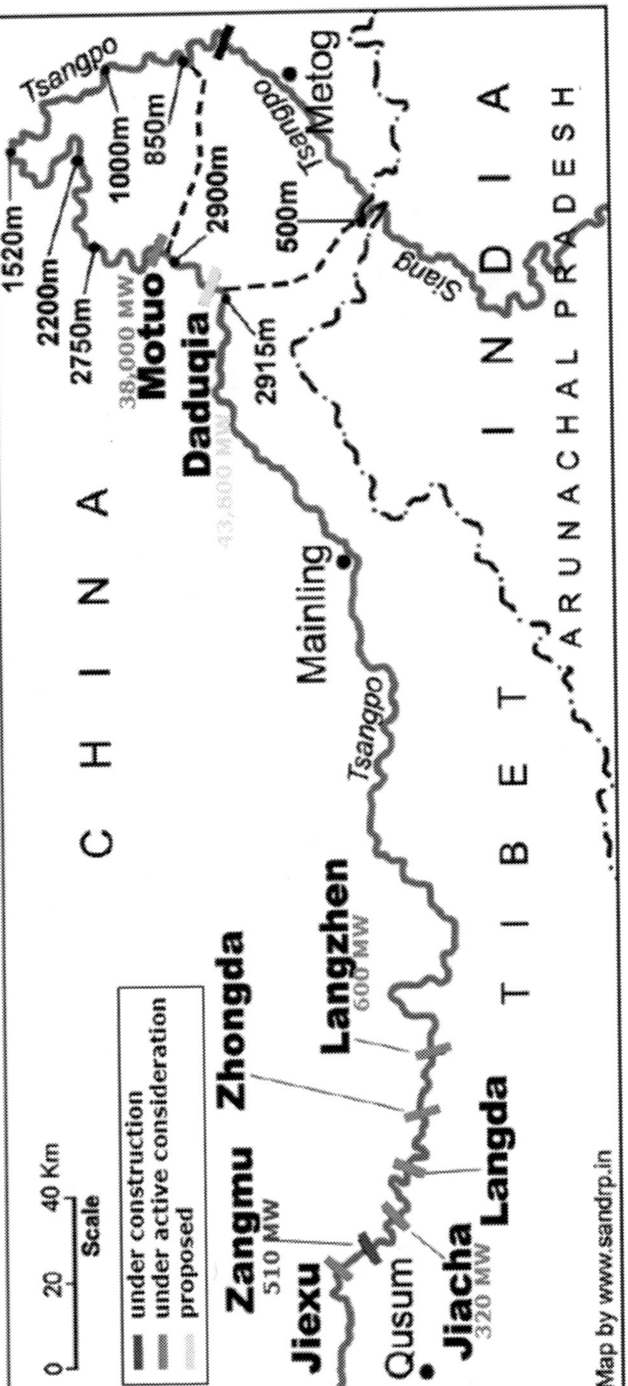

ANNEXURE 7

Composition of India's Trade With China During Financial Years 2016-17 & 2017-18

Value in US$ Million

S. No.	*Commodity*	*2016-2017*		*2017-2018*	
		Export to China	*Import from China*	*Export to China*	*Import from China*
1.	Fish, eggs, honey, animal origin products, plants, cut flowers, vegetables, fruits & nuts	170.24	233.93	181.77	132.12
2.	Coffee, tea, cereals, malts, oil seeds, medicinal plants, lac, gums, vegetable products, fats & oils, meat or fish preparations, sugars, cocoa, vegetable/fruit preparations, beverages, residue and waste from food industries, tobacco	495.97	169.62	606.66	217.20
3.	Salt, Sulphur, lime, cement, ores, slag and ash	2206.83	102.85	1935.75	140.19
4.	Minerals, fuels and oils	789.48	641.54	1507.21	1004.44
5.	Inorganic chemicals, Rare earth metals	122.13	542.36	118.60	667.05
6.	Organic chemicals	882.22	5615.88	2106.24	7091.53
7.	Pharmaceutical products & fertilizers	27.48	1384.64	41.71	1199.14
8.	Dyes, pigments, paints	120.81	390.88	169.00	516.42
9.	Essential oils, soaps, perfumes, photographic goods, glue etc	71.71	289.38	133.94	368.08
10.	Miscellaneous Chemical products	118.99	947.30	127.16	1348.97
11.	Plastic, Rubber & articles	331.92	2222.60	604.48	2704.00
12.	Raw Hides, Leather articles, fur skins	140.52	279.92	129.41	387.78
13.	Wood, cork, straw, wood pulp, paper, books and Newspapers	44.49	566.27	60.12	752.34
14.	Silk, wool and fabric	15.87	195.28	17.01	226.89
15.	Cotton	1342.55	124.37	1003.28	130.63
16.	Textile fiber, Man-made filaments, man-made fibers, ropes & cables, carpets & floor coverings, variety of fabrics	205.24	1583.24	231.53	2082.41
17.	Apparel & Clothing accessories	80.00	220.74	81.69	295.08
18.	Worn clothing and worn textile; rags	23.52	178.24	28.69	170.00
19.	Foot wear, Head gear, Umbrellas etc	35.52	359.71	43.76	511.36
20.	Feathers, Down feathers, articles, artificial flowers, stone, cement, ceramic products, glass ware	215.06	1100.36	189.04	1338.84

S. No.	Commodity	2016-2017		2017-2018	
		Export to China	Import from China	Export to China	Import from China
21.	Natural or Cultured Pearls, stones, imitjewellery	142.98	538.35	235.69	550.60
22.	Iron and steel and its articles	413.82	2580.85	383.85	3094.99
23.	Cu, Ni, Al, Pb, Zn, Sn, other base metals & articles thereof	812.90	1027.29	1871.05	1219.83
24.	Tools, cutlery, miscellaneous articles of base metal	14.26	519.49	16.49	706.32
25.	Nuclear Reactors, Boilers, Machy and Mechanical Appliances	531.72	11121.17	715.65	13540.00
26.	Electrical Machinery & equipment, TV Image & Sound Recorders	395.67	21982.63	479.54	28672.44
27.	Railway & Tramway locomotives & vehicles other than rlys etc	77.35	1180.79	95.65	1579.80
28.	Aircraft, spacecraft, ships, Boats & Floating structures	43.38	1460.41	32.72	1216.65
29.	Optical, photographic, Medical or surgical	152.16	1320.48	155.21	1663.21
30.	Clocks & watches, musical instruments, furniture, mattresses, toys, games & sports requisites	32.20	1399.01	19.83	1820.28
31.	Works of Art	105.41	230.81	1.37	310.90
32.	Miscellaneous goods	8.54	770.80	1.74	613.88
	Total	10171.89	61283.03	13333.53	76380.70

Source: Govt. ofIndia, Ministryof Commerce &Industrysitehttp://commerce-app.gov.in/eidb/default.asp

ANNEXURE 8

Policy Objectives Related to Low Carbon Growth in China and India

Theme	*China*	*India*
Copenhagen accord target	40%–45% by 2020 in comparison to 2005 levels	20%–25% by 2020 in comparison to 2005 levels
INDC target (emission intensity)	60%–65% by 2030 in comparison to 2005 levels	33%–35% by 2030 in comparison to 2005 levels
INDC: peaking	2030 orearlier	–
INDC: non-fossil fuel	Non-fossil fuels in primary energy consumption to be around 20% by 2030	To achieve 40% cumulative electric power installed capacity from non-fossil fuel-based energy resources by 2030
INDC: forestry and land use	To increase the forest stock volume by around 4.5 billion m^3on the 2005 level by 2030	Create additional carbon sink of 2.5–3 billion tonnes of CO_2 equivalent through additional forest and tree cover by 2030
INDC: financing needs	–	US$ 2.5 trillion (at 2014–2015 prices) will be required for meeting India's climate change actions between now and 2030
National climate policy	China's Policies and Actions on Climate Change (2014) National Strategy for Climate Adaptation	National Action Plan on Climate Change (2008) National Adaptation Fund
Key national agency co-ordinating climate change	The National Development and Reform Commission	Ministry of Environment, Forest and Climate Change
Sub-national initiatives	Low carbon Pilot Projects in Provinces and Cities	State Action Plan on Climate Change
Emissions/energy trading	Carbon Emissions Trading Pilot Program	Energy Saving Certificate and Renewable Energy Certificates
Technology development	China's Science and Technology Actions on Climate Change	Climate Change Centres in states
South–South cooperation	Fund for South–South Cooperation on Climate Change	International Solar Alliance

ANNEXURE 9

BRICS Countries' Share of the Total BRICS GDP (2017)

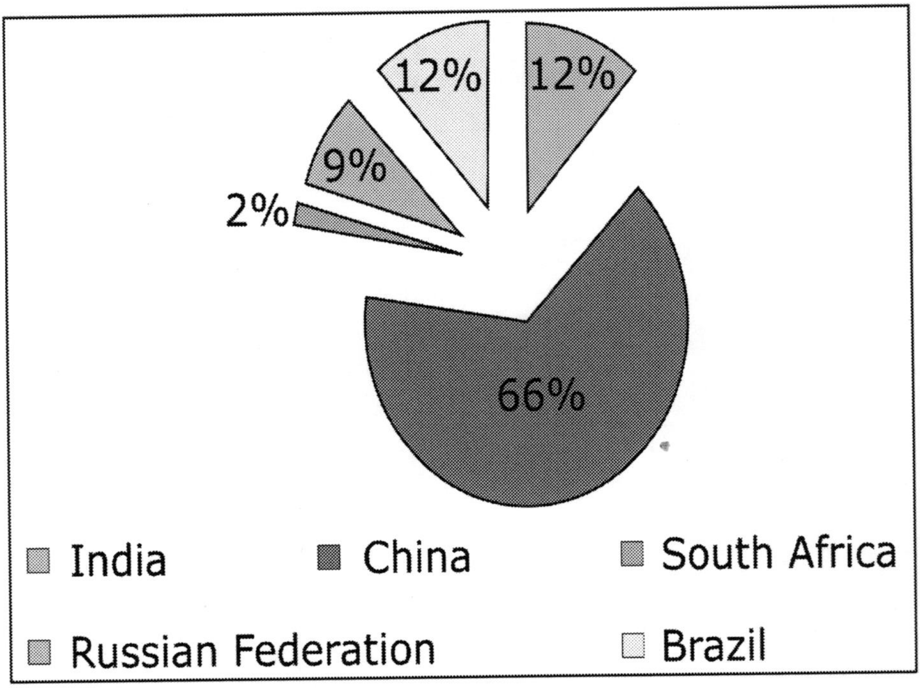

Source: International Monetary Fund.

ANNEXURE 10

Outline Plan of Turkmenistan–Afghanistan–Pakistan–India (TAPI) Pipeline

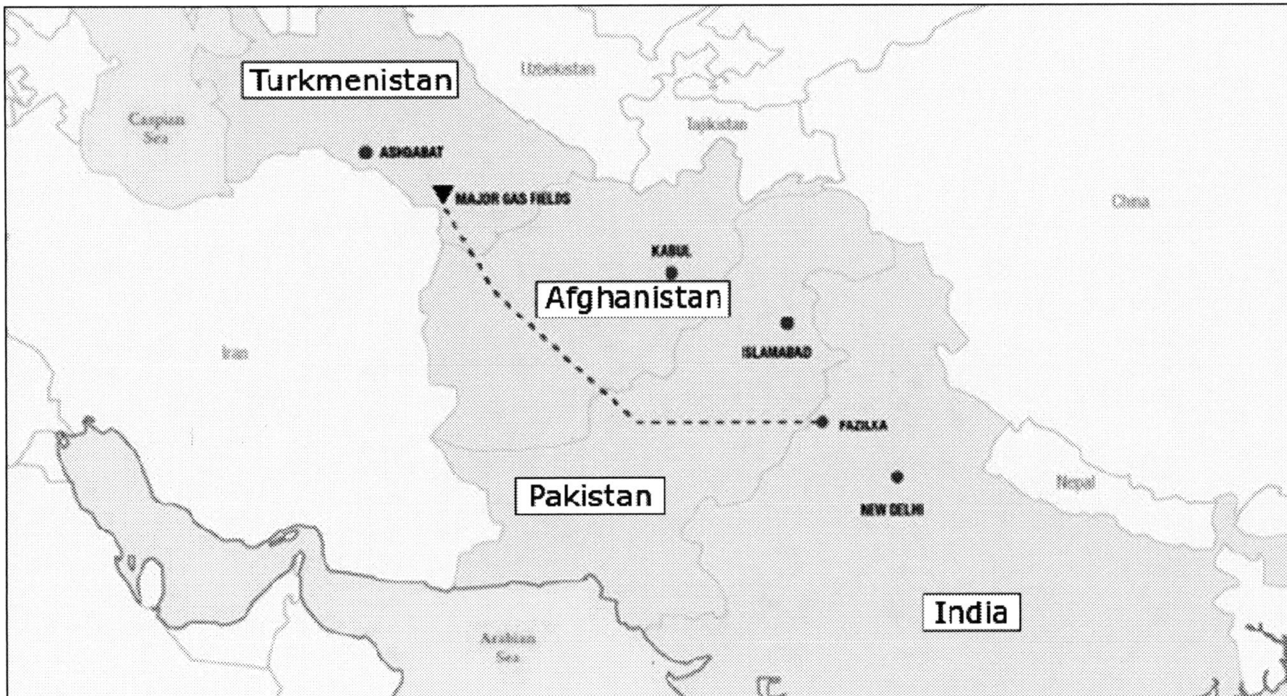

Source: The Energy Information Administration (EIA)

ANNEXURE 11

Wakhan Corridor

ANNEXURE 12

India–Myanmar–Thailand (IMT) Trilateral Highway

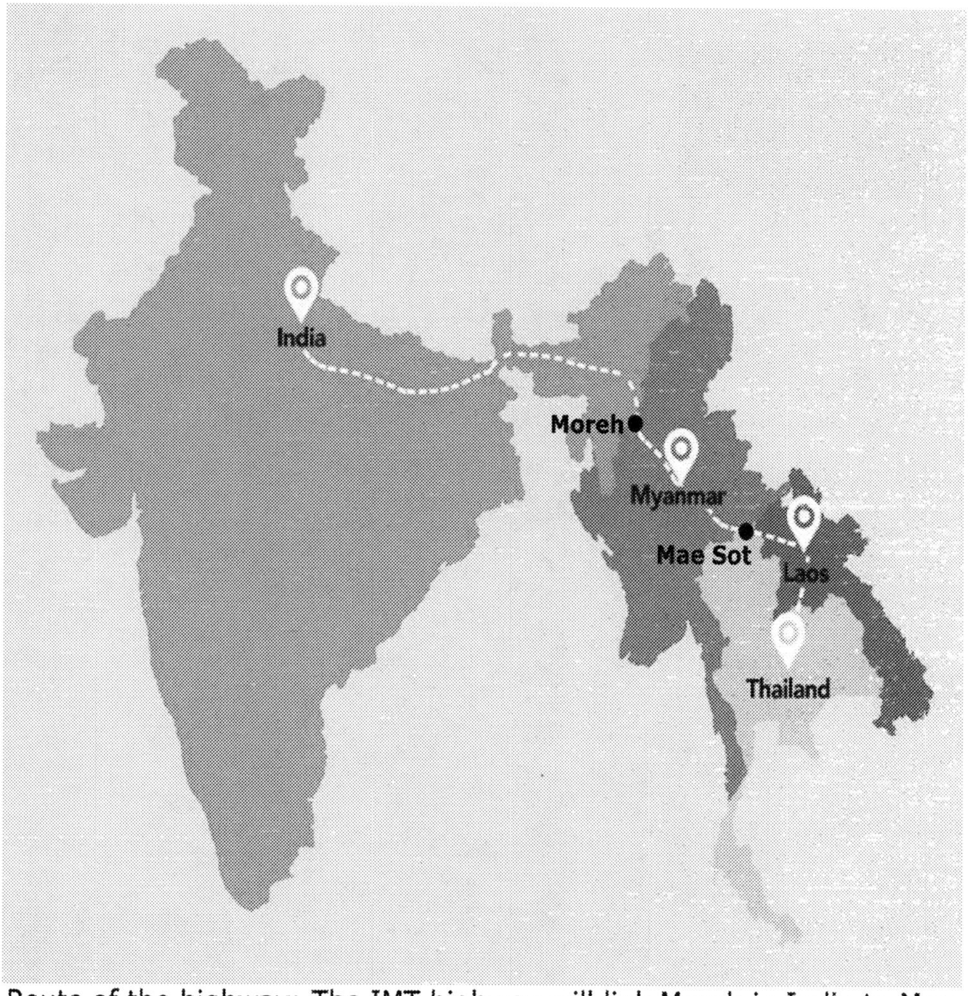

Route of the highway: The IMT highway will link Moreh in India to Mae Sot in Thailand via Myanmar; along route Moreh (India) to locations of Tamu,Kalewa, Yagyi, Monywa, Mandalay, Nay Pyi Taw, Payagyi, Theinzayat, Thaton, Hpa'an, Kawkareik and Myawaddy in Myanmar, further linking to Mae Sot in Thailand.

Source: https://www.ixigo.com/india-myanmar-thailand-on-road-an-iconic-journey-story-1112764

ANNEXURE 13

India's Trade with SAARC Partners

$ 26.1 Billion

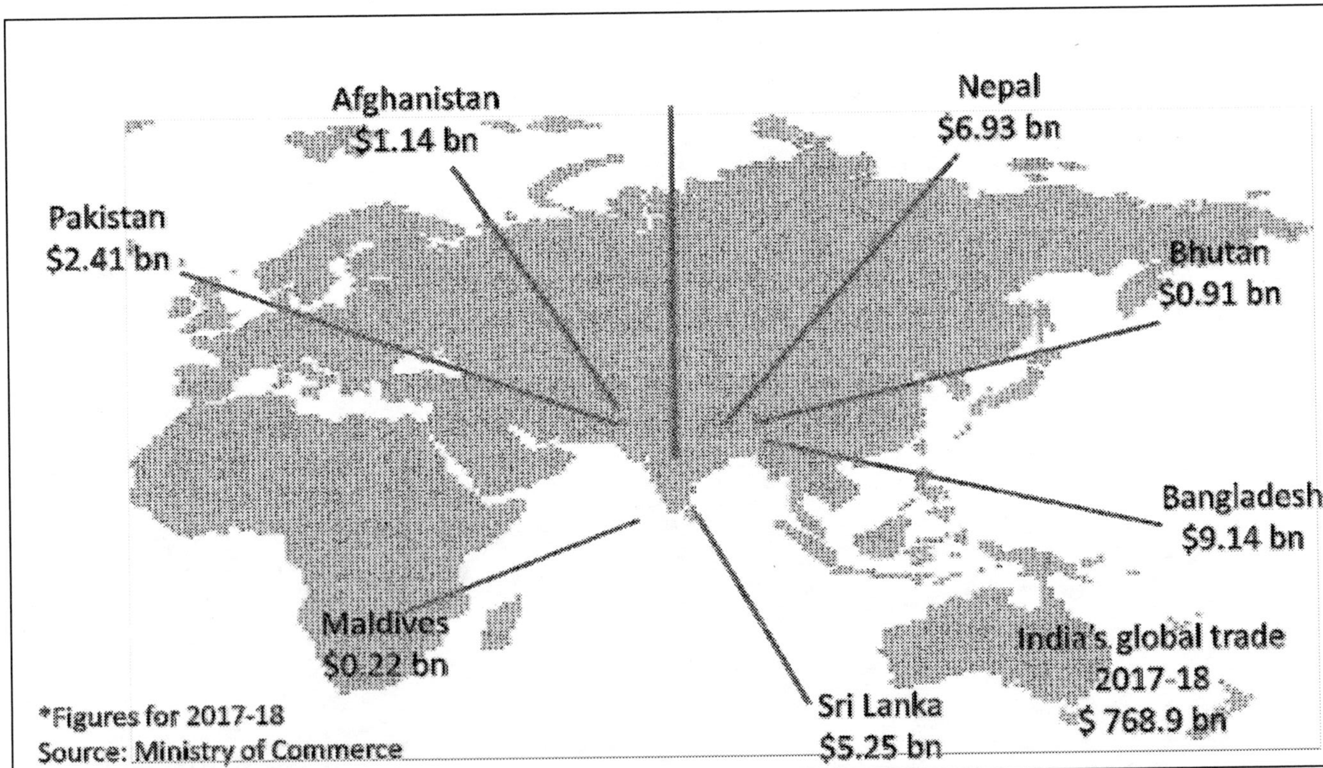

*Figures for 2017-18
Source: Ministry of Commerce

ANNEXURE 14

Chinese Investments in South Asia

Ser	*Country*	*Investments / Contracts*
1.	Afghanistan	US$ 210 Million
2.	Myanmar	US$ 2.52 Billion
3.	Bangladesh	US$ 13.87 Billion
4.	Sri Lanka	US$ 3.11 Billion
5.	Nepal	US$ 1.34 Billion
6.	Maldives	US$ 970 Million
7.	Pakistan	US$ 12.9 Billion

Source: http://www.aei.org/china-global-investment-tracker

ANNEXURE 15

India's Aid to South Asian Neighbors in 2017-18 & 2018-19

Ser	*Country*	*2017-18*	*2018-19*
1.	Bhutan	Rs 1,779 crore	Rs 1,813 crore
2.	Nepal	Rs 375 crore	Rs 650 crore
3.	Afghanistan	Rs 350 crore	Rs 325 crore
4.	Seychelles	Rs 200 crore	Rs 300 crore
5.	Myanmar	Rs 225 crore	Rs 280 crore
6.	Bangladesh	Rs 65 crore	Rs 175 crore
7.	Maldives	Rs 125 crore	Rs 125 crore

Source: The Times ofIndia, 31 May 2018

ANNEXURE 16

Country-wise Details of Migrant Workers and Remittances from South Asian Countries to India and China and vice versa

World Bank Bilateral Remittance Estimates from South Asian Countries to India and China (US$ Million) (2017-18)

Remittance from Country→	*Afghanistan*	*Bangladesh*	*Bhutan*	*India*	*Maldives*	*Nepal*	*Pakistan*	*Sri Lanka*	*Total*
To India	0	126	186	-	81	3016	-	1265	4,674
To China	0	992	6	41	0	139	0	2	1,180

Migrant Workers from India and China in South Asian Countries (2017-18)

South Asian Country	*Indian Workers*	*Chinese Workers*
Afghanistan	0	0
Bangladesh	35,250	1,74,787
Bhutan	48,076	973
India	-	7,035
Maldives	19,801	0
Nepal	4,40,198	24,394
Pakistan	13,95,854*	312
Sri Lanka	10,814	2,482
Total	5,54,139	2,09,683

*Strength of Pakistan excluded from Total

Source: www.worldbank.org/en/topic/migrantremittancesdiasporaissues/brief/migration-remittances-data

World Bank Bilateral Remittance Estimates from India and China to South Asia 2017-18 (US$ Million)

Remittance-Receiving Country→	*Afghanistan*	*Bangladesh*	*Bhutan*	*India*	*Maldives*	*Nepal*	*Pakistan*	*Sri Lanka*	*Total*
From India	0	4033	3	-	1	1021	-	520	5578
From China	0	9	0	64	0	5	22	22	122

Migrant Workers from South Asian Countries in India and China (2017-18)

From South Asian Country	*INDIA*	*CHINA*
Afghanistan	8,005	685
Bangladesh	31,39,311	6,282
Bhutan	6,580	539
India	-	15,051
Maldives	197	0
Nepal	5,37,517	2,401
Pakistan	10,95,149*	7,746
Sri Lanka	1,53,643	6,361
Total	3,845,253*	39,065

*Strength of Pakistan excluded from Total

Source: www.worldbank.org/en/topic/migrantremittancesdiasporaissues/brief/migration-remittances-data

ANNEXURE 17

SAGARMALA: National Perspective Plan

415 Projects; US$123 billion (2015 - 2025)

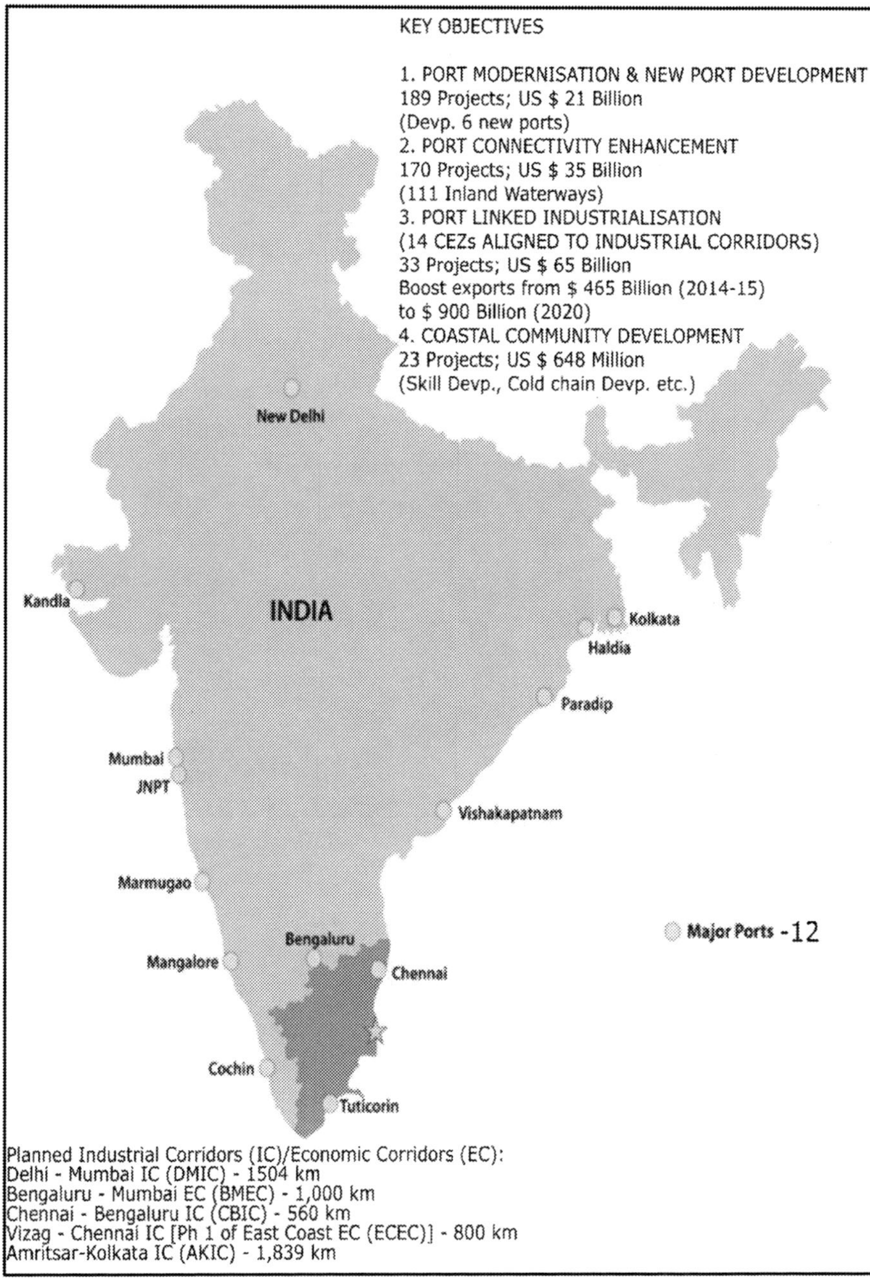

ANNEXURE 18

MAUSAM Map

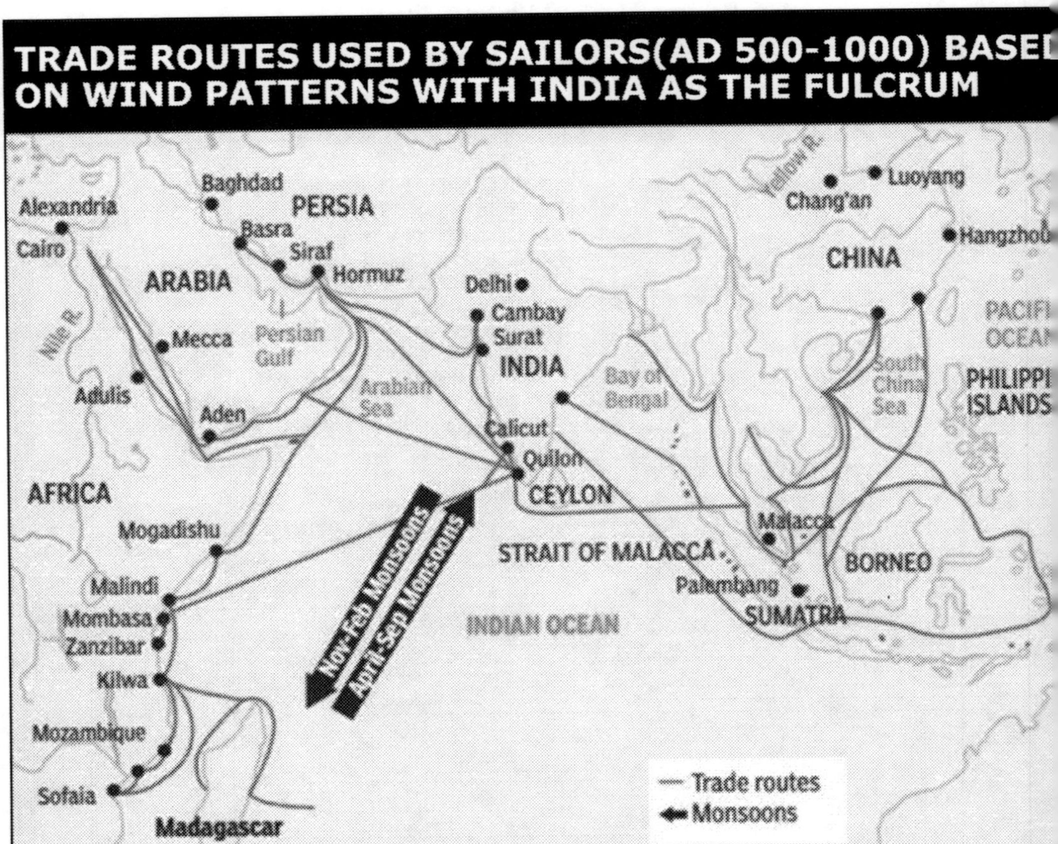

Source: http://strategicstudyindia.blogspot.com/2014/09/narendra-modis-mausam-manoeuvre-to.html

ANNEXURE 19

Outline Plan of International North South Transport Corridor (INSTC)

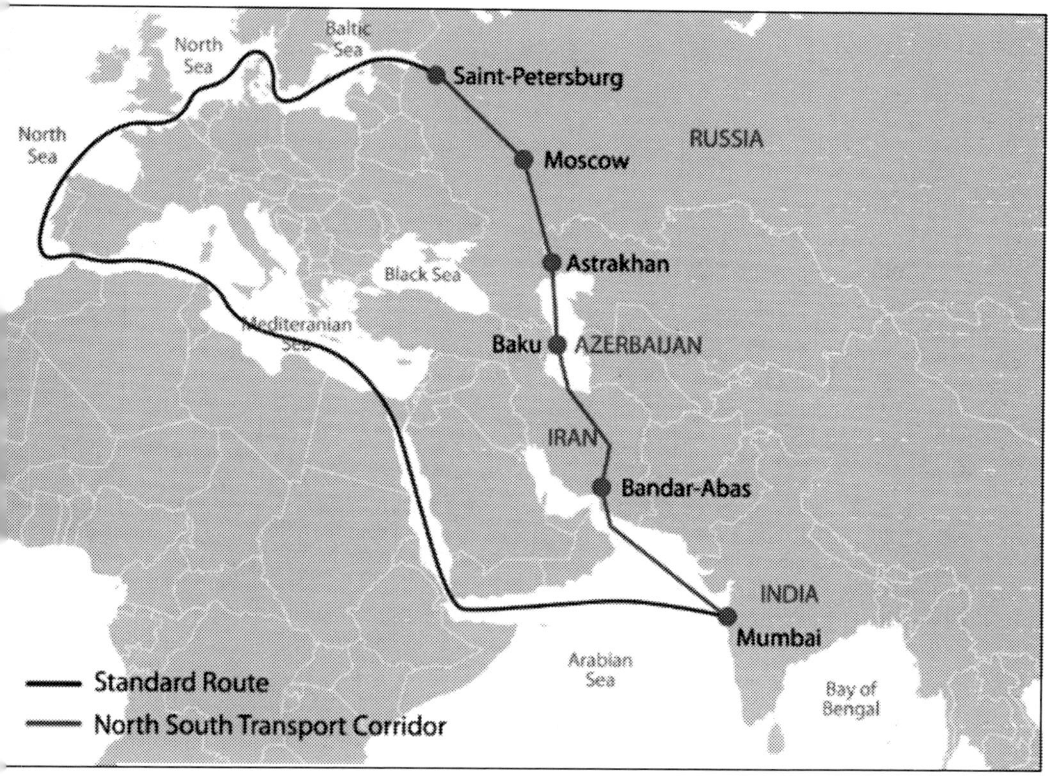

Source: Alena Repkina, www.rbth.com 12 December 2016

Index